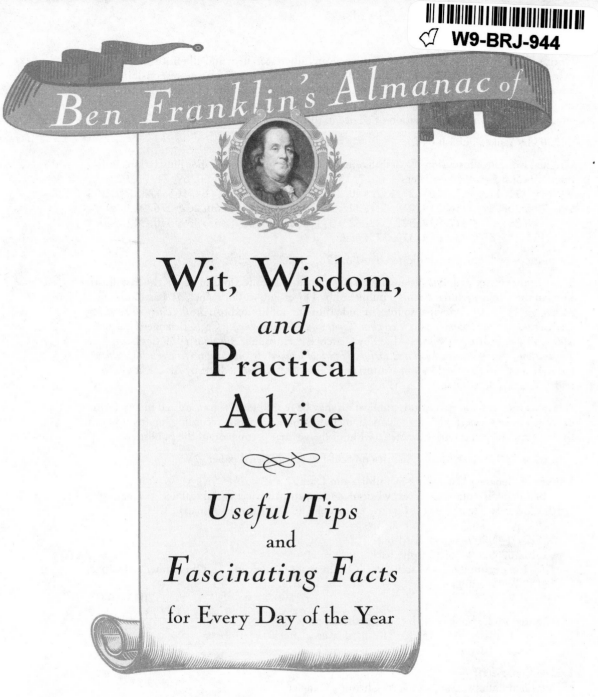

Ben Franklin's Almanac of

Wit, Wisdom, and Practical Advice

Useful Tips and Fascinating Facts

for Every Day of the Year

By the Editors of *The Old Farmer's Almanac*

YANKEE BOOKS

© 2003 by Yankee Publishing Inc.

Original woodcut illustrations © Beth Krommes (chapter openers and spot illustrations indicated by –BK): 5 (and all recurrences), 6, 7, 13, 15, 25, 26, 39, 41, 55, 60, 69, 71, 73, 92, 97, 99, 101, 111, 112, 113, 116, 127, 132, 140, 151, 155, 161, 163 (2), 164, 165, 173, 187, 195, 196, 204, 208, 211, 216, 218, 219, 221, 227, 228, 247, 255, 259, 260, 262, 276, 282, 290, 295, 299, 301, 307, 312, 318, 321, 322, 323, 331, 332, 335, 337, 338, 339, 340, 342, 346, 347, 352, 353, 357, 361, 364, 370, 375, 382.

Illustrations by Jill Shaffer (indicated by –JS): 126, 211, 239, 352.

Many of the uncredited illustrations are taken from various collections of copyright-free illustrations in the Dover Pictorial Archive, published by Dover Publications, Inc., 31 East 2nd Street, Mineola, NY 11501. Principal sources include (but are not limited to): *3,800 Early Advertising Cuts, Deberny Type Foundry,* and *Victorian Goods and Merchandise* by Carol Belanger Grafton; *2000 Early Advertising Woodcuts,* edited by Clarence P. Hornung; *Animals: 1419 Copyright-Free Illustrations, Men, Women, Food and Drink, Hands (Pictorial Archives from Nineteenth Century Sources),* and *Plants,* edited by Jim Harter; and *Plants and Flowers,* edited by Alan E. Bessette and William K. Chapman.

Library of Congress Cataloging-in-Publication Data

Ben Franklin's almanac of wit, wisdom, and practical advice: useful tips and fascinating facts for every day of the year / by the editors of The Old Farmer's Almanac.

p.   cm.

ISBN 0–89909–388–4 hardcover

ISBN 0–89909–389–2 paperback

1. Home economics—Miscellanea.   2. Almanacs, American.   I. Old Farmer's Almanac.

TX158.B395 2003

640—dc21   2003010316

Distributed to the book trade by St. Martin's Press

2 4 6 8 10 9 7 5 3 1 hardcover

2 4 6 8 10 9 7 5 3 1 paperback

Rodale Books Staff

Editor: Ellen Phillips; *Cover Designer:* Christina Gaugler; *Editorial Production Manager:* Marilyn Hauptly

Yankee Publishing Staff

President: Jamie Trowbridge; *Book Editors:* Sarah Elder Hale and Susan Peery

Contributing Writers: Polly Bannister, Christine Halvorson, Randy Miller, Georgia Orcutt, Kenneth M. Sheldon, Martha White

Book Designer: Jill Shaffer; *Indexer:* Nanette Bendyna; *Copy Editor:* Barbara Jatkola

CONTENTS

INTRODUCTION

BEN FRANKLIN, one of the most famous of all Americans, couldn't make the usual claims to fame. He was not a president, eminent professor, professional athlete, or movie star. He did not make a vital medical discovery or write the great American novel. His fame came instead from his being a curious person and an excellent communicator. Ben enjoyed all aspects of life and was as fascinated by the mind and motives of his fellow human beings as he was by unraveling the mysteries of science. And he liked to get the word out. He spent his whole life conveying information and ideas—as a printer, diplomat, inventor, philosopher, civic leader, and revolutionary.

Ben's wit is legendary. He is particularly well known for his maxims—bits of advice he readily doled out in *Poor Richard's Almanack,* published between 1733 and 1758. Like the great thinkers of antiquity, such as Plato and Aristotle, he distilled advice and observations into short sentences and clever couplets. *Poor Richard's Almanack,* like all such annuals, contained astronomical tables—collected observations used to predict the weather for the coming year. But it also provided Ben with a forum to pass along all kinds of information he considered worth sharing. Ben never held back when it came to expressing his opinions on civic progress, affairs of state, or even matters of privacy. His life was an open book. And although he instilled in his audience an ambition toward self-improvement, he never claimed to be perfect himself.

Throughout his life, Ben Franklin seized every opportunity to understand and improve the world. Things we consider basic services—weather forecasts, public libraries, higher education, vaccinations, electricity, the postal service, fire departments—were, in the 18th century, important breakthroughs achieved by the efforts of Ben and others like him.

Ben Franklin's Almanac of Wit, Wisdom, and Practical Advice is a collection of anecdotes, sage advice, and useful information in the form of a perpetual almanac, with selections to read every day of the year. Scattered throughout are many details of Ben's life and interests, including his views on politics, religion, marriage, and a strong work ethic. But Ben wasn't much of a cook, housekeeper, or gardener. So for these matters, we have called on the talents of other almanac writers—veteran contributors to *The Old Farmer's Almanac*, first published in 1792 and now the oldest continuously published periodical in North America.

Like Ben, we wish to share information and provide enjoyment. The ideas herein will inspire you, the history will inform you, the stories will amuse you, and the practical hints will make you a more frugal and industrious person— ideals high on Ben's list of virtues. Although we think that you will find many great suggestions to make everyday life easier and more productive, we also hope that this book will serve as a daily reminder that curiosity is a fine attribute to cultivate. Open your eyes to the changing seasons and the wonders of nature; open your mind to the possibilities that exist to understand the world; and open your heart to all those curious people, such as Ben Franklin, who provide us with a rich and abundant treasure trove of ideas.

JANUARY, *the First Month*

Full Wolf Moon

is the Native American name for January's full moon, evoking wolf packs trotting across the frozen plains or howling in the northern woods. It is also known as the *Full Old Moon.*

Sign of the Zodiac:
Capricorn
(December 22–
January 19)

Element: Earth

Quality: Disciplined

Birthstone: Garnet

Flower: Carnation

JANUARY GETS ITS NAME from the Roman god Janus, the two-faced god of beginnings and entrances—a fitting deity to preside over the start of a new year. A fresh calendar encourages us to fill in the blanks with ambitious projects for home and personal improvement, better known as our New Year's resolutions. Toss out last year's resolutions—they are "so yesterday"—and turn your face to the future.

That all this feeling of excitement and forward motion comes at the coldest and darkest time of year seems like a paradox. A month that brings the best black ice for skating and the most invigorating skiing also sees us sipping lemon tea and chewing garlic cloves to fight off colds and flu. It's the best month for being a homebody, for plowing through thick novels, for trying new recipes for savory soups and yeasty breads. When blustery weather hits, we do just what the creatures of the forest do—hunker down and stay warm.

January, the cold heart of winter, carries the seeds of spring. The first garden catalog arrives in the mail, we gain nearly an hour of daylight, and, usually in the third week, the much-heralded January thaw turns snow to mud. And that's progress!

JANUARY

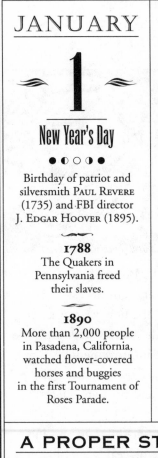

1

New Year's Day

●◐○◑●

Birthday of patriot and silversmith PAUL REVERE (1735) and FBI director J. EDGAR HOOVER (1895).

1788
The Quakers in Pennsylvania freed their slaves.

1890
More than 2,000 people in Pasadena, California, watched flower-covered horses and buggies in the first Tournament of Roses Parade.

Let thy vices die before thee.

—BEN FRANKLIN

AT ONE POINT, Ben Franklin undertook what he called "the bold and arduous project of arriving at moral perfection." From his reading and studies, he developed a list of 13 virtues he considered necessary to a moral life: temperance, silence, order, resolution, frugality, industry, sincerity, justice, moderation, cleanliness, tranquillity, chastity, and humility.

He then devised a plan to become faultless in each of these areas but, he wrote, "soon found I had undertaken a task of more difficulty than I had imagined." He created a small ledger with columns for each day of the week and a row for each virtue, placing a black mark in the book every time he violated one of them. Examining himself at the end of every day, Ben reported, "I was surprised to find myself so much fuller of faults than I had imagined."

Toward the end of his life, Ben admitted that he fell far short of achieving his goal of perfection, but he believed that he was "a better and a happier man than I otherwise should have been if I had not attempted it."

A WORD TO THE WISE

A PROPER START TO THE NEW YEAR

❧ Firstfooters, the first ones through the door of a dwelling on New Year's Day, should always bring a small gift for good luck. Among the traditional offerings are a chunk of coal, a loaf of bread, and a glass of spirits.

❧ Hopping John—black-eyed peas and rice—is the dish for good luck on New Year's Day. Or eat some cabbage, thought to bring good fortune because it is green. Any kind of fish is also a good choice, because fish always swim forward.

❧ To the ancient Saxons, if the new year began on a Saturday, there would be a snowy winter and a rainy spring.

Striving to better, oft we mar what's well.
—William Shakespeare

Laugh Yourself into Shape

If exercise is on your list of New Year's resolutions, all you have to do is laugh. Laughing uses more muscles at one time than any other activity. In fact, 15 muscles are required just to smile.

A Journal of the New Year

IF YOU HAVE ALWAYS intended to keep a journal or diary but have never quite got around to starting one, there's no time like the present. Whether you write in a simple spiral notebook, in a leather-covered tome, or directly to a hard drive, the important thing is to be regular and establish the habit. The best advice for novice journalists is to write for yourself, not for posterity. After all, it's best to know your audience.

PRACTICAL PRIMER

- Perhaps, like Thomas Jefferson, you want to keep a weather and garden journal, noting temperature, precipitation, wind, and natural events, such as the first crocus to bloom or the day you plant an apple tree.

- Or are you more like Leonardo da Vinci? He always kept a notebook hanging from his belt to record or sketch observations and inspirations.

- Place a notebook and pen on your bedside table to keep a journal of your dreams and those middle-of-the-night brilliant ideas.

- Hold a weekly family meeting and record the concerns, news, achievements, and schedules of each family member in a notebook. Rotate the job of scribe so everyone gets a chance. The kids will love to look back at this running log of family life.

JANUARY

2

1788
Georgia became the fourth state.

1920
Author and scientist ISAAC ASIMOV was born.

1941
The ANDREWS SISTERS recorded "Boogie Woogie Bugle Boy."

. . .

I never travel without my diary. One should always have something sensational to read in the train.

—*Oscar Wilde*

BACK TO SIMPLE EATING

❖ Beware of ingredients ending in *ose*. They are almost always some form of added sugar.

❖ To get the most nutrients out of carrots and spinach, cook them rather than eating them raw.

❖ Eat slowly. It takes about 20 minutes for your brain to realize that you've eaten enough food to be satisfied. If you chow down too quickly, you are likely to overeat.

❖ If you crave old-fashioned steel-cut oatmeal for breakfast but don't have time to prepare it, try this shortcut. The night before, bring 4 cups water to a boil, remove from the heat, and add 1 cup oats. Cover tightly and let soak overnight. In the morning, reheat on the stove or in the microwave. Store leftovers in an airtight container in the refrigerator and reheat servings as needed.

❖ Fresh bread is utterly satisfying—to bake and eat. Set aside time to make it the old-fashioned way: mix, knead, rise, shape, rise, and bake.

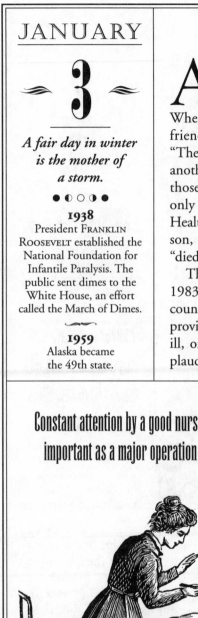

3

*A fair day in winter
is the mother of
a storm.*

● ◐ ○ ○ ●

1938
President FRANKLIN
ROOSEVELT established the
National Foundation for
Infantile Paralysis. The
public sent dimes to the
White House, an effort
called the March of Dimes.

1959
Alaska became
the 49th state.

Visiting the Sick

THE *Inspired* MIND

As A YOUNG MAN newly arrived in Philadelphia, Ben Franklin quickly developed a circle of friends who shared his interest in writing. The group became very close. When Ben suffered a serious attack of pleurisy at age 21, his friends rallied around him. He later wrote, "There are no Kindnesses done by one Man to another, which are remembered so long . . . as those received in Sickness, whether they are only present Comforts, or assist in restoring Health." He also repaid the kindness, reporting that Joseph Watson, whom he considered the most talented man in the group, "died in my Arms a few Years after."

The Visiting Nurse Associations of America was established in 1983, uniting 200 not-for-profit visiting nurse agencies across the country, some of which originated in the 1890s. Visiting nurses provide home health care to people who are disabled, chronically ill, or recovering from illness or accident. Ben would surely applaud their efforts.

Constant attention by a good nurse may be just as important as a major operation by a surgeon.

—Dag Hammarskjold

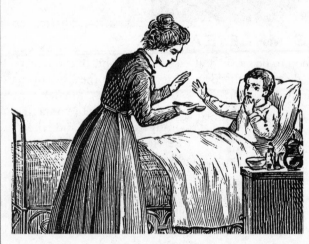

HOME COMFORTS

❦ Try old-fashioned horehound drops to soothe a sore throat. The aerial parts of *Marrubium vulgare* are an expectorant and relaxant.

❦ To relieve aches and pains, make a simple liniment with baby oil and a little powdered mustard. Rub it into arthritic or rheumatic joints, or use it to increase circulation.

❦ Mix a few drops of rose water with a tablespoon of honey to make a sweet and natural balm to help heal chapped lips.

❦ If you've been plagued by stomach ills, such as diarrhea or colitis, try switching to soy milk or goat's milk for a short time.

If thou hast wit & learning, add to it wisdom and modesty.

—BEN FRANKLIN

ON AT LEAST one occasion, Ben Franklin disobeyed his own advice in this regard, though inadvertently. Once, he attended a meeting of a literary group in Paris, where speakers were exchanging fulsome praise for one another in flowery French. Ben's French was only passable, and he was unable to understand much of what was being said, so he opted to follow the lead of an acquaintance, joining in with the applause only when she applauded. Ben's grandson—who apparently spoke better French than Ben—attended the meeting with him.

When it was over, the grandson expressed surprise that Ben had applauded—and loudly at that—only when the speakers were praising *him*.

Some people are born modest, and others have modesty thrust upon them. The great composer Igor Stravinsky was once told by an admirer that of all his works, she enjoyed *Scheherazade* most of all.

"But madame," Stravinsky said, "I did not compose *Scheherazade*."

"Oh, don't be modest," the woman replied.

There's a lot to be said for the fellow who doesn't say it himself.

—*Maurice Switzer*

● ○ ○ ○ ●

If grass grows in January, it will grow badly the whole year.

1809
Birth of LOUIS BRAILLE, who refined a raised-dot alphabet for people who are blind.

1896
Utah became the 45th state.

Gardening—In January?

January's inclement weather is excuse enough to stay indoors. In fact, mild weather in January is regarded with great suspicion by most gardeners and farmers. But there are a few things you can do outside.

❖ Get in the habit of walking around your property and inspecting trees for storm damage. Remove any broken limbs, making a clean cut close to the trunk.

❖ Protect a small tree or shrub from extreme cold by surrounding it with a cylinder of snow fencing and packing straw or shredded leaves inside the cylinder.

❖ Use a broom to gently brush heavy snow off evergreens. If branches are covered with ice, it's best to leave them alone.

❖ Appreciate the insulating qualities of a heavy snow cover on your perennial bed. If you add to it in the course of shoveling, all the better.

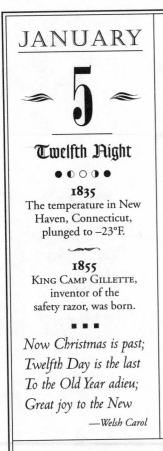

JANUARY

5

Twelfth Night

● ○ ○ ○ ●

1835
The temperature in New Haven, Connecticut, plunged to –23°F.

1855
KING CAMP GILLETTE, inventor of the safety razor, was born.

■ ■ ■

Now Christmas is past;
Twelfth Day is the last
To the Old Year adieu;
Great joy to the New

—*Welsh Carol*

Shavers and Trimmers

THE
Inspired
MIND

IN A 1743 ISSUE of his *Pennsylvania Gazette,* Ben Franklin published an anonymous, satirical essay (his own) titled "Shavers and Trimmers." Inspired by a Philadelphia barber's ad informing the public that he was going out of business, Ben pointed out what a good example this was. He noted that there were "several Shavers and Trimmers at Court, the Bar, in Church and State" who fleeced the public and ought to retire as well. He specifically mentioned "the Reverend Mr. G.W.," but added, "I forbear making farther mention of this spiritual Shaver and Trimmer lest I should affect the Minds of my Readers as deeply as his Preaching has affected their Pockets."

Ben was referring to the charismatic English minister George Whitefield, who at the time was attracting thousands of people throughout the colonies to his open-air ministry and always ended his spellbinding sermons with a collection. Although Whitefield was never accused of fraud, a later charismatic minister and televangelist was indicted in 1988 for defrauding his followers of nearly $4 million for his personal use. The present-day "shaver and trimmer" was convicted, fined $500,000, and sent to prison.

Merrymaking on Twelfth Night

❖ For a winter potluck supper, warm a brick or rock under the woodstove or in a low oven and use it to help keep casseroles or other dishes warm en route. Wrap the stone and covered dish together in a clean bath towel and place them in a basket or sturdy box. For added warmth, toss the towel in the dryer to heat it up as well.

❖ If you have an open bottle of wine left over after the party, plunge the cork into boiling water before reinsert-

ing it in the bottle. This will soften it, making it more pliable.

❖ If you host a dinner party and fear an overabundance of leftovers, have a plan to share the wealth. Be ready with a supply of self-sealing plastic bags and inexpensive food containers. Divide up the leftovers for your guests to take home.

Setting too good an example is a kind of slander seldom forgiven.

—BEN FRANKLIN

WHEN BEN FRANKLIN was 12, his father set him up as an apprentice to his older brother James, a printer. But things didn't work out, and Ben decided to break the terms of his apprenticeship. James countered by speaking ill of Ben to all the other printers in the area, and they refused to hire him.

Seeking work, Ben went to New York and then to Philadelphia, where he eventually became a very successful printer. When he returned to Boston a few years later, he was received with joy by most of his family, but not by James. "I was better dressed than ever while in his service, having a genteel new suit from head to foot, a watch, and my pockets lined with near five pounds sterling in silver," Ben reported. He showed off his possessions to his brother's staff, which angered James. When their mother asked them to reconcile, James said that Ben had insulted him greatly and he could never forgive Ben.

Fortunately, he was wrong. Toward the end of James's life, the brothers did reconcile, and Ben took in James's son and taught him the printing business.

A WORD TO THE WISE

A baby is God's opinion that life should go on.

—*Carl Sandburg*

6

Epiphany

● ○ ○ ●

—BK

Now the days have lengthened one cock's stride.

1759
GEORGE WASHINGTON married MARTHA DANDRIDGE CUSTIS, a widow with two children.

1878
Writer and poet CARL SANDBURG was born.

1912
New Mexico became the 47th state.

FOR LUCK AT EPIPHANY

❦ Epiphany celebrates the visit of the Magi to the baby Jesus and marks the end of the holidays. Traditional fare is a cake with a lucky bean baked in it. Bake a mocha or spice cake with a whole coffee bean in the batter.

❦ As a nod to the three wise men, bring three of anything as a hostess gift. Three bags of spiced

nuts, three bottles of sparkling cider, or three different breads would be appropriate. Noisemakers are also traditional, to discourage evil spirits.

❦ To avoid bad luck, you should take down all Christmas greenery today. Perhaps the family member who finds the lucky bean in the cake can take down the tree.

JANUARY, *the First Month*

13

JANUARY

7

When oak trees bend with snow in January, good crops may be expected.

● ◐ ○ ○ ● ●

1800
Birthday of
MILLARD FILLMORE,
13th president of the
United States
(1850–1853).

1845
President JOHN TYLER
began weekly public
concerts by the U.S.
Marine Corps Band
on the grounds of the
White House.

1990
Up to 5 inches of rain
soaked western Oregon
and Washington.
Wind gusts on
Rattlesnake Ridge in
Washington reached
130 miles per hour.

■ ■ ■

I have sometimes
doubted whether
there could be a
great race without
the hardy influence
of winters in due
proportion.

—*Walt Whitman*

Stick to your winter flannels until your flannels stick to you.

—THE OLD FARMER'S ALMANAC

PRACTICAL PRIMER

IF YOU LIVE in a northern climate where the winters present a near constant chill, you would be wise to keep your flannels handy. The first flannel underwear was used in Boston by Lord Percy's regiment when they were encamped on Boston Common in October of 1774. There was barely enough flannel in town to outfit that one regiment.

Thanks to the severity of New England winters, flannels came to be almost synonymous with long underwear. Union suits followed shortly, being the same idea in a united shirt and pants that wouldn't come untucked and leave the midriff bare.

These days, flannel is more often seen in the form of shirts and sheets, but the idea of layering clothes for winter warmth has remained a tried-and-true method of beating the chill.

❦ To renew the softness of flannel and remove lint, brush it. Ironing flattens the nap, so if you must iron it, brush it afterward.

❦ Before sewing with flannel, soak the fabric in a boiling-water bath. Let stand until cold, then wring out and dry. This avoids shrinkage later.

❦ If you suffer from hot flashes, wear layers of natural fibers (cotton, linen, light flannel, or wool) so you can peel them off when a "power surge" hits.

❦ Recycle old flannel sheets into quilt liners or padding for pot holders. They also make good shoe-shining rags and dustcloths.

KNOW-HOW FOR KNITTERS

Buying European yarn and wondering how much you have? Twenty grams is almost ¾ ounce, 25 grams is not quite an ounce, 40 grams is not quite 1½ ounces, and 50 grams is 1¾ ounces.

> *Since thou art not sure of a minute, throw not away an hour.*
>
> —BEN FRANKLIN

MANY OF US engage in multitasking—talking on the phone while checking our e-mail, or helping the kids with homework while making supper. But a recent study suggests that multitasking is not necessarily an efficient strategy. Researchers at the University of Michigan discovered that test subjects who switched back and forth while completing tasks took longer to complete them than those who stuck to one task at a time. Also, the length of time increased as the complexity of the tasks increased.

A WORD TO THE WISE

According to the authors of the study, switching tasks requires "rule activation"—recognizing and switching to a different set of rules for each task. In many situations, this is merely inefficient. But in some settings, it can be deadly: A moment's inattention while you're driving—talking on your cell phone or looking for a compact disc—can result in an accident if you don't see a car ahead of you change lanes suddenly. Although Ben Franklin encouraged making the most of every minute, we think he'd agree with this bumper sticker: Shut Up and Drive.

CLUTTER CLEANUP

❖ Make a resolution to go after clutter around the house. Work slowly and do one job at a time: Get rid of newspapers and magazines, put away books, or organize photographs.

❖ Go through your closet and weed out any clothing that doesn't fit or that you simply don't like. Take it to a thrift shop or donate it to a homeless shelter.

❖ When you store boxes of ornaments and other holiday decorations, tape a colorful Christmas card to the side of each one for identification and stack them with the card side facing out.

—BK

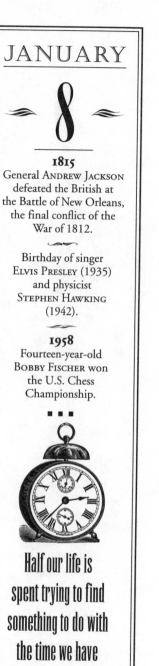

1815
General ANDREW JACKSON defeated the British at the Battle of New Orleans, the final conflict of the War of 1812.

Birthday of singer ELVIS PRESLEY (1935) and physicist STEPHEN HAWKING (1942).

1958
Fourteen-year-old BOBBY FISCHER won the U.S. Chess Championship.

• • •

Half our life is spent trying to find something to do with the time we have rushed through life trying to save.

—*Will Rogers*

9

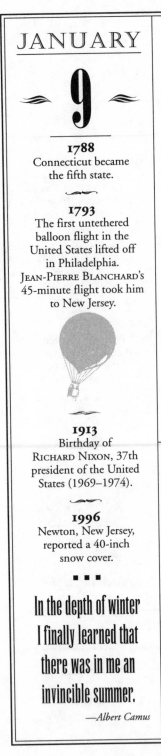

1788
Connecticut became
the fifth state.

1793
The first untethered
balloon flight in the
United States lifted off
in Philadelphia.
JEAN-PIERRE BLANCHARD's
45-minute flight took him
to New Jersey.

1913
Birthday of
RICHARD NIXON, 37th
president of the United
States (1969–1974).

1996
Newton, New Jersey,
reported a 40-inch
snow cover.

■ ■ ■

In the depth of winter
I finally learned that
there was in me an
invincible summer.

—*Albert Camus*

Black Bean Chili

*This slow cooker favorite is easily assembled in the morning
and will be ready to serve for supper. Guaranteed to ward off
January's worst chill.*

1½ pounds boneless pork, cut
   into ½-inch cubes
2 cans (15½ ounces each)
   black beans, drained
1 medium onion, chopped
1 yellow bell pepper, seeded
   and chopped
1 cup chunky salsa
2 cloves garlic, minced
2 teaspoons chili powder, or
   more to taste

1 teaspoon cumin
1 teaspoon coriander
1 teaspoon salt
1 cup water
¼ cup sour cream
½ cup shredded Monterey
   Jack cheese
1 tablespoon finely chopped
   fresh parsley or cilantro

Combine all the ingredients except the sour cream, cheese, and
parsley in a 3½-quart slow cooker. Cover and cook on Low
for 7 to 8 hours. (If you don't have a slow cooker, combine the ingredients in a heavy ovenproof casserole, cover, and bake at 300°F
for 3 hours.) To serve, garnish with the sour cream, cheese, and
parsley. *Makes 4 to 6 servings*

Scrumptious Soups and Stews

❅ For an excellent beef stew, use beer
in place of water or broth.

❅ Add a teaspoonful of honey
to tomato-based soups to coun-
teract the acidity and improve
the flavor.

❅ If a vegetable soup tastes
bland, perk it up with a hearty
dash of Tabasco or Worcester-
shire sauce, a spoonful of Asian
fish sauce, ½ cup red or white
wine, or 1 teaspoon curry
powder or chili powder.

A House Built for Winter

THE *Inspired* **MIND**

WHEN BEN FRANKLIN built a four-story addition to his house in 1786, the hand-hewn timbers were interlocked with mortise and tenon joints, held together by wooden pins. Nails were used only to fasten siding and roofing materials to the timber frame skeleton. Most likely, there was no insulation in the walls or attic, even though Ben had studied conductivity in his experiments with heat and cold. In fact, he suggested that outer garments to warm a person be made of materials with low conductivity to retain body heat longer.

In the 1970s, the long-lost craft of timber framing was revived in America. Once again, post and beam homes were raised just as they had been in Ben's time, but with a concern for energy conservation through insulation. Timber framer Tedd Benson of Alstead, New Hampshire, developed the idea that a timber frame could be enclosed in an insulated skin, eliminating stud walls and fiberglass insulation. The timber frame thus becomes like the skeleton of a mammal. Rigid foam-core panels with a high R-value, patented in 1989, are used to wrap the entire timber frame, serving the same function as Ben's insulating garment of 200 years ago.

STAYING WARM

❖When choosing an overcoat, look for one with a hood that extends well beyond your cheeks to fend off the wind.

❖If you humidify your house during the winter months, you can comfortably turn your heat down to 68°F.

❖For a cozy throw to drape over the back of your couch or easy chair, buy a 2-yard length of colorful polar fleece. It's cheaper than a blanket, needs no hemming, and can be tossed into the washer and dryer as needed.

❖Insert foam liners into your boots or hiking shoes to give your toes an extra layer of insulation when you are outdoors.

JANUARY

~ 10 ~

1904
Birth of actor
RAY BOLGER, best known
for his portrayal of the
Scarecrow in the 1939
movie *The Wizard of Oz.*

1946
The first United Nations
General Assembly opened
in London.

1982
A blizzard in Fargo, North
Dakota, produced a
windchill factor of −98°F.

*I could while away the
hours,
Conferrin' with the
flowers
Consultin' with the rain,
And my head I'd be
scratchin',
While my thoughts were
busy hatchin',
If I only had a brain.*

—Harold Arlen and
E. Y. Harburg, from
The Wizard of Oz

JANUARY

11

1918
A blizzard struck the Midwest, halting mail service for 2 weeks.

1943
President FRANKLIN ROOSEVELT sent to Congress a budget of $109 billion, $100 billion of which was for the war in Europe and the Pacific.

* * *

Money is the root of all evil, and yet it is such a useful root that we cannot get on without it any more than we can without potatoes.

—*Louisa May Alcott*

There is much money given to be laught at, though the purchasers don't know it; witness A's fine horse, and B's fine house.

—BEN FRANKLIN

OR, AS ANOTHER PUNDIT put it, "One man's trash is another man's treasure." Why else would online auction Web sites be so successful? At this writing, the largest online auction site lists millions of items, including old campaign buttons, bobble head dolls, movie props, sunglasses for dogs, Roman coins, white go-go boots, and a Jack Armstrong flashlight. Who would want the leftovers from a plate of nachos eaten by Donny Osmond during a concert? Apparently someone who was willing to bid $22.43 for them.

A WORD TO THE WISE

For sheer oddity, it's hard to beat the $67,000 paid for a single litchi at a Beijing auction in 2002. It came from a 400-year-old litchi tree whose fruit was once enjoyed by emperors of the Qing dynasty. The pricey produce broke the record price of $6,645 paid for a single litchi, which came from the same tree and earned it a spot in the book of *Guinness World Records 2001*. Now that's nutty.

CURING THE CATARRH

Catarrh *(a word derived from the Greek* katarrhein, *"to flow down") was what your grandparents called an overproduc-tion of mucus, generally resulting from a respiratory infection or cold. Before you hasten to call the doctor, try these cures.*

❖ Make a tea by simmering 5 nickel-size slices of fresh ginger in 2 cups water with 1 cinnamon stick, a few whole cloves, and some coriander seeds. Simmer for about 10 minutes, then sweeten with honey.

❖ For a dry cough, heat a lemon (roast or boil it for 10 minutes), juice it, and sweeten the juice with honey. Take by the teaspoonful as needed.

❖ Sweat it out! There's evidence that a sauna may stop cold germs in their tracks.

Fort Chops

W HEN BEN FRANKLIN led 70 woodsmen to Pennsylvania's western frontier to build Fort Allen in January 1756 (see also February 26), he needed it done in a hurry to defend settlers from the French and their Native American allies. Ben's team set to work cutting down trees to build the 6,000-square-foot stockade, completing the task in just five hours. He timed two men chopping down a 14-inch-diameter pine: It took them just 6 minutes.

THE *Inspired* MIND

Today the task would be lightened by chain saws. Loggers first introduced a hand-cranked logging saw in the 1860s. Forty years later, in 1906, Jacob Smith patented a large-toothed "endless chain saw" that could be hooked up to a gasoline engine. By 1950, one-man (portable) gas-driven chain saws were in use, but they were heavy and required lots of filing. Lightweight, high-speed chain saws appeared in the 1960s, followed by antivibration models with electronic ignitions, self-lubricating chains, and coasting brakes. Now there are compact chain saws for farmers and arborists. But Ben's men might choose a more heavy-duty rig that can saw a 14-inch tree in about 30 seconds.

(see also February 26)

JANUARY

12

Cut wood in January in the waning moon.

● ○ ○ ○ ●

1876
Author JACK LONDON
was born.

1932
Democrat HATTIE
OPHELIA WYATT CARAWAY
of Arkansas became
the first woman elected to
the U.S. Senate.

■ ■ ■

*I would rather be a
superb meteor,
every atom of me in
magnificent glow,
than a sleepy and
permanent planet.*

—*Jack London*

NATURE WATCH

We see chickadees, nuthatches, and other small birds at the feeder constantly on the coldest winter days, taking in calories. In the most inclement weather and at night, birds find shelter where they can remain inactive and protected, fluffing their feathers to preserve their body heat until the sun comes up and the feeding cycle begins again.

Fun in the Snow

❧ The new lightweight aluminum snowshoes on the market are engineered to make snowshoeing easy for every member of the family. Watch for late-season sales at sports shops and score a pair for everyone.

❧ For vigorous outdoor activities, dress with a wicking fabric close to your skin and a windproof layer on the outside. Tuck your camera into a pocket where your body heat will keep it from freezing up.

❧ Wear sunglasses or goggles on bright days to avoid getting a headache from the reflection off the snow.

13

St. Knut

● ○ ○ ○ ●

*Traditionally
the coldest day of
the year.*

1559
ELIZABETH I was crowned
queen of England.

1888
Thirty-three men—
explorers, naturalists,
mapmakers, and
educators—decided to
form the National
Geographic Society.

*There have been as many
great souls unknown to fame as
any of the most famous.*

—BEN FRANKLIN

A WORD TO THE WISE

LEONARD SKUTNIK was heading home from work on January 13, 1982, when a traffic jam changed his life. The backup was caused by an Air Florida plane that had crashed into a bridge during a freak blizzard in Washington, D.C. The plane had fallen into the Potomac River, and Skutnik watched with other commuters as survivors clung to the partially submerged plane waiting for rescue.

By the time helicopters arrived, the victims had been in the freezing water for more than 15 minutes. Skutnik saw that one woman was too weak to grab the rescue line lowered to her. "Nobody else was doing anything," he said, so he jumped in and rescued the woman. After the rescue, Skutnik gave his jacket to another victim, although he himself was wet and shivering. When asked to explain his heroic behavior, Skutnik didn't have any profound explanation. "I just did it," he said. "It was the only way."

Take time today to honor an unsung hero in your life.

> The hero is commonly the simplest and obscurest of men.
>
> —*Henry David Thoreau*

Don't Get Nipped (or Bitten)

❦ To avoid frost nip, which precedes frostbite, wear layered clothing, stay dry, and come in out of the cold. Wear a face mask, ear coverings, and mittens rather than gloves.

❦ To prevent frostbite on exposed flesh, do not stay out for more than 15 minutes if the windchill factor is −18°F or below.

❦ To treat frost nip, immerse the affected body parts in tepid to warm water (no hotter than bathwater). Do not rub the skin with snow or anything else.

LORE & LEGEND

King Knut, Sweden's king from 1080 to 1086, decreed that the Christmas season should be celebrated for 20 days—December 25 to January 13. In Sweden, it is still traditional to wait until January 13, known as **ST. KNUT'S DAY,** to discard the Christmas tree.

The Skinny on Dry Skin

WINTER'S LOW HUMIDITY and harsh conditions can do a number on your skin, leaving it flaky, itchy, and dry as an old bone. If you don't want to look like a desert tortoise by the end of the winter, take a few precautionary measures.

PRACTICAL PRIMER

- Moisturize like crazy. As soon as you get out of the shower or tub, while your skin is still damp, slather on lotion. Choose a brand that has petroleum jelly or lanolin high on the ingredients list.
- Don't go outside without using a moisturizer with an SPF of at least 15 on your face and hands.
- Try adding lemon juice or vinegar to your bathwater. Soap, being highly alkaline, may make your skin feel itchy.
- To soften dry skin, add 1 cup powdered milk to your bath. (It worked for Cleopatra.)
- Avoid steaming hot water or lengthy immersions, which will strip your skin of its natural oils.
- Wash gently. Vigorous scrubbing can further irritate sensitive skin.
- Forgo skin products that contain alcohol, which is drying.

> Years may wrinkle the skin, but to give up enthusiasm wrinkles the soul.
>
> —*Samuel Ullman*

JANUARY

14

Propitious day for the birth of women.

● ◐ ○ ◑ ●

1784
The Revolutionary War officially ended when Congress ratified the Treaty of Paris, establishing peace with Great Britain.

1900
The world premiere of PUCCINI's opera *Tosca* took place in Rome.

1935
Birth of LUCILLE WHEELER, alpine skier who won Canada's first Olympic medal for skiing.

Help for Sneezes, Warts, and Itchy Feet

❖ Eat raw garlic to stop a sneezing fit.

❖ To remove a wart, apply a piece of duct tape and leave it in place for 6 days out of 7 until the wart disappears.

❖ To treat athlete's foot, soak your feet in salted warm water (1 teaspoon salt for each cup water), then apply athlete's foot powder or a baking soda paste between your toes.

❖ To avoid athlete's foot, wear a pair of flip-flops or water shoes in locker rooms and public showers.

JANUARY

15

1929
Civil rights leader
MARTIN LUTHER KING JR.
was born.

1932
A record-setting 2 inches
of snow fell on Los
Angeles.

1967
The Green Bay Packers
and Kansas City Chiefs
played Super Bowl I
in Los Angeles. The
Packers won, 35–10.

• • •

Perhaps I am a bear,
or some hibernating
animal underneath,
for the instinct to be
half asleep all winter
is so strong in me.

—*Anne Morrow Lindbergh*

He that riseth late, must trot all day, and shall scarce overtake his business at night.

—BEN FRANKLIN

THE LEGENDARY Paul "Bear" Bryant, head football coach at the University of Alabama, at one point was the winningest coach in college football history, with 323 victories. He was once asked whether it was true that he could walk on water. "I won't say I can or I can't," he replied. "But if I do, I do it before most people get up in the morning."

Many famous writers find that they're able to do their best writing in the morning, when they're fresh. As Ben Franklin noted in *Poor Richard's Almanack,* "The muses love the morning."

One famously creative person who *didn't* see the need of rising early—or rising at all—was Mark Twain, who often wrote while lying in bed. Once, when a reporter arrived to interview Twain at his home, his wife, Livy, asked him, "Don't you think it will be a little embarrassing for him to find you in bed?"

"Why, if you think so, Livy," Twain replied, "we could have the other bed made up for him."

SPEAKING OF BEDS

❧ Make your bedroom a personal retreat. Splurge on luxurious sheets, set a pitcher of fresh water by your bed, and surround yourself with books or whatever else you most enjoy.

❧ If your family pet likes to sleep on your bed, cover your spread with an extra sheet, which is much easier to launder or shake outside than a heavy coverlet.

❧ To avoid waking up with a dry throat in the winter, set up a humidifier in your bedroom.

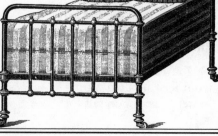

Winter White Chocolate Drink

Think of this as hot chocolate for grown-ups—a rich and warming variation on kids' cocoa. Add a splash of liqueur right before serving, if desired.

4 ounces good-quality white chocolate, finely chopped
½ cup coffee
1½ cups milk
1 cup half-and-half
1 teaspoon pure vanilla extract
Cinnamon sticks or freshly grated nutmeg for garnish

Melt the chocolate in a double boiler or in a heavy saucepan over low heat, stirring constantly. Add the coffee, milk, and half-and-half and heat until hot (do not boil). Add the vanilla right before serving. Serve garnished with cinnamon sticks or nutmeg.

Makes 4 servings

WHITE CHOCOLATE WISDOM

❖ The cocoa butter in white chocolate gives it a mild milk chocolate taste and creamy texture, but it contains no chocolate liquor, which is why it's white. Don't confuse it with white confectionery coating, which has no chocolate taste whatsoever.

❖ White chocolate contains only a very small amount of caffeine and thus is often tolerated well by people who are sensitive to caffeine or allergic to chocolate.

❖ To make a simple **WHITE CHOCOLATE SAUCE** to serve with chocolate cake or ice cream, combine 4 ounces white chocolate, finely chopped; 3 tablespoons butter; and 2 tablespoons heavy cream in a heatproof bowl set in a pan of hot water. Stir until the chocolate melts, then remove from the water bath and stir vigorously until smooth. Makes about ¾ cup.

JANUARY

16

January fog means a wet spring.

● ○ ◑ ●

1909
Birth of singer
ETHEL MERMAN.

1944
In London, General
DWIGHT EISENHOWER was placed in command of the Allied invasion force.

■ ■ ■

LORE & LEGEND
"Beware the pogonip," some almanacs advise. A pogonip is a dense winter fog that freezes on trees but melts on the ground. Native Americans and early settlers alike considered a pogonip extremely unhealthy and a source of respiratory illness. To help ward off coughs and colds, tie a winter scarf around your face when a pogonip hits.

As with most fine things, chocolate has its season. . . . Any month whose name contains the letter A, E, or U is the proper time for chocolate.

—*Sandra Boynton*

~17~

1706

BEN FRANKLIN was born in Boston, the 8th of JOSIAH and ABIAH FRANKLIN'S 10 children and the youngest son.

Birth of British prime minister DAVID LLOYD GEORGE (1863), ballerina NORA KAYE (1920), actor JAMES EARL JONES (1931), and boxer MUHAMMAD ALI (1942).

· · ·

I think, at a child's birth, if a mother could ask a fairy godmother to endow it with the most useful gift, that gift should be curiosity.

—*Eleanor Roosevelt*

We Know He Was Born, but on Which Day?

R EFERRING TO an uncle, Ben Franklin wrote in his *Autobiography,* "He died in 1702, January 6, old style, just four years to a day before I was born." Ben thought his own birthday was January 6, but today we mark it on January 17. Why the difference?

Before 1752, England and the colonies used Julius Caesar's calendar, based on a year that began on the vernal equinox date of March 25. The Julian year lasted 365 days, 6 hours—about 11 minutes longer than the actual solar year. Over the centuries, those minutes added up. The Julian calendar was gaining a full day every 128 years, and the calendar dates no longer matched the seasons.

THE *Inspired* MIND

In 1582, Pope Gregory eliminated several calendar days to make the equinox fall on March 21, but England ignored the new Gregorian calendar. When Parliament fixed the discrepancy in 1752, it changed the beginning of the new year from March 25 to January 1 and "erased" 11 days to align the equinox with March 21. Thus 11 days are now added to Old Style dates that fall between January 1 and March 25, and the year for those dates is advanced by 1.

When Ben Franklin was baptized, his birth date was recorded as January 6, 1705, according to the Julian calendar. Because of Parliament's 1752 decision, we add 11 days and 1 year to come up with the date January 17, 1706.

INGENIOUS TOOLS

❦ Use an emery board to sand small objects or when working in really tight spaces.

❦ If you don't have a Phillips screwdriver, use the tip of a vegetable peeler instead.

❦ Use a bobby pin to hold a nail in place and avoid smashing your fingers with a hammer.

❦ Glue the tab from a soda can to the back of a light picture frame to create a make-do hook.

If you desire many things, many things will seem but a few.

—BEN FRANKLIN

THE CLASSIC short story by Leo Tolstoy titled "How Much Land Does a Man Need?" tells the tale of a man who was offered a great opportunity. For 1,000 rubles, he could have as much land as he could pace off from sunrise to sunset. There was just one condition: He had to return to the exact spot where he started before the sun set, or he would lose his money.

At sunrise, the man set out, marking the edges of his land as he went. The farther he went, the better the land seemed, and he hurried on, growing hot and tired. By the time he headed back to the starting point, the sun was beginning to set. He began running and was soon exhausted and dying of thirst. He pressed on, his heart pounding in his chest, his lungs straining. Finally, just as the sun set, he reached his goal—and collapsed, dead. The man's servant buried him on the spot.

As we strain to acquire more, we would all do well to remember Tolstoy's conclusion to this story: "Six feet from his head to his heels was all he needed."

TIPS FOR WINTER TRAVEL

❖ When traveling, be sure your suitcase has your identification both inside and outside. For easier recognition, add a stripe of bright tape to the outside or tie a colorful ribbon or pom-pom to the handle.

❖ If you're vacationing in a tropical spot and stomach upsets threaten to spoil the fun, add papaya to your diet. Plain black tea (no milk, cream, or sugar) also may help.

❖ For a soothing footbath after a long day of sight-seeing, pack lavender oil in your travel bag and add a few drops to warm water.

–BK

1778
Captain JAMES COOK discovered the Sandwich Islands, which we now know as Hawaii.

1911
EUGENE ELY, a civilian pilot from Iowa, became the first person to land an airplane on a ship when he brought a biplane safely onto the deck of the USS *Pennsylvania* in San Francisco Bay.

■ ■ ■

Life contains but two tragedies. One is not to get your heart's desire; the other is to get it.

—*George Bernard Shaw*

19

1809
Writer EDGAR ALLAN POE
was born.

1825
EZRA DAGGETT and
THOMAS KENSETT of New
York were granted a patent
for the tin can.

1928
ELEANORA SEARS won
the first women's U.S.
National Squash Racquets
Championship.

*Pollio, who values nothing
that's within, buys books as men
hunt beavers—for their skin.*

—BEN FRANKLIN

A WORD TO THE WISE

LITTLE DID BEN know. These days, interior designers often buy books to decorate the libraries of well-to-do patrons, with no regard at all to their content. Antiquarian bookshops specialize in selling antique leather-bound books in a selection of sizes and colors to match any decorating scheme.

In some ways, this is not a new idea. Charles Dickens did something similar when he designed his study at Tavistock House. The study had a hidden doorway that resembled a bookshelf, complete with fake books. Dickens had chosen the titles for the phony books himself. They included:

Five Minutes in China
Noah's Arkitecture
The Gunpowder Magazine
Lady Godiva on the Horse
Heaviside's Conversations with Nobody
The Quarrelly Review
Drowsy's Recollections of Nothing
Cat's Lives (a nine-volume set)

Books are not made for furniture, but there is nothing else that so beautifully furnishes a house.

—*Henry Ward Beecher*

THE INDOOR GARDENER

❖ Let houseplants almost dry out between waterings. If leaves turn yellow and drop, you are overwatering.

❖ Place ficus plants near a sunny window. Keep the soil moist, but don't let water pool in the saucer.

❖ Check root crops and tender bulbs you've stored in the basement or root cellar and discard any that are soft or show signs of decay.

❖ Keep houseplants away from cold windows, and be careful never to pull the curtains and trap them against the glass on a frigid night.

❖ To boost indoor humidity for orchids, place the pots on large saucers filled with pebbles and keep the pebbles wet.

❖ Discourage spider mites by misting under the leaves.

It's Family Game Night!

PRACTICAL

PRIMER

Depending on the ages of your children, they may cheer wildly or roll their eyes at the prospect of playing board games with their parents. But if you provide enough variety and lots of snacks, your game night will be a success. Take comfort in the fact that many of these games go back thousands of years. The ancient Egyptians played *senat* (backgammon), and the Romans rolled *tesserae* (dice) and played *terni lapilli* (ticktacktoe) and *calculi* (checkers). (There is, however, no record of an ancient form of Candy Land.) To ensure a memorable evening, try these ideas.

- Invite another family or two to join you so that you can set up several game stations. Go for a good selection: an abstract game such as backgammon or chess, a classic board game such as Clue or Monopoly, and perhaps a traditional pub game such as checkers or cribbage.

- Keep a copy of Edmond Hoyle's rules for games handy to resolve any arguments.

- Allow variations on the rules as long as everyone involved agrees. For instance, play a round of Scrabble using only invented words that the players have to define.

- Set up a jigsaw puzzle for those who don't like board games.

- Award prizes at the end for "best sport," "most ruthless," and so on.

FOOD FOR GAME NIGHT

❖ Serve classic snacks to go with classic games—Rice Krispies Treats, pretzels dipped in chocolate, salted peanuts in the shell.

❖ At the end of the evening, serve this delicious **HOT FUDGE SAUCE** over peppermint stick ice cream. In a small saucepan, combine 1 cup sugar, ¼ cup unsweetened cocoa, pinch of salt, ⅔ cup milk, and 2 tablespoons butter. Bring to a boil over medium heat and cook for 3 minutes, stirring steadily. Remove from the heat and add 1 teaspoon pure vanilla extract. Makes 2 cups.

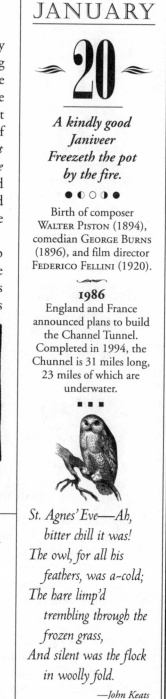

JANUARY

20

A kindly good Janiveer Freezeth the pot by the fire.

● ◐ ○ ◑ ●

Birth of composer WALTER PISTON (1894), comedian GEORGE BURNS (1896), and film director FEDERICO FELLINI (1920).

1986
England and France announced plans to build the Channel Tunnel. Completed in 1994, the Chunnel is 31 miles long, 23 miles of which are underwater.

■ ■ ■

*St. Agnes' Eve—Ah,
   bitter chill it was!
The owl, for all his
   feathers, was a-cold;
The hare limp'd
   trembling through the
   frozen grass,
And silent was the flock
   in woolly fold.*

—John Keats

● ● ○ ○ ●

1738
Patriot and soldier
ETHAN ALLEN was born.

1985
Akron, Ohio, experienced
a record low of –24°F.

● ● ●

**There is no psychiatrist
in the world like a puppy
licking your face.**

—*Bern Williams*

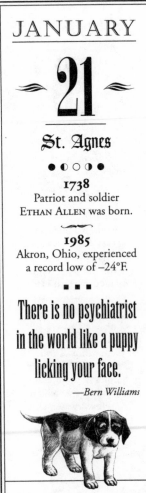

*Let thy child's first lesson
be obedience, and the second may
be what thou wilt.*

—BEN FRANKLIN

D URING THE CIVIL WAR, General Ulysses Grant
had to deal with a young soldier who had abandoned his
post while on guard duty. Grant took pity on the man
and pardoned him, but the general told him that in the future,
"orders must be strictly and promptly obeyed."

ULYSSES S. GRANT

Later, the soldier happened to be guard-
ing a steamboat loaded with ammunition.
He had been instructed not to allow anyone smoking a pipe or cigar aboard the
boat. Along came General Grant with one
of his trademark cigars clamped between
his teeth. The soldier commanded the
general to halt. Amazed by the soldier's au-
dacity, Grant demanded an explanation.
The soldier replied, "I have been taught to
obey orders strictly and promptly, and my orders are to allow no
one to approach this boat with a lighted cigar. You will please
throw yours away."

Grant tossed the cigar into the river, no doubt pleased that the
man had learned his lesson so well.

Teaching Your New Puppy a Few Tricks

❖ The best time to adopt a
new puppy is between 7 and
10 weeks of age. This period
is the middle of a puppy's
"socialization" phase, when
relationships with humans
are formed.

❖ Housebreaking, walking
on a leash, and responding
to the command "Come" are
the first order of business for

a new puppy. Her success depends on the vigilance and
patience of the owner.

❖ To acclimate a puppy to a
crate, it's a good idea to line
the crate with old bath towels. They are easy to wash
and are soft and cozy for the
puppy. Also place a few toys
in the crate so the puppy re-
gards it as a haven. Get in

the habit of saying "Crate
up" and tapping the crate
two or three times when putting the puppy inside, and
he will quickly learn to respond to the command.

❖ Puppies, like children,
love to play. Use these play-
ful periods as a time to practice some simple commands,
such as "Come" and "Stay."

Cask for a Casket

BEN FRANKLIN wrote an account, published in France in 1774, of how a fly, apparently drowned in wine, was rejuvenated by the sun. Ben wished that he could replicate the fly's revival by coming up with a method of embalming drowned people so that they might be revived at a later time—say, 100 years later. "I should prefer to any ordinary death . . . being immersed in a cask of Madeira wine, with a few friends," he wrote, "to be recalled to life by the solar warmth."

THE **Inspired** MIND

If the sun shines today, the vineyards rejoice.

The Michigan-based Cryonics Institute, founded in 1976, offers to prepare, cool, and store patrons—as soon as possible after dying—for later revival. The corpse is immersed in liquid nitrogen at a temperature of −196°C (−321°F), a point at which physical decay all but ceases. According to the institute's Web site (www.cryonics.org), "When and if future medical technology allows, our member patients will be healed and revived, and awaken to extended life in youthful good health."

Alas, although some researchers have found that moderate consumption of red wine may increase longevity, there is no evidence of its suitability for embalming, as Ben fancied. Drat!

Do any human beings ever realize life while they live it—every, every minute?

—*Thornton Wilder,*
Our Town

1901
Great Britain's Queen VICTORIA died, ending a 63-year reign, the longest of any British monarch.

1938
Our Town, a play written by THORNTON WILDER, was performed for the first time in Princeton, New Jersey.

LOW-TECH TOOLS FOR PAINTING

❦ When painting door and window frames, protect windows with dampened strips of newspaper, smoothed flat against the glass. When you are done painting, be sure to peel off the strips before they dry.

❦ For a quick touch-up, use a scrap piece of foam rubber. The paint will go on easily, and you can throw away the foam when you're finished.

❦ Stretch a strong rubber band vertically around your paint can, cutting across the middle of the opening. Use the band to catch excess paint. This will keep the side and rim of the can clean.

❦ Before painting a ceiling, attach a used dry cleaner's bag around each hanging light fixture to protect it from spatters.

❦ Before spray-painting, slip your hands into plastic bags to keep them clean.

23

1737
Birth of founding father
JOHN HANCOCK.

1849
ELIZABETH BLACKWELL
became the first woman to
earn a medical degree in
the United States.

1971
A U.S. record low
temperature was set at
Prospect Creek Camp,
Alaska: −80°F.

▪ ▪ ▪

LORE & LEGEND

Upon signing the Declaration of Independence, John Hancock looked around at his fellow revolutionaries and warned, "We must be unanimous; there must be no pulling different ways; we must all hang together." To which Ben Franklin reportedly answered, "Yes, we must indeed all hang together, or most assuredly we shall all hang separately."

Gingerbread

This is the quintessential winter dessert, best served warm
with real whipped cream.

½ cup molasses
⅓ cup sugar
½ cup butter, cut into
   pieces
1 cup boiling water
1 egg
1¾ cups flour
1 to 2 tablespoons ginger,
   to taste
½ teaspoon cinnamon
½ teaspoon cloves
1 teaspoon baking soda

Preheat the oven to 350°F. Put the molasses, sugar, and butter in a ceramic mixing bowl and pour the water on top. Stir until the butter melts. Add the egg and beat well. In another bowl, whisk together the flour, ginger, cinnamon, cloves, and baking soda and add to the butter mixture. Beat until smooth. Pour into a greased 8- or 9-inch square pan and bake for about 35 minutes, or until a toothpick inserted in the center comes out clean.

Makes 8 servings

Ginger for Warmth and Comfort

Sea captains kept ginger among their rations, and Civil War tonics included it (along with red currants, lemon juice, and whiskey) as a morale booster. Here are some suggestions for using ginger to give yourself a boost.

GINGER
PLANT

❧ After a hard day, mix some ginger into an herbal oil and use it to massage sore muscles.

❧ Try ginger tea for morning sickness or menstrual distress.

❧ Add a few drops of ginger oil or some grated fresh ginger to hot bathwater. A good soak in gingered water will help you sweat away what ails you.

I don't s'pose anybody on earth likes gingerbread better'n I do—and gets less'n I do.

—*Abraham Lincoln*

He that builds before he counts the cost, acts foolishly; and he that counts before he builds, finds he did not count wisely.

—BEN FRANKLIN

JANUARY

24

1848
The discovery of gold at Sutter's Mill in northern California started a gold rush.

1924
The Russian city of St. Petersburg was renamed Leningrad.

Sir WINSTON CHURCHILL (1965) and Supreme Court justice THURGOOD MARSHALL (1993) died.

BEN FRANKLIN learned early on the value of counting the cost before undertaking a project. As a boy growing up in Boston, he spent a lot of time in and around the water. He and his friends loved to fish for minnows at a local millpond, and young Ben once suggested that they build a wharf at the edge of the pond, where they could fish without getting their feet muddy. Nearby was a pile of stones, intended to be used for a new house, which Ben and his friends "borrowed" after the builders had gone home for the day.

The next morning, the workers discovered the stones missing and soon located the culprits, whose parents lectured them sternly. When Ben's father reprimanded him, Ben tried to justify their actions based on the obvious need for their building project. His father quickly convinced him that "nothing is useful which is not honest."

Live so that when your children think of fairness and integrity, they think of you.

—H. Jackson Brown Jr.

Mighty Good Meat Loaf and Meatballs

❖ To keep meat loaf from sticking to the pan, place two strips of bacon on the bottom of the pan before adding the meat mixture.

❖ Add a tablespoonful of horseradish to your next meat loaf mix to perk up the taste.

❖ Meat loaf for company? Try this presentation. Bake your meat loaf in a ring mold. To serve, fill the center of the ring with mashed potatoes and garnish with onion gravy.

❖ For a healthier meat loaf, substitute oatmeal for bread crumbs. You'll add fiber and vitamins.

❖ To save time making meatballs, roll the meat into a log and cut into even slices. Roll the slices into balls.

❖ Before cooking, dredge meatballs lightly in flour seasoned with freshly ground black pepper, garlic salt, and a pinch each of chili powder and curry powder.

25

St. Paul

● ○ ○ ●

*St. Paul fair
with sunshine
Brings fertility to
rye and wine.*

1759
Scottish poet and
songwriter ROBERT BURNS
was born.

1924
Winter games sanctioned
by the International
Olympic Committee were
held in Chamonix,
France. The games lasted
for 11 days and were later
referred to as the first
Winter Olympics.

If evils come not, then our fears are vain; And if they do, fear but augments the pain.

—BEN FRANKLIN

A WORD TO THE WISE

AS A CHILD, Olympic bobsledder Nick Inzerello was afraid of roller coasters. (Fortunately, he overcame that fear.) Another man was so afraid of bridges that he would cross the Chesapeake Bay Bridge only if his wife was driving and he was locked in the trunk of the car. And one woman—think of it—had a fear of canned tomatoes. Other bizarre phobias include chorophobia (fear of dancing), homichlophobia (fear of fog), lachanophobia (fear of vegetables), and pteronophobia (fear of being tickled by feathers).

But for truly bizarre phobias, it's hard to beat the fear of alien abduction. In 1966, a London insurance company offered an insurance policy to cover just such a fear. For a premium of $155 a year, the company promised to pay $160,000 if you were abducted by aliens and $360,000 if you were impregnated by them. (The latter applied to men as well as women. Who knows what those aliens can do?) The company sold 300 policies in the first week.

Fear is that little darkroom where negatives are developed.

—*Michael Pritchard*

Home Remedies for Earaches, Colds, and Headaches

❖ For a mild earache, a warm heating pad can ease the pain. Keep the heat low. Consult your doctor if the pain persists.

❖ To prevent colds and sore throats from circulating in the family, soak toothbrushes in mouthwash. Be sure each

family member keeps his or her toothbrush separate— don't just pile them all in the same cup.

❖ Sinus headaches, common when we're shut up inside with dry indoor heat, respond well to aromatic steam. Boil sprigs of laven-

der, rosemary, pine, or thyme (alone or in combination), make a tent with a towel over your head, and inhale the steam.

❖ If you have a ringing in the ears, it may be tinnitus. Try avoiding quinine, aspirin, and caffeine.

John Bartram's *Franklinia*

A SMALL GROUP of tradesmen and specialists in mathematics, medicine, and the natural sciences met in Philadelphia in 1744 to establish the American Philosophical Society, the nation's first intellectual think tank. The idea of an organization applying practical knowledge to better the lives of people in America had been proposed by Ben Franklin the year before, and he served as the society's first secretary.

THE *Inspired* MIND

Founding member and botanist John Bartram had been trying for several years to raise money by subscription to support his field trips to study wildlife and collect mineral and plant specimens. Ben organized fund-raisers for his friend, who already had established the country's first botanic garden. Bartram also raised wheat, flax, oats, and Indian corn, but it was his harvesting of wild plants, including trees (which he sent to horticulturists in England for replanting), that earned him fame. In 1765, he and his son William discovered a tree with fragrant white blossoms growing in Georgia. They named it *Franklinia alatamaha,* the Franklin tree, in honor of their patron.

HEALING PLANTS

❦ To help fight winter colds and flu, look to herbs known for their strong scents—rosemary, thyme, sage, basil, oregano, hyssop, dill, chamomile, lavender, and others. They have high concentrations of volatile oils that have antiseptic and antibiotic properties, which bolster the immune system.

❦ To ease sore throats, make your own gargle by adding a teaspoon or two of any of the following to warm water: cider vinegar, sage, chamomile, lemon juice, or raspberry leaves.

❦ If you're prone to sinus infections, try sipping a tea made with oregano. Inhale the steamy vapor for the best effect.

❦ When strep or other infections require antibiotics, which kill good bacteria as well as bad, help your body keep its balance by eating lots of yogurt with active cultures. Also boost your vitamin C intake.

JANUARY

26

1784
In a letter to his daughter, BEN FRANKLIN wrote of his disapproval of the eagle as a symbol of the United States. He suggested using the wild turkey.

1837
Michigan became the 26th state.

1915
President WOODROW WILSON signed a bill establishing Colorado's Rocky Mountain National Park.

• • •

Much education today is monumentally ineffective. All too often we are giving young people cut flowers when we should be teaching them to grow their own plants.

—*John W. Gardner*

JANUARY

27

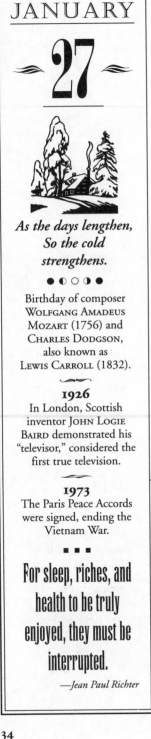

*As the days lengthen,
So the cold
strengthens.*

● ● ○ ● ●

Birthday of composer
WOLFGANG AMADEUS
MOZART (1756) and
CHARLES DODGSON,
also known as
LEWIS CARROLL (1832).

1926
In London, Scottish
inventor JOHN LOGIE
BAIRD demonstrated his
"televisor," considered the
first true television.

1973
The Paris Peace Accords
were signed, ending the
Vietnam War.

■ ■ ■

For sleep, riches, and
health to be truly
enjoyed, they must be
interrupted.

—*Jean Paul Richter*

Early to bed and early to rise, makes a man healthy, wealthy, and wise.

—BEN FRANKLIN

A WORD TO THE WISE

ONE OF Ben Franklin's most popular sayings, this proverb actually came from a book published in 1496. The "olde englysshe prouverbe" cited there goes like this: "Who soo woll ryse erly shall be holy helthy and zely [happy, fortunate.]"

Whatever the origin, now there's a study to back up the advice. Researchers at Brigham Young University surveyed 184 freshmen and correlated their sleep habits with their grades. The results showed that students who went to bed late and slept in the next day tended to have lower grades. For every extra hour (above the average) that students slept in, their grade point averages dropped 0.13 points (on a scale of 0 to 4.0). Why should this make a difference? It appears that our bodies were designed to rest during the hours of darkness. Important functions of the liver, adrenal glands, and other organs occur after dark and are disrupted if we're awake.

Before the discovery of electricity, people slept when it was dark and got up with the sun. If you're having trouble sleeping, try going to bed earlier and getting up earlier.

Clean Your House While You're Asleep

◖ Freshen musty sponges by soaking them overnight in a solution of one part vinegar and two parts water. Repeat periodically to kill mildew.

◖ To get odors out of plastic containers, fill them with crumpled newspaper, cover, and let sit overnight.

◖ Once a month, sprinkle your carpets with baking soda before you go to bed, then vacuum it up in the morning.

◖ Improve the smell of your refrigerator by soaking a cotton ball in a little vanilla extract and leaving it in the fridge overnight.

A Pillow for a Peaceful Night

With the right combination of herbs, a dream pillow can help ward off nightmares and intensify sweet dreams. Be sure that the herbs you use are completely dry. Also, people react differently to fragrances, so you may have to experiment with the combination of herbs to find a blend that suits you.

Two 12-inch squares of cheesecloth or tulle
½ cup mugwort leaves
½ cup lavender flowers
½ cup spearmint or peppermint leaves
2 tablespoons thyme leaves
2 tablespoons rosemary leaves
1 tablespoon orrisroot (a stabilizer)

Sew the pieces of cloth together along 3 sides, then turn so the seams are inside. Toss the herbs together and pour into the bag. Sew to close. Slip the pillow into a washable pillowcase, then place on top of your regular pillow. Sweet dreams!

A ruffled mind makes a restless pillow.
—Charlotte Brontë

1887
Pianist ARTHUR RUBINSTEIN was born.

1915
Congress established the U.S. Coast Guard.

1986
The space shuttle *Challenger* exploded after liftoff. All seven crew members perished.

Celebrating Chinese New Year

❖ The Chinese calendar, which dates back to 2700 B.C., is based on astronomy. Chinese New Year begins at sunset on the day of the second new moon following the winter solstice—sometime between January 21 and February 19.

❖ The Chinese zodiac is a 12-year cycle, in which each year is named after the rat, ox, tiger, hare, dragon, snake, horse, ram, monkey, rooster, dog, or boar. Even so, the good luck food on Chinese New Year is none of the above—it's fish, a symbol of abundance.

❖ **CHINESE FISH STEAKS** make a delicious—and lucky—Chinese New Year meal. In a large self-sealing plastic bag, combine ½ cup soy sauce; ¼ cup rice wine vinegar; 1 clove garlic, minced; 2 teaspoons minced fresh ginger; 1 tablespoon sesame oil; 4 scallions, chopped; and 1 teaspoon grated lemon zest. Place 4 swordfish, tuna, or salmon steaks in the bag and let marinate for 1 to 2 hours. Broil or grill the fish until flaky, about 4 minutes per side. Makes 4 servings.

JANUARY

29

1843
Birthday of
WILLIAM MCKINLEY, 25th
president of the United
States (1897–1901).

1861
Kansas became
the 34th state.

1880
Birth of comedian
W. C. FIELDS.

1921
A violent windstorm,
gusting up to 113 miles
per hour at North Head,
Washington, blasted the
Pacific Northwest.

∎ ∎ ∎

**Winter lies too long
in country towns;
hangs on until it is
stale and shabby,
old and sullen.**

—*Willa Cather*

Cures for Cabin Fever

CABIN FEVER may not give you physical aches and pains, but it sure does make your spirit pine for sun and fun. Especially if you live in the North, you may be feeling downright crabby and confined at this point, with nearly 2 more months of winter to go. In case a trip to Tahiti is not in the budget, here are a few surefire cures.

PRACTICAL **PRIMER**

- Book a weekend for you and your family or friends at a hotel with a big swimming pool, sauna, massage room, and other amenities.
- Rent a pile of movies that transport you to a warmer clime—*Lawrence of Arabia, The African Queen, The Lion King,* whatever appeals.
- Make the best of the cold and snow and go skiing, snowshoeing, or ice-skating—anything that gets you out in the fresh air.
- Make a beautiful fruit salad with the freshest fruit you can find—pineapples, strawberries, grapes, limes, kiwifruit. Re-create your favorite summer meal, even if you look like Nanook of the North while you grill your swordfish outdoors.
- Paint your kitchen or living room yellow, with sparkling white trim. Paint the ceiling, too, and open the drapes to let in the light.

New Ideas for the Lunch Box

❖ Pack clementines instead of large oranges. They're easier to peel and often sweeter.

❖ Tired of the same old sandwich? Try pita bread or tortillas instead of regular bread; roasted red peppers instead of tomatoes; Gouda, Havarti, or feta instead of cheddar; sprouts instead of lettuce; or pesto or hummus instead of mayonnaise.

❖ Buy plain yogurt in quart containers and spoon about a cupful into a reusable container. Drizzle with maple syrup or honey, then add a handful of granola, nuts, or dried cranberries.

Kings and bears often worry their keepers.

—Ben Franklin

MANY PRESIDENTS have chafed under the constraints imposed on them by the need for security. Woodrow Wilson occasionally tried to sneak out of the White House without his escorts. Warren G. Harding purposely hit golf balls into the woods to get rid of the Secret Service agents who followed him around disguised as caddies. Franklin Roosevelt made a game out of going for drives in his Ford phaeton (which was equipped with hand controls) and eluding his keepers as they followed in their more cumbersome touring cars.

A WORD TO THE WISE

But Jimmy Carter may have had more reason to begrudge overzealous security than any other president. Once, he was in a bathroom near the Oval Office and pushed a button that he thought was intended to flush the toilet. It was, in fact, a buzzer the Secret Service had installed for the first family to press if they were in trouble. Within seconds, an agent burst through the door, gun drawn, as Carter was still zipping up his pants.

The agent later reported that the president was "pretty chilly" to him after that.

JANUARY

30

1835
President ANDREW JACKSON survived an assassination attempt after a man fired two pistols at point-blank range. Both guns misfired.

1882
Birthday of FRANKLIN DELANO ROOSEVELT, 32nd president of the United States (1933–1945).

1912
Historian BARBARA TUCHMAN was born.

■ ■ ■

There are many ways of going forward, but only one way of standing still.

—*Franklin Delano Roosevelt*

THE HOUSEHOLD TOOL KIT

Here are the tools and materials you need to handle the basic fix-it projects in your home.

Crosscut saw
Hammer
Nail set
Nail punch
Assorted screws and nails
Tape measure
Bits and hand drill
Awl
Two screwdrivers
   (Phillips and regular)

Pliers
Glue
Paintbrush
Small level
Sandpaper assortment and
   holder for them
Adjustable wrench
Utility knife
Toilet plunger
Household oil

JANUARY

31

*January warm,
the Lord have mercy.*

● ○ ○ ○ ●

1865
General ROBERT E. LEE
was officially named to
lead the Confederate
armies, just months before
their ultimate defeat.

Birth of baseball greats
JACKIE ROBINSON (1919),
ERNIE BANKS (1931), and
NOLAN RYAN (1947).

1949
NBC aired America's
first television
daytime soap opera,
These Are My Children.

Death takes no bribes.

—BEN FRANKLIN

ON HIS DEATHBED, W. C. Fields was found reading a Bible—something he'd never been known to do before. When asked what he was doing, Fields replied, "Looking for a loophole."

The great British writer Rudyard Kipling was once surprised to see a notice of his own death in a newspaper to which he happened to be a subscriber. He wrote a letter to the paper saying, "I've just read that I am dead. Don't forget to delete me from your list of subscribers."

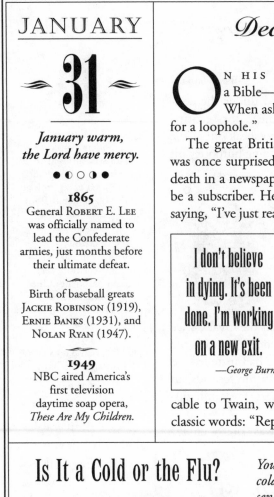

A WORD TO THE WISE

> I don't believe in dying. It's been done. I'm working on a new exit.
>
> —*George Burns*

Once, while Mark Twain was in London, a cousin of his became seriously ill. The cousin recovered, but by the time the story traveled back to New York, it was Twain himself who was at death's door. The *New York Journal* sent its reporter a cablegram asking whether the rumor was true. The reporter showed the cable to Twain, who instructed him to respond with these now classic words: "Report of my death greatly exaggerated."

Is It a Cold or the Flu?

You are achy, tired, and starting to cough. If it's a cold, you can probably tough it out, but the flu will send you straight to bed. Here are a few ways to distinguish the source of your discomfort.

	FLU	COLD
Headache	Always	Sometimes
Aches, fatigue	Always	Usually
Fever	Always	Sometimes
Cough	Usually	Sometimes
Runny nose	Sometimes	Usually
Sore throat	Rarely	Usually

FEBRUARY, *the Second Month*

Full Snow Moon

is the Native American name for this month's moon, a time when forest trails were often impassable. Because hunting could be so difficult, the tribes also called it the *Full Hunger Moon.*

Sign of the Zodiac:
Aquarius (January 20–February 19)

Element: Air

Quality: Inventive

Birthstone: Amethyst

Flower: Violet

ERIVED FROM the Latin *februo,* "to purify through sacrifice," February was a time of atonement for the ancient Romans. It seems a bit premature for spring-cleaning or for any serious regrets about the year just begun, so we might want to hang our hats on a different piece of lore, perhaps Groundhog Day on the 2nd (it means we are halfway to spring) or Valentine's Day on the 14th (a great excuse for smooching and eating chocolate).

February has one leg firmly planted in winter, the other tilting toward spring. A snowstorm can turn to ice or rain and back again on bitter winds, or the brightening sun can set icicles to dripping and frozen streams to gurgling. It's a month to make farmers downright restless. Gardeners design elaborate beds in their minds and content themselves with scrubbing the rust off their tools. Inside, houseplants that have languished for months are beginning to revive.

For a short month, February packs in a lot: the birthdays of George Washington and Abraham Lincoln, cherry pie and Mardi Gras (usually), the deepest snow, the first lambs of the season. Loggers like to fell trees in February's waning moon, before the sap starts to rise. No wonder February needs an extra day every 4 years.

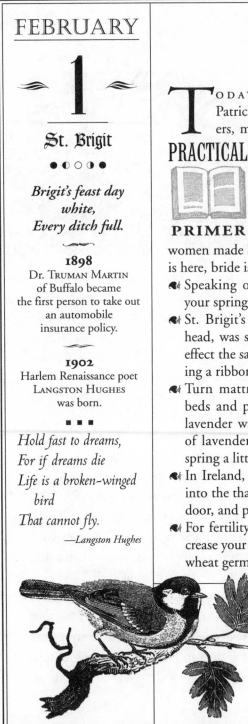

1

St. Brigit

● ● ○ ○ ●

*Brigit's feast day
white,
Every ditch full.*

1898
Dr. TRUMAN MARTIN
of Buffalo became
the first person to take out
an automobile
insurance policy.

1902
Harlem Renaissance poet
LANGSTON HUGHES
was born.

■ ■ ■

*Hold fast to dreams,
For if dreams die
Life is a broken-winged
bird
That cannot fly.*

—*Langston Hughes*

Start the Month with St. Brigit

PRACTICAL PRIMER

TODAY IS the feast day of St. Brigit, second only to St. Patrick in Ireland and patron of poets, blacksmiths, healers, midwives, dairymaids, and newborns. Snow on her day was thought to indicate a wet spring, whereas sunshine prognosticated more snow until May. Either way, Brigit's day is considered the start of spring in Ireland, the legend being that she dipped her finger in the brook to release the hen that hatched the cold. In 18th-century Scotland, women made Brigit's bed on the eve of February 2, saying, "Bride is here, bride is welcome!" to ensure continued fertility.

- Speaking of hens, have you ordered your spring chicks yet?
- St. Brigit's ribbon, worn around the head, was said to cure a headache. To effect the same remedy today, try soaking a ribbon in lavender water first.
- Turn mattresses now, plump feather beds and pillows, and sprinkle some lavender water on pillowcases. Sprigs of lavender in the linen closet bring spring a little closer.
- In Ireland, a little straw cross called St. Brigit's bow is tucked into the thatch roof to protect a house. Hang the same on your door, and perhaps get your chimney swept now as well.
- For fertility, add kelp or dulse to your diet, quit smoking, increase your zinc (found in leafy green vegetables, fish, nuts, and wheat germ), and maintain a good supply of vitamin C.

NATURE WATCH

Even in the northernmost states, birds are beginning to sing at sunrise. What you hear is likely to be a brief, businesslike call, such as the *dee-dee-dee* of the chickadee, but as the month advances and migrants arrive, the dawn choristers will become more melodious.

When Your Candles Have a Meltdown

THERE'S A FRIENDLY glow about a house with tapers on the supper table and votives flickering on windowsills in defiance of the darkness. But even if you buy good-quality candles, the slightest movement can set them to dripping melted wax. Here's how to deal with it.

PRACTICAL PRIMER

- Hardened wax is most easily removed when it's either cold and brittle or warm and soft. Put wooden candlesticks in the freezer for an hour, and the drippings will lift off easily. (By the way, candles stored in the freezer burn longer and drip less.) For brass, pewter, or other metals, immerse the candlesticks in very hot water and rub with a soft cloth.
- Wax stains on a tablecloth or carpet can be rubbed with an ice cube, then scraped off.
- Dye stains made by colored candles can be removed by laundering a piece as usual or using dry-cleaning solution.

There are two ways of spreading light: to be the candle or the mirror that reflects it.

—*Edith Wharton*

LORE & LEGEND

It is no accident that **GROUNDHOG DAY** and **CANDLEMAS** are celebrated together, for both signify the triumph of light over darkness, spring over winter. Candlemas, a Christian feast day that got its name from the candlelit processions that accompanied it, was an overlay on older celebrations marking the astronomical midpoint between the winter solstice and the spring equinox.

Groundhog Day, a Germanic holiday that uses a furry prognosticator to foretell the coming of spring, depends on the presence (or not) of sunshine for its forecast.

Thus the day is known for weather rhymes, such as "Half your wood and half your hay, / Should be gone and be left on Candlemas Day," a reference to the halfway point of wintry weather.

FEBRUARY

2

Candlemas

● ○ ○ ● ●

Groundhog Day

—BK

If Candlemas Day bring snow and rain Winter is gone, and won't come again. If Candlemas Day be clear and bright Winter will have another flight.

1952
A hurricane crossed southern Florida, a highly unusual occurrence for February.

1974
BARBRA STREISAND's song "The Way We Were" topped the charts.

FEBRUARY

3

1894
Birth of painter
NORMAN ROCKWELL.

1947
The temperature at
Snag, Yukon Territory,
dipped to −81°F,
the coldest reading
ever recorded in
North America.

1973
The Endangered Species
Act was passed.

■ ■ ■

Commonplaces
never become
tiresome. It is *we*
who become tired
when we cease to
be curious and
appreciative.

—*Norman Rockwell*

Vanity backbites more than malice.

—BEN FRANKLIN

SOMETIMES THE THINGS we do to make ourselves more attractive backfire. Take the wealthy woman who had her portrait done by the great French painter Hyacinthe Rigaud. Upon seeing the portrait, the woman, who tended to wear far too much makeup, complained that the colors the artist had used were too bright. Unabashed, Rigaud replied, "We buy them at the same shop, madame."

More recently, firefighters in Newton, Massachusetts, had to spend 15 minutes rescuing a woman who had become attached to a parking meter. The problem? One of her long fingernails had become stuck in the coin slot of the meter.

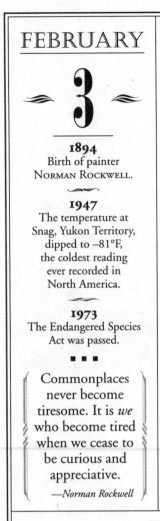

Finally, there's the story of the woman who was putting on face cream while visiting with her young grandson. The boy asked her what she was doing, and she explained that the cream was supposed to prevent wrinkles. The boy looked at her closely and said, "It doesn't work, does it?"

TOOLS AND TIPS FOR PAINTING

❖ Before you paint, remove any dust and dirt from your paintbrush, then condition it by dipping the bristles into paint thinner. Blot the excess, and you will be good to go.

❖ Save empty nail polish bottles and clean them thoroughly with polish remover. After completing a painting project, pour a little of the leftover paint into the bottle and label it. When your painted area gets chipped or scratched, use the paint and tiny brush to fix it.

❖ If your project requires oil-based paint, keep a bottle of nail polish remover nearby. Dip a cotton ball in the remover and dab up small spatters and spills.

❖ After applying wood stain, thoroughly rinse the brush in paint thinner, then squirt a little liquid dishwasher detergent into the bristles. Work up a lather, then rinse thoroughly in warm water. Hang the brush to dry. Wrap the bristles in a paper towel while it's drying to help them hold their shape.

Don't Dote on Your Houseplants

MORE HOUSEPLANTS have been killed by too much attention—too much water, fertilizer, or heat or too large a pot—than by benign neglect. What do houseplants want?

PRACTICAL PRIMER

- All plants want adequate light. Read up on the requirements of each of your houseplants. An east window may suit an African violet, but a geranium prefers midday sun and plenty of it.

- Most indoor environments, especially in winter, are too dry, but nearly all plants will die if their roots are constantly in water. Mist plants daily with lukewarm water to help replace the water they exhale. Water them when the soil feels dry to the touch.

- Most plants like cooler temperatures at night.

- Most blooming houseplants don't need a lot of fertilizer, unless you want big leaves and few blossoms. Many indoor gardeners withhold fertilizer from November to February.

- If a houseplant wilts between waterings and you can see roots growing out of the drainage hole, the pot is too small. Transplant it into a pot 1 to 2 inches in diameter larger and add crushed eggshells to the soil mix. Don't go from a tiny pot to a huge one—it's best to increase gradually.

- When buying a new houseplant, look for uniform leaf size, new foliage close to the base of the plant, and evidence of new growth. Avoid any plants with drooping leaves or spindly stalks.

FEBRUARY

4

There is always 1 fine week in February.

● ◐ ○ ◑ ●

1824
J. W. GOODRICH began selling rubber galoshes.

1913
Civil rights activist ROSA PARKS was born.

■ ■ ■

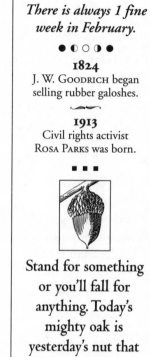

Stand for something or you'll fall for anything. Today's mighty oak is yesterday's nut that held its ground.

—Rosa Parks

WATERING TIPS FOR HOUSEPLANTS

❦ Water carnivorous plants with distilled water to avoid a buildup of toxic salts.

❦ Spray plants with a mixture of ¼ teaspoon castile soap and 1 quart water to deter aphids and other common winter bugs.

❦ If a houseplant's leaves turn brown and crinkly, create a more humid environment. Set the pot on a tray of pebbles and fill the tray with water to add humidity. Keep the water level just below the bottom of the pot.

❦ Save the water when you clean the fish tank and use it for your houseplants.

FEBRUARY

5

Birth of ABRAHAM LINCOLN's mother, NANCY HANKS (1784), and baseball great HANK AARON (1934).

1952
Don't Walk signs were used for the first time in New York City.

• • •

If you reveal your secrets to the wind, you should not blame the wind for revealing them to the trees.

—*Kahlil Gibran*

If you would keep your secret from an enemy, tell it not to a friend.

—BEN FRANKLIN

A WORD TO THE WISE

WHEN BEN FRANKLIN opened his print shop, the only newspaper in Philadelphia was, in his words, "a paltry thing, wretchedly managed, no way entertaining," but nevertheless quite profitable. Ben decided to publish his own newspaper and made the mistake of discussing his intentions with a former coworker. The friend promptly revealed Ben's plans to a competitor, who beat Ben to the punch. Ben learned his lesson and thereafter played his cards close to his chest.

Others have used the inability to keep a secret to their advantage. A minister who had $30,000 to invest came to railroad magnate Jay Gould looking for advice. Gould suggested that the minister put the money into Missouri Pacific railroad stock. The stock did well for a while, then tumbled, and the minister lost everything. When he complained to Gould about the advice, the financier pulled out a checkbook and wrote the minister a check to cover his entire loss. Relieved, the minister confessed that he had told a few others—members of his congregation—about Gould's advice. "I know that," Gould said. "They were the ones I was after."

HINTS FOR HEALTHY EATING

❖ If you can afford only a few organic food items, choose milk products, apples, cantaloupes, strawberries, grapes, green beans, spinach, and cucumbers. These tend to have higher pesticide levels when grown nonorganically.

❖ Avoid foods made with trans fats or hardened vegetable oils, including margarine, vegetable shortening, and partially hydrogenated oils. But don't avoid all fats. Moderate consumption of unsaturated fats (most liquid plant oils) actually helps prevent heart attacks and strokes.

❖ Avoid foods made with palm oil, palm kernel oil, or coconut oil. These cooking oils are extremely high in saturated fats and are commonly found in prepared baked goods and candy.

❖ To cut your fat intake, substitute half applesauce, prune puree (the latter available in a can), or even pureed junior baby fruit for cooking oil in baked goods such as muffins, cakes, and quick breads.

Stout Honesty

Lost last Saturday Night, in Market Street, about 40 or 50 shillings. If the Finder will bring it to the Printer hereof, who will describe the Marks, he shall have 10 s. Reward.

—Pennsylvania Gazette, *March 30, 1732*

BEN FRANKLIN'S hopeful ad to the Philadelphia citizenry seems hopelessly outdated today. We laugh at the writer's naive assumption that lost cash could so easily be reclaimed. Later, in *Poor Richard's Almanack* for 1750, Ben admitted, "'Tis hard to be poor and honest: An empty Sack can hardly stand upright; but if it does, 'tis a stout one!"

THE *Inspired* MIND

In 2002, a 72-year-old businessman on a golfing vacation in Tampa lost four envelopes containing a total of $4,000. Jarvarious Jones and Oscar Carter, both 13, found the money near a bus stop and turned it over to their school principal. The man's name was on the envelopes, he got his money back, and he rewarded the boys with cash and clothes. For their stout honesty, the two also received bicycles, college scholarship funds, and the keys to the city of Tampa.

Maybe Ben was onto something.

> Make yourself an honest man, and then you may be sure there is one less rascal in the world.
>
> —*Thomas Carlyle*

St. Dorothy gives the most snow.

1788
Massachusetts became the sixth state.

1895
Baseball legend BABE RUTH was born.

1911
Birthday of RONALD REAGAN, 40th president of the United States (1981–1989).

1935
The board game Monopoly first went on sale.

SQUELCHING SQUEAKS AND CREAKS

❧ For squeaky floorboards or stairs, sprinkle talcum powder over the noisy area, then sweep the powder into the cracks between the boards.

❧ If a wooden drawer creaks or sticks when you pull it out, run a bar of soap or a candle along the edges of the drawer and pull it back and forth a few times.

❧ Silence a squeaky door hinge by cutting a washer out of felt and saturating it with light oil. Remove the hinge pin, put the washer on the pin, and reinsert it in the hinge. Add more oil if the squeak returns.

❧ Remember to oil your sewing machine once a year so the moving parts run quietly.

7

Birthday of novelist
CHARLES DICKENS (1812)
and FREDERICK DOUGLASS
(1817).

1926
The average wage for
common labor in the
United States was reported
to be 54 cents an hour.

1964
The BEATLES arrived in
New York City for their
first American tour.
Thousands of cheering
fans were on hand
to greet them.

• • •

Have a heart
that never hardens, and
a temper that never
tires, and a touch that
never hurts.

—*Charles Dickens*

What Seed Catalogs Sell

WHO AMONG US has not spent many a happy winter hour lost in the latest garden catalog, imagining the juicy red tomatoes, crisp peppers, fragrant roses, or prizewinning sunflowers we will grow as soon as all this darned snow melts? A good garden catalog excels at selling the potential of the next growing season. But along with the romance, catalogs hold lots of hard information to help gardeners make a workable plan for their locations.

PRACTICAL

PRIMER

Before you order seeds or plants, read the fine print to determine these limitations for each item.

- **Gardening zone(s) and length of growing season:** A 120-day tomato will never make it past green if your growing season averages only 100 days. A Georgia peach won't survive in North Dakota, and a Wisconsin lilac will shrivel up and die in Texas.

- **Amount of sunlight required:** Many blooming plants, herbs, and garden vegetables need at least 6 hours of direct sun a day. If you have a shady yard, garden catalogs will help you find suitable alternatives.

- **Water and soil requirements:** Be sure you have the ability to furnish irrigation for water-loving crops such as tomatoes, peppers, and squash. If your soil is mostly clay, carrots, which thrive in sandy loam, won't be happy.

- **Space requirements:** Catalogs note the ultimate size of a perennial. Account for this in planning, and fill in with annuals until the plant has reached maturity.

POPPY LOVE

When winter lingers too long, find a packet of poppy seeds and scatter them over the snow. They'll do best in a previously cultivated spot, but even a grassy slope is apt to show their determined germination come spring.

Get the Lead Out

PRINTERS IN THE 1700S sometimes heated their pieces of lead type to make them easier to handle in cold weather. Ben Franklin tried this trick but found that at the end of the day, his fingers ached painfully. He later learned that veteran typesetters accustomed to heating their type often lost all use of their hands. In 1745, Ben wrote an essay on the "dry gripes," a bellyache he attributed to chronic exposure to lead. In 1768, he blamed the metal for poisoning tradesmen such as letter founders, plumbers, and painters, all of whom worked with lead.

In 1978, Wayne Matson patented a system for measuring lead in human blood, and that year the United States finally banned lead-based paint from housing. Federal regulatory programs have helped reduce the amount of lead in consumer products, the environment, and the workplace (the Department of Labor lists 900 occupations associated with lead use), but lead poisoning continues to be a health problem, particularly in children, more than 200 years after Ben's pioneering diagnosis.

The Old Cat and Mouse Game

❖ If you need an incentive to catch the mice you hear rustling in your cupboards at night, consider this: The common house mouse lives for about 1 year and leaves behind about 18,000 droppings.

❖ Use peanut butter to bait mousetraps. Mice can't resist the smell, and you can reset the traps and catch additional mice on one application of the bait.

❖ Inspect your cellar and sill plate for openings, then plug them up with caulking. Remember, a mouse can squeeze through a ¾-inch-diameter hole.

❖ To help your cat catch mice, leave cupboard doors open at night if you see signs of mouse occupation. A Norwegian proverb counsels, "It's better to feed one cat than many mice."

When the cat in February lies in the sun, she will creep behind the stove again in March.

● ○ ◐ ◑ ●

1828
Birth of science fiction writer JULES VERNE.

1969
After nearly 150 years of publication, the *Saturday Evening Post* published its final issue.

■ ■ ■

I believe cats to be spirits come to earth. A cat, I am sure, could walk on a cloud without coming through.

—*Jules Verne*

9

1773
Birthday of WILLIAM
HENRY HARRISON, ninth
president of the
United States (1841).

1819
LYDIA E. PINKHAM,
patent medicine
proprietor, was born.

1870
The U.S. Weather Bureau
was established. It was
renamed the National
Weather Service in 1970.

∎ ∎ ∎

**Wishing to be friends
is quick work, but
friendship is a slow
ripening fruit.**

—*Aristotle*

Tart words make no friends: a spoonful of honey will catch more flies than a gallon of vinegar.

—BEN FRANKLIN

A WORD TO THE WISE

A YOUNG MILITARY OFFICER learned the problem with tart words when he needed change to buy a soda from a vending machine. He stopped a private and asked if he had any change. "I think so," the private said. "Let me check." The officer proceeded to reprimand the private for not addressing him properly. "We'll start all over again," he said. "Do you have change for a dollar?" This time the private stood at attention, saluted, and said, "Sir, no, sir!"

Then there's the story of the foulmouthed parrot who was warned by his owner to clean up his act. The parrot persisted in uttering obscenities, until one day the owner said, "If you keep it up, I'm going to stick you in the freezer." The parrot responded with a vulgar oath, so the owner stuck him in the freezer for a few minutes.

After the parrot had cooled off, the owner asked if he was ready to come out and behave. "Y-y-yes," the parrot said, shivering. "J-j-just one question. What did that t-t-turkey do?"

COOKING OIL CAUTIONS

❦ Oil stored in a dark container (or dark cupboard) has a longer shelf life than oil exposed to light.

❦ Prolonged exposure to heat and air can turn olive oil rancid quickly, so be careful not to leave your opened bottle of oil next to the stove.

❦ Most oils can be stored at room temperature for 2 months. Keep them tightly sealed. Oils with a high proportion of mono-unsaturates (olive oil and peanut oil) are more perishable and benefit from refrigeration after 1 month.

Fire Insurance

Over 100 MILLION American households are members of mutuals, cooperatives, and credit unions," notes David Thompson, president of Twin Pines Cooperative Foundation in Davis, California. Cooperatives are voluntarily owned and operated by the people who use them.

The very first cooperative in America was Ben Franklin's Philadelphia Contributionship for the Insurance of Houses from Loss by Fire, formed in 1752. He printed the insurance policies and oversaw the distribution of fire

THE *Inspired* MIND

marks—metal identification plates decorated with a logo of four clasping hands, which were fastened over the front doors of members' homes. The contributionship is thought to have been modeled after a mutual fire insurance group begun in London in the 1690s.

In 1768, the contributionship was granted permission to incorporate by the Pennsylvania assembly, and in 1897 for the first time it began paying cash dividends on deposits. Beginning in 1960, several subsidiary insurance entities were added, and today Ben's enterprise, the oldest property insurance company in America, includes five subsidiaries known collectively as the Contributionship Companies.

1763
The Treaty of Paris was signed, ending the Seven Years' War. Most French territory in North America was ceded to Britain.

1863
ALANSON CRANE patented the first fire extinguisher.

1893
Comedian JIMMY DURANTE was born.

■ ■ ■

Your own safety is at stake when your neighbor's wall is ablaze.

—Horace

FIRE SAFETY IN THE HOME

❖ To reduce your risk of suffering a disastrous home fire, pay special attention to the leading causes of home fires: cigarette smoking, faulty heating systems, kids playing with matches and lighters, faulty electrical systems and extension cords, and cooking accidents.

❖ Never use extension cords with high-wattage appliances such as toasters, irons, and space heaters.

❖ Clean out the dryer's lint filter every time you use it. Once a year, vacuum behind the dryer and check the flexible vent.

❖ Be sure to allow air space around the television set,

which can get very warm with extended use.

❖ Keep all combustibles at least 3 feet away from woodstoves, heaters, and furnaces.

❖ Install smoke detectors, replace the batteries faithfully, and make an exit plan for each room in case of fire. Pick a spot outside where your family will meet.

FEBRUARY

11

Violent north winds in February herald a fertile year.

● ○ ○ ● ●

1847
Inventor THOMAS EDISON was born.

1990
NELSON MANDELA was released from prison.

■ ■ ■

Opportunity is missed by most people because it is dressed in overalls and looks like work.

—*Thomas Edison*

Industry, perseverance, and frugality, make fortune yield.

—BEN FRANKLIN

A WORD TO THE WISE

PROBABLY NO ONE epitomizes the spirit of perseverance more than Thomas Edison. As a young person, he spent just 3 months in school, where his teachers didn't think him very bright. At age 12, he developed progressive deafness. His first patented invention, an electric vote recorder, was a commercial failure. But Edison went on to invent the lightbulb, the phonograph, the kinetoscope (forerunner of the movie camera), the stock ticker, and many other devices.

Edison was stubbornly tenacious on the trail of a new discovery. It took him 10 years to develop a better storage battery for electric cars, in the course of which he conducted 50,000 experiments. When someone commented on the number of failures he'd had before he saw any results, Edison replied, "Why, I have gotten a lot of results. I know fifty thousand things that won't work." By the time he perfected his alkaline battery, electric cars were becoming passé, but even so, it was one of his most successful commercial products, used in lighting railroads and mines.

"Genius is 1 percent inspiration and 99 percent perspiration," Edison said, and Ben Franklin would surely have agreed.

Ingenious Tricks for Nailing and Drilling

❖ When drilling holes into drywall, control the dust by taping an envelope to the wall just below the area to be drilled. Pull the envelope open, and the dust will drop right in.

❖ When nailing into brick to hang a picture, always drill a pilot hole with a car-

bide tip drill or a star drill, and always wear goggles. Masonry nails tend to break rather than bend.

❖ To get a stripped screw out of its hole, hold a putty knife under the screw head while

turning the screwdriver.

❖ If you can't find a stud and have no stud finder, use an electric razor. Run it along the wall, and when the sound changes, you've found the stud.

Don't go to the doctor with every distemper, nor to the lawyer with every quarrel, nor to the pot for every thirst.

—BEN FRANKLIN

O NE DAY WHEN Abraham Lincoln was practicing law, an irate client came in, demanding that Lincoln sue a poverty-stricken man who owed him $2.50. Lincoln tried to talk the client out of pursuing the case, but to no avail. Finally, Lincoln agreed to take the case and charged him a fee of $10. He promptly gave half of the fee to the debtor, who paid off the debt, thereby satisfying all parties concerned, including himself.

ABRAHAM LINCOLN

Unfortunately, many lawsuits are equally pointless. A lawyer tells of a couple getting a divorce who argued over the ownership of a set of canisters that had come free with a purchase they'd made. It occurred to the lawyer —but apparently not to the combatants—that at the rate they were paying their attorneys, they could each have bought several very expensive sets of canisters instead of arguing about the old ones.

Before you bring a lawyer into a fight, make sure the end result is worth the expense. Revenge—which is often the prime motive in lawsuits—is never worth the price.

Sunshine today is good for apples.

● ● ○ ○ ●

1809
Birthday of
ABRAHAM LINCOLN,
16th president of the
United States
(1861–1865).

1909
The National Association
for the Advancement of
Colored People (NAACP)
was founded.

■ ■ ■

As a peacemaker the lawyer has a superior opportunity of being a good man. There will still be business enough.

—*Abraham Lincoln*

NUTS TO YOU!

❦ To grind nuts for baking, use a hand grinder for the best results. A blender tends to release too much of the oil.

❦ *Do* use a blender to make nut butters from cashews, peanuts, and other nuts. Add a dash of salt and perhaps a spoonful of honey, if desired.

❦ Spread a thin layer of finely ground nuts on the bottom crust of a pie to keep it from becoming soggy.

❦ Nuts are a delicious meat extender. Try adding ¼ cup ground or finely chopped nuts to meat loaf to boost taste and nutrition.

13

1899

The temperature was a frigid –2°F in Tallahassee, Florida. It was the state's all-time coldest reading.

1920

Birth of soprano EILEEN FARRELL.

■ ■ ■

When I write of hunger, I am really writing about love and the hunger for it, and warmth and the love of it and it is all one.

—*M. F. K. Fisher*

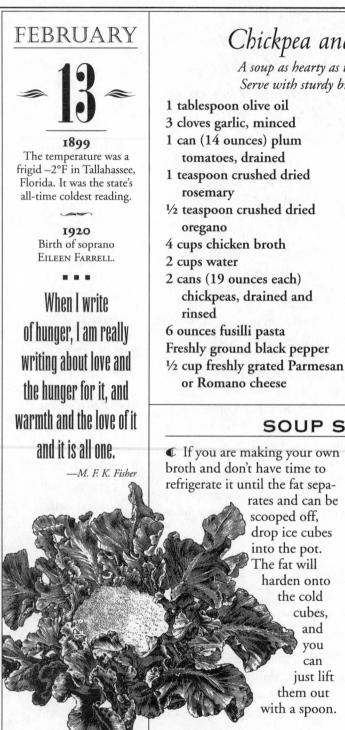

Chickpea and Fusilli Soup

A soup as hearty as this one makes a meal.
Serve with sturdy bread and sweet butter.

1 tablespoon olive oil
3 cloves garlic, minced
1 can (14 ounces) plum tomatoes, drained
1 teaspoon crushed dried rosemary
½ teaspoon crushed dried oregano
4 cups chicken broth
2 cups water
2 cans (19 ounces each) chickpeas, drained and rinsed
6 ounces fusilli pasta
Freshly ground black pepper
½ cup freshly grated Parmesan or Romano cheese

Heat the oil in a soup pot over low heat. Add the garlic and sauté for 2 minutes. Add the tomatoes, rosemary, and oregano and simmer for 5 minutes. Add the chicken broth and water and bring to a simmer. Add 1 can of the chickpeas. Mash the chickpeas and tomatoes with a potato masher. Bring to a boil, add the fusilli, and cook until tender, about 10 minutes. Stir in the remaining chickpeas and heat through. Add pepper to taste. Serve topped with the cheese.

Makes 6 servings

SOUP SUCCESS

❧ If you are making your own broth and don't have time to refrigerate it until the fat separates and can be scooped off, drop ice cubes into the pot. The fat will harden onto the cold cubes, and you can just lift them out with a spoon.

❧ Avoid using strong-flavored vegetables, such as cauliflower, cabbage, or turnips, in broth. Also avoid starchy vegetables, such as potatoes or corn, which will cloud the liquid.

❧ If you soak dried mushrooms to rehydrate them, be sure to save the water to use in soup or gravy.

❧ Make canned broth taste almost like homemade by simmering it for 15 minutes with a large handful of chopped carrots, celery, and scallions and a splash of wine. Strain and use.

> ## *Where there's marriage without love, there will be love without marriage.*
>
> —BEN FRANKLIN

BEN FRANKLIN had heard a rumor that the Moravians, a religious group residing in Pennsylvania, arranged marriages for their young people, choosing the partners by lot. When he asked some members of the group if this was true, they explained the process to him. A young man who wished to marry told the elders of the church, who then spoke to the older women charged with bringing up the young women. Since the elders knew the young people and their temperaments, they were generally able to make a good match. Occasionally, however, two or three matches might seem equally suitable, in which case they drew lots.

A WORD TO THE WISE

> ## The heart has its reasons which reason knows nothing of.
>
> —*Blaise Pascal*

Ben objected, saying, "If the matches are not made by the mutual choice of the parties, some of them may chance to be very unhappy."

The Moravians replied, "And so they may if you let the parties choose for themselves"—which, Ben had to admit, was quite true.

FEBRUARY

14

Valentine's Day

● ○ ◐ ◑ ●

Oregon became the 33rd state (1859), and Arizona became the 48th state (1912).

1894
Comedian JACK BENNY was born.

1929
Rivals of AL CAPONE'S gang were gunned down in Chicago's St. Valentine's Day Massacre.

Heartfelt Hints

❖ Make a heart-shaped cake for your valentine. Bake a round cake and a square cake. When cool, cut the round cake in half. Turn the square cake to make a diamond shape and place each half round on the upper sides of the diamond.

❖ Do your heart a favor and take the dog for a daily walk. No dog? Borrow one!

LORE & LEGEND

The first person of the opposite sex you see today—except your family—must be your valentine. Important note: It is permissible to keep your eyes shut until the right person happens by.

15

*If you wish to live
and thrive,
Let a spider run
alive.*

● ○ ○ ● ●

Birthday of astronomer
and physicist
GALILEO GALILEI (1564)
and social reformer
SUSAN B. ANTHONY
(1820).

1898
The battleship USS *Maine*
exploded in Havana,
Cuba.

1965
Canada adopted a new
flag that featured a maple
leaf against a red and
white background.

■ ■ ■

I have never met
a man so ignorant
that I couldn't learn
something from him.

—Galileo Galilei

Getting Clarity
on Clarified Butter

CLARIFIED BUTTER, also known as drawn butter, is butter heated until it separates from its milk solids and most of its water, leaving a clear, golden fat with a mild butter taste. The advantage of clarified butter is that it withstands higher cooking temperatures than regular butter and can be stored up to three times longer.

The traditional way to make clarified butter is to heat unsalted butter in a heavy pan over very low heat until it separates, then carefully pour off the clear layer, discarding the milk solids. Here's an even easier way,

PRACTICAL

PRIMER

Cut 1 cup (2 sticks) unsalted butter into small pieces and place in an ovenproof glass bowl. Cover the bowl, place in a 200°F oven, and let melt completely for about 1 hour. Do not stir. Set the covered bowl in the refrigerator until the clear top layer has coagulated. This is your clarified butter. Gently lift the clarified layer and rinse it quickly under cold water. Pat dry and store in a covered jar for up to 1 month in the refrigerator. Because clarified butter turns grainy with refrigeration, it is better used for frying than as a spread. Makes about ¾ cup.

Butter Makes It Better

❖ For the most flavorful sauces, use clarified butter in the roux.

❖ For a perfect omelette or delicate scrambled eggs, cook them in clarified butter.

❖ To keep regular butter from burning when sautéing, add a little canola, safflower, or corn oil to the pan to raise the smoke point.

❖ If you use whipped butter instead of stick butter in a recipe, increase the amount by about one-third to compensate for the air in this product.

❖ If you're counting calories, use whipped butter instead of sticks. It spreads more easily, and you'll tend to use less of it.

Take courage, mortal; death can't banish thee out of the universe.

—BEN FRANKLIN

OVER THE AGES, human beings have developed all kinds of methods to attain immortality, from the embalming techniques of the Egyptians to today's cryogenics. Following are some of the odder ways to seek immortality.

A WORD TO THE WISE

- An entrepreneur in Des Moines, Iowa, places the ashes of hunters in shotgun shells, which the loved one's family can then shoot at targets. He also has put ashes in fishing lures, duck decoys, and golf clubs.
- The family of inventor Ed Headrick, who perfected the aerodynamic design of the Frisbee, had his ashes placed in "memorial flying discs" for distribution to family and friends.
- A Chicago company promises to convert human ashes into diamonds. Under intense heat and pressure, the carbon-based remains actually turn into artificial diamonds. A quarter-carat diamond costs about $4,000, which gives a whole new meaning to the saying "Diamonds are a girl's best friend."

How to Tell the Temperature by Looking at Your Rhododendron

You can tell how cold it is outside by checking out the leaves on your rhododendron.

- Leaves begin to cup and curl below 35°F.
- Half the leaf surface disappears into the curl at 24°F.
- Leaves curl tightly, turn brownish green, and dangle at temperatures in the teens.

–BK

For every thunderstorm in February will be a cold spell in May.

● ○ ○ ◑ ●

1883
The *Ladies' Home Journal* began publication.

1923
In Egypt, the tomb of KING TUTANKHAMEN was opened.

Because I could not stop for Death,
He kindly stopped for me.
The carriage held but just ourselves,
And immortality.

—Emily Dickinson

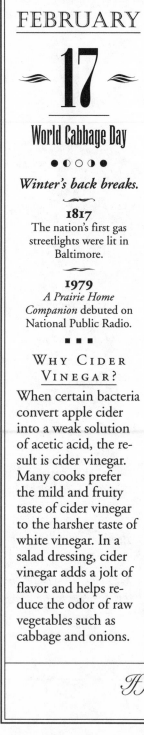

FEBRUARY

17

World Cabbage Day

● ○ ○ ● ●

Winter's back breaks.

1817
The nation's first gas streetlights were lit in Baltimore.

1979
A Prairie Home Companion debuted on National Public Radio.

■ ■ ■

WHY CIDER VINEGAR?

When certain bacteria convert apple cider into a weak solution of acetic acid, the result is cider vinegar. Many cooks prefer the mild and fruity taste of cider vinegar to the harsher taste of white vinegar. In a salad dressing, cider vinegar adds a jolt of flavor and helps reduce the odor of raw vegetables such as cabbage and onions.

The Healthiest Slaw You'll Ever Eat

Not only is it healthy, but it looks beautiful on the plate, tastes fresh, and has a satisfying crunch.

½ cup plain yogurt
½ cup mayonnaise
2 teaspoons cider vinegar
4 to 5 cups thinly sliced green cabbage
1 cup finely shredded carrots
1 Granny Smith apple, cored and chopped
½ cup seedless red grape halves
½ cup chopped dates
Salt and freshly ground black pepper to taste
¼ cup toasted walnut halves

Blend the yogurt, mayonnaise, and vinegar in a large bowl. Add all the remaining ingredients except the walnuts and toss to coat well with the dressing. Refrigerate for about 30 minutes. Before serving, taste for salt and pepper, then sprinkle with the walnuts.

Makes 4 to 6 servings

Cabbage Facts

❦ Cabbage is packed with immunity-boosting phytochemicals that are not damaged by cooking. Eat it raw in salads, stir-fried, in soups, or on pizza. That's right—in county Sligo, Ireland, they top pizza with cabbage, ham, cheese, and nutmeg.

❦ When you select cabbage at the store, look for a tight, firm head. If the leaves and bottom stems have begun to separate, the cabbage may have a coarse texture and strong flavor.

❦ A favorite cabbage dish in England is called bubble and squeak. To make it, mix together equal parts mashed potatoes and chopped cooked cabbage and fry the mixture in butter or bacon fat. Listen closely while it fries to hear it bubble and squeak.

❦ Red cabbage will hold its color during cooking if you acidify the cooking water. Add 1 tablespoon vinegar or lemon juice for every 2 cups water.

If food is poetry, is not poetry also food?

—*Joyce Carol Oates*

> *A quiet conscience sleeps in thunder, but rest and guilt live far asunder.*
>
> —BEN FRANKLIN

FEBRUARY

18

1885
MARK TWAIN'S *Adventures of Huckleberry Finn* was published.

1932
SONJA HENIE won her sixth women's world figure skating championship.

1933
Birth of artist YOKO ONO, wife of JOHN LENNON.

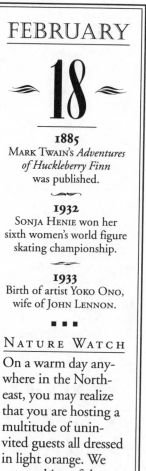

S IR ARTHUR CONAN DOYLE, creator of Sherlock Holmes, was a devious practical joker. He once sent the same telegram to 12 well-known and respected associates. The telegram read simply, "Fly at once; all is discovered." By the next day, all of the men had suddenly discovered urgent business that required them to leave the country.

A prosecuting attorney questioned a witness at a burglary trial in San Diego. "Were you at the scene when the robbery took place?" he asked. When the witness said yes, the attorney asked, "And did you observe the two robbers?" The witness again said yes. Finally, the attorney said dramatically, "Are these two men present in court today?" To his surprise, the two defendants in the case raised their hands. The prosecutor didn't need to ask any further questions.

As Ben Franklin once said, "Keep conscience clear, then never fear."

A WORD TO THE WISE

> **Humor is the great thing, the saving thing.**
>
> —*Mark Twain*

NATURE WATCH

On a warm day anywhere in the Northeast, you may realize that you are hosting a multitude of uninvited guests all dressed in light orange. We are speaking of the Asian lady beetle *(Harmonia axyridis),* a nonnative relative of the common red ladybug. These lady beetles winter inside our walls, having entered through the tiniest of crevices, and emerge en masse on warm days in search of an exit. You can simply open the windows to set them free.

ADD COLOR TO YOUR LIFE

❖ If a room has many windows and doors, be sure the trim is not painted an intense color, or the room will look too broken up.

❖ Paint a room from the top down. Start with the ceiling, continue with the walls, and then move on to the doors and trim. If you want to paint the floor, do it last.

❖ Keep track of the brand and color of the paint in a room by writing the information on the back of a light switch plate before you put it back on.

❖ To paint behind a radiator, buy a small paint roller (about 1 inch in diameter) with a 24-inch handle made just for this use.

FEBRUARY

19

1473
Astronomer NICOLAUS COPERNICUS was born.

1730
"The great Snow we had here, was so much greater in New-England, as to prevent all Travelling on the Roads for a considerable Time," reported BEN FRANKLIN's *Pennsylvania Gazette.* The storm delayed publication of the newspaper by 2 days.

• • •

Books let us into their souls and lay open to us the secrets of our own.

—*William Hazlitt*

There is much difference between imitating a good man, and counterfeiting him.

—BEN FRANKLIN

PLAGIARISM IS nothing new. In 1734, a young preacher arrived at Ben Franklin's church in Philadelphia and began attracting a large following with his strong voice and dynamic preaching. His sermons aimed at inspiring virtue and good behavior but had little in the way of dogmatic advice. Although this appealed to listeners like Ben, many of the old guard accused the preacher of being unorthodox and even heretical.

A WORD TO THE WISE

Ben and others rallied to the preacher's side, until it was discovered that he had borrowed large portions of his sermons from other ministers. Most of his followers abandoned him, but Ben stuck with him, saying, "I rather approved his giving us good sermons composed by others, than bad ones of his own manufacture."

The great Italian political philosopher Niccolò Machiavelli echoed this opinion: "A prudent man should always follow in the footsteps of great men and imitate those who have been outstanding. If his own prowess fails to compare with theirs, at least it has an air of greatness about it."

The Reluctant Reader

If a child you know avoids reading books, you may be able to encourage a love of reading with a new approach.

❧ Keep on reading aloud to the child long after she has learned to read. Many children love the coziness and relaxation of sitting with you rather than reading alone.

❧ Limit TV and computer use. If necessary, offer rewards for reading.

❧ Find a chapter book that is exciting to the child and get in the habit of reading a chapter a night aloud.

❧ Go with a child's interests rather than your own. If your son thinks of nothing but baseball, go to the library and find books about the game.

❧ Children love to receive mail, so subscribe in their names to suitable magazines and book clubs.

The Image of Lightning

THE GEORGE EASTMAN HOUSE in Rochester, New York, possesses within its photography collection the first photograph of lightning. At least that's what William N. Jennings thought it was when he wrote those words on his gelatin silver print showing lightning striking the ridge of a distant hill. The spectacular photograph is thought to  have been made in 1885, when Jennings was 25 years old.

Wouldn't Ben Franklin have been impressed with that fixed image of the electric discharge he studied so intently? In fact, the whole development of photography would surely have fascinated him, starting with the first photographic image, by Joseph Niepce in 1816, and the first daguerreotype, by Louis Daguerre in 1837.

A 1930 photograph in the Eastman House collection documents the groundbreaking ceremony for the new Franklin Institute Science Museum in Philadelphia. The picture was taken by William Jennings, the man who photographed lightning.

THE Inspired MIND

FEBRUARY
20

It takes 3 cloudy days to bring a heavy snow.

● ◐ ○ ◑ ●

1902
Birth of photographer
ANSEL ADAMS.

1962
JOHN GLENN became
the first American
to orbit Earth.

■ ■ ■

When words
become unclear,
I shall focus with
photographs. When
images become
inadequate, I shall
be content
with silence.

—*Ansel Adams*

Cleaning Up around the House

❖ To remove spray starch from the bottom of an iron, rub the plate with a baking soda and water paste. Wipe it off with a clean cloth.

❖ To clean cobwebs from hard-to-reach corners, slip an old sock over the end of a yardstick and fasten it with a rubber band. Reach up into corners and twirl the yardstick to gather up the cobwebs.

❖ A beer can opener is a handy tool for removing old grout from between tiles.

❖ Don't be in a big hurry to sweep all the ashes out of the fireplace. An inch or two of ashes makes a good base for a fire.

❖ To remove a bloodstain from carpet, sprinkle it with salt, then cold water. Gently blot the area with a wet sponge (do not rub), then dab it with paper towels until dry.

FEBRUARY

21

1878
The first telephone book was published, in New Haven, Connecticut.

1885
The Washington Monument was dedicated.

1893
Guitarist ANDRES SEGOVIA was born.

• • •

The first duty of love is to listen.

—*Paul Tillich*

A pair of good ears will drain dry an hundred tongues.

—BEN FRANKLIN

MOST OF US think we're better listeners than we actually are, according to psychologist Michael Nichols, author of *The Lost Art of Listening*. "It is one of the most powerful forces in human relationships," he says.

Why don't we listen better? Nichols blames the hectic pace of modern life, which leaves us too tired and with too little time to listen to one another carefully.

What's the secret of being a good listener? Focus on the speaker, making eye contact and using body language that tells the person you're interested. Don't let your mind wander, and don't think about what you're going to say next. Don't interrupt, but do ask questions to amplify or clarify a point. When you respond, watch your tone so that it doesn't sound accusatory or critical; no one responds well to that. Listening can be hard work, but the good news is that people who listen well are more likely to be listened to.

THINGS TO DO OUTDOORS

For gardeners and landscapers who are itching to get to work outside despite the snow cover, there actually are a few tasks best done now.

❦ Prune up to a quarter of a mature peach tree.

❦ Prune grapes now, removing most of the old wood.

❦ If you see coal black knobs on fruit tree branches —a fungus called black knot—prune and immediately burn all affected limbs. (Spores can develop and spread if prunings are left on the ground or in a brush pile.) Disinfect your pruning shears with bleach.

❦ Sharpen all your garden tools, especially shovels and edgers, to make work easier in the spring.

❦ When stacking brush for burning, arrange it compactly and all in the same direction. This makes the pile denser and easier to burn.

❦ Take advantage of frozen ground by trucking loads of manure out to the garden.

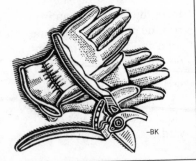

—BK

Little Cherry Cheesecakes

Make these individual desserts in honor of George Washington and his inspiring (if apocryphal) cherry tree.

24 vanilla wafers or Oreo cookies

1 pound cream cheese, at room temperature

¾ cup sugar

1 teaspoon pure vanilla extract

2 eggs

1 can (20 ounces) cherry pie filling

Preheat the oven to 350°F. Line 24 muffin cups with paper liners and place a wafer or cookie in the bottom of each. In a medium bowl, beat the cream cheese, sugar, vanilla, and eggs until smooth. Fill each muffin cup three-quarters full with the mixture. Bake for 15 minutes, remove from the oven, and let cool for 30 minutes. (At this point, you can wrap the cheesecakes and freeze them for up to 1 month. Defrost before topping.) Place a spoonful of cherry pie filling on each little cheesecake and refrigerate until ready to serve.

Makes 2 dozen

NATURE WATCH

In the North, only the earliest migrating birds are starting to return. In the Southwest, it is mating season for many birds, including hummingbirds, which love to hang around the chuparosa shrubs now in bloom. Also in the Southwest, you can hear pairs of breeding great horned owls hooting in the evening and just before dawn.

Cherry Trivia

❖ Most sour or pie cherries sold in this country are Montmorency cherries, grown mainly in New England, around the Great Lakes, and in the Great Plains.

❖ Adding ¼ teaspoon almond extract to cherry pie results in a richer flavor.

❖ Cherry pie or cobbler may help combat bloating, gout, or trouble with swollen joints.

FEBRUARY

February fills the dike, Be it black or be it white.

● ● ○ ○ ●

1732
Birthday of
GEORGE WASHINGTON,
first president of the
United States
(1789–1797).

1766
In London, BEN FRANKLIN's defense of America's opposition to the Stamp Act helped win its repeal and established him as the leading representative of the colonies.

■ ■ ■

One must ask children and birds how cherries and strawberries taste.

—*Johann Wolfgang von Goethe*

FEBRUARY

23

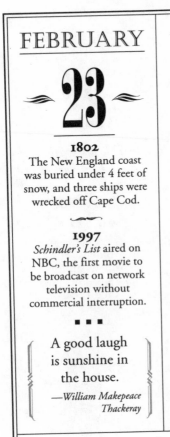

1802
The New England coast was buried under 4 feet of snow, and three ships were wrecked off Cape Cod.

1997
Schindler's List aired on NBC, the first movie to be broadcast on network television without commercial interruption.

■ ■ ■

A good laugh is sunshine in the house.
—*William Makepeace Thackeray*

Innocence is its own defense.

—BEN FRANKLIN

A WORD TO THE WISE

THAT MAY BE TRUE, but there are other approaches. Take the credit union manager in Eugene, Oregon, who was charged with embezzling $630,000 from her company over the course of 6 years. The woman admitted to a jury that although her hands had indeed taken the money, her heart, mind, and spirit were innocent because it was one of her multiple personalities that had committed the crimes.

And how about the soccer fan in London who was convicted of threatening a well-known French soccer star? When the guilty verdict was handed down, the fan grabbed the prosecuting attorney in a headlock and attempted to punch him, screaming, "I am innocent! I promise! I swear on the Bible!"

Finally, a man in Bay City, Michigan, pleaded not guilty to the charge of stealing some rings. He changed his mind when he learned that his girlfriend was in the hallway outside the courtroom showing off the rings. Oops.

A Few Lines on Laundry Day

❆ Use either powdered or liquid laundry detergents. They work the same way but may need to be used in different amounts. Personal preference reigns here.

❆ Before you launder anything, close all zippers, hooks, and buttons; empty all pockets; and remove pins or belt buckles. Even better, train your family members to do this for themselves.

❆ Don't overload your washer. The clothes simply won't get clean, and overloading puts too much stress on the machine.

❆ If your water is hard, add ½ cup white vinegar to the rinse. Vinegar softens the water, reduces lint, and keeps hard-water scale from building up inside the machine.

Be True to Your Teeth,
or Your Teeth Will Be False to You

"SHE LAUGHS AT everything you say. Why? Because she has fine teeth," Ben Franklin wrote, echoing others of his day who valued every tooth as if it were a diamond. In Ben's time, people who lost their teeth tried awkward replacements made from carved wood, wads of cloth, and even teeth pulled from corpses. A person whose teeth survived through adulthood was lucky indeed.

For centuries, people had cleaned their teeth with "chew sticks" (twigs with rough ends that could get into crevices) and rubbed them with all manner of substances, from honey to nutshells to dead mice. In Ben's youth, a rough linen cloth was the most common tooth cleaner. George Washington added chalk to his rag, as recommended by his dentist. Some toothpastes were so corrosive that they sanded off the enamel, dooming the teeth.

THE *Inspired* MIND

The invention of the toothbrush is credited to an Englishman, William Addis, who was languishing in prison in 1780. With nothing but time on his hands, he bored holes into a meat bone and glued tufts of natural bristles into them to create his toothbrush. Unfortunately, his invention did nothing to help George Washington, whose ill-fitting dentures (so much for the chalk) caused him much pain.

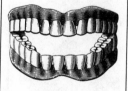

A smile is the universal welcome.
—*Max Eastman*

FEBRUARY
24

February makes a bridge, and March breaks it.

● ○ ○ ○ ●

1836
Birth of painter
WINSLOW HOMER.

1857
The first perforated U.S. postage stamps went on sale.

1938
DuPont sold its first nylon-bristle toothbrush.

TOOTH TIPS

❖ Instead of commercial tooth whiteners, make a paste of baking soda and a few drops of hydrogen peroxide. Brush gently with it to remove tooth stains, then rinse well.

❖ Let teething babies chew on a frozen bagel to ease their swollen gums.

❖ If a child knocks out a permanent tooth, immerse it in milk and take it (and the child) to the dentist immediately. Sometimes the tooth can be reimplanted.

❖ To combat bacteria that proliferate in the mouth during sleep, brush teeth immediately upon awakening and

again after breakfast. Go one step further: Brush your tongue or gently scrape it with the edge of a spoon to keep bacteria at bay.

❖ Choose desserts that won't stick to your teeth for hours. A milk chocolate bar is easier on the enamel than a chewy granola bar.

25

1842
Birth of IDA LEWIS,
legendary keeper of the
Lime Rock Light in
Newport, Rhode Island.
She assumed her duties at
age 15 and rescued many
people from the sea.

1919
Oregon became
the first state to impose a
gasoline tax.

■ ■ ■

From December
to March, there are
for many of us
three gardens—
the garden outdoors,
the garden of pots
and bowls in the
house, and
the garden of
the mind's eye.

—*Katherine S. White*

Grow Your Own Houseplants—From Garbage

DON'T THROW those avocado pits, grapefruit seeds, and pineapple tops into the compost—and certainly not into the garbage. Plant them to make beautiful, long-lived houseplants.

PRACTICAL PRIMER

To start an avocado plant, put the pit in a self-sealing plastic bag partially filled with slightly damp sphagnum moss. Cover the pit with more damp moss, seal almost all the way, and place in a warm, dark spot for a week or more until roots form. (The top of the refrigerator is perfect for this.) When the roots are 4 inches long, plant the pit in potting soil, flat end down, with the top third above the soil. When the shoot is about 6 inches high, cut the plant back to two leaves to force it to branch. Avocados love sun and moisture.

Grapefruit seeds can take a long time to germinate, but they'll eventually grow into large houseplants. Choose the largest seeds and plant them about ½ inch deep in sterile potting soil. Keep the soil moist but not wet. Pinch the young plant back so that it branches out.

Before you cut a fresh pineapple, twist off the leafy top. Pull off all but the top 8 to 10 leaves and root the top in water. When roots form, plant in a mixture of equal parts sand and peat moss, with a handful of coffee grounds mixed in. Spray diluted fertilizer on the crown and cut off any brown tips. Pineapples like warmth and light.

BOOST THE BLOOMS

☾ To give houseplants a boost of energy, rig up a fixture with two 40-watt fluorescent tubes (one cool, one warm). Hang it 6 inches above the plants and keep it on 12 to 14 hours a day.

☾ When Christmas cactus blossoms fade, pinch off a few sections of each stem to stimulate branching and increased bloom during the next flowering cycle. Propagate new plants with cuttings.

☾ After a period of prolonged cold weather, cut long branches of forsythia, crab apple, pussy willow, or flowering quince. Put them in warm water and keep them in a cool, shady spot.

Idleness is the dead sea, that swallows all virtues: Be active in business, that temptation may miss her aim: The bird that sits, is easily shot.

—BEN FRANKLIN

DURING THE French and Indian War (1754–1763), Ben Franklin was commissioned to head up the militia defending Pennsylvania's northwestern frontier. Among their tasks was building a fort at the site of the Moravian settlement of Gnadenhutten (now Weissport, Pennsylvania). It was hard work, requiring the men to fell timbers, cart them to the site, and erect a rudimentary stockade, all the while fearful of attack by Native Americans. On top of that, it rained every other day, delaying the work.

A WORD TO THE WISE

Oddly, Ben noted that the men were happiest on the days when they could work. On the rainy days, with idle time on their hands, they argued, fought, and complained about the food. This put Ben in mind of a sea captain who always tried to keep his men busy for just that reason. When told that all the work was done and there was nothing else for them to do, the captain told the first mate, "Make them scour the anchor," a pointless task. But as Ben also learned, "when men are employed, they are best contented."

—

FEBRUARY

26

1852
Health food pioneer and cereal maker JOHN KELLOGG was born.

1919
Grand Canyon National Park in Arizona was established.

1972
After 3 days of rain and melting snow, Buffalo Creek Dam in West Virginia broke. A 50-foot wall of water slammed down the narrow valley, killing 125 people.

A CLEAN AND SHINING BATHROOM

❖ To clean stained rubber tub mats, nonskid strips, or appliqués, dampen with water, then sprinkle with baking soda. Let sit for 15 minutes, then scrub and rinse.

❖ Buy a toilet bowl brush just for scrubbing the bathtub. It's much easier to use than a traditional hand-held scrub brush.

❖ To eliminate a stubborn hard-water ring in your toilet, shut off the water supply to the tank and flush. Spray the stain with warm white vinegar and sprinkle with borax. Wait at least 15 minutes, then scrub the area with fine steel wool.

The bathroom is out of this world ... which makes it a little inconvenient.

—*Jimmy Durante*

FEBRUARY, *the Second Month*

65

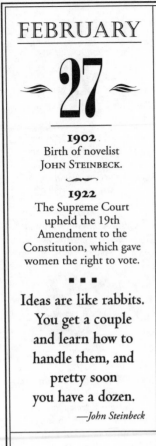

1902
Birth of novelist
JOHN STEINBECK.

1922
The Supreme Court
upheld the 19th
Amendment to the
Constitution, which gave
women the right to vote.

• • •

Ideas are like rabbits.
You get a couple
and learn how to
handle them, and
pretty soon
you have a dozen.

—*John Steinbeck*

Printing Partners

A FTER BEN FRANKLIN retired from active printing in 1748, he formed silent partnerships with several other printers. A typical arrangement was for Ben to provide a press and type, pay one-third of the business expenses, and receive one-third of the profits. Ben's far-flung chain included a dozen printers in Philadelphia, New York, Boston, Rhode Island, Connecticut, North Carolina, Georgia, Antigua, and Jamaica.

THE
Inspired
MIND

More than 200 years later, in 1970, the first Kinko's opened with one copy machine in Isla Vista, adjacent to the University of California at Santa Barbara. ("Kinko" is founder Paul Orfalea's nickname, given to him for his curly reddish hair.) Within 2 years, a second store opened, and by 1979 the copy and document-printing chain had 80 stores in 28 states. By 1985, customers were able to make color copies on recycled paper at any hour of the day or night. Today there are more than 1,100 Kinko's worldwide, offering fax, e-mail, videoconferencing, and computer rental services in addition to photocopying. Kinko's does not franchise, but instead partners with owners who share the bottom-line profits. Sound familiar?

How to Jazz Up Everyday Foods

◖ Add a dash of soy sauce or tamari to gravy. It seasons at the same time it enriches the color.

◖ If you use packaged corn bread mix, add one or all of the following to boost the flavor: corn kernels, chopped jalapeño peppers, or grated cheddar cheese.

◖ Transform leftover mashed potatoes by adding 1 beaten egg for every 2 cups potatoes.

Mound or pipe the mixture on a parchment-lined baking sheet and bake in a 350°F oven for 15 minutes, or until golden.

◖ To jazz up white rice, put a cinnamon stick in the pot, or boil the rice in chicken

broth. Experiment by adding herbs, raisins, nuts, or minced vegetables to the cooking liquid.

◖ To enhance canned soup, add chopped fresh herbs to vegetable soup; sautéed fresh mushrooms and a splash of sherry to mushroom soup; balsamic vinegar to bean soup; or fresh lemon juice, diced tomato, and a dollop of pesto to tomato soup.

Keep flax from fire, youth from gaming.

—BEN FRANKLIN

GAMBLING IS big business these days, thanks in part to the millions of dollars the gambling industry pumps into advertising and the campaign coffers of friendly politicians. But what are the odds of the average person hitting it big in the lottery or at a casino? According to the Consumer Federation of America, the odds of winning the lottery are about 1 in 10 million to 20 million.

Just for comparison's sake, here are some other scenarios.

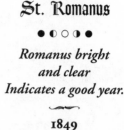

A WORD TO THE WISE

- Odds that you will be hit by lightning: 1 in 3 million
- Odds that you will be attacked by a shark: 1 in 350,000
- Odds that you will choke to death on something you're eating: 1 in 100,000
- Odds that you will marry an actor: 1 in 5,000
- Odds that you will marry a dentist: 1 in 3,000

But don't gamblers win sometimes? Sure they do. A friend of the French novelist Tristan Bernard once admired a new yachting cap that Bernard had purchased with some gambling winnings. When the friend commented on his good luck, Bernard said, "Ah, but what I lost would have bought me the yacht."

PET CARE POINTERS

❖ Cats will usually keep themselves clean, although very old cats may stop grooming. Rather than shocking a cat with a tub bath, rub her coat gently with a hand towel rinsed in warm water and wrung out well.

❖ If your dog chews on his paws out of boredom or anxiety, you can deter him by painting the spot he likes to chew with oil of cloves, available at drugstores.

❖ When choosing a puppy, especially if there are children in the house, you should disregard the trendy breeds (which often become inbred) and select a mellow puppy with mellow parents. The breeding matters much less than the temperament.

FEBRUARY

28

St. Romanus

● ● ○ ○ ● ●

Romanus bright and clear Indicates a good year.

1849
The ship *California* sailed into San Francisco Harbor, carrying the first of the gold seekers known as the 49ers.

1901
Birth of chemist LINUS PAULING.

. . .

I care not much for a man's religion whose dog and cat are not the better for it.

—*Abraham Lincoln*

29

Leap Day

● ○ ○ ○ ●

1736

Birthday of ANN LEE, founder of the Shakers in America.

2000

Ninety-year-old DORIS "GRANNY D" HADDOCK arrived in Washington, D.C., completing a 14-month cross-country walk to publicize the issue of campaign finance reform.

■ ■ ■

We are sick with the desire for the sun And the grass on the mountain.

—Paiute Song

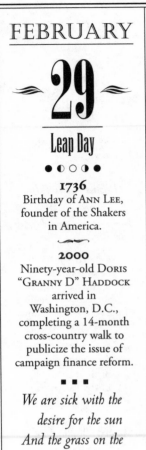

The Unredeemed Captives

DURING A SURPRISE ATTACK on Deerfield, Massachusetts, on February 29, 1704, French soldiers and Mohawk warriors captured more than 100 settlers. After an 8-week forced march to Montreal, some of the survivors of the attack were ransomed by English authorities in Boston and returned to their families. Others stayed in Canada with their Native American captors.

THE *Inspired* MIND

Mercy Carter (age 11) and Eunice Williams (age 7), whose mothers had died during the march, were two of those who stayed. Despite repeated attempts by their fathers to "redeem" them, they remained in Canada, eventually marrying Native

American men and raising families there. They never returned to New England.

In a 1753 letter, Ben Franklin noted the difficulty of repatriation when "white persons of either sex have been taken prisoners young by the Indians and lived a while among them." One reason for this, Ben speculated, was that "they become disgusted with our manner of life, and the care and pains that are necessary to support it."

Unconventional Wisdom about Beans

Forget what you've heard about storing, soaking, salting, and cooking dried beans. As it turns out, most of the old advice is wrong.

❖ Always soak beans? It's necessary only if the beans are old or large. Small, recently harvested beans can be cooked without soaking.

❖ Never salt beans during cooking? A recent test showed that beans salted during cooking stayed just as tender as unsalted ones and required only half as much salt to taste good.

❖ Dried beans will keep forever on the shelf? Perhaps they won't rot away, but after

about 6 months, they will become progressively tougher, taking longer and longer to cook.

❖ Keep beans at a boil so they cook thoroughly? No! Once they reach a boil, simmer them tenderly and gently so the skins don't split and toughen.

MARCH, *the Third Month*

Full Sap Moon

is the traditional name for this month's full moon. For premium maple syrup, a good sap run needs warm days and cold nights. *Full Worm Moon,* an alternative name sure to please gardeners, celebrates the reemergence of earthworms as the ground thaws.

Sign of the Zodiac: Pisces (February 20–March 20)

Element: Water

Quality: Creative

Birthstone: Aquamarine

Flower: Daffodil

THE ROMANS NAMED this month for Mars, the god of war (it was a traditional time to resume military campaigns), and made it the first month of their year. It often *is* a month of firsts—the first daffodil, robin, earthworm, skunk cabbage—but the early settlers of our country dreaded it as a time of deprivation. Graveyards attest that many a pioneer, weakened by the rigors of winter and lack of vitamin-rich foods, could not quite make it to spring but instead died on "March Hill."

If you are Irish (or wish you were), a highlight of March is the feast day of St. Patrick on the 17th. The patron saint of Ireland was born in Britain around A.D. 389, and in his name we bake Irish soda bread, eat corned beef and cabbage, and proudly wear the green.

March is notoriously temperamental weather-wise. According to old weather proverbs, if it comes in like a lion, it will go out like a lamb. The month is alive with fast-moving weather systems, tantalizing warm days, and record-breaking storms, such as the Blizzard of 1888, which paralyzed the East Coast. In the country, March means mud and maple syrup, skeins of migrating geese, and spring-cleaning. Pick a warm day, fling open the windows, and let spring blow in.

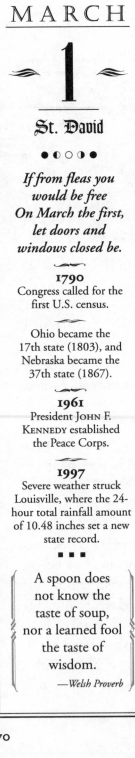

1

St. David

● ○ ○ ◑ ●

*If from fleas you
would be free
On March the first,
let doors and
windows closed be.*

1790
Congress called for the
first U.S. census.

Ohio became the
17th state (1803), and
Nebraska became the
37th state (1867).

1961
President JOHN F.
KENNEDY established
the Peace Corps.

1997
Severe weather struck
Louisville, where the 24-
hour total rainfall amount
of 10.48 inches set a new
state record.

■ ■ ■

A spoon does
not know the
taste of soup,
nor a learned fool
the taste of
wisdom.

—*Welsh Proverb*

Cream of Leek Soup

*In honor of the patron saint of Wales, St. David, whose symbol is the
leek, here is a soup that will warm the cockles of the coldest heart.*

4 **medium leeks**
3 **tablespoons butter**
2 **tablespoons flour**
4 **cups chicken broth**
1 **teaspoon salt, or to taste**
½ **teaspoon ground white
pepper**
2 **cups whole milk**
2 **ounces vermicelli or thin
spaghetti, broken up**

Trim the leeks, retaining the
white and light green parts.
Slice lengthwise in half and wash
thoroughly under running water to
remove any grit. Slice crosswise
about ¼ inch thick. Melt the butter
in a heavy soup pot and sauté the
leeks gently over low heat for about
15 minutes. Do not let them brown.
Sprinkle with the flour, stir, and
cook over very low heat for 10 minutes, stirring occasionally.

Add 1 cup of the chicken broth
to the leeks and stir. Add the salt,
pepper, and milk and cook gently,
stirring often, for 10 minutes. Remove from the heat. Bring the remaining 3 cups chicken broth to a
boil in a medium saucepan and add
the vermicelli. Cook for about 5
minutes, until the pasta is soft. Pour
the broth and vermicelli into the
soup and heat through.

Makes 6 servings

SOUP SAVVY

☾ If you have oversalted your soup,
add a quartered raw potato to absorb the excess salt. Discard the potato pieces before serving the soup.

☾ If you have leftover wine from a
party, freeze it in ice cube trays for a
zesty addition to sauces and soups.

☾ Shine your copper soup pots with
a paste made from vinegar and salt.

Growing Leeks

❖ Start leek seeds indoors 12
weeks before the last frost.

❖ When it's time to plant the
seedlings, dig a trench 1 foot
deep and 1 foot wide. Fill the
bottom with a 5-inch layer of
compost and transplant
seedlings into holes 6 inches
apart. As they grow, gradually
fill in the trench with more
soil, keeping the tips of the
plants exposed.

Proportion your charity to the strength of your estate, or God will proportion your estate to the weakness of your charity.

—BEN FRANKLIN

A MAN PROMISED to give 10 percent of his income to charity if God would bless him financially. At first, when he had little money, that was an easy promise to keep. But as his wealth grew, so did his charitable contributions, until the man began to begrudge the arrangement. He went to his minister and asked if he could decrease the percentage.

"I have a better idea," the minister said. "Why don't we ask God to lower your income so it doesn't hurt so much?"

Today the average American gives about 3 percent of his or her income to charity. Poorer Americans (those earning less than $10,000 a year) give more, around 5 percent.

Before you write out that check to the Mother of the Unknown Soldier Society, check with the Better Business Bureau's Wise Giving Alliance (www.give.org) to find out how much of your gift actually goes to programs, as opposed to fund-raising and administration.

THREE WAYS TO HELP

1. Consider volunteering in your town for something you *don't* know how to do. Organizations will happily train you, so you will learn a new skill while helping others.

2. Keep an "outgrown" box under each child's bed. When it's full, pass it along.

3. Routinely look through your books and magazines and donate those you won't read again to libraries or nursing homes.

A month that comes in good, goes out bad.

● ● ○ ○ ●

1904
THEODOR SEUSS GEISEL (aka Dr. Seuss) was born.

1917
The United States granted Puerto Ricans citizenship.

■ ■ ■

–BK

STRAIGHT FROM THE HEART

❧ Send flowers to a loved one for no particular reason. Never use flowers or other gifts only to say you're sorry. If you do, the recipient will cringe every time the florist's van approaches.

❧ Looking for a special way to say "take care" to someone you love? Present a basketful of small gifts for pampering: lip balm, aromatic oil of roses or lavender for the bath, a few sweets, and a scented candle.

3

*Manure your garden,
and marry if
you dare.*

● ◐ ○ ◑ ●

1842
Massachusetts enacted a
law limiting the workday
for children under
age 12 to 10 hours.

1845
Florida became the
27th state.

1911
Birth of actress
JEAN HARLOW.

1931
"The Star-Spangled
Banner" became the
official U.S. national
anthem.

■ ■ ■

Then, in that hour
of deliverance, my
heart spoke. Does
not such a country,
and such defenders
of their country,
deserve a song?

—*Francis Scott Key*

The Printer's Devil

THE *Inspired* MIND

BEN FRANKLIN'S apprenticeship to his brother James, a printer, may have given him a solid training in the craft, but it came at a price. At the age of 12, Ben became a printer's devil, spending long, unpaid hours in the shop learning (and later performing) the tasks of a printer: hand-setting type, engraving metal blocks, mixing ink, printing, collating, folding, and binding. Unhappy with the tedious work and tired of the beatings his older brother administered, Ben cut his 9-year term short by running away to Philadelphia at age 17 to begin his own successful printing career.

The apprentice tradition, which dates to the guilds of the Middle Ages, was soon to change anyway as the rise of the factory system transformed the workplace. No longer was the extended family, complete with apprentices like Ben, the primary unit of production. Factory workers found strength in numbers, and working conditions were gradually improved. Paid apprenticeships in the skilled trades were augmented by trade and technical schools.

Ben Franklin eventually reconciled with his brother. After James died, Ben raised his nephew Jimmy and in 1740 apprenticed him—with a gentler hand—to the printer's trade.

KEEPING PRINTED (AND PRINTING) MATTER

❦ Organize recipes clipped from magazines and newspapers into photo binders that contain clear plastic self-adhesive pages. Just peel back the plastic and smooth the recipe in place.

❦ Look for old magazines with interesting artwork or covers at yard sales, flea markets, and giveaway boxes at your library. These can be an inexpensive source of framable art for the home or office.

❦ Keep a rubber stamp collection in a printer's type tray mounted on the wall.

Speak little, do much. He that speaks much, is much mistaken.

—BEN FRANKLIN

PRESIDENT CALVIN COOLIDGE was the living embodiment of taciturnity. At a dinner one evening, a woman who knew of his reputation for reticence said to him, "I have made a bet, Mr. Coolidge, that I could get more than two words out of you."

"You lose," Coolidge replied.

Another time, an old colleague came to visit him and noted that, despite receiving a steady stream of callers every day, Coolidge was always able to finish work by 5:00 P.M. The colleague, who often had to work late to see all his visitors, asked Coolidge what the difference was.

"You talk back," Coolidge said.

But the most famous story about Coolidge concerns the day he returned from church. His wife, who hadn't attended that day, asked what the minister had preached about.

"Sin," Coolidge replied.

Hoping for a bit more detail, his wife asked, "What did he say about sin?"

"He was against it."

A WORD TO THE WISE

1791
Vermont became
the 14th state.

1888
Notre Dame football
coach KNUTE ROCKNE
was born.

. . .

It takes a great man to be a good listener.

—*Calvin Coolidge*

THE SAP IS RUNNING

—BK

❖ Tap maple trees when daytime temperatures reach 40° to 50°F and nighttime temperatures still drop below freezing.

❖ To tap a sugar maple, drill 2 to 4 inches into the south side of the tree at any convenient height, making a hole ⅜ to ⅝ inch in diameter (larger holes for larger trees). The hole should slant upward slightly. Drive a metal sap spigot (available at hardware stores) into the hole, stopping short of the full distance of the hole.

Hang a bucket on it to collect the sap. It takes about 40 gallons of sap to make 1 gallon of maple syrup.

❖ For a treat, boil syrup until it spins a thread, then pour it over clean packed snow (or crushed ice).

❖ If your maple syrup crystallizes, place the container in a pan of very hot water for a few minutes to restore it to its liquid state.

1770
British soldiers opened fire
on a taunting, snowball-
throwing crowd, killing
five colonists in what
became known as the
Boston Massacre.

1872
GEORGE WESTINGHOUSE
JR. patented a braking
system for trains.
His air brake became a
standard feature on all
heavy vehicles.

1908
Birth of actor
Sir REX HARRISON.

■ ■ ■

Like people,
plants respond to
extra attention.

—*H. Peter Loewer*

■ ■ ■

NATURE WATCH

In the Southwest, be
on the lookout for
desert tortoises and
desert box turtles
emerging from their
winter burrows.

A Guide to Spring Pruning

PRUNING KEEPS plants symmetrical and encourages strong new growth. Here are some general rules for a wide variety of commonly grown plants. Buy yourself a good pair of pruners and get to work.

PRACTICAL PRIMER

- **Apple and other fruit trees:** Prune in late winter or early spring before new growth starts. Cut back any suckers (water sprouts) that develop throughout the growing season, and remove any dead or diseased branches.

- **Flowering shrubs:** Prune summer- and fall-blooming shrubs before growth begins. Never remove more than one-third of the total growth unless the plant is seriously overgrown. Prune spring-flowering shrubs (lilacs, forsythias, and others) soon after the flowers fade.

- **Holly:** Prune in winter or early spring to give plants a desirable shape. Shorten any straggly stems and remove all dead growth.

- **Hydrangea:** Prune climbing hydrangeas and others that flower on new growth in early spring before growth begins. Prune oak-leaf hydrangeas and lacecaps after the flowers fade. For both types, prune back to the strongest pair of new shoots, thin older woody stems, and remove any crossed or dead branches.

- **Rose:** Prune in winter or early spring when plants are dormant. Cut back last year's growth by one-third. Cut off any branches that cross and remove all dead canes.

TOOL TIPS

❖ Clean rusty tools by wiping them with kerosene or motor oil and scrubbing them with steel wool.

❖ Prevent rust on the blades of spades, shovels, and hoes by plunging them into a box of sand moistened with motor oil. Do this after each use to double the life of your tools.

❖ Paint your tool handles a bright color, and you'll locate them more easily in the shed or on the ground. If you lend tools, the paint will help identify them as yours.

Content makes poor men rich;
discontent makes rich men poor.

—BEN FRANKLIN

1836
The Alamo in
San Antonio fell to
the Mexicans.

1926
Birth of economist
ALAN GREENSPAN.

1987
Record high temperatures
occurred in 28 cities in the
north-central United
States, including 83°F in
Pickstown, South Dakota,
the nation's hottest spot.

GEORGE III, king of England during the American Revolution, was in the stables at Windsor Castle one day when he came upon a boy and asked what he did there. "I help in the stable," the boy said. "But they give me only my food and clothing."

"Be content," the king said. "I have no more."

Perhaps the king was thinking of the apostle Paul's words in a letter to Timothy: "We brought nothing into the world, and we can take nothing out of it. But if we have food and clothing, we will be content with that." Paul went on to warn Timothy that people who want to get rich are prey to all kinds of disasters, and he added these famous words: "For the love of money is a root of all kinds of evil."

One man who knew what money could and couldn't provide was the pioneering conservationist John Muir, who once stated that he was richer than railroad magnate E. H. Harriman. When asked how that could be, Muir noted, "I have all the money I want and he hasn't."

KING GEORGE III

Make the Most of It

❦ To increase your supply of dahlias, plant each tuber indoors in a pot in March and take cuttings in April to set out as plants after the danger of frost has passed.

❦ If you have a room with a less-than-great view but you need the light, line the window with glass shelves and display decorative glassware, such as bottles or vases, on the shelves. Or hang baskets of plants in front of the window.

❦ Take some of those annoying Styrofoam packing peanuts (the nonbiodegradable kind) and encase them in a terry cloth cover to make a bathtub pillow for a more relaxing soak.

Yes, in the poor man's garden grow
Far more than herbs and
flowers—
Kind thoughts, contentment, peace
of mind,
And joy for weary hours.

—*Mary Howitt*

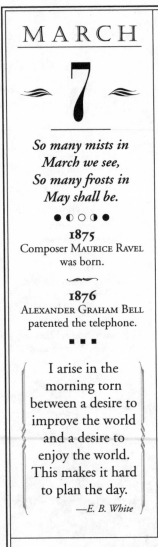

*So many mists in
March we see,
So many frosts in
May shall be.*

● ◐ ○ ◑ ●

1875
Composer MAURICE RAVEL
was born.

1876
ALEXANDER GRAHAM BELL
patented the telephone.

■ ■ ■

I arise in the
morning torn
between a desire to
improve the world
and a desire to
enjoy the world.
This makes it hard
to plan the day.

—*E. B. White*

The Long Arm
or, Gizmos That Retrieve Things
from the Oddest Places

RETURNING FROM EUROPE after the Revolution to live with his daughter and her family, Ben Franklin found his quarters cramped, so he built an addition in 1786. One room was his library, with shelves from floor to ceiling. Finding it difficult to retrieve books from the highest shelves, Ben invented a mechanical claw attached to a long wooden arm.

Since then, other grasping devices for out-of-reach objects have been invented, including an 1867 "fruit gatherer," an 1891 pruning tool with interchangeable cutting devices, Peter Christman's 1903 "store goods lifter" with a sliding metallic clamp, and Lawrence and Walter Metzler's electric bulb changer in 1924. The last had a bulb gripper that could be twisted by an attached cable, thus unscrewing the lightbulb.

THE *Inspired* MIND

On a smaller scale and designed to retrieve objects such as bladder stones inside the human body, inventor Frederick Wappler's 1936 endoscopic forceps used a tiny spring to open and close the pincers attached to the end of a flexible tube. Ben Franklin, plagued by a stone at the time of his book-retrieving invention, would have appreciated this miniature grasper.

INFORMATION RETRIEVAL

❧ Keep clothing sizes, blood types, Social Security numbers, and other vital statistics in the back of your address book for quick access.

❧ Keep an emergency information card near the busiest phone. List the numbers for the family doctor and dentist, ambulance, poison control center, police, and fire department, and make sure everyone in the family knows it's there.

❧ Attach a strip of self-adhesive Velcro next to your calendar or telephone, wrap its complementary strip around a pen or pencil, and keep the two together to eliminate hunting when you need to write down important items.

Best is the Tongue that feels the rein;—
He that talks much, must talk in vain;
We from the wordy torrent fly: Who
listens to the chattering pye [magpie]?

—BEN FRANKLIN

ACCORDING TO LEGEND, the young Albert Einstein was slow to speak, which made his parents worry that there might be something wrong with him. Finally, at the dinner table one evening, the boy piped up and said, "This soup is too hot."

His parents were astonished. "You can talk!"

"Of course I can talk," he said.

"But you never said anything before. Why?"

"Because up until now everything has been fine."

A WORD TO THE WISE

Some professions seem to be more inclined to garrulousness than others. Take barbers, for instance. As far back as 400 B.C., Archelaus, the king of Macedon, was asked by his barber how he wanted his hair cut. "In silence," Archelaus replied.

Of course, for true verbosity, it's hard to beat politicians. The late Hubert Humphrey was noted for being a bit long-winded. His political adversary Barry Goldwater once said, "Hubert has been clocked at 275 words a minute, with gusts up to 340."

1841
Birthday of OLIVER WENDELL HOLMES JR., Supreme Court justice known as the Great Dissenter.

1917
Rioting and strikes in St. Petersburg marked the start of the Russian Revolution. It would be known as the February Revolution because of the Old Style calendar used in Russia at the time.

1917
The U.S. Senate approved the use of cloture, a way to limit the obstructive speechifying known as filibuster.

• • •

They say women talk too much. If you have worked in Congress you know that the filibuster was invented by men.

—*Clare Boothe Luce*

HOUSEHOLD HINTS

❖ Designate a drawer in your house for keeping all warranties, instruction booklets, and other information that comes with appliances, computers, TVs, radios, sound systems, and other electronic devices.

❖ Cover your computer keyboard with a cloth when not in use to keep out dust.

❖ Keep a highlighter pen near your phone book and mark any numbers you're apt to look up again. You'll find them more quickly.

MARCH

9

Thunder in March betokens a fruitful year.

● ● ○ ◐ ●

1822
New Yorker CHARLES GRAHAM received a patent for artificial teeth.

1901
A fire destroyed the Olds Motor Works in Detroit.

1987
A 60-mile-per-hour gale produced waves as high as 15 feet on Lake Michigan.

■ ■ ■

Look around for a place to sow a few seeds.

—*Henry Van Dyke*

NATURE WATCH
Migrant birds are returning from the South. In the Great Plains, look for white-fronted, snow, and Canada geese; bald eagles; robins; and meadowlarks by mid-month.

Starting Seeds Indoors

GROWING FLOWERS and vegetables from seeds provides a head start for your garden plants. It also allows you to grow varieties that you might not be able to buy as seedlings.

PRACTICAL PRIMER

1. Before relying on last year's leftover seeds, test their germination rate. Place a few between damp paper towels, put them in a dark place, and keep them moist. Viable seeds will sprout in 5 to 10 days.

2. Buy a bag of seed-starting soil or make your own mix, using one part sieved compost and one part vermiculite.

3. Wet the soil, let it drain, and fill flats or individual containers. Make shallow indentations with a pencil or chopstick, plant several seeds per pot, cover with soil, and mist lightly with water.

4. Cover with plastic wrap or seal in a plastic bag to keep the soil from drying out. Place in a warm spot for 4 to 10 days, checking to be sure the soil doesn't dry out.

5. As soon as seedlings emerge, remove the plastic, move containers to bright light, and keep the soil evenly moist.

SUCCESSFUL START-UPS

❖ When starting coleus, impatiens, petunia, primula (primrose), or snapdragon seeds, make an indentation in the potting soil and sow thinly, but don't cover the seeds with soil. They need light to germinate.

❖ When starting cucumber seeds indoors, place the pots in a tray and put the tray on top of the refrigerator. The seeds will sprout faster with the heat given off by the

fridge. But once they sprout, move them into bright light.

❖ Grow real Easter grass table ornaments. About three weeks before Easter, fill small terracotta pots with potting soil, sprinkle with grass seeds, place in bright light, and keep watered. When the grass is up and growing, add a decorated egg, wrapped candy, small toy, or any other Easter trinkets you can nestle in the grass.

Mighty Moist Chocolate Cake

Bake this cake for a birthday party—or for no reason at all except to perk up a late-winter day.

1¾ cups flour

2 cups sugar

¾ cup cocoa (Dutch is recommended)

1½ teaspoons baking soda

1½ teaspoons baking powder

1 teaspoon salt

2 eggs

1 cup milk

½ cup canola oil

2 teaspoons pure vanilla extract

1 cup boiling water

½ cup confectioners' sugar

Preheat the oven to 350°F. Grease and flour a Bundt pan or a 9- by 13-inch cake pan. In a large mixing bowl, combine the flour, sugar, cocoa, baking soda, baking powder, and salt. Mix well. Add the eggs, milk, oil, and vanilla. Beat with an electric mixer at medium speed for 2 minutes. Stir in the boiling water by hand—the batter will be thin. Pour into the prepared pan and bake for about 40 minutes for the Bundt pan or 30 to 35 minutes for the cake pan, or until a tester inserted in the cake comes out clean. Cool in the pan on a wire rack for 10 minutes, then remove from the Bundt pan (this is optional for the cake pan) and continue cooling on the rack. Dust with the confectioners' sugar when cool.

Makes 12 servings

It's a Cakewalk

❖ If you have to make a cake and know you will be pressed for time, measure out the ingredients ahead of time (up to 3 days). Place the wet ingredients in a screw-top glass jar in the refrigerator. Place the dry ingredients in an airtight container.

❖ For extra flavor in your chocolate cake and cupcakes, dust your greased cooking pan or tin with sifted cocoa instead of flour.

❖ To keep a fresh cake from sticking to the serving plate, sprinkle the plate with granulated sugar before placing the cake on it.

❖ To keep leftover layer cake from drying out, attach pieces of bread with toothpicks to the exposed edges of the cake.

MARCH

10

1785
THOMAS JEFFERSON succeeded BEN FRANKLIN as minister to France.

1862
The United States issued its first paper money.

1979
GLORIA GAYNOR's song "I Will Survive" topped the pop music charts.

■ ■ ■

A compromise is the art of dividing a cake in such a way that everyone believes he has the biggest piece.

—*Ludwig Erhard*

11

1888
The Blizzard of 1888 struck the Northeast. Four hundred lives were lost.

1903
Birth of bandleader LAWRENCE WELK.

1918
The Spanish flu epidemic hit the United States.

1985
MIKHAIL GORBACHEV was elected general secretary of the Communist Party of the Soviet Union.

■ ■ ■

There are good days and there are bad days, and this is one of them.

—*Lawrence Welk*

ST. JOHN'S WORT

Read's Ointment for the ITCH

THE *Inspired* MIND

SARAH READ sold homemade Family Salve or Ointment, for Burns or Scalds from a Market Street shop in Philadelphia in the 1730s. She also marketed her well-known Ointment for the ITCH, but we are left guessing at the nature of the itch meant to be soothed.

For burns, Native Americans made ointments out of red clover, the inner bark of elderberry trees, and mashed cattail stems. Maybe Read had learned about these herbal remedies or knew the recipe for a burn salve made by boiling jimsonweed and hog fat.

In the 1700s, ointments made from aloe vera, slippery elm, comfrey, St. John's wort, and evening primrose were used to relieve itching from vaginitis and yeast infections. To soothe itchy hemorrhoids, butcher's-broom, witch hazel, or poplar unguent was prescribed. Today clinical studies show positive results from treating hemorrhoids with pennywort (*Centella asiatica*) or horse chestnut seed extract.

Sarah Read probably shared her ointments with her daughter Deborah, with whom she lived on Market Street, and with Deborah's husband, Ben Franklin.

HELP FOR AILING INNARDS

❦ If you need a remedy for hemorrhoids, apply witch hazel or aloe vera with a cotton ball several times a day. More expensive hemorrhoid pads, sold commercially, often contain the same thing.

❦ Once again, your mother was right: "Eat your prunes!"

For constipation, diverticulitis, and other digestive ills, prunes offer a naturally sweet, high-fiber cure. Prune juice works, too, and both are good sources of iron. For the best flavor, serve them very cold.

❦ Try yoga to relieve hemorrhoids. The half shoulder stand and plow postures are supposed to be particularly effective in increasing natural circulation and reducing the swelling and itching.

❦ If you expect digestive difficulties after a big or spicy meal, sip a small cordial of balsamic or cider vinegar.

A true friend is the best possession.

—Ben Franklin

Lord Byron, the romantic poet, may have been a Don Juan and a cad. But he could also be a good friend. While attending prep school, he saw a friend being beaten up by an older boy. Byron, who was born with a clubfoot, could do nothing to help. Nevertheless, he bravely asked the bully how many stripes he intended to give his friend. When the bully asked why he wanted to know, Byron replied, "Because, if you please, I would take half."

Not too many years ago, a young Nebraska boy named Mike won a contest in which the first prize was a new bike. Mike already had a bike, so he decided to give the prize to a friend

who didn't. The restaurant that sponsored the contest was so impressed by his generosity that they gave him a gift certificate for $100 to replace the bike. Mike promptly went out and bought his friend a safety helmet to go with the new bike. In years to come, the bike and the helmet went the way of most possessions, but the friend never forgot Mike, who cared so much about him.

1912
Juliette Low founded the Girl Guides, precursor of the Girl Scouts.

1933
The first of President Franklin D. Roosevelt's fireside chats was broadcast on national radio.

■ ■ ■

Hold a true friend with both hands.

—*Nigerian Proverb*

■ ■ ■

Nature Watch

It's breeding season for opossums, skunks, flying squirrels, and muskrats across the North. And that eerie howling noise? It could be a coyote calling for a mate.

FRIENDLY FAVORS

❦ Keep photo albums in a hinged chest that doubles as a living room coffee table. They'll be within easy reach to share with family and friends.

❦ Before any big occasion, whether a birthday, an anniversary, or a reunion, consider assembling a photo display of the honored guest(s). Ask friends, family, and neighbors to con-tribute to the display. Set it up on a corkboard and identify the photos with sticky notes on the back, so it's easy to return the originals.

❦ Carry a few notecards and stamps with you in your car or purse. When you are delayed or waiting for an appointment, write an impromptu note to a friend or relative.

13

1852
Uncle Sam first appeared in a political cartoon.

1947
LERNER and LOEWE's musical *Brigadoon* opened on Broadway.

1986
SUSAN BUTCHER and her canines won the Iditarod dogsled race from Anchorage to Nome, Alaska, in the record time of 11 days, 15 hours.

• • •

To his dog, every man is Napoleon; hence the constant popularity of dogs.

—*Aldous Huxley*

How Old Is Your Dog?

MULTIPLYING your dog's age by seven is easy, but it isn't accurate. "Human years" accumulate more quickly in a dog's life during the dog's early years. As the dog ages, the rate of maturity in equivalent human years slows down. (As of this writing, the world's record for dog longevity is 29 years 5 months.)

Dog Age (Years)	Equivalent Human Age (Years)	Dog Age (Years)	Equivalent Human Age (Years)	Dog Age (Years)	Equivalent Human Age (Years)
½	10	13	68	26	100½
1	15	14	70½	27	103
2	24	15	73	28	105½
3	28	16	75½	29	108
4	32	17	78	30	110
5	36	18	80½		
6	40	19	83		
7	44	20	85½		
8	48	21	88		
9	52	22	90½		
10	56	23	93		
11	60	24	95½		
12	64	25	98		

RULE OF THUMB: After the 2nd year, add 4 human years for each dog year. After the 13th year, add 2½ human years for each dog year.

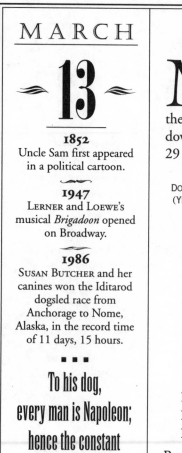

DOGGY DO'S AND DON'TS

❖ Let leftover bagels dry until rock hard, then give them to your dog for a good session of gnawing. They're beneficial to teeth and gums, and nutritious to boot.

❖ When greeted at a door by a barking dog, remain calm and quiet. If the dog is wagging its tail, extend your hand in a friendly gesture so the dog can sniff it. Do *not* try to pat its head. Many dogs find this threatening. If the dog is making aggressive sounds or looks ready to pounce, stay still and avoid eye contact until its owner arrives on the scene.

❖ Sprinkle baking soda on a rug after a pet accident to kill the odor and remove the stain. Scrub gently into the rug with warm water and a brush. Vacuum when dry.

❖ Keep several old towels in a box near the back door to dry off a wet dog.

Pitch upon that course of life which is most excellent, and custom will make it the most delightful.

—BEN FRANKLIN

A bushel of March dust is worth a king's ransom.

● ○ ○ ○ ●

1879
Birthday of
ALBERT EINSTEIN.

1989
High winds in the central plains carried dust as far east as Kansas City, Missouri. In Hill City, Kansas, windblown dust reduced visibility to one city block.

■ ■ ■

I never think of the future. It comes soon enough.

—*Albert Einstein*

AFTER GIVING this advice, Ben Franklin went on to say, "But many pitch on no course of life at all, nor form any scheme of living by which to attain any valuable end; but wander perpetually from one thing to another." Or, as another old saying goes, "if you fail to plan, you are planning to fail." Too many people act as if life owes them a living and are surprised and upset when good things don't just come their way.

Here are some simple rules for achieving success in any field.

- Set goals. Decide what things are important to you. Keep in mind that you can't do everything, so prioritize and choose.

- Stay focused. Don't waste time on tasks that don't advance your goals.

- Break big goals down into little ones. As the old joke goes, "How do you eat an elephant? A little at a time."

Let's Get Organized

❦ To avoid being overwhelmed on weekends, use the old-time but effective system of allotting certain days of the week to specific household chores. Do the laundry on Monday, shop for groceries on Tuesday, vacuum the house on Wednesday, and so on. With any luck, you won't wake up on Saturday morning with an impossible agenda.

❦ Organize household tasks for your family with a master chart. List the days of the week across the top and the names of parents and children along one side. In the blank spaces, write in the jobs for each person: feed pets, set table, wash dishes, take out trash. Write down who is responsible for each job on each day, leaving some free spaces for everyone.

❦ Create a master list for grocery shopping organized by category or store aisle. Make several copies at a time and post one to check off needed goods.

15

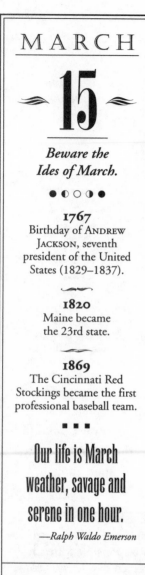

*Beware the
Ides of March.*

● ◐ ○ ◑ ●

1767
Birthday of ANDREW
JACKSON, seventh
president of the United
States (1829–1837).

1820
Maine became
the 23rd state.

1869
The Cincinnati Red
Stockings became the first
professional baseball team.

■ ■ ■

Our life is March
weather, savage and
serene in one hour.

—*Ralph Waldo Emerson*

Paving the Way
with Cobblestones

IN DESCRIBING Philadelphia in his *Autobiography*, Ben Franklin noted that the city "had the disgrace of suffering [its] streets to remain long unpaved, and in wet weather the wheels of heavy carriages plowed them into a quagmire." Ben lobbied to get Market Street paved with cobblestones, and when the towns-people applauded the improvement, he introduced successful legislation in 1757 for paving the entire city.

A big improvement in road surfaces came in 1819, when macadamized roads, named after their inventor, John McAdam, were constructed in England. They consisted of small broken stones in a 10-inch-thick layer bound together with hardened mud.

THE *Inspired* MIND

In 1870, the first asphalt road in the United States (probably made of crushed stone, tar, and pitch) was laid in Newark, New Jersey. The first concrete pavement was laid in Bellefontaine, Ohio, in 1894. About this time, "noiseless" asphalt pavement containing india rubber was

used near dwellings and hotels. Modern-day rubber-impregnated asphalt appeared in 1955, and asphalt using recycled rubber was developed in 1995.

Today 90 percent of America's roads are paved with asphalt, but Ben Franklin might have appreciated Darrel Adamson's 1995 invention of a machine that produces a "cobblestone-like pattern" in concrete pavement.

DEALING WITH MUD SEASON

When frozen ground turns to mud, and the mud gets tracked indoors, here's how to cope.

❖ Beat rugs, doormats, and car mats from the wrong side, then vacuum or wipe with a damp sponge.

❖ Sprinkle a damp sponge with baking soda and use it to remove water spots on wood floors.

❖ Use a neutral pH cleaner —not oil soaps—on your hardwood floors.

❖ To remove mud from suede shoes, let them dry thoroughly, then brush with a stiff-bristle brush.

As we enjoy great advantages from the inventions of others, we should be glad of an opportunity to serve others by any invention of ours.

—Ben Franklin

MARCH

1751
Birthday of
James Madison, fourth
president of the United
States (1809–1817).

1830
It was a slow day—the
slowest ever—at the New
York Stock Exchange:
Only 31 shares were
traded.

1909
A federal court ruled
that a 1907 movie
production of *Ben-Hur*,
filmed without the
author's permission, was
a copyright violation.

In this day of patent and copyright battles, it's hard to believe that Ben Franklin refused to accept a patent for the invention of the Franklin stove. The governor of Pennsylvania was so impressed by its design that he offered Ben the exclusive right to produce it for a period of time. Ben declined, believing that anyone should have the right to benefit from his work. Others felt no such scruples. One Englishman made minor adaptations to Ben's design, patented it, and earned a good deal of money. It was not the first instance of someone stealing Ben's ideas, but Ben never sought legal redress, because he hated disputes. As he said, "A quarrelsome man has no good neighbours."

Similarly, Jonas Salk never patented the polio vaccine for which he became famous. When asked why, he responded, "Could you patent the sun?"

A WORD TO THE WISE

> *Daring ideas are like chessmen moved forward; they may be beaten, but they may start a winning game.*
>
> —*Johann Wolfgang von Goethe*

BRIGHT IDEAS THAT COST NOTHING

❖ Save the cardboard tubes from toilet paper and use them to hold detachable cords from electric frying pans, waffle irons, and other kitchen appliances.

❖ Tired of ironing and reironing your good tablecloths? Slit a paper towel or wrapping paper tube lengthwise, then fit it over a wire hanger. Reclose the tube using sturdy tape. Hang your tablecloths on the hanger, and the creases will be softened.

❖ Don't throw out a worn or stained linen tablecloth. With a little cutting and sewing, you can recycle it into linen dishcloths (they'll already be soft and absorbent) or use the unstained parts to make napkins.

❖ To keep jewelry or other small, valuable items safe, cut a slit in a tennis ball, tuck them inside, and put the ball in your top drawer.

❖ Use old neckties to tie up sleeping bags and bedrolls.

St. Patrick

● ○ ○ ◑ ●

On the high day of Patrick, every fold will have a cow-calf, and every pool a salmon.

1776
The British evacuated Boston.

1901
The paintings of VINCENT VAN GOGH, who died in 1890, went on display in Paris, causing a sensation in the art world and recognition of his genius.

■ ■ ■

LORE & LEGEND

ST. PATRICK, who lived in the fifth century A.D., was kidnapped and enslaved but escaped by walking to freedom.

How to Make Milk Paint

MILK PAINT was once an inexpensive finish for woodwork and furniture. The old recipe required curdled milk or cottage cheese, but this one, using skim milk, will do the trick. It makes an excellent medium when you're experimenting with custom colors or crafts.

PRACTICAL PRIMER

1 ounce, by weight, hydrated lime (available at hardware stores; do not substitute quicklime, which is caustic)
1 quart skim milk, at room temperature
Powdered pigment (available at art stores)

Put the hydrated lime in a clean plastic bucket. Stir in just enough skim milk to make a creamlike solution. Stir some more, then add the rest of the milk. Add enough powdered pigment to get the desired color. Apply using a natural-bristle brush. Stir frequently while using. Let dry between coats. When the top coat is dry, apply a finish such as polyurethane.

Support the Arts

March is Youth Arts Month. Here's how you can celebrate it.

❧ Take your child's class to an art museum, or bring an artist into the classroom for some hands-on fun. Invite a local pro to teach the basics of watercolors, drawing, or collage.

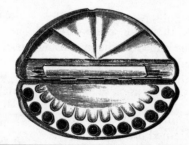

❧ String some fishing line along a playroom or family room wall and use tiny clothespins to hang up your kids' artwork.

❧ Use a lunch box or sturdy old purse to assemble portable art supplies for kids—markers, small pads of paper, stickers, little maze books—and take it along whenever you go out for dinner, to church, or to visit friends and relatives.

You've got to do your own growing, no matter how tall your grandfather was.

—*Irish Proverb*

Take this remark from Richard poor and lame, Whate'er's begun in anger ends in shame.

—BEN FRANKLIN

A WOMAN DRIVER in Tustin, California, was angry that a truck in front of her was moving too slowly. She grabbed an aluminum baseball bat, pulled up next to the truck, and began swinging at it. The truck was unhurt, but the woman was arrested, at which point the police noted that her vanity plate read Peace 95. She told them she'd chosen it because there was so much violence going on in society.

A peace activist in Santa Rosa, California, was angry about a series of articles criticizing him, so he found the newspaper's editor and belted him.

A WORD TO THE WISE

And a man in Santa Monica, California, lost his cool when a bird sitting on a nearby lamppost messed on his head. He began violently shaking the lamppost and loosened its large lightbulb, which fell on his head and fractured his skull.

Generally, the faster you become angry, the more likely you are to regret your actions. Take three deep breaths, count to 10, and remember that this, too, shall pass.

> Be the change you want to see in the world.
>
> —*Mahatma Gandhi*

MARCH

18

1837
Birthday of
GROVER CLEVELAND,
22nd and 24th president
of the United States
(1885–1889, 1893–1897).

1922
In India, spiritual
and political leader
MAHATMA GANDHI was
sentenced to prison for
civil disobedience.

1932
Birth of writer
JOHN UPDIKE.

1970
Postal workers went on
strike in New York City,
and within 2 days
200,000 other postal
workers joined them
nationwide.

KITCHEN WISDOM

❖ To keep rolls, muffins, and biscuits warm longer, line your bread basket with aluminum foil, then wrap warm baked goods in a towel and pop them in the basket.

❖ Freshen your kitchen (or cover up odors) by simmering 1 teaspoon whole cloves,

1 cinnamon stick, and grated orange peel in 1 cup water.

❖ Butter the rim of the pan in which you are cooking rice or pasta to prevent the water from boiling over.

❖ Cook artichokes in a nonreactive pot. Aluminum or

iron will turn the artichokes a grayish color.

MARCH

19

St. Joseph

● ○ ○ ○ ●

Clear today betides a fertile year.

1918
Congress approved daylight saving time.

1931
Nevada legalized gambling. The move was an attempt to spur the state's economy during the Great Depression.

⁘

You cannot just waste time. Otherwise you'll die to regret it.

—*Harriet Doerr*

⁘

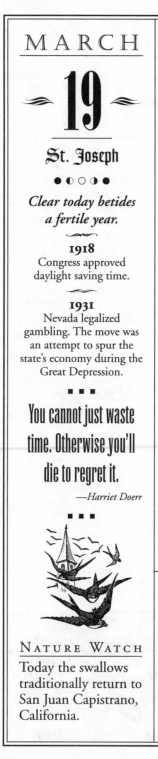

NATURE WATCH
Today the swallows traditionally return to San Juan Capistrano, California.

Money lost may be found; what we are robb'd of may be restored: the treasure of time once lost, can never be recovered.

—BEN FRANKLIN

IN THE 1751 EDITION of *Poor Richard's Almanack,* Ben Franklin told the story of a cobbler who was prone to wasting time, much to his wife's dismay. When he was out drinking with his friends, she would send word to him when the clock struck midnight. "Tell her to be easy," he instructed the messenger. "It can never be more" (meaning it can't get any later than that). If she sent word that the clock had struck one, he responded, "Bid her be comforted, for it can never be less."

One man who set a higher value on his time was Jean Louis Rodolphe Agassiz, a naturalist famous for his studies of fossil fish. Agassiz was once asked to address the members of an important society, but he declined, saying that lectures took too much time away from his research and writing. The organizers of the meeting pressed him, explaining that they would pay him well for speaking to the group. "That's no inducement to me," Agassiz responded. "I can't afford to waste my time making money."

TIPS FOR CLOCK WATCHERS

☾ Keep your alarm clock on the other side of your bedroom so you have to get out of bed to turn it off.

☾ If you have trouble getting places on time, put a clock in every room (including the bathroom) and check the clocks periodically to be sure they're in agreement.

☾ Save time on the phone. When you send out invitations, instead of asking for an RSVP, request regrets only.

Ink Blot Jottings

PRINTERS IN Ben Franklin's day used a variety of inks, depending on the printing job and the season. Cold weather required thinner ink, warm weather dictated thicker ink, and the type of fiber in the paper (from linen to cotton rag) affected the ink's spreadability. Ben made up his own formulas or used other printers' inks and advertised inks for sale at his print shop. In the 1730s, he sold Aleppo ink (a "true staining Black" with the quality of "Lastingness" for use in deeds and documents requiring longevity), japan ink, common ink, and Persian ink (made of water, gum arabic, iron sulfate, honey, and tannin).

THE *Inspired* MIND

Oil from petroleum eventually replaced vegetable oil as the main ingredient in ink, with a typical formula for news ink containing about 65 percent oil and 20 percent carbon black (pigment made from oil). But the oil embargo of the 1970s spurred interest in the revival of vegetable oil–based inks. John Moynihan of New Jersey patented a non-petroleum-based newspaper ink in 1983, but it still contained carbon black. In 1992, Sevim Erhan and Marvin Bagby patented a soybean oil–based ink containing no petroleum-derived components.

MARCH

1852
HARRIET BEECHER STOWE's *Uncle Tom's Cabin* was published in book form.

Birth of educator and children's TV personality FRED "MISTER" ROGERS (1928) and actor/director SPIKE LEE (1957).

1971
Singer JANIS JOPLIN's recording of "Me and Bobby McGee" topped the charts.

But words are things, and a small drop of ink,
Falling like dew, upon a thought, produces
That which makes thousands, perhaps millions, think.

—Lord Byron

OUT, DAMNED SPOT!

❖ Use your regular liquid laundry detergent to pretreat stains. Store it in an empty sport top water bottle or shampoo bottle and keep it in the bathroom. When you take your clothes off at the end of the day, check for stains and squirt any you find with detergent. Wash within 24 hours and dry as usual.

❖ Mix together 1 quart water and ¼ cup salt and sponge the solution onto laundry stains, then launder as usual.

❖ For stubborn wine stains on washable fabrics, sponge with hydrogen peroxide, then wash.

❖ For old stains on clothes, apply white vinegar using a spray bottle. Let dry, then rinse and launder as usual.

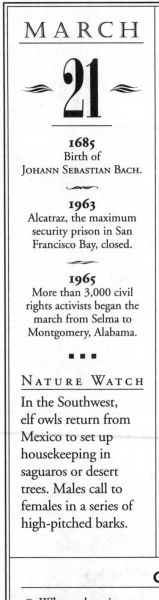

MARCH

21

1685
Birth of
JOHANN SEBASTIAN BACH.

1963
Alcatraz, the maximum
security prison in San
Francisco Bay, closed.

1965
More than 3,000 civil
rights activists began the
march from Selma to
Montgomery, Alabama.

• • •

NATURE WATCH

In the Southwest,
elf owls return from
Mexico to set up
housekeeping in
saguaros or desert
trees. Males call to
females in a series of
high-pitched barks.

---

*The cunning man steals a horse,
the wise man lets him alone.*

—BEN FRANKLIN

IT DOESN'T TAKE a lot of brains to be a criminal. In fact, intelligence could disqualify you. Take the bank robber who tried to push open the door of the Security Federal Savings Bank in Durham, North Carolina. The masked man pounded on the door, but alarmed employees refused to open it. The robber fled, apparently not realizing that he had been pushing on a "pull" door.

A WORD TO THE WISE

A man in Norfolk, Nebraska, tried to cash a check for $22 million—which he had printed on his home computer—at a bank's drive-up window. Tellers refused to cash the check, which was missing the name of an issuing bank. Undaunted, the man wrote Reality Perspective Bank on the check and tried again. This time, tellers called the police.

In Hartford, Connecticut, a thief stole a purse with a cell phone in it. Police called the number, and the thief answered but neglected to turn off the phone when returning it to the purse. Police listened in and located the thief from the music playing in a store where he was shopping. "I've had a few names in my book of dumb criminals," the arresting officer said, "but this guy goes right to the top."

The first day of
spring is one thing,
and the first spring
day is another.
The difference
between them is
sometimes as great
as a month.

—*Henry Van Dyke*

GARDENING KNOW-HOW

❧ When planning a vegetable garden, arrange the rows on a north-south axis so crops will receive the most sun. If geography dictates east-west rows, situate the tallest plants on the north side.

❧ Experiment with short garden rows of different crops, or plant crops in squares to deter insect pests that can easily spot expanses of their favorite crops.

❧ As a rule of thumb, when you see your lawn starting to green up, start planting cold-hardy seeds in your vegetable garden. Note that grass starts to grow when the soil temperature reaches 43°F.

Patching Things Up with Homemade Spackle

FOR A SMOOTH FINISH, fill in small holes and cracks in walls before painting or papering. You can make your own hole filler and patching compounds. To fill small nail holes and fine cracks in wallboard or plaster, combine 2 tablespoons cornstarch, 2 tablespoons salt, and 4 to 5 teaspoons water. Stir the mixture until it becomes a pliable paste. Fill the holes or cracks with a spackling knife, then let dry. Sand the area, if necessary, then paint. Another easy way to fill nail holes is to combine equal parts white toothpaste or baking soda and white glue. Very small holes can be filled with a baking soda and water paste.

PRACTICAL PRIMER

The Wonder of Cornstarch

❖ For cooking, use cornstarch to thicken sauces. It has almost twice the thickening power of flour. Sauces thickened with cornstarch will be clear, not opaque as with flour-based sauces.

❖ Make goo! (A fun project for kids.) Measure 1 cup cornstarch into a bowl. Slowly add up to ½ cup water, stirring constantly, until the mixture resembles pancake batter. Add a few drops of food coloring, if you wish. The goo will act like a liquid until you handle it; then it magically turns into a solid. Kids love goo's tactile qualities. It's nontoxic, and cleanup is easy.

CELLAR SMARTS

With cinder blocks and boards, build a raised platform in your basement to keep boxes and other items well above the floor or ground. Even the driest of basements can sometimes get flooded in the spring.

> Time spent laughing is time spent with the gods.
>
> —*Japanese Proverb*

1841
Cornstarch was patented. (Starch from potatoes was already in common use.)

1893
The first women's collegiate basketball game was played at Smith College in Massachusetts.

1920
A brilliant display of the northern lights (aurora borealis) was seen in Detroit.

• • •

NATURE WATCH

In New England and the Middle Atlantic states, spring has irrefutably arrived when the peepers begin to sing, usually in mid- to late March. A single peeper makes a repetitive "peep" sound, while many peepers together sound like a continuous shaking of sleigh bells. The small frogs live in and near wetlands and moist woodlands.

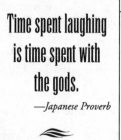

23

—BK

*The winds of
the daytime wrestle
and fight
longer and stronger
than those of
the night.*

● ◐ ○ ◑ ●

1775
"Give me liberty, or give
me death!" declared
PATRICK HENRY at
Richmond, Virginia.

1908
Birth of actress JOAN
CRAWFORD.

■ ■ ■

NATURE WATCH

As temperatures rise
above 60°F, march
hares and spring rab-
bits get frisky. Males
will fight for mates
and chase each other
in a wild breeding
frenzy. The litters
will be born within
a month.

Grow a Giant Pumpkin

IF YOU WANT a prizewinning pumpkin this year, you have
to start now. Your pumpkin (or squash) will pack on the
pounds if you follow these tips.

1. Buy seeds with a built-in genetic ability to
produce giants.
2. Start seeds indoors 6 to 8 weeks before the
last expected frost.
3. When the ground is tillable, prepare the
planting area, digging 14 to 16 inches deep.
Enrich it with well-rotted cow or sheep manure.
4. Move the seedlings to the garden after any
danger of frost has passed. Space them at
least 10 feet apart and protect them from
wind and cold nights.
5. When blossoms appear, allow just one to
bear fruit, then pinch off all the others.
6. Fertilize weekly with manure or compost tea
and side-dress every 2 weeks with a balanced
organic fertilizer.

A little Madness
in the Spring
Is wholesome even
for the King.

—*Emily Dickinson*

Spring Tonics for Spring Fever

*Spring fever occurs when a cool spell is followed by sudden warmth
and the body is slow to catch up. The resulting lassitude, or weari-
ness, is a physiological change. To combat it, try the following tactics.*

☾ Add these spring tonic greens to your
salads: dandelion, burdock (roots or stems
and leaves), asparagus, early cresses, or
parsley. Keep leftover greens (not dressed)
fresh by wrapping them in a damp paper
towel and storing them in a plastic bag
with ventilation holes.

☾ For exercise and a fresh outlook, take a
noontime walk as part of your lunch break.

☾ Eat some fiddleheads. Shake them in a
wire basket to remove the papery chaff.

PARSLEY

He that spills the rum, loses that only;
He that drinks it, often loses both
that and himself.

—BEN FRANKLIN

B EN FRANKLIN had good reason to advise against excessive drinking: He'd seen its disastrous effects too often. A childhood friend took to drink and, after borrowing a great deal of money from Ben, went off to Barbados and was never heard from again. Ben's first partner in the printing business, Hugh Meredith, was seldom sober, and they eventually dissolved their partnership.

A WORD TO THE WISE

As a member of the Pennsylvania assembly, Ben was once sent to negotiate a treaty with Native Americans at Carlisle. The Native Americans demanded rum, which the negotiators promised to give them only after the treaty was completed. That night, the Native Americans drank all the liquor and demanded more. The next day, the elders of the tribe apologized for their conduct, and Ben despaired of their future if they kept on drinking. "If it be the design of Providence to extirpate these savages in order to make room for cultivators of the earth, it seems not improbable that rum may be the appointed means," he noted ruefully. "It has already annihilated all the tribes who formerly inhabited the sea-coast."

1955
Cat on a Hot Tin Roof
premiered on Broadway.

1987
A blizzard struck parts of Nebraska. Wind gusts created 12-foot snowdrifts.

1989
The *Exxon Valdez* ran aground in Prince William Sound, Alaska, spilling 11 million gallons of oil.

. . .

Most of the confidence which I appear to feel, especially when influenced by noon wine, is only a pretense.

—*Tennessee Williams*

TEMPERANCE TIPS

❖ At any gathering, include a choice of nonalcoholic sparkling cider, seltzer or other fizzy water, or fruit punch for designated drivers or others who prefer not to indulge.

❖ To make an easy FRUIT PUNCH, combine 1½ cups cranberry juice, ½ can frozen orange juice concentrate, and 1 can (7 ounces) crushed

pineapple in a blender. Blend until smooth, then add 2 cups ginger ale. Chill and serve. Makes 1 quart.

❖ If you have trouble sleeping, avoid alcohol, chocolate, and caffeine. Instead, have a cup of hot chamomile tea or warm Ovaltine before turning in.

25

1775
GEORGE WASHINGTON
planted pecan trees at
Mount Vernon, Virginia.

1802
Dr. JAMES SMITH of
Baltimore, Maryland, gave
free smallpox vaccines to
the poor.

1942
Birthday of singer
ARETHA FRANKLIN.

> Labor to keep alive
> in your breast
> that little spark
> of celestial fire
> called conscience.
>
> —*George Washington*

• • •

NATURE WATCH

Chipmunks end their
hibernation as the
days get warmer. The
striped eastern chip-
munk, actually a
small terrestrial squir-
rel, is not a true hi-
bernator. It spends
the winter in its ex-
tensive underground
chambers, snacking
on a stash of nuts,
seeds, and berries.

Smallpox Inoculation, Then and Now

THE
Inspired
MIND

SMALLPOX, with a 30 percent fatality rate, became epidemic in Boston in the early 1720s. James Franklin and his
younger brother Ben, apparently believing that inoculation
spread the disease, published numerous essays
and letters criticizing the practice. After Ben
moved to Philadelphia, he came out in support of inoculation in 1731, but he neglected
to treat his own son Francis, who died of
smallpox at the age of 4 in 1736. A remorseful Ben later penned a
strong statement in support of inoculation in the preface to a 1759
pamphlet on the disease, which he distributed free of charge.

During the 1970s, the World Health Organization (WHO)
used mass vaccination, in which the smallpox vaccine was given to
large numbers of people, and ring vaccination, in which the vaccine was given to an exposed person and those who had come in
contact with that person, to fight the disease. By 1980, WHO
achieved the global eradication of smallpox.

Although the vaccine is no longer given to the general population, in 2002 the U.S. Centers for Disease Control stockpiled
15.4 million doses of the vaccine for emergency use.

NUT KNOWLEDGE

❖ Store walnuts and pecans,
which can turn rancid more

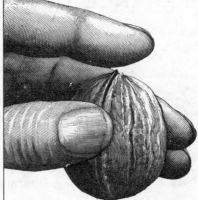

quickly than other nuts, in airtight containers in the freezer
for up to 2 years.

❖ To shell pecans, use a nutcracker and crack them end to
end rather than across the middle. One pound of pecans in
the shell yields about 1¼ cups
chopped nuts.

❖ Before adding nuts to cake
or muffin batter, warm them
in the oven or microwave, and
they won't be as apt to sink.

Tricks and treachery are the practice of fools, that have not wit enough to be honest.

—BEN FRANKLIN

THEODORE ROOSEVELT was riding near his North Dakota ranch with a hired hand, looking for mavericks (calves without brands). They found one and prepared to brand it. But they were on a neighbor's land, and the rules of the range dictated that the calf was his. Even so, the hired hand started heating up Roosevelt's branding iron. When Roosevelt questioned the hand, he said that he always put his boss's brand on mavericks. Roosevelt fired him at once. "Any man who steals for me will steal from me," he said.

A WORD TO THE WISE

A student at George Washington University thought that he could outsmart a professor with a plagiarized term paper. The professor called him into his office and accused him of having someone else type the paper for him, copying it verbatim from an encyclopedia entry. The audacious student told the professor he couldn't prove the charge. Then the professor pointed to the last line of the paper, which read, "Also see article on communism."

MARCH

26

Birth of poet ROBERT FROST (1874) and Supreme Court justice SANDRA DAY O'CONNOR (1930).

1885
The first commercial film for motion pictures was manufactured in Rochester, New York.

1979
ANWAR EL-SADAT and MENACHEM BEGIN signed the Camp David Accords between Egypt and Israel.

Oh, give us pleasure in the flowers today;
And give us not to think so far away
As the uncertain harvest;
keep us here
All simply in the springing of the year.

—*Robert Frost*

What's That Awful Smell?

❦ If your dog is sprayed by a skunk, clean him with a mixture of 1 quart hydrogen peroxide, 1 cup baking soda, and 1 teaspoon mild dishwashing liquid. Rub the mixture through his coat, avoiding his eyes, then bathe him with a regular dog shampoo. This solution works better than tomato juice at neutralizing the smell.

❦ Keep a pretty dish filled with baking soda on a shelf or the top of the toilet tank as a natural air freshener for your bathroom.

❦ To rid your hands of an onion or fish odor, rub them against a stainless steel sink.

27

1855

ABRAHAM GESNER received a patent for kerosene.

1912

Two Yoshino cherry trees were planted in Washington, D.C., the first of more than 3,000 given to the United States as a gift from Japan.

1994

A deadly tornado struck Alabama. Twenty people died during the Palm Sunday service at Goshen United Methodist Church.

• • •

NATURE WATCH

A massive spring migration is under way as birds move north along the Atlantic and Mississippi Flyways. Watch for warblers, robins, field sparrows, red-winged blackbirds, turkey vultures, killdeer, ducks, geese, and great blue herons.

Salmon Teriyaki

A simple teriyaki sauce is a perfect foil to salmon. Turn the fish carefully to keep the pieces intact.

12 ounces salmon fillets, skinned
1 tablespoon soy sauce
1 teaspoon grated fresh ginger
1½ teaspoons brown sugar
1 tablespoon rice wine or lime juice
1 tablespoon peanut oil

Cut the salmon into 1- to 1½-inch chunks. In a small bowl, combine the soy sauce, ginger, brown sugar, and rice wine. Heat the oil in a heavy skillet over medium-high heat and add the salmon. Fry until cooked through and crisp on all sides, about 6 minutes. Brush the salmon with the soy sauce mixture and fry for 1 minute more.

Makes 2 servings

FISH COOKERY

❖ Dark red spots on fish are bruises that reflect poor handling. They affect the flavor and can hasten deterioration.

❖ If you thaw frozen fish in milk, it will taste fresher and sweeter.

❖ Fish does not have to be tenderized before cooking because its flesh doesn't have the same muscle mass as animal meat. If you do marinate fish, keep the total time to less than 2 hours.

❖ Poaching fish can be tricky. Always let the water or stock return to a simmer after placing the fish in the pan, then begin timing.

❖ Whether poaching, frying, grilling, broiling, or steaming a fish fillet or steak, it should be cooked for about 10 minutes per inch (measured at the thickest part).

Govern a family as you would cook a small fish—very gently.

—*Chinese Proverb*

Each age of men new fashions doth invent.

—Ben Franklin

There's no accounting for taste. Fashions that would have got their wearers laughed off the street at one time are all the rage at another. People who came of age in the era of bell-bottom pants and peasant blouses have been astonished to see those fashions return.

Among the more daring fashion trends was one that swept French society during the time of Napoleon I. Fashionable women took to wearing dresses made of transparent gauze, a practice that offended Napoleon's sensibilities. He once ordered his servants to build up the fire in his drawing room until the temperature reached tropical levels. "It is extremely cold," he explained, "and these ladies are almost naked." The empress Josephine got the point and soon introduced a more modest style of dress.

A WORD TO THE WISE

Every generation laughs at the old fashions, but follows religiously the new.

—*Henry David Thoreau*

Laundry Day

❧ Start an extra-dirty load of clothes in the washer as usual, but turn the machine off after a few minutes and let the load soak for several hours or overnight before restarting the machine.

❧ To deodorize a washing machine that smells musty, fill the machine with water and add 1 quart white vinegar. Run it through a full cycle, with no detergent. This also helps clean out the hoses.

❧ Brighten and soften yellowed nylon or linen items by adding ¼ cup baking soda to your wash along with the detergent, then adding another ¼ cup during the rinse cycle.

MARCH

28

1793
Birth of Henry Rowe Schoolcraft, explorer who discovered the source of the Mississippi River.

1881
Barnum and Bailey combined their circuses.

1987
Maria von Trapp, whose life inspired the musical *The Sound of Music*, died in Vermont.

■ ■ ■

–BK

NATURE WATCH
While robins are winging their way northward, earthworms are migrating, too. Worms travel upward through the soil as the ground gradually thaws, moving about 3 vertical feet from their winter quarters to the surface. Their appearance above ground usually coincides with sightings of the year's first robins.

MARCH

29

1790
Birthday of John Tyler,
10th president of the
United States
(1841–1845).

1943
Meat, cheese, and cooking
fat were rationed in the
United States.

1973
The last U.S. troops left
South Vietnam.

1999
The Dow-Jones average
closed above 10,000 for
the first time.

*How happy is he, who can
satisfy his hunger with any food,
quench his thirst with any drink,
please his ear with any musick,
delight his eye with any painting, any
sculpture, any architecture, and divert his
mind with any book or any company!*

—Ben Franklin

Ben Franklin's father often invited company to join his family for dinner, as he loved intellectual discussions that would improve his children's minds. In fact, he was so interested in the conversation that he paid little attention to the food. The meal might be good or bad, in or out of season, and the elder Franklin never seemed to notice. As a result, Ben grew up to be indifferent to the food set before him. "To this day if I am asked I can scarce tell a few hours after dinner what I dined upon," he once said. Although his traveling companions often complained about the food they were served, Ben's appetite was more easily pleased than their "more delicate, because better instructed, tastes."

The Careful Cook

❖ If meat in a display case is sitting in a large pool of juice, pick another package. The juice indicates that the meat was previously frozen. Freezing bursts the cell walls, allowing liquid to escape. This hurts both flavor and texture.

❖ To keep cottage cheese and yogurt fresh longer, store them upside down in the refrigerator before they are opened. This helps keep air away from the surface of the product, which in turn prevents bacteria from growing.

❖ Store all dairy products in the coldest part of the refrigerator—that is, in the back, away from the door.

❖ Wrap leftover cheese in waxed paper rather than plastic wrap to keep it fresh. As cheese ages, its living cultures need to breathe.

*Some hae meat and canna eat,
And some would eat that
want it;
But we hae meat, and we can eat,
Sae let the Lord be thankit.*

—*Robert Burns*

The Best Means of Relieving the Distressed

IN 1750, when Dr. Thomas Bond of Philadelphia resolved to start a hospital for poor people with physical and mental diseases, he knew his plan had a much better chance to succeed with Ben Franklin's help. Convinced of the plan's wisdom, Ben solicited private subscriptions and introduced a fund-raising bill in the legislature. The bill was passed on the condition that matching private donations be raised, and when this was accomplished in 1751, the Pennsylvania Hospital "for the relief of the sick and miserable" was founded. It was the first hospital in the nation.

In 1803, the hospital established a maternity department, and the next year it opened a surgical amphitheater. By 1847, the Medical Library was the largest of its kind in the United States, containing rare works dating from 1483. In 1879, the hospital instituted its first training program for nurses. In 1997, Pennsylvania Hospital merged with the University of Pennsylvania Health System.

HEALTH HINTS

❧ Suck on an ice cube before you take a bad-tasting medicine. Ice helps deaden the tastebuds.

❧ If your hearing is fading fast, try cutting way back on salt. Sodium is sometimes implicated in hearing loss. You'll know quickly whether salt is the culprit.

❧ If you're pregnant, sleep on your left side. Not only does this improve blood flow to the fetus, but it also may help keep you from getting varicose veins. Sleeping on your back may cause the fetus to put more pressure on the veins in your pelvic area.

❧ If you have high blood pressure, consider eating these foods, which have natural chemicals that help reduce blood pressure: carrots, tomatoes, celery, garlic, onions, broccoli, and virtually anything that contains magnesium (such as leafy greens, legumes, or whole grains).

–BK

1842
DR. CRAWFORD LONG was the first to use ether as an anesthetic in the United States.

1858
HYMAN LIPMAN patented the first pencil with an eraser top.

1968
Chanteuse CELINE DION was born.

■ ■ ■

Listen or thy tongue will keep thee deaf.
—*Native American Proverb*

■ ■ ■

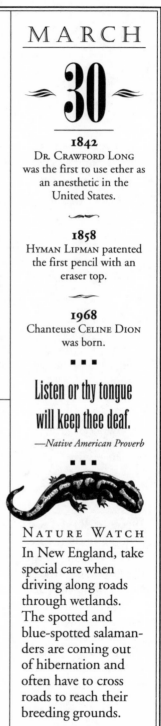

NATURE WATCH
In New England, take special care when driving along roads through wetlands. The spotted and blue-spotted salamanders are coming out of hibernation and often have to cross roads to reach their breeding grounds.

31

*If March comes in
with adder's head,
it goes out with
peacock's tail.*

● ○ ○ ● ●

1896
The zipper (originally
for fastening shoes)
was patented by
WHITCOMB JUDSON.

1923
The first dance
marathon was held in
the United States.

1927
Birth of migrant
farmworker and union
organizer CÉSAR CHÁVEZ.

■ ■ ■

NATURE WATCH

If you live in the east-
ern half of the United
States, it's time to set
up a bluebird nesting
box in an open field
or clean out an exist-
ing box. To deter
predators such as
snakes, raccoons, and
cats, install a predator
guard on the pole
below the box.

A Garden for Butterflies

AS YOU PLAN this year's garden, consider dedicating an area to butterflies. To attract a variety of visitors, plant an assortment of nectar-rich flowers. Choose plants appropriate to your locale. Here are some suggestions: aster, bee balm, borage, black-eyed Susan (rudbeckia), butterfly bush, butterfly weed, coreopsis, daylily, gayfeather, hibiscus, joe-pye weed, lantana, lavender, lilac, marigold, nicotiana, phlox, pineapple sage, privet, purple coneflower, rosemary, sweet william, verbena, and zinnia.

PRACTICAL PRIMER

Butterflies cannot live on nectar alone. They also need a sunny spot to soak up warmth, such as a large rock. A shallow pan of water, a mud puddle that's kept damp, or a birdbath provides drinking water. Butterflies require a sheltered spot to rest until the energizing sun comes out. A pile of rocks with plenty of crevices, some old boards, or a fallen limb works well.

Take butterfly gardening one step further and research the host plants that different species need for laying eggs and feeding caterpillars. For example, monarch butterflies prefer to lay eggs on milkweeds. Having these plants nearby will provide everything the butterflies need for their full life cycle.

The butterfly
counts not months but
moments, and has
time enough.

—*Rabindranath Tagore*

The Designing Gardener

❦ For sweet scents from foliage, try these plants: achillea (yarrow), artemisia, lemon balm, monarda (bee balm or wild bergamot), salvia (sage), basil, and the mints and thymes.

❦ Lay out your perennial garden so that its width is no more than twice the height of the tallest plant.

WILD
BERGAMOT

APRIL, *the Fourth Month*

Full Pink Moon

(for the wild ground phlox) is the traditional name for April's full moon, although some Native Americans called it the *Full Sprouting Grass Moon* or the *Full Egg Moon,* all curtsies to the promise of spring.

Sign of the Zodiac: Aries (March 21–April 20)

Element: Fire

Quality: Assertive

Birthstone: Diamond

Flower: Sweet pea

ARE YOU AN APRIL FOOL? In France, the gullible ones are called *poisson d'avril,* or "April fish," perhaps because of the folklore that says "April fish are easily caught." Throughout the northern hemisphere, this month of capricious weather is an optimist's dream and a poet's inspiration. The Latin word *aperire,* meaning "to open or bud," gives us the name April, and spring festivals around the world, from Easter and Passover to our own Arbor Day, celebrate the season's renewal of life.

We like to mark the month in practical ways: bake a rhubarb pie, plant peas and potatoes, toss the first green leaves of dandelions into a salad. The fresh greens are an irresistible tonic, and not just to humans. Since medieval times, dairy farmers have known they could make the finest cheese from the milk of cows that grazed on April's verdant pastures.

Naturalist Hal Borland wrote, "April is a promise that May is bound to keep." With that in mind, plant shade trees now to please posterity; dwarf fruit trees, lilacs, and roses to please yourself. Teach a child to fish; adopt a kitten; volunteer at your community soup kitchen. Play hopscotch; fly a kite; build a tree house; learn to throw a curveball. It's April, after all!

1

April Fools' Day

● ○ ◑ ○ ●

Birthday of silent film star LON CHANEY (1883) and singer-dancer-actress DEBBIE REYNOLDS (1932).

1946

A tsunami, or tidal wave, struck the Hawaiian Islands with devastating force, killing 170 people.

■ ■ ■

NATURE WATCH

If you see a brown bird with a long, narrow bill shoot straight up in the air in a spiral, fly in a circle, and then plummet to the ground, you have witnessed the courtship dance of the male American woodcock. Its courting call is a loud buzz: Bzeep! Woodcocks breed from New England west to the Mississippi River.

Daylight Saving Time

BY CHANGING our clocks in the spring and fall, we save energy because less electricity is used for lighting and appliances. Daylight saving time (DST) allows us to take advantage of longer sunlight hours during half of the year. Congress enacted the first standard time law, which included a provision for DST, in 1918, but it proved unpopular and was repealed in 1919. In 1966, Congress passed legislation (modified in 1986) establishing DST as we know it today (from the first Sunday in April until the last Sunday in October).

In a 1784 letter to a Paris newspaper, Ben Franklin described an economical project containing the first proposal for DST. In his humorous self-parody, he professed shock at seeing sunlight at 6:00 A.M. when accidentally awakened—6 hours before his usual time of rising. He calculated the amount of money Parisians could save on candles "if the light of the Sun was used from the moment it rises each day." To pry sleeping citizens from their beds, he proposed measures ranging from ringing church bells and firing cannons to levying a tax on each window with shutters. Ben claimed that his proposal rested on his startling discovery that the sun "gives light as soon as he rises."

> *In winter I get up at night*
> *And dress by yellow*
> *   candle-light.*
> *In summer, quite the*
> *   other way,*
> *I have to go to bed by day.*
>
> *—Robert Louis Stevenson*

How to Spring Forward Gracefully

❖ If your outdoor lights are on timers, remember to adjust them for daylight saving time.

❖ Drive carefully. It takes about 1 week for our circadian rhythms to adjust to a 1-hour time loss, so the beginning of daylight saving time each spring is marked by a 7 percent increase in traffic accidents. More coffee, please!

Dressed-Up Asparagus

You'll never cook asparagus any other way. That's an extravagant claim for a recipe, but wait until you taste the results.

2 bunches asparagus, about
   2 pounds
1 tablespoon extra-virgin
   olive oil
Freshly ground black pepper
3 tablespoons soy sauce
3 tablespoons sesame oil
¼ cup fresh lime juice
1 tablespoon finely grated
   fresh ginger
1 large clove garlic, pressed
2 scallions (green and white
   parts), minced
1 teaspoon brown sugar

Trim the tough ends off the asparagus: Hold each spear three-quarters of the way down the stalk, then with the thumb and index finger of the other hand, bend the stalk until it snaps. In a large bowl, toss the asparagus with the olive oil and pepper to taste and place in a single layer in a baking pan. Broil about 4 inches from the heat for about 8 minutes, shaking the pan halfway through to turn the asparagus. The cooking time will depend on the thickness of the spears; they are done when lightly browned and tender.

Transfer the asparagus to a serving platter. In a small bowl, whisk together the soy sauce, sesame oil, lime juice, ginger, garlic, scallions, and brown sugar. Pour over the asparagus and serve warm.

Makes 4 servings

Getting Ready for Easter Dinner

❦ Use a collection of china teacups or demitasse cups to display decorated eggs. Place a little floral foam in each cup, add some water, set a decorated egg on the foam, and add sprigs of green around the edges. Display one cup at each place setting.

❦ Instead of plastic grass, use a skein of green yarn to line Easter baskets. You can use it again for knitting projects or to tie up packages next Christmas.

❦ Place celery and carrot sticks under a roast to make an edible roasting rack. They will add flavor to the gravy.

1722
The first of
BEN FRANKLIN'S 14
commentaries—America's
first essay series—was
published under the name
Silence Dogood.

1878
The Easter egg roll at the
White House was begun.

1914
Birth of actor
Sir ALEC GUINNESS.

■ ■ ■

*Winter's done, and
   April's in the skies,
Earth, look up with
   laughter in your eyes!*
—Charles G. D. Roberts

■ ■ ■

AVOID CATASTROPHE

Cats that ingest any part of an Easter lily (or another member of the lily family) can develop kidney damage within hours, so keep those Easter lilies out of reach. If your cat nibbles a lily, call your vet right away.

APRIL

3

1860
The Pony Express began
mail delivery.

1934
Birth of ethologist
JANE GOODALL, known
for her study of
chimpanzees.

1988
Easter Sunday
thunderstorms in
Michigan and Indiana
spawned five tornadoes.
A wind gust of 114 miles
per hour was recorded at
Ann Arbor, Michigan.

• • •

NATURE WATCH

Great blue herons
return now to Vinal-
haven, Maine, and
other summer desti-
nations. Largest and
heaviest of the North
American herons, this
solitary and noctur-
nal bird wades slowly
in quiet waters, hunt-
ing for fish and other
food.

Let the letter stay for the post, and not the post for the letter.

—BEN FRANKLIN

THIS MAXIM about waiting for the mail brings to mind an incident in the life of Kenneth Perkins, a young man serving with the U.S. Navy in 1945 in Florida. Perkins met a young woman named Rosalie Tellerman, who had come to Miami on vacation. The two corresponded after she returned home, but suddenly Rosalie's letters stopped coming.

In 2002, to his shock, Perkins received a package from Rosalie—one she'd sent him on December 13, 1945. Somehow, the package had been waylaid and had sat in a dead letter vault in a courthouse in Indianapolis for all those years. The Postal Service tracked down Perkins, who was 79 at the time, and delivered the package to him. Inside were some aftershave, talc, and hairdressing. Whatever happened to Rosalie? "She probably got mad at me for not sending her a card thanking her for the gift," Perkins said.

> The post is
> the consolation
> of life.
> —*Voltaire*

Department of Tiny (and Easily Lost) Objects

❖ Do your kids have thousands of little trinkets cluttering up their rooms? Buy a large glass container with a top (such as an old penny candy or apothecary jar) and toss the trinkets in there.

❖ Store games, puzzles, and other toys that have lots of little pieces in self-sealing plastic bags.

❖ Organize a Lego collection by storing smaller pieces in 9- by 13-inch cake pans with plastic lids, in plastic shoe boxes, or in other shallow containers with lids. Use plastic sweater boxes for larger pieces.

❖ Sort buttons by color or size and store them in glass jars.

The Water-American

D URING B EN F RANKLIN'S first visit to England, he found work at a London printing house, where his imbibing habits earned him the derisive nickname of the Water-American. As related in his *Autobiography,* "I drank only water; the other workmen, near fifty in number, were great guzzlers of beer." Ben reported one coworker's daily 6-pint consumption: upon rising, at breakfast, before and during lunch, at 6:00 P.M., and when the day's work was done. Six British pints of beer is about 1 gallon. Today it is recommended that for good health, a person drink eight 8-ounce glasses of water a day—½ gallon.

THE
Inspired
MIND

Ben was doing himself a favor by drinking water. It accounts for 85 percent of the brain, 78 percent of the blood, and 75 percent of the muscles. Water carries nutrients and oxygen to cells and helps convert food into energy. After a graduate of Ben's University of Pennsylvania, Nathaniel Wyeth, patented the plastic beverage bottle in 1973, water could be consumed conveniently on the run. Sales of small bottles of water increased from 4.4 million gallons in 1984 to 750 million by 1997, and they continue to grow as "water-Americans" act on their health and pollution concerns.

Five Great Reasons to Drink Water

1. Dehydration is a problem for 75 percent of Americans. For many, what feels like a hunger pang is actually thirst.

2. Drinking water boosts the metabolism while lessening food cravings.

3. Dehydration is the chief contributor to daytime fatigue.

4. Most people who suffer from back and joint pain find relief if they drink 8 to 10 glasses of water per day.

5. To keep mental faculties sharp—memory, computation, mental focus—stay hydrated.

Thousands have lived without love, not one without water.

—*W. H. Auden*

APRIL

4

Rain from the south prevents the drought, But rain from the west is always best.

● ● ○ ○ ●

1902
C ECIL R HODES left a scholarship fund in his will providing for Americans to attend Oxford University in England. To this day, Rhodes scholars are chosen for their exemplary scholarship, athleticism, and character.

1915
Bluesman M UDDY W ATERS was born.

1932
C. C. K ING isolated vitamin C at the University of Pittsburgh.

■ ■ ■

N ATURE W ATCH
In the northern Great Plains, watch for American white pelicans in marshy areas as soon as the ice melts. A flock of these huge birds is an amazing sight as they take off and soar in circles.

5

*April snow
breeds grass.*

● ● ○ ○ ● ●

1614
POCAHONTAS married
JOHN ROLFE.

1870
A state law reorganized
the Metropolitan Fire
Department into the Fire
Department of the City of
New York. The Board of
Fire Commissioners
ordered the placement of
"F.D.N.Y." on all
apparatus.

1900
Actor SPENCER TRACY
was born.

■ ■ ■

**Many a bear
going out on
a warm day like this
would never have
thought of bringing
a little something
with him.**

—*A. A. Milne,*
Winnie-the-Pooh

The Bear Facts
or, Sleepers, Awake!

BEARS ARE WAKING from their winter slumber, and they have a fierce appetite. To keep hungry bears away from your yard:

**PRACTICAL
PRIMER**

- Bring in your bird feeders and keep them in through October. (Don't worry about the birds; they'll find food.)
- Do not store birdseed, food, or trash on porches (including screened porches).
- Keep barbecue grills clean.
- If you feed your pets outdoors, bring any leftover food in.
- Wait until morning to put trash out for collection.
- When camping, store food in the car, never in your tent. If a car is not nearby, store food in airtight containers and up out of a bear's reach, not in a cooler set on a picnic table.

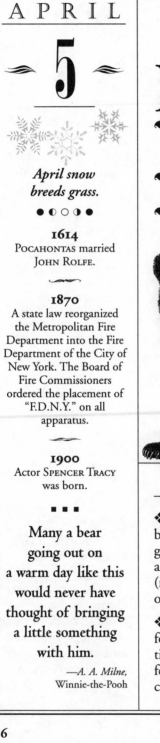

TRASH TALK

❖ In the spring when you bring your bird feeders indoors, give them a good washing with a 10 percent bleach solution (nine parts warm water and one part chlorine bleach).

❖ To deter mice and keep pet food fresh, store large quantities of dry pet food or livestock feed in plastic or metal trash cans with tight-fitting lids.

❖ After emptying the trash, sprinkle baking soda in the can to control odors.

❖ Keep trash cans tightly covered in the spring and summer to cut down on flies around your house.

The brave and the wise can both pity and excuse; when cowards and fools shew no mercy.

—BEN FRANKLIN

IN 1923, a college student visiting Washington, D.C., ran out of money and couldn't pay his hotel bill or buy a train ticket home. He decided to steal the money he needed and broke into the room of another guest. It was early in the morning, and the occupant of the room awoke, saw the young man rifling through his clothes, and said, "I wish you wouldn't take that," referring to a watch chain with a charm attached. He explained that it had been given to him when he was Speaker of the Massachusetts House of Representatives.

The man was Calvin Coolidge, who explained to the astonished burglar that he was the newly elected president of the United States (so new that he had not yet moved into the White House). Coolidge learned of the young man's financial plight and gave him enough money to cover his bill and return to campus. He told the student to consider it a loan.

Coolidge told few people about the incident, which came to light only in 1982. The young man did repay the loan.

Hard-Boiled Eggs

❦ You can prevent hard-boiled eggs from cracking while cooking by bringing refrigerated eggs to room temperature and gently easing them into boiling water. Simmer for 15 minutes, then cool immediately in cold water.

❦ Can't remember which eggs are the hard-boiled ones?

Gently spin the egg on the counter. If the egg spins easily, it is cooked. If it wobbles and stops, it's raw. Next time, mark the cooked eggs.

❦ Eggs a week or two old are easier to peel when hard-boiled than perfectly fresh eggs.

❦ Hard-boiled eggs are easier to peel when hot (the egg white begins to stick to the shell's lining as it cools).

1909
The first credit union in the United States opened in Manchester, New Hampshire.

1973
On opening day, the Boston Red Sox beat the New York Yankees 15–5 in the first American League baseball game played using the designated hitter rule.

■ ■ ■

Remember, people will judge you by your actions, not your intentions. You may have a heart of gold— but so does a hard-boiled egg.

—*Author Unknown*

■ ■ ■

NATURE WATCH
Carp, white bass, and largemouth bass are spawning now in cold northern streams and lakes.

Washboard sky, not three days dry.

● ◐ ○ ◑ ●

1862
Union forces under General ULYSSES S. GRANT defeated the Confederates under General ALBERT SIDNEY JOHNSTON at the Battle of Shiloh in Tennessee, with staggering casualties on both sides.

1915
Birth of jazz singer BILLIE HOLIDAY.

1957
New York City's last electric trolley made its final run from Queens to Manhattan.

■ ■ ■

NATURE WATCH

Old-timers in the upland South believe that frost will not occur after the dogwoods have bloomed. The white blossoms "floating" in the woods beside the soft pink redbud blossoms is a beguiling sight, but tradition holds that full blooms foretell a cold winter.

How to Grow Great Tomatoes

To FULLY APPRECIATE the taste of a tomato, try growing it yourself. Follow these steps for success.

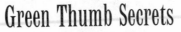

PRACTICAL PRIMER

1. Start seeds indoors 6 to 8 weeks before the last expected frost.
2. Transplant seedlings to the garden when they have only five to seven leaves. If you have tall, leggy plants, plant them deep, with only the top few leaves sticking out of the ground.
3. For each seedling, dig a deep hole, put well-rotted manure in the bottom, cover with an inch or two of rich soil, and then plant the seedling, disturbing its roots as little as possible.
4. Pinch off suckers as the plants grow.
5. Fertilize every 3 weeks once small tomatoes have formed.
6. If Mother Nature does not bring regular, adequate rain, provide irrigation—an inch of water per week, more if it is hot and dry.

Green Thumb Secrets

❦ Plant the seeds of perennials directly in the garden when the maple trees put out their first leaves.

❦ When Easter lilies stop flowering, cut off the stems and store the bulbs in a cool, dark place. Plant the bulbs 4 to 6 inches deep outdoors in a sunny spot after any danger of frost has passed.

❦ Early in the season, scratch some pulverized limestone into the soil around lavender plants, which like alkaline soil.

❦ Prune overwintered potted azaleas to keep them shapely, then repot into containers that are about an inch larger.

❦ Sow hollyhock seeds in early spring in a sunny spot along a garage, outbuilding, or fence, where they can self-sow freely in succeeding years.

One of the healthiest ways to gamble is with a spade and a package of garden seeds.

—*Dan Bennett*

Proportional Taxation
Something to Think about While You Do Your Taxes

P HILADELPHIA'S unfair night watch system caught Ben Franklin's attention in the 1730s. To avoid night watch duty, each resident paid six shillings a year to the neighborhood constable, who was supposed to hire a substitute. Ben circulated an essay outlining "the inequity of this six-shilling tax . . . since a poor widow housekeeper, whose property to be guarded by the watch did not perhaps exceed the value of fifty pounds, paid as much as the wealthiest merchant, who had thousands of pounds' worth of goods in his stores." This led to a reform law for hiring professional watchmen

THE *Inspired* MIND

and, Ben revealed in his *Autobiography*, "as a more equitable way of supporting the charge, the levying [of] a tax that should be proportioned to the property."

Ben's proportional tax—the greater the wealth, the higher the percentage assessed—resembles the federal income tax, enacted in 1913, with its progressive rate. Today's advocates for a flat tax (everyone would pay the same percentage regardless of wealth or poverty) argue for its simplicity, but Ben might argue against its inequity.

● ○ ◐ ● ●

1935
Congress approved the Works Progress Administration (WPA).

1974
HANK AARON blasted home run number 715, breaking BABE RUTH'S career record.

■ ■ ■

The art of taxation consists in so plucking the goose as to obtain the largest possible amount of feathers with the smallest amount of hissing.

—*Jean-Baptiste Colbert*

The Frugal Household

❖ Save money and add flavor to recipes with a modest-priced drinking sherry. Ounce for ounce, cooking sherry is more expensive than the sipping kind. (It also can be salty and barely drinkable.)

❖ Make inexpensive tablecloths by using flat bedsheets. If the sheets are too plain, decorate them with stencils, fabric paints, or appliqués, perhaps in a holiday theme.

❖ To keep cereal and crackers from getting limp and stale as the weather becomes more humid, transfer them to plastic containers with tight-fitting lids.

9

1833
The first tax-supported public library in the United States was founded in Peterborough, New Hampshire.

1872
Dried milk was patented by New Yorker SAMUEL R. PERCY.

1963
Sir WINSTON CHURCHILL was made an honorary U.S. citizen.

When death puts out our flame, the snuff will tell, if we were wax, or tallow by the smell.

—BEN FRANKLIN

A WORD TO THE WISE

SOMETIMES it's hard to tell whether someone's life is as sweet as beeswax or as rank as tallow. As a young child, the English poet Charles Lamb went for a walk in a cemetery with his older sister. As they strolled, they read the engravings on the tombstones, which extolled the many virtues of the departed. After reading about all the exemplary people buried in that cemetery, the young Lamb turned to his sister and asked, "Where are all the naughty people buried?"

Sir Winston Churchill was more forthcoming about his faults. It was no secret that he was a heavy drinker. Once, while visiting the White House, he asked a butler—who had been serving him drinks all day—if he could be depended on. When the butler asked what Churchill wanted him to do, Churchill replied, "If I am ever accused of being a tee-totaler, I want you to come to my defense."

"Mr. Prime Minister," the butler said, "I'll defend you to the last drop."

> I am prepared to meet my Maker. Whether my Maker is prepared for the great ordeal of meeting me is another matter.
>
> —*Sir Winston Churchill*

Watching Your Waistline?

❖ Yogurt cheese is a great low-fat alternative to cream cheese with only about one-third the calories. Make it by lining a mesh strainer with cheesecloth. Put 2 cups plain yogurt in the strainer, cover, and let drain into a bowl overnight. Pour off the liquid (whey) and store the "cheese" in a covered container in the refrigerator. Use as is or stir in chopped herbs to make a quick dip for raw vegetables.

❖ Low-fat cheese used for sauce or as a baked topping does not melt as well as full-fat cheese. For the best results, grate low-fat cheese very finely for melting.

❖ In a restaurant, learn to interpret "menu-speak." Meat that is braised or flame-seared will be lower in fat and calories than meat that is panfried, crispy-seared, or presented fritto misto (coated in batter and deep-fried).

Revolutions in Typesetting

STARTING WITH Johannes Gutenberg's movable type in the 15th century, typesetting has gone through several transformations. As a typesetter, Ben Franklin used Gutenberg's painstaking process of setting each metal character by hand. Then in 1884, Ottmar Mergenthaler of Baltimore developed a machine that could cast a whole line of metal type on command. Mergenthaler's machine created a sensation in 1893 at the Chicago World's Columbian Exposition, and within 20 years 100,000 Linotype machines were in use across the country.

THE **Inspired** MIND

Although Linotype machines continued to be used into the 1980s, their days were numbered. Phototypesetters (introduced in 1945) and later, computers radically changed the industry. Most newspapers and magazines quickly switched over to computers and laser printers. With personal desktop publishing, anyone can be a typesetter and never get ink under his fingernails.

POINTERS FOR THE DESKBOUND

❦ To cut down on eyestrain, avoid computer marathons, the wrong glasses, or not using your glasses, and make sure you have adequate light.

❦ Have you done your carpal tunnel exercises today? Close and open your fist a dozen times with each hand. Put your hands over your head and rotate them from the wrists, first clockwise, then the other way. Gently stretch your fingers back toward your wrist.

❦ Use a silverware organizer in your desk drawer to hold pens and pencils, stamps, paper clips, and other small items.

❦ Save your old toothbrushes and use them to scour computer keyboards.

❦ Keep a small spiral-bound notebook and a pen or pencil next to the phone at all times. Get in the habit of writing names and phone numbers in it so you can easily find the information later.

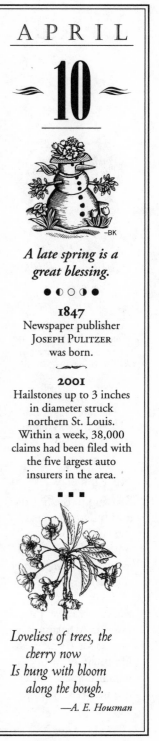

–BK

A late spring is a great blessing.

● ◐ ○ ◑ ●

1847
Newspaper publisher
Joseph Pulitzer
was born.

2001
Hailstones up to 3 inches in diameter struck northern St. Louis. Within a week, 38,000 claims had been filed with the five largest auto insurers in the area.

■ ■ ■

*Loveliest of trees, the cherry now
Is hung with bloom along the bough.*
—*A. E. Housman*

11

—BK

**A cold April
the barn will fill.**

● ● ○ ◐ ●

1945
American soldiers
liberated the Buchenwald
concentration camp in
Germany.

~

1970
The song "Let It Be"
by the BEATLES topped
the charts.

■ ■ ■

NATURE WATCH

Starting in the South
and moving toward
the colder zones,
broods of the periodi-
cal cicada (*Magicicada*
species) begin to
emerge. These large,
extremely noisy but
essentially harmless
insects have a 17-year
life cycle, most of
which is spent under-
ground as a nymph.

*Up, sluggard, and waste not life;
in the grave will be
sleeping enough.*

—BEN FRANKLIN

A WORD TO THE WISE

THESE DAYS, we may be getting too little sleep rather than too much. Some studies indicate that humans may need as much as 10 hours of sleep per night, but fewer and fewer people are getting even the recommended 8 hours. Our busy schedules just don't allow it. Meanwhile, researchers have learned that sleep deprivation (getting less than 6 hours of sleep a night) increases our susceptibility to infection, depression, diabetes, weight disorders, and heart trouble. It may even cause traffic accidents.

Here are some tips for getting a good night's sleep.

- Sleep in complete darkness in a quiet room.
- Wear socks if your feet get cold.
- Avoid sugary snacks just before bed. Instead, eat a piece of fruit or a high-protein snack a few hours before sleeping.
- Avoid alcohol and caffeine in the hours before sleep.
- Avoid decongestants and appetite suppressants.
- Take a hot bath or shower before bed.
- Get regular exercise.

> **People who say
> they sleep like
> a baby usually
> don't have one.**
>
> —*Leo J. Burke*

One Man's Snore Is One Woman's Insomnia

It happens the other way around, too, but twice as many men snore as women. In fact, there are more than 300 antisnoring devices registered with the U.S. Patent and Trademark Office, including chin harnesses and straitjackets. During the Revolutionary War, soldiers sewed a small cannonball in a pocket on the back of a comrade's nightshirt to make him turn over—a variation on today's advice to use a tennis ball (cannonballs being in short supply).

A Hero's Welcome

THE HERO'S WELCOME accorded Ben Franklin upon his return from France in 1785 after having helped secure the Treaty of Paris that ended the Revolution was probably the first of its kind in the United States. When Ben's party docked at Market Street wharf in Philadelphia, he later wrote, "we were received by a crowd of people with huzzas, and accompanied with acclamations quite to my door." Newspapers called him the "father of American independence."

THE
Inspired
MIND

A hero's welcome was also given to astronaut John Glenn in 1962 when hundreds of thousands lined the streets of New York City to honor the first American in space. Other Americans given ticker tape parades through New York City's "Canyon of Heroes" include Charles Lindbergh in 1927 (for the first solo flight across the Atlantic), Amelia Earhart in 1932 (the first woman to duplicate Lindbergh's feat and in less time), and General Douglas MacArthur in 1951, when an estimated seven million people filled Broadway.

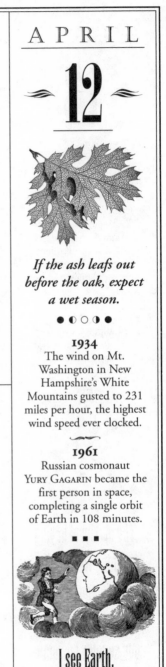

If the ash leafs out before the oak, expect a wet season.

● ○ ○ ◑ ●

1934
The wind on Mt. Washington in New Hampshire's White Mountains gusted to 231 miles per hour, the highest wind speed ever clocked.

1961
Russian cosmonaut YURY GAGARIN became the first person in space, completing a single orbit of Earth in 108 minutes.

● ● ●

I see Earth. It's so beautiful!
—*Yury Gagarin*

Picture Perfect: Tips for Hanging Art

❖ To decide how to hang an arrangement of paintings or photos, cut out templates in the same sizes as your frames. Black construction paper works well for this. Tack them to the wall with a temporary puttylike adhesive and move them around until you're happy with the arrangement.

–BK

❖ If your painting or framed print weighs between 20 and 40 pounds, you have three choices of hanger, depending on what your wall material is.

A *plastic anchor* has a screw driven into it, and it grips the wall material (such as wallboard) as it goes in.

A *hollow wall anchor* goes through the wall material and grips from behind, making a sturdy attachment. Avoid drilling into wall studs.

A *toggle bolt* opens its wings into the wall material as it is drilled. As with hollow wall anchors, you must avoid the wall studs.

APRIL

13

1743
Birthday of
THOMAS JEFFERSON, third
president of the United
States (1801–1809). The
Jefferson Memorial in
Washington, D.C., was
dedicated on this day in
1943, with President
FRANKLIN ROOSEVELT
giving the main address.

1972
Ballplayers went
back to work as major
league baseball's
first strike ended.

· · ·

The maxim of buying
nothing without the
money in our pockets to
pay for it would make of
our country one of the
happiest on earth.

—Thomas Jefferson

Rather go to bed supperless, than run in debt for a Breakfast.
—BEN FRANKLIN

THOMAS JEFFERSON, or Long Tom, as he was called, stood 6 feet 2½ inches tall and had red hair, hazel eyes, and freckles. He invented the revolving chair, pedometer, rope machine, and revolving music stand. Jefferson also suffered from incapacitating headaches, which sometimes lasted for 2 weeks or more. "Indolence and extravagance" irked him, and he saw "the abolition of all credit" as its remedy. (Ironically, he died deeply in debt.) If tax time is giving you a headache, consider this medicine.

THOMAS JEFFERSON

◄ To curb impulse spending, freeze your credit cards in a block of ice to reduce the temptation to use them. (Don't try to thaw them fast in a microwave—they melt.)

◄ The average family of four spends more than $5,000 a year at the grocery store. Resolve to spend no more than 5 percent of each week's grocery budget on convenience and junk foods, and you'll see your expenditures (and maybe your waistline) shrink.

TOP TIGHTWAD TIPS

❆ To make your own wood-polishing formula, find a handful of rusted nails or other rusted metal parts. Dump them into an old bucket, then add 1 quart white vinegar and 1 quart water. Let the rusted parts soak in this mixture for several weeks. Discard the metal pieces, then use the remaining solution and a soft cloth to polish wood finishes and restore dried-out wooden furniture.

❆ When discarding a down comforter or coat, salvage the down. Open the seams and vacuum the down into a brand-new vacuum cleaner bag. Save the bag (it may take more than one), and you'll have down stuffing for a future craft or blanket project of your own.

❆ When you're ready to discard a crusty paintbrush, snip an inch off the brush tips and use what's left of the brush for household dusting.

A Soil Improvement Plan

PRACTICAL PRIMER

BEFORE YOU PLANT your garden, go to work improving the soil. Lush growth will be your reward.

1. Using a spading fork, turn the soil over so that what was on top is now underneath. Shake out and discard any roots or clumps of grass.

2. Let the soil sit undisturbed for a few days, then rake it smooth, removing rocks and any roots you missed.

3. Cover the soil with a layer of compost about 2 inches deep. (As a guideline, you will need a 3-cubic-foot bag to cover 18 square feet to this depth.) Work the compost into the soil with a rake until it is well blended.

4. Work in some well-rotted cow manure, available from your local nursery. (A 25-pound bag will be enough for a garden bed that measures 12 by 4 feet.) Your garden is now ready for planting.

GARDEN BASICS

❖ Improve heavy clay soil by mixing in generous amounts of sand and leaf mold or compost.

❖ To sift rocks and debris out of soil, shovel it into a plastic milk crate and shake.

❖ Don't overfertilize your vegetable garden. Soil that is too rich in nitrogen will produce lush growth but no fruit.

❖ To remove stumps that keep sprouting, cut them as low to the ground as possible, apply an organic fertilizer such as bloodmeal or cottonseed meal or a thick layer of chicken manure, then cover with a thick layer of soil. (Mound it up, if necessary.) Once the stump has rotted, you can level the area again.

> Weather is not as important as good soil, and good soil is not as important as human harmony.
> —*Chinese Proverb*

● ○ ◐ ○ ●

1828
NOAH WEBSTER obtained a copyright for the first edition of his dictionary.

1886
A tornado ripped through St. Cloud, Minnesota, killing 74 people. The bottom of the Mississippi River—normally 15 feet deep—was said to have been seen during the tornado's crossing.

1939
JOHN STEINBECK's *Grapes of Wrath* was published.

■ ■ ■

NATURE WATCH
In the West, bobcats, coyotes, and foxes are giving birth to litters. In the breeze, you will start to see hackberry, skipper, blue, and queen butterflies.

15

1817
The first school for the deaf in the United States was established in Hartford, Connecticut.

1912
The *Titanic* sank.

> There was a time when a fool and his money were soon parted, but now it happens to everybody.
>
> —*Adlai Stevenson*

• • •

LORE & LEGEND

If a wren chooses to nest in your yard, be on the alert for feathers it may drop. If you find one, offer it to anyone with a boat. Folk wisdom says that a wren's feather brought aboard ship will prevent a shipwreck.

In this world nothing can be said to be certain, except death and taxes.

—BEN FRANKLIN

POPULAR RESENTMENT about taxes is nothing new. Back in Ben Franklin's time, a disagreement over a tax on tea helped spark the Revolution, which gave us the ability to tax ourselves. (We showed *them!*) Ever since then, people have been coming up with novel ways to avoid paying taxes. Here are a few of the more inventive ideas.

A rock and roll singer told the IRS that her deductions for clothes were high because she had to throw her outfits away after every performance. Apparently, the "energy levels of her performances and the heat generated on stage from lights and physical exertion" ruined the clothes. Right.

A WORD TO THE WISE

A Massachusetts man tried to avoid paying taxes on lottery winnings by claiming $65,000 in gambling losses from lottery tickets he'd purchased. To support his deduction, he rented a truck full of losing tickets from a lottery ticket collector and claimed they were his. The IRS was not amused.

If you hear of a way to beat taxes that seems too good to be true, it probably is. To check out whether a "pay less taxes" scheme is legitimate, call the IRS fraud hotline at (800) 829-0433.

A CHICKEN IN EVERY POT

❦ If poultry meat is stacked in the grocery cooler, don't buy the package on top—it is the one most likely to be warm enough to grow bacteria.

❦ You should always freeze raw chicken if you're not going to use it within 2 days of purchase. Never thaw chicken at room temperature.

❦ Here are two quick and delicious condiments for poultry.

1. Add 1 tablespoon prepared horseradish to 2 cups pink applesauce and mix well.

2. Add 2 teaspoons grated fresh ginger to 1 can (8 ounces) whole-berry cranberry sauce and stir with a fork until blended.

—BK

With Liberty for All

NOTHING OCCUPIED Ben Franklin more in his later years than the antislavery cause. In 1787, he was named president of the Pennsylvania Society for Promoting the Abolition of Slavery (the nation's first abolitionist organization) and wrote its 1789 protest to Congress against slavery. Just 3 weeks before his death in April 1790, Ben wrote his final public piece, a satire opposing slavery.

THE *Inspired* MIND

He had not always frowned on slavery. Beginning in 1731, his newspaper published ads announcing sales of slaves, and Ben himself bought two slaves in 1748. By 1752, however, he was writing of his dislike for owning slaves, and in a will drawn up in 1758, he provided for the freeing of his slaves. Just before the Revolution, Ben published his views on the injustices of slavery and the educational needs of Blacks.

Soon after the American Anti-Slavery Society was formed in Philadelphia in 1833, the abolitionist movement coined the name Liberty Bell for the famous bell hanging in Independence Hall. They were inspired by the biblical inscription on the bell—"Proclaim liberty throughout all the land unto all the inhabitants thereof"—and adopted the bell as a symbol of their cause.

APRIL

16

St. Bernadette

1862
A bill abolishing slavery in the District of Columbia was passed, providing up to $300 in compensation to slave owners for each freed slave.

1889
Birth of actor CHARLIE CHAPLIN.

. . .

Be ashamed to die until you have won some victory for humanity.

—*Horace Mann*

GARDEN REMINDERS

❖ Plant horseradish roots at the edge of the garden in early spring, in a spot where they can be left undisturbed. The following spring, dig up several main roots to harvest what you need.

❖ Keep cabbage maggots from devouring your broccoli and cabbage by covering plants with floating row covers as soon as you transplant them or as soon as seedlings emerge.

❖ Lay sheets of aluminum foil around cabbage plants to deter aphids. Anchor the foil with stones.

❖ To plant carrots, parsnips, and other root crops in poor, stony soil, drive a stake or crowbar into the ground and rotate it in a circle to form a pit. Remove all the soil, replace it with compost, and plant three or four seeds in each hole.

❖ Start zinnia seeds indoors 3 to 4 weeks before the last frost.

❖ Welcome frogs and toads into the garden. They eat cutworms and other insect pests.

17

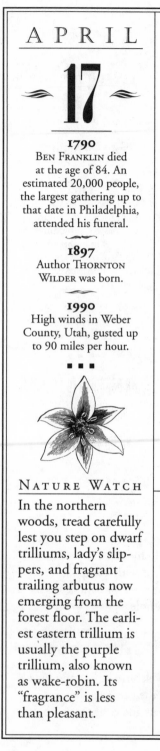

1790
BEN FRANKLIN died
at the age of 84. An
estimated 20,000 people,
the largest gathering up to
that date in Philadelphia,
attended his funeral.

1897
Author THORNTON
WILDER was born.

1990
High winds in Weber
County, Utah, gusted up
to 90 miles per hour.

• • •

NATURE WATCH

In the northern
woods, tread carefully
lest you step on dwarf
trilliums, lady's slip-
pers, and fragrant
trailing arbutus now
emerging from the
forest floor. The earli-
est eastern trillium is
usually the purple
trillium, also known
as wake-robin. Its
"fragrance" is less
than pleasant.

Pleurisy and Other Distempers

AT THE AGE OF 21, Ben Franklin suffered a serious illness. "My distemper was a pleurisy, which very nearly
carried me off," he wrote. Thirty years later, a severe bout
of the flu—fever, headache, delirium—lasted for 2 months. He was
treated by bleeding and given tea brewed from a medicinal bark. In

THE
Inspired
MIND

early April 1790, Ben developed a pulmonary
infection possibly related to his earlier illnesses.
For his pleuritic condition, he was given opium
as a sedative, but his fever continued, and his
breathing grew labored. An abscess inside his
chest filled with fluid, and when it burst, he lost consciousness and
died quietly at the age of 84.

In the 20th century, influenza, pneumonia,
and tuberculosis caused the largest number of
infectious disease deaths in the United States.
According to the Centers for Disease Control,
16,000 tuberculosis and 2 million pneumonia
cases were reported in 2000. These two bacterial diseases are often accompanied by symp-
toms such as fever, coughing, and chest pain
due to inflammation of the lining of the
lungs, known as pleurisy. Treatment includes
fighting the infection with antibiotic drugs
and draining fluid from the chest.

*If of this plant you
don't see many,
Then be a good guy
and don't pick any.*
—Author Unknown

For Those Who Love Wildflowers

❖ In mid-April, go walking
through the woods in search of
trilliums, trailing arbutus, wild
ginger flowers, jack-in-the-
pulpits, and wood anemones.
Bring along a pocket guide and
any child who is willing.

❖ If you love wildflowers,
always buy nursery-propagated
plants from a reputable nurs-

ery. Don't collect your own
specimens from the wild.

❖ To plant a meadow garden,
turn the soil to loosen it and
dislodge weeds. Mix four parts
sand and one part seeds and
broadcast the mixture as if
you were feeding chickens.
Water regularly until the seeds
germinate.

Give Your House a Rainy Day Checkup

DURING A HEAVY rainstorm, put on your sturdiest rain gear and go outside to look for trouble areas. Walk the entire perimeter of your house, garage, and outbuildings. Take note of every place you see water hitting the structures rather than the ground. Water should roll down the roof into gutters and downspouts. If rain gushes onto any part of the building, it could eventually erode that surface and cause big problems. In trouble areas, install downspouts or fix the gutters as soon as the sky clears up.

PRACTICAL PRIMER

> Millions long for immortality who do not know what to do with themselves on a rainy Sunday afternoon.
>
> —*Susan Ertz*

Every spring before the rainy season and every fall after the leaves have fallen, remove all the leaves, twigs, and other debris from gutters, then check them for rust or corrosion. If gutters are sagging or have low spots, lift them section by section. Adjust the hangers to improve the water flow.

Don't Let a Rainy Day Get You Down

☾ Looking for a pH-balanced hair rinse? Try rainwater. It has a pH of 5.6 to 6.0. (Acid rain may be 2.0 to 5.6, so watch out for that.) Beer, another old-time hair rinse, logs in at 4.0 to 5.0.

☾ Let children record a "time capsule" video or cassette tape describing what's going on in their world. You might learn a thing or two about them.

☾ Keep a stash of wooden clip-type clothespins in the kitchen drawer and use them to seal bags of chips, bread, and dry cereal so they won't get stale or soggy during humid weather.

☾ Look for umbrellas designed with vents that let the wind blow through without letting water in.

APRIL

18

April showers bring May flowers.

● ◖ ○ ◗ ●

1746
Facing a spring smallpox epidemic, BEN FRANKLIN had his youngest child, 2-year-old Sarah, inoculated.

1775
PAUL REVERE and WILLIAM DAWES rode from Boston to Lexington to warn of the British force under way.

1906
The deadliest earthquake in American history struck San Francisco, resulting in the deaths of more than 500 people and leaving half a million people homeless. The quake registered 8.3 on the Richter scale. (The most violent earthquake recorded in the United States, in Prince William Sound, Alaska, in 1964, registered 8.4.)

19

Patriots' Day
(Massachusetts)

● ○ ○ ○ ●

Plant your peas by Patriots' Day.

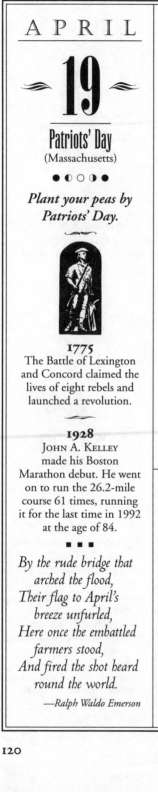

1775
The Battle of Lexington and Concord claimed the lives of eight rebels and launched a revolution.

1928
JOHN A. KELLEY made his Boston Marathon debut. He went on to run the 26.2-mile course 61 times, running it for the last time in 1992 at the age of 84.

■ ■ ■

*By the rude bridge that arched the flood,
Their flag to April's breeze unfurled,
Here once the embattled farmers stood,
And fired the shot heard round the world.*

—Ralph Waldo Emerson

What you would seem to be, be really.

—BEN FRANKLIN

AFTER WORLD WAR II, General Douglas MacArthur and General Dwight D. Eisenhower were both named as possible candidates for the presidency. MacArthur was serving in Tokyo at the time, and Eisenhower went to visit him. In the course of their conversation, Eisenhower offered the opinion that no military man should ever be president of the United States. MacArthur assessed his old colleague for a moment and said, "That's the way to play it, Ike."

JAMES MONROE

A veteran of an earlier war, James Monroe, became the fifth president of the United States. Monroe, who had dropped out of college at William and Mary to fight in the American Revolution, was never considered to be a brilliant man, but his honesty and integrity were beyond reproach. In the words of Thomas Jefferson, "He is a man whose soul might be turned wrong side outwards without discovering a blemish."

How does one go about gaining such a reputation? Will Rogers advised, "Live in such a way that you would not be ashamed to sell your parrot to the town gossip."

PEA-PLANTING PRINCIPLES

❖ Plant peas, spinach, lettuce, and turnips as soon as the soil is thawed enough to be turned over.

❖ If you're worried about dedicating too much of your garden space to early peas, consider planting or transplanting your early lettuce, radishes, and spinach around the pea plants. They're good companions.

❖ Nick sweet pea seeds with a nail file before planting and soak in warm water for an hour. You'll get faster and better germination.

He that would catch fish, must venture his bait.

—BEN FRANKLIN

A YOUNG CLERK who worked for a department store had an idea for a store that would sell only items costing a dime or less. The clerk approached his boss and asked him to invest in the plan, but the boss dismissed the idea as being too risky. "There aren't enough items to sell for five and ten cents," he told the clerk. The young man opened his first store without his boss's help. Eventually, F. W. Woolworth's stores stretched across the nation, and his former boss commented, "As far as I can figure out, each word I used to turn Woolworth down cost me about a million dollars."

A WORD TO THE WISE

Studies of older Americans have shown that those who take risks are the healthiest, live the longest, and remain in the best of spirits. Extreme risk taking has its own hazards, of course, but a moderate level of risk taking is crucial to emotional and physical health. Too much self-protection can hinder our growth.

FITNESS FAVORITES

❦ To erase calories, try brisk walking (3 miles per hour): a slice of pizza, 40 minutes; a small package of potato chips, 33 minutes; an ice cream cone, 30 minutes; a 12-ounce beer, 30 minutes; a blueberry muffin, 25 minutes.

❦ If you would rather work around the homestead, try these chores that burn a lot of calories and make you feel productive at the same time.

- Vigorous chopping with an ax (equivalent to uphill cross-country skiing)
- Mowing the lawn with a push mower (equivalent to a brisk game of tennis)
- Stacking firewood (equivalent to playing golf—without a cart)
- Scrubbing floors (equivalent to bicycling at 5.5 miles per hour)

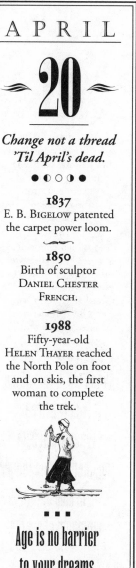

APRIL

20

*Change not a thread
'Til April's dead.*

● ◐ ○ ◑ ●

1837
E. B. BIGELOW patented the carpet power loom.

1850
Birth of sculptor
DANIEL CHESTER
FRENCH.

1988
Fifty-year-old
HELEN THAYER reached the North Pole on foot and on skis, the first woman to complete the trek.

• • •

Age is no barrier to your dreams and goals.... Once people start thinking they're over the hill, they are.

—*Helen Thayer*

1960

Brazil's new capital city, Brasilia, was christened, moving the seat of government from Rio de Janeiro.

1987

Record high temperatures were set in 29 cities from the Gulf of Mexico to New England. The 93°F recorded at New Orleans and 82°F at Caribou, Maine, were records for the month.

• • •

When we dream alone, it is only a dream. When we dream together, it is no longer a dream but the beginning of reality.

—*Brazilian Proverb*

Classic Crab Cakes

The key to memorable crab cakes is a light hand in mixing and handling.

1 extra-large egg
⅓ cup mayonnaise (homemade is best)
1 tablespoon Dijon mustard
1 teaspoon prepared horseradish
1 teaspoon grated or minced lemon zest
2 tablespoons fresh lemon juice
1 tablespoon minced fresh parsley
1 small red onion, finely chopped

1 tablespoon capers, drained and chopped
Dash of Tabasco
½ cup fresh, soft bread crumbs
1 pound fresh jumbo lump crabmeat, picked over for cartilage and shells
Flour
Clarified butter or peanut oil for frying
Cocktail sauce or tartar sauce for serving

In a large mixing bowl, whisk together all the ingredients except the crabmeat, flour, butter, and cocktail sauce. Fold in the crabmeat, taking care not to break it apart too much. Form 6 cakes about 2½ inches in diameter and refrigerate for 1 hour. Sprinkle flour in a pie plate and coat both sides of each crab cake with flour. Refrigerate for at least 1 hour.

Heat the butter in a large skillet over medium-high heat until very hot but not smoking. Fry 3 cakes at a time for 3 minutes per side, or until golden brown. Transfer to paper towels to drain. Serve immediately with the sauce.

Makes 6

EATING WELL

❖ Robert B. Thomas, the original publisher of *The Old Farmer's Almanac*, wrote, "Live chastely, if you wish to live long." But if it's vim and vigor you require, eat oysters, crabmeat, clams, lobster, lima beans, caviar, or herring.

❖ Studies indicate that slow background music at mealtimes helps people eat more slowly and consume less.

❖ Glass and ceramic dishes keep food warm longer. When entertaining, avoid metal serving dishes, if possible. If you insist on using the heirloom silver, preheat it with hot water.

Dig a $100 Hole for a $50 Tree

SPRING IS in the air and "a hole is to dig," as Ruth Krauss pointed out in her 1952 children's book of first definitions. And when it comes to planting trees, the hole is all-important. Before planting, spend some time preparing the hole itself.

PRACTICAL PRIMER

- To test an area for drainage, use a crowbar to dig several narrow holes 3 feet deep. Fill them with water, watch, and repeat several times. If the water remains in any of the holes for a day or more, or if it drains away in less than 3 minutes, find another site.

- Dig a bowl-shaped hole three to four times wider than the tree's rootball or container, but just slightly deeper than the rootball, loosening the soil below.

- Do not add manure or nitrogen additives to the planting hole. Let the new seedling get a year's growth first, then add fertilizer in a circle that follows the dripline.

TREE-PLANTING TIPS

❦ Here's some age-old advice on which trees to plant: "He who plants a walnut tree expects not to eat of the fruit," because the growing time is lengthy, as with the oak. By contrast, "The willow will buy a horse before the oak will buy a saddle."

❦ Fruit trees need full sun (or nearly so) and rich soil to support the production of healthy fruit. Add compost, manure, or other nutritive mulches annually after the first year.

❦ Nut trees require special attention. To delay flowering and protect them from a late frost, plant them on a north slope.

❦ Worried that your backyard is too small? Dwarf fruit trees grow only 8 to 12 feet tall, but once mature, they can produce bushels of fruit. Even in a large yard, you may want to consider dwarf or semidwarf (12 to 18 feet tall) varieties. They're easier to spray, prune, and harvest than full-size trees, which grow 18 to 25 feet tall, sometimes taller.

❦ A tree is not just for fruit. As you make your landscaping plans, consider sites for a clothesline, hammock, swing, or maybe even a tree house. To attract wildlife, consider the ornamental crab apple.

APRIL

22

1721
The *Seahorse* arrived in Boston from the West Indies carrying smallpox. The inoculation crusade mounted by Dr. ZABDIEL BOYLSTON was bitterly opposed. The epidemic claimed 844 lives.

1832
Birth of J. STERLING MORTON, founder of Arbor Day.

1889
The Oklahoma land rush began.

• • •

Acts of creation are ordinarily reserved for gods and poets. To plant a pine, one need only own a shovel.

—*Aldo Leopold*

23

St. George

● ○ ○ ◑ ●

*At St. George,
the meadow turns
into hay.*

1564
Birth of
WILLIAM SHAKESPEARE
(traditionally accepted).

1791
Birthday of JAMES
BUCHANAN, 15th
president of the United
States (1857–1861).

1987
Thunderstorms in
Anderson, South
Carolina, produced
golf ball–size hail and
wind gusts up to
67 miles per hour.

■ ■ ■

*O! how this spring of
love resembleth
The uncertain glory of
an April day!*
—William Shakespeare

---

*Souse down into prose again,
my muse; for poetry's no more thy
element, than air is that of the flying-
fish; whose flights, like thine, are
therefore always short and heavy.*

—BEN FRANKLIN

DESPITE THIS low estimation of his poetic abilities (*souse* means to plunge or dip), Ben Franklin's first commercial success was as a creator of popular ballads. While he was a printer's apprentice to his older brother, he began composing ballads based on current events, such as the capture of Blackbeard the pirate. Ben printed the ballads and sold them on the street. Although they sold very well, he admitted that they "were wretched stuff." His father ridiculed his ballads and told him verse makers were generally beggars. Ben wrote in his *Autobiography,* "So I escaped being a poet, most probably a very bad one." In the 1739 edition of *Poor Richard's Almanack,* he included the following couplet titled "A Cure for Poetry."

*Seven wealthy towns contend for Homer, dead,
Thro' which the living Homer beg'd his bread.*

Helping Kids Keep Order

❖ In a bedroom closet, move the clothes rod down to a child's height and install low hooks inside the door to help her maintain a neat bedroom.

❖ For children hooked on toys with many small pieces (Legos, Lincoln Logs, and oth-ers), use a bottom dresser drawer for storage and include a wide plastic shovel (or dustpan) as the cleanup tool.

❖ Use a clear fishbowl as a handy storage container for girls' scrunchies, headbands, and hair clips.

> *Reading makes a full man,*
> *meditation a profound man,*
> *discourse a clear man.*
>
> —Ben Franklin

BEN FRANKLIN once attended a dinner party at which the topic of discussion was "What condition of man most deserves pity?" Other guests put forth their opinions of the most tragic situation a person could find himself in, but Ben suggested this: "A lonesome man on a rainy day who does not know how to read."

In 1731, Ben founded the first circulating library in North America. The idea caught on, and similar libraries were soon established in all the colonies. As a result, Ben noted, "our people, having no publick amusements to divert their attention from study, became better acquainted with books." He credited libraries with making "common tradesmen and farmers as intelligent as most gentlemen from other countries" and even suggested that libraries may have contributed to the colonists' readiness to fight for their rights.

Today the last week in April is TV-Turnoff Week. Why not celebrate by turning off the tube and reading a book? If you don't have one, go to the library—the librarian will have plenty of suggestions.

1800
The Library of Congress was established.

1898
Spain declared war on the United States.

1905
ROBERT PENN WARREN, first poet laureate of the United States, was born.

• • •

I find television very educational. The minute somebody turns it on, I go to the library and read a good book.

—*Groucho Marx*

For the Librarian in All of Us

❦ Keep books in the room where you use them—cookbooks in the kitchen, leisure time reading in the living room or den, craft books and home improvement manuals in your work area.

❦ Put up a single high shelf (12 to 18 inches from the ceiling) around the perimeter of a room and use it for infrequently read books, baskets, tins, or collections.

❦ Surround a window that has an unpleasant view with bookshelves. This will make the window appear recessed and take the focus off the view.

1792
The guillotine was used
for the first time in Paris.

1932
Basketball player
Meadowlark Lemon
was born.

1959
The St. Lawrence Seaway
opened to shipping.

■ ■ ■

There is no kind of herb,
but somebody or other
says that it is good.

—Henry David Thoreau

Divide—and Share!—Your Herbs

Except for the woody herbs that tend to form a single main stem, most perennial herbs are easy to divide. Bee balm, catnip and other mints, chives, horehound, lemon balm, oregano, pennyroyal, sorrel, sweet woodruff, tansy, tarragon, many thymes (especially the sprawlers), watercress, winter savory, wormwood, and yarrow are just a few of the plants that can be divided now and passed among your friends.

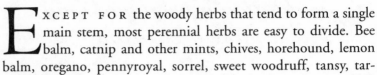

PRACTICAL PRIMER

The woody herbs—lavender, rosemary, rue, sage, and others—can be propagated by layering. Choose a flexible branch near the base of the plant and strip the leaves from the part that will touch the ground. Make a slashing cut through two-thirds of the bare stem and pin the open cut to the soil until new roots form (see illustration).

Bee balm, catnip and other mints, and white yarrow are invasive. Consider planting them in tubs or other containers, in sunken pots, or with underground metal barriers to keep them from spreading out of control.

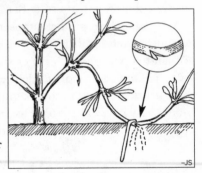

Oregano, pennyroyal, tarragon, thyme, and wormwood can be rooted from cuttings placed in a moist seed-starting medium. Keep the soil lightly moist and cover the pot with a clear plastic "tent" to prevent evaporation and encourage speedy rooting.

HERBAL HINTS

❖ Use a clothes-drying rack to hang bundles of herbs or flowers to dry.

❖ When you buy dried herbs or spices, write the date on the container. Herbs lose their flavor in 6 months; spices last up to a year. Add

spent herbs and spices to potpourris, compost them, or—if you're really frugal—just use a little more than the recipe calls for.

❖ Consider lemon balm, bee balm, basil, sage, or oregano as an alternative to peppermint

to help soothe heartburn. Experiment with various combinations in a mild tea.

❖ When substituting fresh herbs for dried, remember that 1 tablespoon minced fresh herbs equals 1 teaspoon dried.

The Warm Gulf Stream

ALTHOUGH BEN FRANKLIN did not discover the Gulf Stream, he was the first to systematically study the warm current that flows up the southeastern coast of the United States, crosses the Atlantic Ocean, and warms the climate of northwestern Europe. At its origin in the Gulf of Mexico, the water temperature is about 80°F—42°F warmer than the average temperature of all ocean water.

THE *Inspired* MIND

To help British mail packets sail faster to America by avoiding the east-flowing current, Ben got his cousin, a Nantucket whaling captain, to draw a Gulf Stream map, but it was ignored by postal officials in London. Undaunted, Ben recorded sea and air temperatures, water color, and weed content

in the Gulf Stream on three transatlantic voyages. His research culminated in 1786 with an engraved Gulf Stream chart, the first accurate mapping of the current. He advised captains to carry thermometers with them: To go eastward, they should find the warmer water; to go westward, they should follow the colder water.

Today the University of Rhode Island Graduate School of Oceanography maintains an Internet archive of daily sea surface temperature images of the Gulf Stream taken by satellite cameras from 1979 to the present.

Potatoes and Onions

❧ Plant potatoes in a 6-inch-deep trench and cover with a 2-inch layer of soil. Gradually fill in the trench as the shoots get taller.

❧ When any danger of frost has passed, plant sweet potato slips through slits cut in clear plastic mulch, which warms the soil and retains heat.

❧ Because many onions are sensitive to daylength, plant long-day varieties north of the Kansas-Oklahoma border and short-day varieties south of it.

❧ To grow big, sweet onions, give them plenty of water.

APRIL

26

—BK

A cold and wet April fills the cellar and fattens the cow.

● ◗ ○ ◖ ●

1785
Birth of artist
JOHN JAMES AUDUBON.

1865
Confederate general
JOSEPH JOHNSTON
surrendered to Union
general WILLIAM T.
SHERMAN at Durham
Station, North Carolina,
17 days after the official
end of the Civil War.

1993
The U.S. Holocaust
Memorial Museum
opened in
Washington, D.C.

● ● ●

A man who thinks
too much about
his ancestors is
like a potato—the
best part of him is
underground.

—Henry S. F. Cooper

APRIL

1822
Birthday of
ULYSSES S. GRANT, 18th
president of the United
States (1869–1877).

1865
The steamship *Sultana*
exploded on the
Mississippi River, killing
more than 1,400 Union
prisoners of war.

1947
At Yankee Stadium in
New York City,
BABE RUTH Day was held
to honor the ailing
baseball star.

• • •

'Tis better
to remain silent
and be thought a
fool, than open
one's mouth and
remove all doubt.

—*Samuel Johnson*

• • •

NATURE WATCH

In the Ohio River
valley and nearby
states, zebra butter-
flies are emerging
from chrysalides on
papaw trees. Your
porch lights also may
attract the glamorous
luna moth now.

Teach your child to hold his tongue, he'll learn fast enough to speak.

—BEN FRANKLIN

A WORD TO THE WISE

THE WRITER Dorothy Parker was once talking with a friend about a well-known and talkative celebrity. "She's so outspoken," the friend said.

"By whom?" Parker quipped.

If talk were water, some people could drown you. You know whom we mean—the people who make you remember sudden engagements, edge toward the door, and imagine you hear people calling.

Why do some people talk too much? They may simply be insecure and nervous, covering their lack of confidence with a blanket of chatter. Other people seem unable to gauge a listener's level of interest and so go on for hours about a trip that some distant relative made to some place you've never heard of and never care to see.

Finally, there are those who dominate conversations because they are convinced they are the most interesting person in the room. Theodore Roosevelt once invited a famous hunter to dine at the White House and give him some pointers about hunting. The dinner lasted for 2 hours, and the hunter came out of it with a dazed look on his face. When asked what he had told the president, he replied, "My name. After that he did all the talking."

TELEPHONE TIPS

❦ If you spend a lot of time on the phone, line up a few chores to do while chatting. You can do the dusting, match socks, unload the dish drainer or dishwasher, and wipe down counter-tops, all while chatting with your mom halfway across the country.

❦ Keep paper towels or napkins next to the telephone in the kitchen for wiping your hands before picking up a call. This will keep the phone clean and cut down on transferring bacteria.

Rhubarb Crumb Bars

Sweet rhubarb filling topped with golden crumbs makes these bars a favorite in the spring.

1 cup + 1½ tablespoons flour
½ cup oatmeal
½ cup wheat germ (plain or honey-flavored)
1 cup brown sugar, packed
½ cup butter, melted
2 cups rhubarb cut into ½-inch pieces
¾ cup granulated sugar
¼ teaspoon nutmeg
1 tablespoon butter, softened
1 egg, beaten

Preheat the oven to 350°F. In a medium bowl, combine the 1 cup flour, oatmeal, wheat germ, brown sugar, and melted butter. Press one-half of this mixture into a greased 9-inch square baking dish. Sprinkle the rhubarb on top. In a small bowl, combine the granulated sugar, remaining 1½ tablespoons flour, nutmeg, and softened butter. Add the egg and beat until smooth. Pour evenly over the rhubarb and top with the remaining crumb mixture. Bake for 20 to 25 minutes. Cool and cut into bars. *Makes 2 dozen*

RHUBARB ROUNDUP

Rhubarb is also known as pie-plant or wine plant and is excellent in both of those applications. Combine with strawberries in a pie, jam, or sauce for greater sweetness and a redder color. Rhubarb leaves and roots contain oxalic acid and are not edible, but the stalks are divine.

❖ If your rhubarb plants are 8 inches or more in diameter, divide them as early as possible in the spring.

❖ Plant rhubarb where it will be shaded from the hot afternoon sun.

Work in lots of compost. Once plants emerge, mulch around them with straw or shredded leaves.

❖ Pull rhubarb so that the stalks slip out of the base, or cut with a sharp knife. Spring rhubarb is juicier and more tender than plants that have endured hot weather.

❖ Remember that 1 pound rhubarb yields about 3½ cups chopped. For a 9-inch pie, you should have at least 6 cups chopped rhubarb.

APRIL

28

1758
Birthday of JAMES MONROE, fifth president of the United States (1817–1825).

1788
Maryland became the seventh state.

1789
A mutiny occurred on the ship *Bounty* in the South Pacific.

1947
THOR HEYERDAHL launched the balsa wood raft *Kon-Tiki* on a voyage from Peru to Polynesia.

1967
MUHAMMAD ALI refused induction into the U.S. Army.

• • •

The optimist proclaims that we live in the best of all possible worlds; and the pessimist fears this is true.

—*James Branch Cabell*

29

St. Catherine of Siena

1899
Composer DUKE ELLINGTON was born.

1967
The temperature in Los Angeles sank to 47°F, an all-time low for the city on this date.

● ● ●

I merely took the energy it takes to pout and wrote some blues.

—*Duke Ellington*

A lie stands on one leg, truth on two.

—BEN FRANKLIN

ACCORDING TO A recent study, almost two-thirds of Americans believe that truth is always relative to the situation and the person involved. Among teens, more than 80 percent believe that. So how do people make moral and ethical decisions these days? The most common response (38 percent of teens and 30 percent of adults) was "whatever feels right or comfortable in a situation." Teenagers also said they would decide based on whatever would produce the most positive outcome for them, while adults would fall back on values taught to them by their parents.

As a young reporter, Mark Twain was cautioned never to report anything that he couldn't personally verify as factual. Somewhat chafed by this stricture, he reported on a social gathering as follows: "A woman giving the name of Mrs. James Jones, who is reported to be one of the society leaders of the city, is said to have given what purported to be a party yesterday to a number of ladies. The hostess claims to be the wife of a reputed attorney."

The Handyperson Kit

❧ Be prepared! Every household needs a toolbox that contains basic items for routine jobs around the house. Buy a small metal toolbox or a plastic tote bin and put the following tools in it.
• Assorted screwdrivers (or one four-way model)
• Cordless drill
• Hammer (12 to 16 ounces)

• Pliers
• Nails and screws
• Small pry bar
• Small saw
• Tape measure (at least 20 feet long)
• Utility knife

❧ As a secondary measure (and to avoid trips to the basement or workshop for little repairs), put a small hammer, pliers, several sizes of screwdrivers, assorted nails

and screws, and picture hooks in a shoe box or plastic bucket. Store the box under the sink or in a kitchen cabinet or closet. Don't forget to throw in a roll of duct tape and a can of WD-40.

❧ If you haven't fixed an item in 3 months, throw it out or give it away.

Lupines Forever

NATIVE AMERICANS ate lupines steamed, both leaves and flowers, and accompanied them with acorn soup. Often called wild peas or Quaker bonnets, lupines (*Lupinus* species) also were used to make a tea to relieve rheuma-

PRACTICAL PRIMER

tism. In 1640, the great British herbalist John Parkinson recommended lupine seeds to deter gnats. Mixed with meal and honey into a salve, the seeds were used to treat bruises and to heal the umbilical cord stub of newborns.

Today we mainly think of the lupine as a beautiful harbinger of spring in the upper Northeast and Northwest. Hybridized by George Russell of Yorkshire, England, in 1911, lupines are perfect in the perennial bed and in wildflower meadows.

- Lupines tend to die out after a few years, but they self-sow naturally or can be resown.
- Like all legumes, lupines create their own nitrogen and grow happily in poor soils.
- For faster and better germination, lupine seeds should be soaked in water overnight and nicked with a nail file before planting.
- Lupines tolerate transplanting but much prefer to stay put.
- The Texas bluebonnet is a close relative of the garden perennial.

"Lupines," said Miss Rumphius with satisfaction. "I have always loved lupines the best."

—*Barbara Cooney,*
Miss Rumphius

GARDEN ADVICE

❖ As you work in the garden, change your position every 15 minutes to avoid backaches.

❖ To make an instant compost bin, form a 12-foot length of 13-gauge kennel wire into a cylinder and fill with grass clippings, shredded leaves, garden debris, household vegetable peelings, eggshells, coffee grounds, and the like (no meat or fat). Water it along with your garden if it doesn't rain.

1789
GEORGE WASHINGTON was inaugurated as the first president of the United States.

1803
The United States purchased the Louisiana Territory—800,000 square miles from the Mississippi River to the Rocky Mountains—from France for $15 million.

1812
Louisiana became the 18th state.

1939
The New York World's Fair opened.

■ ■ ■

LORE & LEGEND

Strong ale and oatcakes with nine knobs, each to be broken off and eaten as an offering, are the traditional fare of **MAY DAY EVE.** This date is also marked by bonfires and fertility rites.

MAY, *the Fifth Month*

MAY IS NAMED for the Roman goddess Maia, who ruled over the growth of plants. The ancient Celts inaugurated this month with the festival of Beltane to encourage fertility in the newly sown fields. Their exuberance lives on in May baskets, morris dancing, and cries of "Play ball!" at Little League fields in every community. The month that begins with dancing around the maypole ends with Memorial Day, a poignant reminder of the fragility and tenacity of life.

In temperate northern latitudes, farmers and gardeners alike try to complete all seeding and planting by the end of the month, working around May's unpredictable weather in a race with the calendar. Old-timers get suspicious if the weather in May is *too* balmy: "A snowstorm in May is worth a wagonload of hay," they counsel.

May brings a surge of energy that sets us to scrubbing, organizing, and airing out every corner of the house. Outside, we clean and sharpen tools, load the wheelbarrow with plants, and trundle off to the garden. By the end of the month, even those who live in the North are enjoying more than 15 hours of daylight each day. We need every minute of it as we dance through the merry month of May.

Full Flower Moon
is the name
Native Americans gave to
the full moon in May.
It was also known as the
Full Corn Planting Moon,
or the *Full Milk Moon,*
references to the fertility
of the season.

Sign of the Zodiac: Taurus
(April 21–May 20)

Element: Earth

Quality: Practical

Birthstone: Emerald

Flower: Lily of the valley

Window Boxes

CELEBRATE a new season of flowers by installing and planting a couple of window boxes to beautify the house. The boxes work particularly well beneath double-hung windows. Be sure to buy sturdy boxes that can stand up to the weight of soggy soil and be reused season after season. For hanging the boxes, select brackets and hooks that are made with solid welds, not rivets.

PRACTICAL PRIMER

Purchase or make window boxes that are at least 10 inches deep to give roots enough room to grow. Add drainage material in the bottom and fill with a good potting mix. Combine several different kinds of trailing plants that will flower or put out colorful leaves, including variegated nasturtiums and pale green, purple, or variegated sweet potato vines. Fragrant foliage and flowers such as heliotropes and scented geraniums are particularly appealing, too. A few herb plants, including parsley, mint, and basil, will add greenery and come in handy when the cook needs just a sprig or two. Remember to design your window boxes with the tallest plants in back and the trailing ones where they can spill over the edge.

Once plants have been placed in the window boxes, the keys to lush growth are to water faithfully (as often as once a day in hot weather) and to fertilize with a foliar spray of compost tea or liquid seaweed once a week.

MAY

1

May Day

● ○ ○ ○ ●

1830
Birth of labor activist
MARY HARRIS
"MOTHER" JONES.

1931
The Empire State Building, the world's tallest skyscraper until 1974, opened.

■ ■ ■

The world's favorite season is the spring. All things seem possible in May.

—*Edwin Way Teale*

A Green Thumb

☙ Make your own potting soil by mixing together five parts loam; two parts screened compost, coir fiber, or peat moss; and one part sand or perlite.

☙ After spring-flowering bulbs have blossomed outdoors, let their tops die down and turn yellow. Don't cut off the leaves—they need time to transfer energy to the bulb.

LORE & LEGEND

Traditional **MAY DAY** rituals celebrated the sun's victory over winter. Young maidens filled baskets with flowers and greens and bathed their faces in the May Day dew to enhance their complexions. If the sun depletes your dewy glow, try an eye compress of cool cucumbers or a refreshing facial mask made with grated cucumber and plain yogurt, blended well.

<table>
<tr><td>

MAY

2

1903
Baby- and child-care specialist Dr. Benjamin Spock was born.

1933
As reported in the local newspaper, a couple saw an enormous creature cavorting along the surface of Scotland's Loch Ness, initiating the modern era of Loch Ness Monster sightings.

1989
Juneau, Alaska, registered a record high temperature of 72°F, while Honolulu equaled its record low for the month with a reading of 60°F.

• • •

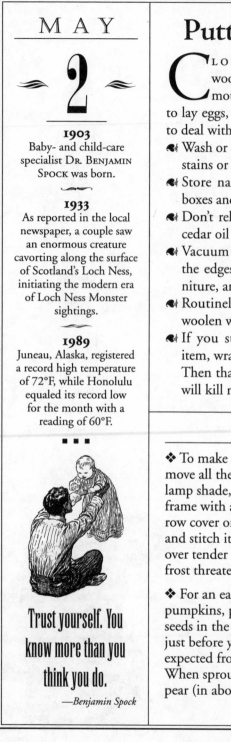

Trust yourself. You know more than you think you do.

—*Benjamin Spock*

</td><td>

Putting Away Your Woollies

CLOTHES MOTHS can cause serious damage to stored woolens, as well as to silk, fur, felt, and feathers. The adult moths, which do no damage, settle into the folds of fabrics to lay eggs, which hatch into fabric-munching larvae. Here's how to deal with them.

- Wash or dry-clean clothing before storing it to remove any food stains or perspiration odors, both of which attract moths.
- Store natural-fiber clothing in tight-sealing sweater bags or boxes and add small cloth bags of cedar chips or dried lavender.
- Don't rely on a cedar chest, which rarely maintains sufficient cedar oil to serve as a repellent.
- Vacuum carpets regularly, especially around the edges, under baseboards, underneath furniture, and in closets.
- Routinely vacuum and inspect the backs of woolen wall hangings.
- If you suspect moth infestation in a small item, wrap it in a plastic bag and put it in the freezer for 2 days. Then thaw it out and freeze it again. The temperature changes will kill moth eggs and larvae.

PRACTICAL PRIMER

GARDEN TRICKS

❖ To make a garden cloche, remove all the fabric from an old lamp shade, then cover the frame with a piece of floating row cover or 4-mil clear plastic and stitch it in place. Put it over tender young plants when frost threatens.

❖ For an early start with pumpkins, plant about half the seeds in the garden just before your last expected frost. When sprouts appear (in about 10 days), plant the other half of the seeds. If the first planting doesn't get nipped by frost, pull out the second.

❖ Plant slow-sprouting seeds such as onions, parsley, and beets outdoors under a strip of burlap. Check under it daily and remove it as soon as you see sprouts.

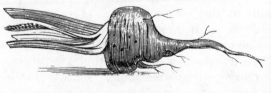

</td></tr>
</table>

An Elegant Death

BLOOPERS ARE as old as writing itself. An article in Ben Franklin's own *Pennsylvania Gazette* mentioned Governor Belcher's important meeting with several London merchants, "after which his Excellency . . . died elegantly at Pontack's." An alert reader wrote to Ben, pointing out that Pontack's was a tavern and the word *died* should doubtless have been *dined*.

An error occurred on a few of New Jersey's 1787 copper coins, the first minted with the national motto *E Pluribus Unum* (One Out of Many). The faulty coins read *E Pluribs Unum*—a goof that makes the coins worth up to $1,850 today if in "extra fine" condition.

The U.S. Postal Service has mistakenly printed pictorial vignettes on stamps upside down, including locomotives and even Old Glory, one of which recently fetched $104,500 at auction.

When Israel Baline immigrated to America and began writing music, his first published song in 1907 listed him as "I. Berlin." Rather than correct the printer's error, he called himself Irving Berlin ever after.

THE *Inspired* MIND

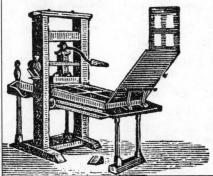

LAWNS: GROWING AND MOWING

When planting a new lawn, drag a flexible doormat over the prepared area to work seeds into the top layer of soil.

For brighter, healthier grass, combine used coffee grounds and aged manure and spread it over patchy areas of the lawn. Mulch with rotted hay. If you need more coffee grounds, ask at a coffee shop or large business near you.

Save a dishwashing liquid bottle and fill it with motor oil for the lawn mower and other garden power tools. The pull top makes it easy to squirt just the amount you need. (Be sure to rinse out all the soap before adding the oil.)

MAY

3

1919
Birth of songwriter
PETE SEEGER.

1933
NELLIE TAYLOE ROSS became the first woman director of the U.S. Mint.

1948
The *CBS Evening News* television program premiered.

• • •

If all else fails, immortality can always be assured by spectacular error.
—*John Kenneth Galbraith*

• • •

NATURE WATCH

In lakes and streams, watch for a hatch of mayflies, delicate winged creatures that are among the most primitive of all insects. Of the order Ephemeroptera, the lovely creatures don't live long, but they drive fish crazy and are the models for many fishing lures.

4

*A cold May is kindly,
And fills the barn
finely.*

1932
Gangster AL CAPONE was
jailed for tax evasion.

1970
On the campus of
Kent State University
in Ohio, four students
were killed by National
Guardsmen during a
demonstration protesting
the Vietnam War.

How can we expect
another to keep our
secret if we have been
unable to keep it
ourselves?

*—François, Duc de La
Rochefoucauld*

*Three may keep a secret,
if two of them are dead.*

—BEN FRANKLIN

SOMETIMES even death isn't enough to protect a secret. Take the staff member of a Norwegian museum who died without recording the password to the museum's database of books and documents. When computer experts were unable to crack the password, the museum offered a reward to anyone who could come up with it. The winning respondent suggested they try the librarian's last name, spelled backward. It worked, and the anxious museum administrators were back online.

A WORD TO THE WISE

Most computer systems aren't that well protected. Despite increased sensitivity about security, the most common password for computer and voice mail systems is "password"—not exactly a challenge for a determined hacker.

Want to keep something secret? If so, don't do what the employees of a bakery in Davenport, Iowa, did. When burglars broke into the bakery, they found that getting into the company safe was a piece of cake. The staff had posted the combination on a nearby bulletin board so they wouldn't forget it.

Fish Facts and Fancy

❖ A fillet of fish has less flavor than a whole fish, because the bones hold flavor and transmit taste to the flesh.

❖ When poaching fish, add an acidic ingredient such as lemon juice or wine to the liquid to keep the fish from discoloring.

❖ Use fresh dill as a companion to fish. Dill gets its name from the Saxon word *dilla*, meaning "to lull," for it was thought to put witches to sleep. The English boiled it in wine and inhaled the aroma to stop the hiccups.

❖ To rid your hands of onion or fish odor, rub them with the back of a stainless steel spoon.

❖ Remove store-bought fish from its packaging, rinse, and pat dry. Place it on ice in a covered container and keep it in the refrigerator. Cook the fish within a day or two.

Success with Strawberries

EW THINGS IN LIFE are as rewarding as growing your own sweet strawberries. Select a variety known to do well where you live. June-bearing plants produce one heavy crop in early summer, while day-neutral plants yield a lighter but steady crop of berries from early summer to fall.

- Prepare the bed in a sunny spot by turning the soil over and working in plenty of compost, rotted leaves, or aged manure. Avoid areas where tomatoes, eggplants, or potatoes have recently grown. These crops are hosts for nematodes and viruses that can attack strawberries.
- Select a disease-resistant variety at your local nursery or from a mail-order company that specializes in strawberries.
- Dig a hole deep enough to accommodate the roots, but be sure the crown is at the surface when you fill in with soil. Set plants 10 to 12 inches apart in rows.
- Water well throughout the growing season and mulch with straw to deter weeds.
- At the end of the growing season (2 weeks after your final harvest if you're growing day-neutral berries), run a lawn mower at the highest setting over the tops of your plants to clip the leaves and stimulate new root growth for the following year.
- Once temperatures drop below freezing, protect the bed with a thick layer of mulch.

MAY

5

1862
Mexico's General
IGNACIO ZARAGOZA
defeated the French at
Puebla de los Angeles,
commemorated today
with the Mexican holiday
Cinco de Mayo.

1891
Carnegie Hall opened in
New York City.

■ ■ ■

**An optimist is the
human personification
of spring.**

—*Susan J. Bissonette*

PLANTING PERENNIAL FAVORITES

❧ Before planting daylilies, turn the soil over to a depth of 1 foot. Set the crown just an inch below the soil surface, and as you cover the plant, press the soil down firmly.

❧ Plant irises so the roots are underground but the rhizomes (the thick, fleshy stems from which the fans of leaves emerge) are covered with just a thin sprinkling of soil.

❧ Plant asparagus in trenches 8 inches deep, spacing the roots 1 foot apart. Let the spears grow for 2 years to make the plants strong, then harvest the third spring. Asparagus beds can bear for 50 years.

6

*Cool and dour,
but each shower
brings a flower.*

● ● ○ ○ ● ●

1889
The Paris Exposition
opened, featuring the new
Eiffel Tower.

1954
ROGER BANNISTER was the
first to break the 4-minute
barrier in the mile run
with a time of 3:59.4.

■ ■ ■

A man gazing on the
stars is proverbially
at the mercy of the
puddles in the road.
—*Alexander Smith*

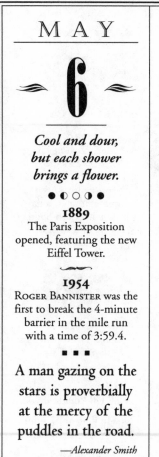

The Transit of Mercury

THE *Inspired* MIND

POOR RICHARD'S ALMANACK for 1753 contained astronomical information about Mercury's transit of the sun on May 6. Ben Franklin eagerly awaited the event, arranging to have a 3-foot telescope for viewing the planet's path between Earth and the sun. He printed a pamphlet urging others throughout North America to take notes and measurements. The pamphlet was a translation of a French astronomer's letter urging that the study be used as a practice for the really significant upcoming transits of Venus, whereby it was hoped that data from different points on Earth could (through geometry) determine the distance to the sun, which was not known at the time.

"You will see Mercury rise in the Sun, and will appear like a small black Patch in a Lady's Face," wrote Ben in his almanac. Bad luck prevailed: The only successful observation of the 1753 transit of Mercury was made in Antigua, which had a cloudless sunrise. Ben stopped publishing his almanac after 1758, but the transits of Venus in 1761 and 1769 were successfully observed in enough places for astronomers to determine, for the first time, Earth's distance from the sun (roughly 93 million miles).

KITCHEN MEASUREMENTS

❖ If you find yourself without measuring devices, bear in mind that a handful of dry ingredients (rice, pasta, cereal, nuts, and so on) equals about ¼ cup.

❖ A clenched fist held upright approximates the volume of a 1-cup liquid measure and can be used to guess at the volume of an unmarked container.

❖ In old cookbooks, a "pinch" is about ⅛ teaspoon; "butter the size of an egg" means about 4 tablespoons, or ¼ cup; and a "teacupful" means about ½ cup.

❖ Here are some oven temperature equivalents every cook should know:
• A low oven is 250°F.
• A slow oven is 300°F.
• A moderate oven is 350°F.
• A hot oven is 400°F.
• A very hot oven is 450°F.
• Broil is 550°F.

The royal crown cures not the headache.

—BEN FRANKLIN

MAY

7

1789
President and Mrs. GEORGE WASHINGTON had a ball—the first inaugural ball.

1847
The American Medical Association was founded.

1945
Germany surrendered to the Allies, ending World War II in Europe.

■ ■ ■

In America any boy may become President, and I suppose it's just one of the risks he takes!

—*Adlai Stevenson*

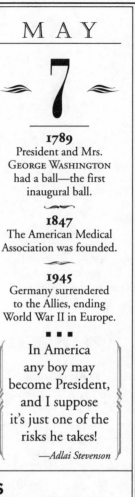

I N FACT, power and authority often bring headaches with them. No one knows that better than the families of those elected to the presidency of the United States.

John Quincy Adams's mother, Abigail—a former first lady herself—once wrote that she would rather see her son "thrown as a log on a fire than see him president of the United States."

A WORD TO THE WISE

Martin Van Buren's wife said after his election, "I wish that my husband's friends had left him where he is, happy and contented in retirement."

Zachary Taylor's wife prayed that her husband would not be elected and called his nomination "a plot to deprive me of his society and shorten his life."

The daughter of William Howard Taft said of his term in office, "Those years in the White House were the only unhappy years of his entire life."

When Vice President Harry Truman was told of the death of Franklin Roosevelt, he asked Mrs. Roosevelt, "Is there anything we can do for you?" The weary first lady replied, "Is there anything we can do for *you?* For you are the one in trouble now."

WHEN YOUR HEAD HURTS

❦ For sinus headaches, you might try a hot compress made by soaking a washcloth in chamomile or peppermint tea and applying it to the forehead. You can reheat the compress in the microwave for a few seconds to keep it soothingly warm.

❦ Some headaches can be eased by drinking the juice of one-half lemon in a cup of coffee. In Europe, a twist of lemon peel is often served in a small demitasse cup of espresso. For some migraine and vascular headache sufferers, the combination of a cup of coffee and aspirin or an-

other analgesic can stop a headache in its tracks.

❦ To prevent migraine headaches, recent research suggests avoiding "trigger" foods, including aged meats, anchovies, avocados, bananas, chocolate, hot bread, liver, nuts and seeds, onions, plums, processed meat, ripened cheese, sour cream, red or brown vinegar, and yogurt.

MAY

8

1884
Birthday of
HARRY S. TRUMAN, 33rd
president of the United
States (1945–1953).

1987
The record high of 95°F
at Redding, California,
was the fifth record-high
day in a row. Redding was
in the grip of a heat wave
lasting nearly 2 weeks.

• • •

There is nothing new in the world except the history you do not know.

—Harry S. Truman

There never was a good war nor a bad peace.

—BEN FRANKLIN

A WORD TO THE WISE

IN HIS SATIRICAL NOVEL *Gulliver's Travels,* Jonathan Swift mocked the political and religious foibles of his day, including the propensity to go to war over trivial offenses. Among Gulliver's encounters were the Big-endians, who were convinced that the best place to break their eggs was at the large end. Opposed to them were the Small-endians, who broke the small end of an egg.

At the end of the American Revolution, Ben Franklin wrote to Sir Joseph Banks, offering the sentiment above and rejoicing at the return of peace between England and its former colonies. He went on to say, "What vast additions to the conveniences and comforts of living might mankind have acquired, if the money spent in wars had been employed in works of public utility!"

We might say the same today. And couldn't the same words be said about the personal squabbles that often rob our lives of time, money, and peace with our neighbors?

SOME EGG-CELLENT TIPS

❖ When a recipe directs you to beat egg yolks and whites separately, always do the whites first. The tiniest trace of yolk in egg whites can ruin the frothy texture, but a bit of egg white in the yolks does no harm.

❖ Leftover egg whites? Store them in an airtight container in the refrigerator for up to a month. They also freeze well. Next

time you have a recipe that calls for yolks, save the whites. When you have 10 or 12, you have enough for an angel food cake.

❖ To separate the yolks from the whites of eggs, be sure the eggs are cold. They separate more easily that way.

—BK

Keeping Ants Out

❆ If you can tell where ants are coming into your house, plug the hole with petroleum jelly or soft soap.

❆ Surround anthills with used coffee grounds, and the ants will not cross the barrier.

Ben Franklin, Freemason

SHRINERS, WHO OPERATE children's hospitals and whose red fezzes can be seen at Shriners parades, are Masons of an advanced degree in a secret male-only society with some five million members worldwide. Freemasons, originally a guild of stoneworkers who built medieval cathedrals, espouse religious tolerance and political compromise.

THE *Inspired* MIND

In 1731, Ben Franklin became a Philadelphia Freemason in the first regular lodge established in the United States, and later he was elected grand master of Pennsylvania. (John Hancock, Paul Revere, and George Washington also joined the Masons.) In 1737, some friends of Ben's who were not Masons tricked a young man into undergoing fake initiation ceremonies. The "initiate" died of the abuses heaped on him, and Ben was forced to deny any participation. His parents, alarmed at seeing his name associated with the tragedy in the papers, wrote to him. He replied that Freemasons "have no principles or practices that are inconsistent with Religion or good Manners," but he conceded that the society's discrimination against women gave his mother "some reason to be displeas'd with it."

> Men have become the tools of their tools.
>
> —*Henry David Thoreau*

MAY

9

1754
In response to French military action on the western frontier, BEN FRANKLIN printed in the *Pennsylvania Gazette* his "Join, or Die" illustration depicting a snake cut into pieces. It was America's first political cartoon.

1800
Birth of militant abolitionist JOHN BROWN.

1960
The Food and Drug Administration approved the sale of birth control pills.

HOSE SENSE

❖ Never throw out a worn garden hose. Instead, cut portions to cushion bucket and watering can handles, wooden shafts on shovels or rakes, ropes that stake out fruit trees, the top of fencing that cuts under berry bushes, and the places where rowboat oars meet the oarlocks. You'll soon think of many other uses.

❖ Cut short pieces of narrow hose or flexible plastic tubing (available at hardware stores) and fit them over the ends of your screwdrivers. The covers will protect the tips while the screwdrivers are stored.

❖ If you don't have a safe place to hang your saw, protect the teeth with a length of garden hose slit lengthwise.

NATURE WATCH

Is mama woodchuck leading her babies on a tour of your garden? The creatures may look endearing, but they will raise havoc with your crops. Place a couple of mirrors upright in the garden to scare the woodchucks away, or scatter hair clippings around the perimeter. Some say unwrapped sticks of Juicy Fruit gum laid in the garden paths will distract the woodchucks so they won't come back.

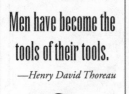

10

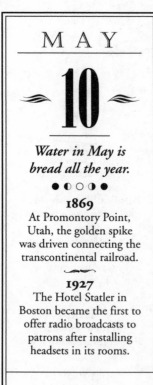

*Water in May is
bread all the year.*

● ◐ ○ ○ ●

1869
At Promontory Point,
Utah, the golden spike
was driven connecting the
transcontinental railroad.

1927
The Hotel Statler in
Boston became the first to
offer radio broadcasts to
patrons after installing
headsets in its rooms.

For Much More Than Shoes

ONE OF THE BEST home storage devices you can buy is a multipocket vinyl shoe organizer with grommets, designed to hang on the back of a door. Of course, you can always keep your shoes in it, but here are a few other ways to use this clever organizer.

❧ Store socks, panty hose, or underwear in the pockets.

❧ In the bathroom, fill the pockets with shampoo, brushes, shaving lotion, and other toiletries.

❧ Keep mittens, gloves, hats, and scarves organized in a hall closet or on the porch.

❧ Hang it in your camper and use it for bathing suits, goggles, sunglasses, sunscreen, and other small items that often go astray.

❧ In a child's room, use it to hold Beanie Babies, Barbie dolls, small stuffed animals, or action figures.

❧ Stash balls of yarn or other craft supplies in it.

❧ Fill it with kids' paints, brushes, crayons, and markers.

PRACTICAL PRIMER

Painting Shortcuts

❦ Before beginning a painting project, protect doorknobs, glass doors, hardware, switch plates, and windowpanes from paint spatters by rubbing them with bar soap. This makes it easy to wipe them clean when the job is finished.

❦ Add 2 capfuls of hair conditioner to a pint of warm water and use this mixture to soften your hardened paintbrushes. When the bristles soften, rinse them thoroughly and hang the brushes to dry.

❦ When you have only a small amount of paint left over after an indoor painting project, store it in a clear glass jar and label it with the date and the name of the paint color, the brand, and the room you painted.

Painting. The art of protecting flat surfaces from the weather and exposing them to the critic.

—*Ambrose Bierce*

CAR CARE

❖ To remove bumper stickers and decals from car chrome or windows, paint the stickers with vinegar, let it soak in, and then scrape the stickers off.

❖ To remove bugs and tar from your car without hurting the paint, use a paste of baking soda and water on a damp cloth. Let the paste sit for a few minutes, then wipe and rinse.

> *There was never any great man
> who was not an industrious man.*
>
> —BEN FRANKLIN

PABLO DE SARASATE was a brilliant violinist and composer from the Basque region of Spain. Toward the end of his life, a critic acclaimed Sarasate as a genius. "A genius!" the great violinist responded. "For thirty-seven years I've practiced fourteen hours a day, and now they call me a genius."

For industriousness personified, it's hard to beat Theodore Roosevelt. The youngest president in history kept a small army of clerks, secretaries, and stenographers busy

with his speeches and correspondence. He read, on average, one book a day. He wrote 40 books and numerous articles himself. The once sickly child pursued physical activity with a passion, on one occasion playing 91 games of tennis on the White House courts in a single day. As an English visitor to the United States once wrote, "I have seen two tremendous works of nature in America. One is Niagara Falls and the other is the President of the United States."

> **The world is always ready to receive talent with open arms. Very often it does not know what to do with genius.**
>
> —*Oliver Wendell Holmes*

WHEN IS IT TIME TO PLANT?

Gardeners love to debate the best times for all sorts of garden activities. Does nature give us certain signs that indicate it's safe to plant? These rules of thumb may help.

❦ Plant potatoes when dandelions bloom in the fields.

❦ Plant seeds of cold-tolerant garden crops when the soil crumbles through your fingers and you can step in it without

sinking in over the toes of your shoes. If the soil is muddy and water stands on top, or if you can grab a handful and easily shape it into a ball, it's too early.

❦ Plant cold-sensitive crops such as corn, beans, squash, and tomatoes when lilacs are in full bloom (that is, the flowers are open on at least 95 percent of the clusters).

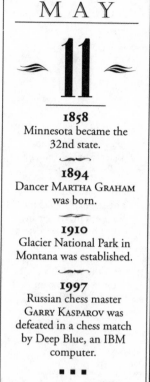

MAY

11

1858
Minnesota became the
32nd state.

1894
Dancer MARTHA GRAHAM
was born.

1910
Glacier National Park in
Montana was established.

1997
Russian chess master
GARRY KASPAROV was
defeated in a chess match
by Deep Blue, an IBM
computer.

• • •

LORE & LEGEND
May 11, 12, and 13 were known collectively to old-time almanac makers as the **THREE CHILLY SAINTS**, named for three early Christian martyrs whose feast days occur now. These days are traditionally cold. Sensitive crops were usually not planted until after the 13th.

1922

A 20-ton meteor crashed to Earth near Blackstone, Virginia.

❧

2002

The Leonard P. Zakim Bunker Hill Bridge in Boston opened on Mother's Day with 250,000 people strolling across the world's widest cable-stayed span. Vehicular traffic had to wait several months before using the 10-lane bridge.

● ● ●

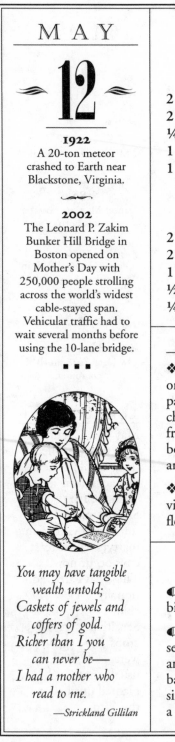

*You may have tangible
wealth untold;
Caskets of jewels and
coffers of gold.
Richer than I you
can never be—
I had a mother who
read to me.*

—*Strickland Gillilan*

Multigrain Blender Pancakes

*Surprise Mom with a stack of delicious (and healthy)
pancakes for breakfast.*

2 eggs
2 cups plain yogurt
¼ cup vegetable oil
1 cup all-purpose flour
1 cup whole wheat flour (or
   a combination of plain
   wheat germ, cornmeal,
   and oat flour)
2 tablespoons sugar
2 teaspoons baking powder
1 teaspoon baking soda
½ teaspoon salt
¼ teaspoon cinnamon

In a blender, combine the eggs, yogurt, and oil. In a large mixing bowl, whisk together the flours, sugar, baking powder, baking soda, salt, and cinnamon. Pour the yogurt mixture into the dry ingredients, mixing with a spoon until just combined. Heat an oiled griddle or skillet over medium-high heat until very hot. Ladle the batter on the griddle and cook until golden on both sides.

Makes about ten 3-inch pancakes

FOR PERFECT PANCAKES

❖ After you've ladled the batter onto the griddle, sprinkle each pancake with blueberries, chopped banana, or other small fruit, if desired. Cook until the bottom is golden, then turn and cook the other side.

❖ Don't mix pancake batter too vigorously, or the gluten in the flour will overdevelop, resulting in tough pancakes. Blend the ingredients until some small flour lumps remain, then refrigerate the batter for 1 hour before cooking. Cold slows down gluten development.

❖ Make extra pancakes on the weekend, freeze them, and pop them in the toaster for a quick, healthy weekday breakfast.

Pampering Mom

℄ Instead of giving Mom something for Mother's Day or her birthday, try taking something away—such as housework.

℄ Want to give Mom a homemade floral arrangement? Keep several floral foam bricks on hand for anchoring cut flower arrangements in baskets and containers. Put the brick in a basin of water and let it absorb its fill. When it has, it will sink to the bottom. Then cut it to the desired size, place it on a plastic tray in the container, and arrange your flowers.

Rocking Chair Fan

IN HIS LAST YEARS in Philadelphia, surrounded by grandchildren, Ben Franklin could take his ease after years of travel and public service. Although his material wants were never extravagant, he did have one of his large armchairs fitted with curved runners to make a comfortable rocking chair for his hours of reading. To cool himself and keep the flies away, he rigged up an overhead fan that was activated by the rocker's motion.

THE *Inspired* MIND

Although more than 250 rocking chair patents have been issued in the United States, only a few imitate Ben's fan rocker. Four of these designs appeared between 1915 and 1920—the era of the

gigantic ocean liner. One offered a small fan clamped to the arm of the rocker; a series of hand-operated gears turned the fan's blades. Another had a fan permanently mounted on the rocking chair arm and was spring-activated by a lever running under one of the rockers. The two others used standing fans bolted to the floor (or deck) directly behind the rocking chair. As in Ben's design, the fan was activated by the motion of the chair.

If Dust You Must

❖ When dusting, work from the top of the room downward. Dust first, then vacuum.

❖ Keep those single mittens that seem to accumulate and wear them for dusting. They work especially well on venetian blinds and other hard-to-reach areas. Old cotton socks worn like mittens work, too.

❖ Focus your attention on places that distribute the most dust, such as radiators, heat registers, and wood-burning stoves, and vacuum them frequently.

❖ Carry one or two small paintbrushes with you while dusting and use them to get into tight corners and window jambs.

MAY

13

St. Juliana of Norwich

● ○ ◐ ○ ●

1607
One hundred English colonists settled on the banks of the James River in Virginia to found Jamestown, the first permanent English settlement in North America.

1914
Birthday of boxing champion JOE LOUIS.

1918
The first U.S. airmail postage stamps were issued.

• • •

Drop the question what tomorrow may bring, and count as profit every day that fate allows you.

—*Horace*

14

1804
LEWIS and CLARK set out
from St. Louis, bound for
the Pacific Ocean.

1904
The United States hosted
its first Olympic Games,
an ancient Greek festival
revived in 1896.
The games opened on
this day in St. Louis.

*Hard is the heart that
loveth nought
In May.*

—The Romance of
the Rose, *13th century*

• • •

LORE & LEGEND

One of the many
plants collected in the
Rocky Mountains by
Lewis and Clark was
the small, sprawling,
eponymous *Lewisia
rediviva,* or bitterroot,
now a staple of rock
gardens. The starchy
root is tasty in the
spring but bitter and
inedible by summer.

Hear no ill of a friend, nor speak any of an enemy.

—BEN FRANKLIN

IN 1996, an Orthodox rabbi named Joseph Telushkin asked
Congress to designate May 14 Speak No Evil Day. Telushkin
argued that words are the source of much of the pain and suffering in the world. He envisioned a national day on which people
would be encouraged not to insult, backbite, gossip, or make personal attacks on others. Although some people thought it was a
silly idea, at least three senators (Connie Mack, Joseph Lieberman,
and Tom Harkin) were willing to sign on. Unfortunately, the idea
never gathered enough support for passage, but Telushkin did
offer some advice for taking the sting out of
harsh words.

• If a person angers you, talk to him about it,
not to someone else.
• Don't dig up past events.
• In arguments, avoid the words *always* and
never, which are rarely true.
• Don't get upset about little things.
• If you're really furious, wait until you cool
down before speaking.

A WORD TO THE WISE

ROSE SECRETS

❦ Root a rose cutting by sticking it into a raw potato and
planting it, potato and
all, where you want
the rose to grow.

❦ Plant roses where
they will receive at
least 6 hours of sun
per day.

❦ Save hair
clippings and
sprinkle them
near roses. They
make a great fertil-

izer, with 16 times as much nitrogen as cow manure.

❦ Fertilize roses when you see
the first signs of new
growth.

❦ As soon as climb-
ing roses start to leaf
out, secure them to a
trellis or arbor with
twist ties, plastic-
coated wire, or
strips cut from
an old green
T-shirt.

Your Backyard
Department of Agriculture

READY TO PLANT your garden? Remember not to make it any bigger than you can handle. A small, well-tended plot will surprise you with its bounty. Here are a few tips to help you along.

PRACTICAL PRIMER

- When planting tiny seeds that are hard to see, roll out a length of white toilet tissue, scatter the seeds evenly on it, cover with another layer of tissue, spray lightly with water, and sprinkle it all with soil.

- Keep newly planted seeds warm and speed their germination by covering them at night with plastic or newspaper. Anchor the cover with stones or bricks and remove it in the morning. Do this until sprouts appear.

- Before planting okra seeds, rub them gently between two pieces of sandpaper. Plant them outdoors when the soil is warm.

- Never grow more than six zucchini plants unless you're feeding an army.

- Don't use fresh manure or nitrogen-heavy fertilizer when planting carrot or parsnip seeds. Root crops will produce forked and misshapen roots if the soil is too rich.

- Work coffee grounds into the soil when you plant carrots.

*Oh, Adam was a gardener,
And God who made
him sees
That half a proper
gardener's work
Is done upon his knees.*
—*Rudyard Kipling*

*A swarm of bees
in May is worth a
load of hay.*

● ○ ○ ● ●

1834
Three feet of snow
fell on Haverhill,
New Hampshire, in the
greatest May snowstorm
on record along the
North Atlantic coast.

1862
Congress passed
legislation creating the
Department of
Agriculture.

1942
Wartime gasoline
rationing began, limiting
sales to 3 gallons a week.

TAKING CARE OF THE GARDENER

❖ If you suspect you've come in contact with poison ivy roots while turning over the soil, gently swab your skin with rubbing alcohol within 4 to 6 hours.

❖ Load hand tools, garden gloves, insect repellent, water bottle, and other small things you may need into a tote bag, basket, or plastic pail and take them to the garden on your first trip of the day.

❖ To remove garden grime from your hands, add a teaspoon of salt to the lather as you wash them.

MAY

16

St. Brendan

● ○ ○ ○ ●

1866
Congress authorized a
new coin—the nickel.

1939
Food stamps were
introduced.

■ ■ ■

**The only mystery
about the cat is
why it ever decided
to become a
domesticated animal.**

—*Sir Compton Mackenzie*

---

*Be always asham'd
to catch thy self idle.*

—Ben Franklin

A WORD TO THE WISE

HOW DO YOU picture retirement? As a time to kick back and take it easy? If you've led an active life, you might want to rethink that plan. Studies conducted by the insurance industry seem to indicate that people who retire from active work and do nothing die sooner than those who keep busy.

Of course, figuring out how you're going to keep busy can be a challenge for some people. Golfer George Archer won 19 Champions Tour tournaments during his lifetime. When asked what he was going to do when he retired, he said, "Baseball players quit playing and take up golf. Basketball players quit and take up golf. Football players quit and take up golf. What are we supposed to do when we quit?"

If you want to enjoy an active retirement, start now. Develop a hobby that you love. Begin donating time as a volunteer to a charity, hospital, or nonprofit organization. Become involved in community affairs. Remember, it's better to wear out than to rust out.

WHAT CATS WANT

❖ Cats like milk, but it is not good for them and can cause diarrhea. Cut back to little or no milk in your cat's diet. If you just can't resist treating your cat, give her a spoonful of plain yogurt or cottage cheese or a tidbit of hard cheese instead.

❖ If you are considering declawing your cat but are reluctant to do so, ask your veterinarian about a painless alternative: claw covers. The vinyl caps, which are glued onto your cat's claws, have rounded points. Each application lasts for up to 6 weeks.

❖ Give your older cats some help with grooming. As they age, cats spend less time grooming themselves. Comb them frequently to remove loose hair and dirt and to help distribute the natural oils that keep them looking sleek.

Thunderstorm Threat

On AVERAGE, 93 people in the United States are killed each year by lightning and another 300 are injured by it, according to the National Weather Service, which also estimates that the United States experiences 100,000 thunderstorms annually. If you are caught outdoors during a thunderstorm, become the lowest point around—lightning strikes the tallest object. Avoid sheds and picnic shelters. Move to a sturdy building or hardtop car and avoid touching metal. Or outfit yourself with a portable lightning rod, a 1984 invention by Norman Drulard of Portland, Oregon. The insulated rod extends and retracts, can be grounded, and has an umbrella that demarcates the area of lightning protection.

THE *Inspired* MIND

To determine how far a lightning bolt is from where you are standing, count the number of seconds between seeing the flash and hearing the next clap of thunder. Since sound travels at roughly 0.2 mile per second, multiply the seconds by 0.2 to get the number of miles you are from the lightning. For example, if you count 10 seconds between flash and thunder, you are about 2 miles away.

WATERING BASICS

❦ Use a rain gauge or mark off inches on a straight-sided can to keep track of rainfall. If you receive less than an inch a week, get out the sprinkler.

❦ When putting flower or vegetable transplants into the garden, lessen the shock to their roots by soaking the plants and the place where you're putting them until the soil has the consistency of mud.

❦ Water all transplants twice a day during their first week in the garden.

❦ To set up an efficient system for watering thirsty plants, dig a 12-inch hole in the garden and sink a large unglazed clay pot into it. Plant a ring of vegetables or flowers around the pot. When you fill the pot to the top with water, it will slowly seep out to the nearby roots.

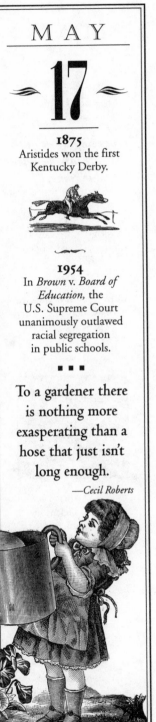

1875
Aristides won the first Kentucky Derby.

1954
In *Brown v. Board of Education,* the U.S. Supreme Court unanimously outlawed racial segregation in public schools.

• • •

To a gardener there is nothing more exasperating than a hose that just isn't long enough.

—*Cecil Roberts*

18

*Frogs singing at dusk
indicate fair weather
to come.*

● ● ○ ○ ●

1804
Napoleon Bonaparte
was proclaimed emperor
of France.

Birthday of film director
Frank Capra (1897) and
Pope John Paul II
(1920).

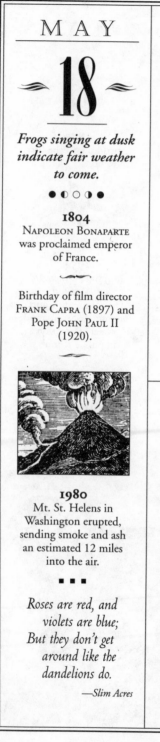

1980
Mt. St. Helens in
Washington erupted,
sending smoke and ash
an estimated 12 miles
into the air.

■ ■ ■

*Roses are red, and
violets are blue;
But they don't get
around like the
dandelions do.*

—*Slim Acres*

Federal Salaries

At the Constitutional Convention held in Philadelphia in May 1787, Ben Franklin asked the delegates to consider the issue of federal salaries. With firsthand knowledge of how monarchies worked in England and France, he pushed the idea that the president and other officials not be given compensation other than expenses. He believed that "making our posts of honor places of profit" would invite corruption, but his plea was ignored.

President George Washington was given a salary of $25,000 in 1789, a fabulous sum in that day. (It works out to about $500,000 in today's dollars.) The presidential salary has been changed only four times since then, but each time it has doubled: to $50,000 in 1873; $100,000 in 1949; $200,000 in 1969; and $400,000 in 2001.

Between 1856 and 1955, the salary for a congressman was only $6,960, but then the figure started to climb. By 2000, congressional paychecks were set at $141,300.

Outwitting Weeds

❦ Go after crabgrass as soon as it appears in the garden by digging it out by the roots with a spading fork or smothering it with black plastic. Don't let it go to seed.

CRABGRASS

❦ Use a 4-inch-deep layer of organic mulch such as grass clippings, straw, or chopped leaves to cover dirt walkways and deter weeds in the vegetable garden. Turn them over with the soil in the fall.

❦ Keep weeds away from young crops during the first 4 weeks. The crops will stand a better chance of competing. (Not that you should relax after that!)

❦ While weeding, hold the trowel vertically (like a child holding a crayon) to eliminate strain on your wrist.

❦ If digging out weeds is difficult for you, at least resolve to keep them from setting seed. Sharpen a hoe and chop off their heads once a week.

A Bennie Shaved . . .

HAPPINESS, Ben Franklin believed, could be experienced in "small conveniences" that occur daily rather than in "great pieces of good fortune that happen but seldom." In a 1768 letter, he noted one such daily felicity: "I can set [hone] my own razor and shave myself perfectly well," thus avoiding "the dirty fingers or bad breath of a slovenly barber."

THE *Inspired* MIND

Ben's straight razor, a tongue of forged metal that required frequent sharpening and stropping, was the facial tool of choice well into the 1800s, but its long exposed blade could be dangerous to handle. In 1864, Philadelphian John Kinloch invented a toothed metal guard for the razor that offered some safety to users. Then in 1880, New Yorkers Frederic and Otto Kampfe patented a T-shaped safety razor, although it still required sharpening.

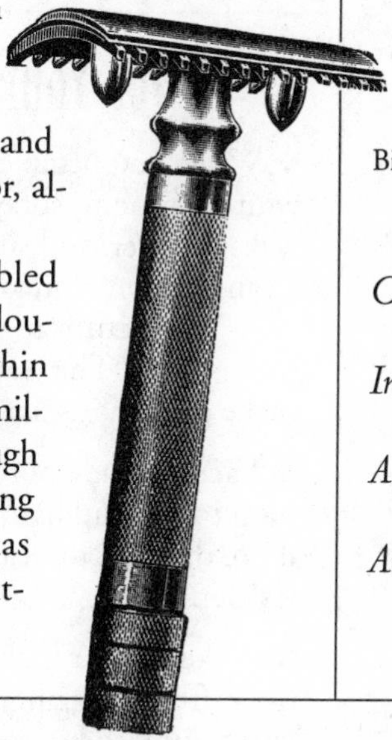

King Camp Gillette's 1904 razor resembled the Kampfe model but included disposable double-edged blades, a startling innovation. Within 5 years, Gillette's company had passed the million mark in annual razor sales, and although disposability did away with Ben's happy honing routine, the hundred-year-old invention has provided daily satisfaction to countless do-it-yourself barbers.

MAY

19

1780
A dark day occurred in New England. At noon, it was nearly as dark as night. Although people were convinced that this was a manifestation of divine wrath, the dimming was a result of smoke from forest fires to the west.

1925
Birth of civil rights activist MALCOLM X.

■ ■ ■

Commuter—one who
spends his life
In riding to and from
his wife;
A man who shaves and
takes a train,
And then rides back to
shave again.

—E. B. White

Look Sharp, Feel Sharp, Be Sharp

❖ If you keep a metal can of shaving cream on your sink or in your shower, store it upside down. This will prevent rust rings caused by the can.

❖ For fewer nicks, soften your beard with a hot shower before shaving. While you shower, set your can of shaving cream or gel on its side near the drain. The water will warm it up, and it will be easier to apply.

❖ If you're a new shaver, practice your technique on a lathered-up party balloon (if you won't be too startled if the balloon pops) or a smooth beach ball.

❖ If shaving creams and gels cause irritation, try substituting shower gel or hair conditioner.

–BK

20

*If there is enough
blue sky to patch a
Dutchman's breeches,
expect clearing
weather.*

● ○ ○ ◑ ●

1830
The fountain pen was
patented by D. HYDE of
Reading, Pennsylvania.

1902
Cuba gained its
independence from Spain.

1932
AMELIA EARHART became
the first woman to fly solo
across the Atlantic Ocean.

■ ■ ■

NATURE WATCH

In the desert West,
king snakes, gopher
snakes, Sonoran whip
snakes, and diamond-
back and tiger rattle-
snakes lay eggs or bear
live young now. In
the skies above them,
lesser nighthawks fill
the nights with their
trilling calls.

Make-It-Yourself All-Purpose Cleaner

Here's a way to make your own spray cleaner using safe, old-fashioned ingredients—and save the money you'd otherwise spend on a commercial product. You can use it on countertops,

2 teaspoons vinegar or
 lemon juice
1 teaspoon borax
1 teaspoon baking soda
A squirt (say, ¼ teaspoon)
 of dishwashing liquid
2 cups hot water

PRACTICAL PRIMER

sinks, glass, and other hard surfaces.
 Combine all the ingredients in a clean spray bottle and shake well. For a really sticky mess, spray on the cleaner and let it sit for a few minutes before wiping.

Get Your Bathroom Squeaky Clean

❖ When you begin cleaning your bathroom, spray the tubs, walls, shower, and sink with cleaner before doing anything else. Then return to these as the last task. The wait will make cleaning easier.

❖ Vacuum the floor before you mop to pick up hair, which is more difficult to deal with once it's wet.

❖ To keep your bathroom drain from clogging, pour in ½ cup baking soda, followed by 1 cup vinegar. After 20 minutes, flush with very hot water. Do this every 3

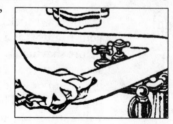

months, more often if the drain seems sluggish.

❖ Remove old bathtub decals or nonskid strips by covering them with aluminum foil and heating them with a hair dryer. Scrape while heating, using a credit card or the dull edge of a knife. To remove any sticky residue, use nail polish remover.

❖ Sprinkle borax into the toilet bowl before going to bed. In the morning, stains will be easier to scrub away. A couple of denture tablets or vitamin C tablets also work for overnight cleaning.

When the sun rises, it rises for everyone.
—*Cuban Proverb*

*Don't judge of men's wealth
or piety, by their
Sunday appearances.*

—BEN FRANKLIN

A MAN IN SHABBY construction clothes came into the Old National Bank in Spokane, Washington, and asked to cash a check for $100. Upon receiving his cash, he asked the cashier to validate his parking ticket, which was worth 60 cents. The cashier refused, saying the man hadn't conducted a transaction. The man explained that he was a depositor, but the cashier still refused to validate the parking ticket. He then insisted on seeing the manager, who also turned down his request. The man went to the headquarters of the bank and said he would withdraw all his money unless someone apologized for the incident. No one ever called, so he did just that—all $2 million of it.

A farmer had a successful apple orchard. But one of the trees was somewhat misshapen. A friend mentioned that he should remove that tree, as it was disrupting the neat, orderly appearance of the orchard. "That's the most productive tree I have," the farmer explained, "much more productive than any of the others."

Do you judge people or things by their appearance? If so, perhaps you should take a different tack.

MAY

21

1881
The American Red Cross
was founded by
CLARA BARTON.

1944
Human rights activist
MARY ROBINSON
was born.

*May is a green as no other,
May is much sun
   through small leaves,
May is soft earth,
And apple-blossoms,
And windows open to a
   South wind.*

—Amy Lowell

No More Runs

Pretreat your new panty hose to resist running. Wash and dry them first, then mix 2 cups salt and 1 gallon water. Add the panty hose and soak for 3 hours. Rinse in cool water and let dry.

CLOSET FRESHENERS

☙ To deodorize hardwood closet floors, wash with a mixture of ½ cup vinegar, ½ cup baking soda, and 1 gallon warm water.

☙ Put a mixture of equal parts baking soda and borax in a shoe box. Punch holes in the lid.

Tape the lid onto the box and store it in a closet or any closed space that needs deodorizing.

☙ Keep your cedar closet dry by installing a dehumidifier or a low-wattage lightbulb that can stay on for a few hours at a time.

22

1843
A wagon train with 1,000 people of all ages left Independence, Missouri, for Oregon to start the Great Migration of 1843. A herd of 5,000 oxen and cattle lumbering behind helped carve out the Oregon Trail.

1859
Birth of Sherlock Holmes's creator, SIR ARTHUR CONAN DOYLE.

A man should keep his little brain attic stocked with all the furniture that he is likely to use, and the rest he can put away in the lumber-room of his library, where he can get it if he wants it.

—*Sir Arthur Conan Doyle*

How to Run a Yard Sale

WHEN THE BASEMENT, attic, or garage threatens to overflow, consider holding a yard sale. Your clutter and castoffs may be a boon to someone looking for secondhand bargains.

PRACTICAL PRIMER

- Pick a day and time. Invite friends to join you with their extra stuff.
- Decide how you will dispose of any leftovers. If you or one of your friends has a truck, reserve it for a trip to the Salvation Army (or the dump) after the sale.
- Be sure all items are clean and looking their best. If something is broken, attach a note that says As Is.
- Display sets of glasses or encyclopedias in cardboard boxes. Have extra boxes and sturdy bags on hand for customers to use.
- Use sticky labels to assign a reasonable price to every item. Group small items, such as kids' action figures, in a box and label the box.
- Put up signs several days in advance and advertise a large sale in the local newspaper (check for deadlines).
- Get at least $5 worth of quarters before the sale starts. Wear an apron with pockets to hold the money and easily make change.
- Arrange items on tables or on blankets or sheets on the ground.
- Be willing to bargain. Remember, you want to get rid of this stuff!

The Stuff You Can't Part With

◖ If you must keep your record albums, clean them by squirting dishwashing liquid on a fingertip, then running your finger around the grooves. Rinse well and let air-dry before playing.

◖ Use a metal trash can or ceramic umbrella stand to store baseball bats, lacrosse and hockey sticks, skis and poles, and tennis rackets.

◖ Organize a comic book collection in a filing cabinet. Use file folders and hanging files to keep the pages flat.

Sight Lines

AS HIS EYESIGHT grew weaker with age (and after years of setting small type by hand as a printer), Ben Franklin resorted to wearing glasses—one pair for reading and another for distance. In 1784, bothered by the constant switching between pairs, he thought of the idea of cutting the lenses in half horizontally and joining the tops of his everyday lenses to the bottoms of his reading glasses, thereby inventing bifocals.

THE *Inspired* MIND

Trifocals were introduced in London in 1827 by John Hawkins, but it wasn't until late in the century that multifocal lenses became commercially standardized, although they were fragile and collected dirt at the dividing lines. By 1908, fused rather than cemented bifocals were available. Lenses that came in direct contact with the eye were invented in 1888 and made commercially available in the 1890s, with bifocal soft contact lenses first being introduced in 1982. As for Ben's traditional bifocals, a remarkable improvement occurred in 1988 when Frenchman Bernard Maitenaz patented progressive lenses without bifocal lines for distance, midrange, and near vision.

FURNITURE SPIT AND POLISH

❖ Remove white rings left by wet drinking glasses with a mixture of equal parts olive oil and white vinegar. Rub with the grain of the wood. Let stand for an hour or two, then wipe off and apply a coat of polish. Or cover the rings with petroleum jelly, let stand for 24 hours, and wipe off.

❖ Restore the shine and luster of old wooden furniture by rubbing it with a piece of salt pork.

❖ Remove scuff marks on the legs of wooden chairs and tables by rubbing gently with very fine steel wool (grade 0000) dipped in vegetable or olive oil.

❖ Use cooled, plain tea to polish furniture. Just dip a soft cloth in the tea and wipe the wood.

In the old of the moon, a cloudy morning bodes a fair afternoon.

● ○ ○ ○ ●

1784
BEN FRANKLIN described his new invention, bifocal glasses.

1788
South Carolina became the eighth state.

1870
Trains ran between San Francisco and Boston to provide the first transcontinental railway service.

■ ■ ■

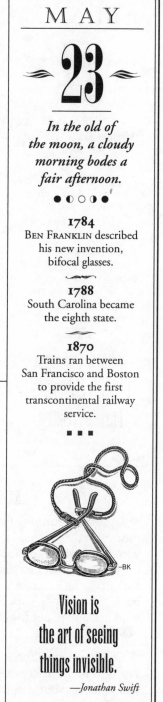

—BK

Vision is the art of seeing things invisible.

—*Jonathan Swift*

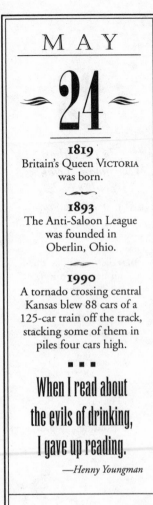

MAY

24

1819
Britain's Queen VICTORIA was born.

1893
The Anti-Saloon League was founded in Oberlin, Ohio.

1990
A tornado crossing central Kansas blew 88 cars of a 125-car train off the track, stacking some of them in piles four cars high.

• • •

When I read about the evils of drinking, I gave up reading.

—Henny Youngman

Life with fools consists in drinking; With the wise man living's thinking.

—BEN FRANKLIN

WHAT'S THE CONNECTION between drinking and thinking? According to a report by Columbia University's National Center on Addiction and Substance Abuse, there is an inverse relationship—that is, the more you drink, the less you think. Researchers at Columbia studied the drinking habits of college students and came up with these findings.

A WORD TO THE WISE

- The average student consumes 34 gallons of alcoholic beverages per year.
- Students consume the most alcohol in their freshman years.
- The more students drink, the lower their grade point averages are. Students who get A's drink the least.

All colleges and universities have active abuse prevention programs to help students focus on education rather than inebriation. Learning to handle alcohol responsibly—or to avoid it altogether—can have a big payoff later in life. As playwright Jean Kerr wrote, "Even though a number of people have tried, no one has yet found a way to drink for a living."

Take the Grind Out of Grocery Shopping

❖ Draw up a running list of grocery and household items you need and try to shop only once or twice a week. Buy items such as toothpaste, toilet paper, paper napkins, and paper towels before you run out.

❖ Store grocery coupons in a box next to the place where you write out your shopping list and carry them with you in your purse only when you go to the store. Keep a magnifying glass in the box, too, and check the dates often, discarding any that have expired.

❖ If you bring and pack your own grocery bags (it's worth it), consolidate items according to where they will ultimately go when you unpack them. Pack freezer items together, keep pet foods in one bag, consolidate cleaning supplies and personal items, and so forth. This will save time when you get home.

The Desk Rules

IF YOU DON'T have a desk, set one up wherever you can. It will give you a place to store papers and keep track of important letters and bills. Here are a few tips.

- Always use your desk for paperwork. Don't try to get by with a multipurpose surface such as a table that has to be cleared off for meals or other projects.

- To make an instant desk, buy a pair of two-drawer filing cabinets and put a hollow-core door or piece of plywood on top.

- Put a wastebasket nearby. Go through papers as soon as you put them on your desk and discard or recycle anything you don't need.

- Keep a number of blank birthday and special occasion cards in your desk drawer so that you don't need to make a trip to the store every time a birthday comes around.

PRACTICAL

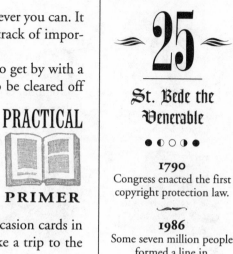

PRIMER

KEEPING ORDER

❦ Establish a folder for all incoming bills and file them as soon as they arrive. Keep a list of when they're due and post a reminder on your calendar a week before the deadline.

❦ File paid bills and receipts according to category—auto, credit cards, medical expenses, utilities, mortgage, and so on—so you can find them easily if a question arises or if you want to analyze your spending habits.

❦ Use checks to pay for school fees, charitable donations, and other tax-deductible expenses so you'll have a record of what you spend. Write "deductible" in the memo line, and you can quickly pull them out of your pile of canceled checks each month.

1790
Congress enacted the first copyright protection law.

1986
Some seven million people formed a line in Hands Across America to raise money for the nation's hungry and homeless.

■ ■ ■

I write down everything I want to remember. That way, instead of spending a lot of time trying to remember what it is I wrote down, I spend the time looking for the paper I wrote it down on.

—*Beryl Pfizer*

MAY

26

1956
ALTHEA GIBSON won the
French Open tennis
tournament.

1981
S. PAL ASIJA received
the first patent for a
software program.

All things are easy to industry, all things difficult to sloth.

—BEN FRANKLIN

A WORD TO THE WISE

IN HIS RAGS-TO-RICHES autobiography, Edward Bok tells how he got his first job. As a boy, he was standing in front of a bakery window admiring the pastries on display when the baker came out and said, "Look pretty good, don't they?"

"They would if your windows were clean," the young Bok replied, displaying a passion for cleanliness and order typical of his Dutch heritage.

The baker decided the boy was right and hired him on the spot to wash the windows. Bok put so much energy into his work that the baker gave him a regular job of washing the windows twice a week. The pay was 50 cents. From that meager beginning, Bok went on to become editor of the *Ladies' Home Journal,* founder of *Cosmopolitan,* and winner of a Pulitzer Prize for *The Americanization of Edward Bok*. His was a long and successful career that began with a dirty window.

> Give me the splendid silent sun with all his beams full-dazzling.
>
> —*Walt Whitman*

A Great Day for Washing Windows

❖ To make an inexpensive window cleaner, combine about ½ cup ammonia, 2½ cups rubbing alcohol, 1 teaspoon dishwashing liquid, 1½ quarts water, and blue food coloring (if desired) in a clean half-gallon jug. Shake well and label. To use, transfer to a clean spray bottle.

❖ When washing windows, use horizontal strokes inside and vertical strokes outside,

or vice versa. When it comes to figuring out where the streaks are, you'll know which side is which.

❖ Spray windows, then wipe immediately using loosely wadded newspaper. (Do not

use coated paper, such as advertising inserts.)

❖ To prevent bird collisions with windows, float helium balloons in front of the windows on 2- to 3-foot lengths of string. Birds often fly into windows during nesting season. Male birds, in particular, confuse their reflections with invaders. Once baby birds hatch, adults tend not to display such aggressive behavior.

Ben Franklin, Storyteller

SAMUEL JOHNSON, England's literary giant and a contemporary of Ben Franklin, wrote an essay in 1751 about leaving home. In it, he said, "My eagerness to distinguish myself in public, and my impatience of the narrow scheme of life to which my indigence confined me, did not suffer me to continue long in the town where I was born. I went away as from a place of confinement." Johnson, mentioning himself numerous times, long-windedly described his relief at escaping home. There is nothing here to grab our interest in what the future holds for him.

Contrast this with Ben's autobiographical description of his own hometown flight, written in 1771: "In three days I found myself in New York, near three hundred miles from home, a boy of but seventeen, without the least recommendation to or knowledge of any person in the place, and with very little money in my pocket." Using crisp phrases and subordinating himself to the tale, Ben makes us curious to know what will happen next. Ben was a master storyteller, and his *Autobiography* was the original model for the American rags-to-riches story.

> There is no greater agony than bearing an untold story inside you.
>
> —*Maya Angelou*

MAY

27

Birth of writers DASHIELL HAMMETT (1894) and RACHEL CARSON (1907).

1926
Bronze statues of Huck Finn and Tom Sawyer were dedicated in Hannibal, Missouri.

1937
The Golden Gate Bridge opened in San Francisco.

TIPS FOR CHILLY MICROCLIMATES

Gardeners in USDA Zone 4 or colder, especially those who live in cold pockets (you know who you are), are often reluctant to plant tender crops such as tomatoes, melons, and peppers until the very end of May. If you fear a late frost, here are a few tricks.

❧ Lay red plastic mulch (available at garden centers and from garden supply catalogs) around tomato plants to hold in the soil's heat and increase productivity.

❧ Plant tomatoes at the base of a stone or brick wall. They'll benefit from the heat it retains.

❧ Mound a pile of compost 2 feet deep and plant melon seeds in it. The compost will generate warmth in addition to providing nutrients and good drainage.

❧ To protect young peppers, use black plastic to warm the soil and cloches or a light covering on chilly nights. Peppers will not set fruit if temperatures are below 65°F during the day.

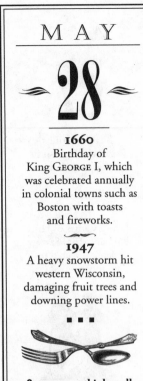

MAY

28

1660
Birthday of
King GEORGE I, which
was celebrated annually
in colonial towns such as
Boston with toasts
and fireworks.

1947
A heavy snowstorm hit
western Wisconsin,
damaging fruit trees and
downing power lines.

• • •

One cannot think well,
love well, sleep well,
if one has not
dined well.

—*Virginia Woolf*

Dine with little, sup with less.
Do better still; sleep supperless.

—BEN FRANKLIN

NOT ALL GREAT MEN have been as indifferent about food as Ben Franklin was. The great composer George Frideric Handel once sent word to a restaurant requesting dinner for two. When he arrived alone, the proprietor expressed some confusion, saying that he understood the maestro would be arriving with company. "I *am* the company," Handel said, and proceeded to eat both meals.

Another creative genius who enjoyed a good meal was film director Alfred Hitchcock. He once attended a dinner at which he was dismayed by the small size of the portions. When the meal was over, the host said, "I do hope you will dine with us again soon."

"By all means," Hitchcock replied. "Let's start now."

Andrew Mellon, the wealthy financier and philanthropist, was very fond of the pancakes and sausages his cook prepared for him. One morning, as his breakfast was being served, a servant brought in a telephone and announced that France's minister of finance wished to speak with him. "Not with the hotcakes," Mellon said. Then he added, "These foreigners have no sense of propriety."

Today modern dietary wisdom is in agreement with Ben, who held to this advice: To stay slim and live long, eat your biggest meal for breakfast, have a moderate lunch, and eat a light supper.

Party Pointers

❖ More guests than you expected? Use a little ingenuity to stretch your dessert. For example, layer crumbled cake or cookies, fruit, or pudding with ice cream or whipped cream in decorative glasses.

❖ Dress up pureed or cream-style soups by swirling in a dollop of sour cream or yogurt. Use a knife to make a marbleized effect.

❖ For a new twist on entertaining, host a "tasting." Does bottled water really taste better than tap water? Is one brown mustard better than another? Is the expensive wine more flavorful than the cheap one? Explore the possibilities and have fun.

❖ Give your guests (and yourself) the gift of time. State both beginning and ending times for a party in the invitation.

Simple Cheese Strata

This savory layered dish makes a wonderful breakfast or brunch offering. You can construct it the night before.

4 eggs

2½ cups milk

1 teaspoon salt

1 tablespoon Dijon mustard

4 cups cubed day-old bread, crusts removed

1 small Vidalia onion, chopped

8 ounces sharp cheddar cheese, grated

In a medium bowl, beat together the eggs, milk, salt, and mustard. In a greased 9- by 13-inch casserole, layer one-third of the bread, one-third of the onion, and one-third of the cheese. Repeat to make 2 more layers. Pour the milk mixture over all and refrigerate for at least 1 hour or overnight. Preheat the oven to 350°F and bake for 1 hour, or until golden brown.

Makes 6 servings

ENJOYING CHEESE

❧ For full flavor, bring cheese to room temperature before serving. Allow about 2 hours per pound to raise the temperature from 40°F to 70°F.

❧ To make your cheese grater easier to clean, grate a raw potato or onion right after you grate some cheese.

❧ To keep cheese moist, coat the exposed end of the block with butter.

❧ Cut firm cheese such as cheddar with a cheese plane (for thin slices) or a strong chef's knife.

❧ Cheese and wine are natural partners, but beer also goes well with cheese. Try stout or dark ale with a dry, aged cheese; pair lagers with Swiss or mild cheddar.

Poets have been mysteriously silent on the subject of cheese.

—*G. K. Chesterton*

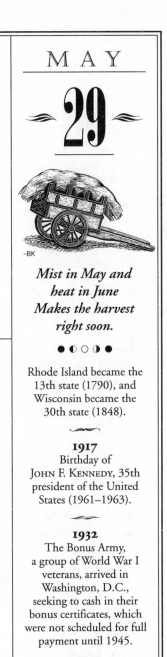

MAY

29

—BK

Mist in May and heat in June Makes the harvest right soon.

● ◐ ○ ◑ ●

Rhode Island became the 13th state (1790), and Wisconsin became the 30th state (1848).

1917
Birthday of
JOHN F. KENNEDY, 35th
president of the United
States (1961–1963).

1932
The Bonus Army,
a group of World War I
veterans, arrived in
Washington, D.C.,
seeking to cash in their
bonus certificates, which
were not scheduled for full
payment until 1945.

1953
EDMUND HILLARY and
TENZING NORGAY reached
the summit of
Mt. Everest.

30

1868
The graves of Civil War soldiers were decorated at Arlington National Cemetery on the first official observance of Memorial Day.

1922
The Lincoln Memorial was dedicated.

1977
JANET GUTHRIE became the first woman to race in the Indianapolis 500.

● ● ●

LORE & LEGEND

Rosemary is a symbol of remembrance. Instead of geraniums for the memorial plot, consider a fragrant rosemary bush. It likes humidity, so bring a spray mister to the plot.

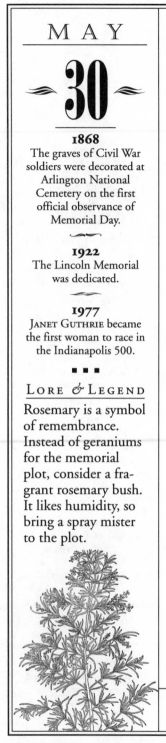

Colonial Potherbs for a Kitchen Garden

PRACTICAL

PRIMER

A KITCHEN-GARDEN don't thrive better or faster in any part of the Universe than there," said Robert Beverly in a 1705 book intended to lure prospective settlers to Virginia. Beverly was referring to the potherbs (medicinal and culinary herbs), small fruits, and berries that were commonly grown in the protected dooryards of American households. Try these flavorful culinary herbs in your kitchen garden.

Basil: Native to India, basil is grown as an annual and has become America's most popular herb. Set plants out after any danger of frost has passed, and pinch them back to encourage bushy growth.

Chives: A clump of chives will come back year after year. Although the purple seedheads are lovely, the leaves get tougher after the plants flower.

Mint: A rampant grower, mint is an ideal container plant. If you plant it in a bed, contain it in a large plastic pot with the bottom removed. Sink the pot into the soil at ground level.

Parsley: If you like to cook, put in six parsley plants and cut them to the ground as you harvest them. Give plants 2 to 3 weeks to regrow between cuttings. Many cooks prefer the taste of flat-leaf parsley to the curly varieties. Buy new plants every year.

Rosemary: In USDA Zones 2 through 6, grow rosemary in a big pot and keep it well-watered. Bring it indoors to a cool, sunny spot when the first frost is predicted in fall. Move it outside when warm weather arrives. In Zones 7 through 11, you can grow rosemary in the ground all year.

Tarragon: Cooks love French tarragon, with its smooth, narrow, pointed leaves hinting of anise and lemon. Make sure you buy plants—you can't grow true French tarragon from seeds. It's a slow grower, so put in at least four plants. Treat it as a tender perennial in the North.

Thyme: Common or garden thyme is the most useful in the kitchen. In a sunny or semishaded spot, it will last for years.

The soldier, above all other people, prays for peace.
—*Douglas MacArthur*

'Tis easy to see, hard to foresee.

—BEN FRANKLIN

OVER THE YEARS, people have used all kinds of methods to predict the future: tea leaves, crystal balls, oracles, entrails, tarot cards, palm reading. A blind German, the clairvoyant Ulf Buck, even claimed that he could read people's futures from the lines on their buttocks. But perhaps the most disastrous prognosticator of all was John Partridge, a British cobbler, self-styled weather forecaster, and—like Ben Franklin—publisher of an almanac.

A WORD TO THE WISE

One day while traveling, Partridge stopped to rest at an inn. As he prepared to leave, the innkeeper warned him that he would be caught in a rainstorm if he left just then. Ignoring the innkeeper's advice, Partridge went on his way and was indeed caught in a downpour. Curious as to the innkeeper's forecasting method, Partridge returned to the inn and gave the man a large tip in exchange for his secret. The innkeeper explained that he always referred to his copy of Partridge's almanac, which had predicted settled weather for the day. He added, "The fellow is such a notorious liar that whenever he promises fine weather we can be sure it will rain."

–BK

For the Younger Set

❖ Grow an outdoor room or playhouse for young children by planting sunflowers in a square and leaving an opening for a door. For extra fun and blooms, let morning glories climb up the sunflower stems.

❖ To cure a young child of hiccups, ask her to hold her breath, raise her arms above her head, and promise not to laugh. Then gently tickle her around the ribs.

❖ Remove pine pitch from hands by rubbing well with mayonnaise, then washing.

❖ Help young children snip out their images from duplicate photos and paste them over those of characters in an inexpensive children's book. Suddenly, the book is about them.

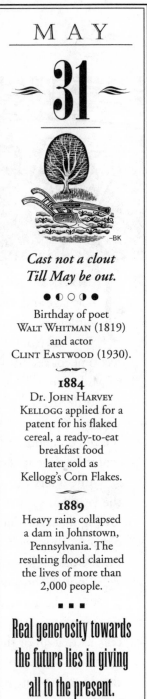

MAY

31

–BK

*Cast not a clout
Till May be out.*

● ● ○ ● ●

Birthday of poet
WALT WHITMAN (1819)
and actor
CLINT EASTWOOD (1930).

1884
Dr. JOHN HARVEY
KELLOGG applied for a
patent for his flaked
cereal, a ready-to-eat
breakfast food
later sold as
Kellogg's Corn Flakes.

1889
Heavy rains collapsed
a dam in Johnstown,
Pennsylvania. The
resulting flood claimed
the lives of more than
2,000 people.

■ ■ ■

Real generosity towards
the future lies in giving
all to the present.

—*Albert Camus*

JUNE, *the Sixth Month*

J UNE, NAMED FOR the Roman goddess Juno, patron of marriage and women, is a month embraced by brides and gardeners, schoolchildren and strawberry growers. Since ancient times, cultures have adopted June as the perfect time for revelry, weddings, and feasts, especially on the eve of Midsummer Day, June 24, when people from Scandinavia to North Africa celebrated the summer solstice with wild parties and bonfires. While high school seniors look forward to the end of school and a June graduation, we remind them that "commencement" simply means a new beginning.

June offers the most hours of daylight of any month of the year. For farmers and gardeners, this is a great boon, allowing them to concentrate on their fields and flowers. One old proverb says, "Calm weather in June sets corn in tune." Like Goldilocks, gardeners hope for weather that is just right: not too hot, not too cold; not too wet, not too dry.

Even the most tender plants—softies like basil, impatiens, and tomatoes—are in the ground now. Folk wisdom tells us that all of the plants will catch up by the end of the month regardless of how early we got them in the ground, thanks to the long hours of sunshine and, with any luck, the gentle rains of June.

Full Strawberry Moon

is the traditional name that pays homage to the sweetest of our ground fruits, especially the tiny, fragrant wood strawberries beloved by Linnaeus. June's moon is also called the *Full Rose Moon.*

Sign of the Zodiac: Gemini (May 21–June 20)

Element: Air

Quality: Intelligent

Birthstone: Pearl

Flower: Rose

The First Lightning Rods

We hear from Malden, that the Lightning on Tuesday last enter'd in at the Door of an House there, and very much scorch'd a Man and a Boy, Kill'd a Dog, and melted some Pewter in the Cellar.

—New England Courant, *April 16, 1722*

IN JUNE 1752, 30 years after Ben Franklin helped print this newspaper report, he performed the kite experiment proving that lightning is an electrical discharge. Ben fixed an iron rod to a silk kite, flew the kite in a thunderstorm to attract lightning and electrify the kite's hemp twine and a metal key tied to the twine, and then generated a spark by placing his knuckle near the key. The effect was identical to what happened in his laboratory experiments with electrical charges.

THE Inspired MIND

Ben applied this knowledge in a practical, inventive way. Two public buildings in Philadelphia were immediately outfitted with protective (grounded) lightning rods, and in September a third went atop the Franklin home. In *Poor Richard's Almanack* for 1753, Ben explained the new device and gave instructions on how to install a grounded, pointed, metallic rod on buildings and ships.

*The Lightning showed
a Yellow Beak
And then a livid Claw.*

—Emily Dickinson

NOTES FOR GARDENERS

❖ Instead of using chemical herbicides, pour boiling water on pesky weeds.

❖ Don't handle plants immediately after a rainstorm, or you might spread fungal diseases.

❖ In late spring, as soon as flowers fade, prune forsythias by selectively cutting a third of the oldest and thickest stems to within a foot of the ground.

This will maintain the natural fountain shape.

❖ Rejuvenate overgrown rhododendrons after flowering by cutting the stems back to 6 to 12 inches. If a plant has multiple stems, cut back one-third of them each year.

*A dry May and
a leaking June
Make the farmer
whistle a merry tune.*

● ○ ○ ○ ●

–BK

1752
Sometime early in the month of June, BEN FRANKLIN, with the help of his son WILLIAM, a silk kite, and a key, performed an experiment during a thunderstorm proving that lightning is electrical.

Kentucky became the 15th state (1792), and Tennessee became the 16th state (1796).

1926
Actress MARILYN MONROE was born.

● ● ●

Thunder is good, thunder is impressive; but it is lightning that does the work.

—Mark Twain

2

1886
GROVER CLEVELAND
married FRANCES FOLSOM,
the first presidential
couple to wed in the
White House.

1924
Congress granted
Native Americans
U.S. citizenship.

■ ■ ■

**Woodchucks are as
fond of the fruits of
our gardens as we
are, and even better
at harvesting them.**

—*Ruth Page*

The Well-Equipped Toolshed

I F Y O U ' V E I N H E R I T E D a spacious garage or toolshed or just wish that yours contained more useful things, consider this checklist. Look for many of these items at yard sales.

PRACTICAL

PRIMER

- **A sturdy ladder**—or maybe two: one tall enough to reach your gutters, plus a smaller stepladder
- **Gardening tools:** spading fork, pointed shovel, hoe, cultivator, trowel, hand weeder, pruners, clippers
- **Lawn rake:** with rubber tines, which are durable and efficient

- **Wheelbarrow:** for carrying heavy loads, transporting trees and shrubs to be planted, delivering mulch and compost to the garden beds, and myriad other uses
- **Stiff broom:** for sweeping sidewalks, driveway, stairs, deck, or patio
- **Large bucket:** for washing the car (or the dog) or collecting the harvest
- **Hose:** one long enough to reach the garden, plus nozzles or a sprinkler

COMBATING CRITTERS IN THE GARDEN

❖ To see a mole "run out, astonished" (according to the 16th-century herbalist John Gerard), put a bulb of garlic in its hole.

❖ Sprinkle ground red pepper in the entrances to mole tunnels.

❖ To keep rabbits out of your garden, surround it with fencing at least 3 feet tall and bury the fencing to a depth of 8 inches below the surface.

❖ Surround your garden with garlic plants to deter woodchucks and raccoons.

❖ To keep cats and raccoons away, scatter broken eggshells around your plants.

❖ Plant rue to keep cats out of your garden.

❖ Tie old sneakers and clothes that smell of human perspiration to posts in the vegetable garden to deter deer and raccoons.

❖ To discourage deer, scatter rotten eggs and garlic around your garden.

❖ If your neighbors don't mind, play a radio at low volume all night long.

The Franklin Medal for Scholarship

BOSTON LATIN SCHOOL, the oldest public school in the United States, was founded in 1635. Ben Franklin was 8 years old when he enrolled there in 1714, rising quickly to the rank of first in his class. After a year, however, his father withdrew him from the school. At the end of his life, Ben remembered the school in his will, establishing a trust to earn interest, "which interest annually shall be laid out in silver medals" to be awarded to worthy students in the public schools.

THE *Inspired* MIND

If Ben were enrolled in one of Boston's 131 public schools today, he would be one of 63,000 students, including Blacks, Latinos, Whites, Asians, and Native Americans. Now 16 out of every 100 students speak Spanish, Chinese, or another language besides English. Those who exhibit good conduct and scholarship throughout high school are eligible to receive the Franklin Medal, given annually to a male and female scholar in each of Boston's 19 public high schools.

JUNE

3

Birth of singer JOSEPHINE BAKER (1906) and actress COLLEEN DEWHURST (1924).

1965
The silver in U.S. dimes and quarters was eliminated.

・・・

You know that children are growing up when they start asking questions that have answers.

—*John J. Plomp*

SCHOOL'S OUT!

❦ As the school year comes to a close, thank your child's teacher with a gift from the classroom. Instead of 20 small gifts (so many mugs!), have each family contribute a small amount toward a gift certificate to a bookstore, garden center, or other appropriate store.

❦ Buy a box of large kraft envelopes (18 by 23 inches) at your stationery store and use them to store your children's artwork. Label them by name and year (or grade and teacher) and store them flat.

A Place for Everything

❖ Use a shoe box to hold all the items you need to send packages: packing tape, cellophane tape, labels, scissors, string, pens, and markers. Make sure you label the box.

❖ Use clear zippered pouches to organize cosmetics, pens and notepads, and other things you carry in your purse.

❖ Fold a multipocket chef's apron over the front of a senior citizen's walker and secure it with snaps or safety pins to provide storage space for glasses, tissues, medicines, and other items.

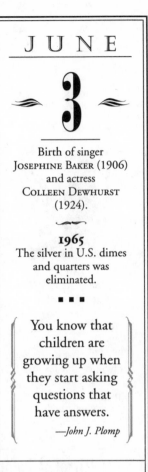

4

1892
The Sierra Club
was organized in
San Francisco.

1992
The U.S. Postal Service
announced the results of
the ELVIS PRESLEY stamp
poll: People preferred
the young Elvis to
the Vegas era Elvis.

Coping with Drought

BECAUSE THE WEATHER rarely announces its long-range intentions, the gardener needs to be prepared to cope with the inevitable problems of a dry season. To help your garden survive a long dry spell, keep these tips in mind.

🌿 When you water, give plants a thorough soaking to encourage roots to grow deep. Water during the twilight hours, not in the heat of the day.

🌿 Keep all garden plants well-weeded so they won't have to compete with weeds for moisture. (When water is scarce, the weeds are bound to win.)

🌿 Mulch all plants, including those in containers, to keep weeds down and to slow the evaporation of water. Straw, hay, peat moss, grass clippings, or shredded leaves will do the job.

🌿 Loosen hard-packed clay soils to allow water to penetrate.

🌿 Cover garden paths with a thick layer of hay, straw, boards, old carpeting—anything that will cut down on water evaporation and discourage weeds.

🌿 Install a rain barrel at the base of your gutters and dip out bucketfuls to water plants near the house.

PRACTICAL

PRIMER

A Sage Bit of Wisdom

*The mind should be sound
and gay, yet sage withal.*

—THE OLD FARMER'S
ALMANAC, *1792*

If the mind is not naturally sage, try culinary sage for the mind. Sage tea is recommended by old-timers for headaches, insomnia, colds, coughs, asthma, dieting, and any number of other ills.

NATURE'S HOME REMEDIES

❦ Remember witch hazel *(Hamamelis virginiana),* which grows wild in eastern North America, for its astringent properties. Boil the bark or leaves well, strain the liquid, and let it cool. Use it for stings or sunburns or as a complexion aid.

❦ For the tastiest, iron-rich salads, pick dandelion leaves when they're young and less bitter. They're a mild diuretic and help guard against urinary infections.

❦ To cure warts, pick dandelions two or three times a day and rub the milky juice from the stems on the warts.

WITCH HAZEL

Quick Curried Chicken on the Grill

Marinating chicken in a mixture of spicy herbs and plain yogurt tenderizes it and gives it the flavors of India. Serve this with white or basmati rice and a salad of chopped cucumbers and tomatoes.

⅓ cup plain yogurt
1 large clove garlic, minced
1 teaspoon coarsely ground black pepper
½ teaspoon cayenne pepper, or to taste
2 teaspoons cumin
1 tablespoon mild curry powder
2 tablespoons fresh lemon juice
4 to 6 boneless chicken breast halves
Salt

Combine the yogurt, garlic, black pepper, cayenne, cumin, curry powder, and lemon juice in a bowl. Rub the mixture all over the chicken breasts. Cover and let marinate in the refrigerator for 30 minutes to 1 hour.

Preheat the grill to medium and place the chicken pieces about 5 inches from the heat source. Grill for about 6 minutes per side, or until browned and cooked through. Season with salt to taste.

Makes 4 to 6 servings

1859
Frost was reported from the Midwest to New England, and 2 inches of snow fell on parts of Ohio. The cold and snow damaged the wheat crop.

1934
Birth of TV commentator BILL MOYERS

■ ■ ■

Be first at the feast, and last at the fight.

—*Indian Proverb*

PUTTING OUT THE FIRE OF CURRY

If you go overboard on the cayenne, or if you order curry in a restaurant and find your lips burning, don't reach for a glass of water. Milk, yogurt, bread, or beer will be more effective at extinguishing the burn.

Be the Guru of Grilling

❖ Remember the 4-by-4 rule to determine how hot the grill is. If you can keep your palm 4 inches over the coals for 4 seconds, it's at medium heat.

❖ Whether grilling or broiling, always turn meat with a spatula or tongs. A fork will pierce the meat, allowing precious juices to escape.

❖ Use fresh lemon juice in your marinades. It tenderizes meat, blends well with many different flavors (from soy sauce and ginger to barbecue sauce), and accents other tastes.

❖ If you prefer to remove the skin from chicken before grilling, be sure to keep the meat moist by marinating first, then basting frequently with leftover marinade during grilling.

❖ If you grill over charcoal, a chimney starter is a must. You'll have glowing coals in 20 minutes and can spare the expense, stench, and taste of lighter fluid.

6

EMILY GREENE BALCH was awarded a graduate fellowship in sociology by Bryn Mawr College, becoming the first woman to receive a graduate fellowship in the United States. She went on to win the Nobel Peace Prize in 1946.

1942
ADELINE GRAY became the first person to jump with a nylon parachute. (Testing with dead weights was used previously.)

1944
Allied forces stormed the beaches of Normandy, France.

A perfect method for adding drama to life is to wait until the deadline looms large.

—*Alyce P. Cornyn-Selby*

Procrastination is the thief of time.

—BEN FRANKLIN

BEN FRANKLIN wasn't the first person to say that (the honor goes to Edward Young, an English poet and dramatist), and he certainly won't be the last. According to counseling centers at colleges and universities (who deal with a lot of procrastinators), we tend to procrastinate when:

- We're following other people's goals instead of our own.
- We're overwhelmed by the size of a project.
- We manage time poorly.
- We're perfectionists.
- We put too much value on others' responses to our work.

How can we deal with procrastination? Here are a few tips.

A WORD TO THE WISE

- Set goals, making sure they're goals *you* want to accomplish.
- Break major tasks down into smaller, bite-size segments that you know you can do.
- Set priorities. Try to avoid minor tasks that don't contribute to your main goals.
- Don't be afraid to fail on your way to success. Thomas Edison tried dozens of filaments before he found the right one for the lightbulb.

A Procrastinator's Inspiration . . .

❦ Pull out your junk drawer, dump it on a nearby tabletop, and discard everything you don't absolutely need. Use silverware organizers or muffin tins to hold small items. Do this every 6 months.

❦ Put clothes that need to be mended or dry-cleaned into a basket and schedule a time to deal with them within a week. Don't hang them in the closet, where they'll be forgotten.

. . . and Salvation

❦ Never start a household project after noon on Saturday. Invariably, you'll need something from the hardware store just as it closes for the weekend. Wait until next week.

Ant Communication

ONE DAY, Ben Franklin found ants inside a small pot of molasses. He shook out all but one of the ants and hung the pot by a string from the ceiling. He watched the lone ant feast on the molasses, then climb the string, make its way across the ceiling, descend a wall, and disappear. Within 30 minutes, a small army of ants appeared, retraced the lone ant's path to the pot, and ate its collective fill. Ben believed that ants use some form of speech to communicate.

THE *Inspired* MIND

In the book *Journey to the Ants,* Bert Hölldobler and Edward O. Wilson conclude that although a majority of ant species use sound—signals delivered by tapping another ant—to communicate, pheromone scents are the favored mode of communication. Chemical trails begin with a single winding, scented path that is straightened by other ants overlaying the quickest route to the food with more scent.

When British Telecom experienced overloaded phone networks in 1997, the firm invented a software program modeled on ant colonies. Thousands of impulses, or "ants," are sent out to explore alternate routes through the network until the jammed configuration is bypassed.

JUNE

7

1909
Actress JESSICA TANDY was born.

1939
King GEORGE VI visited Niagara Falls on the first trip to the United States by a reigning British monarch.

• • •

The two words "information" and "communication" are often used interchangeably, but they signify quite different things. Information is giving out; communication is getting through.

—*Sydney J. Harris*

Ants in Your Plants?

❖ Don't disturb ants that crawl on peony buds and blossoms. They're enjoying the flowers' nectar and protecting the buds from aphids and other pests.

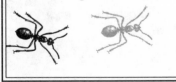

❖ To repel ants in the kitchen, put a few drops of clove or peppermint oil on a cloth and wipe countertops and backsplashes.

❖ Sponge your tabletops and counters with white vinegar and water to discourage houseflies from landing. Keep a vase of mint in the room for the same reason.

❖ Ladybugs are beneficial insects, but when they overpopulate your house, they become, well, pests. To remove them from your home so they can live to eat another aphid, put a clean bag in your vacuum cleaner, suck up the ladybugs, take the vacuum cleaner outside, and reverse the airflow to blow the ladybugs out.

8

1786

An advertisement for ice cream appeared in the *New York Gazette*.

1869

IVES W. McGAFFEY of Chicago patented the vacuum cleaner.

1940

The bald eagle was protected as an endangered species.

• • •

NATURE WATCH

If you see a baby robin alone on the grass or in a shrub, it may not be an orphan; often its parents are close by. If you know where the baby's nest is, simply pick it up and put it back. Despite rumors to the contrary, robins identify their young by sight and sound, not by smell, and will not be turned off by any human scent you leave on the chick.

Ready to Grow Up?

PLANT VINES and climbing plants to create a graceful living screen for privacy, hide an unwanted feature or view, provide shade on a sunny patio, add beauty through flowers and foliage, or simply add interest to your backyard.

PRACTICAL PRIMER

- Plant vines in rich, moist, well-drained soil about 3 inches away from a trellis, arbor, or other support.
- Keep vines well-watered until established—you'll know they've settled in when they start sending out vigorous new growth—and prevent them from drying out during the heat of summer.
- If branches look leggy, pinch them back to encourage bushiness.
- In early fall, prune vines to limit growth and remove dead or damaged wood.

Social Climbers

❦ For quick color to cover a pillar or back wall, plant one of the many varieties of clematis. Plant clematis so that the crown is buried at least 4 to 5 inches below the soil surface. For a stunning, sophisticated medley, plant a climbing rose and a clematis with complementary flower colors on the same trellis or arbor; they'll bloom beautifully together.

❦ Coax a wisteria vine to bloom by removing any stray shoots and cutting vertically into the soil all around the base with a sharp shovel to prune the roots.

❦ Consider perennial hops for a quick-growing vine that will climb up a string without attaching to a wall for support. The most beautiful variety is the golden hop vine; combine it with purple clematis for a dazzling display.

❦ To screen a large patio for shade, invest in perennial stalwarts with woody stems, such as wisteria, climbing hydrangea, trumpet vine, or Boston ivy.

Keep your eyes wide open before marriage, half shut afterwards.

—BEN FRANKLIN

HOLLYWOOD ACTORS are notorious for multiple marriages and quick divorces, but there are exceptions. Robert Mitchum, who appeared in films such as *The Friends of Eddie Coyle* and *The Sundowners,* was happily married for 30 years. To what did he attribute the stability of his marriage? "Mutual forbearance," Mitchum said. "We have each continued to believe that the other will do better tomorrow."

A WORD TO THE WISE

Academy Award–winning actor Charles Laughton (Captain Bligh in *Mutiny on the Bounty*), who was married to actress Elsa Lanchester, was once asked if he would ever consider marrying again. He rejected the idea firmly. When asked why, he replied, "During courtship, a man reveals only his better qualities. After marriage, however, his real self gradually begins to emerge, and there is very little his wife can do about it. I don't believe I would ever put a woman through that again."

EASY ENTERTAINING

❖ Freeze green and red grapes separately in plastic bags. Use them as "ice cubes" to chill wine or punch.

❖ Hollow out red cabbages, colorful bell peppers, or round loaves of bread and fill them with your favorite dips. These creative containers look pretty, and there are no bowls to wash after the party.

❖ Use edible flowers to decorate platters. Apple, borage, calendula, clover, dandelion, daylily, elderberry, lavender, marigold, nasturtium, orange, primrose, rose, violet, and zucchini blossoms are just a few possibilities.

❖ For evening entertaining, set small clusters of votive candles on a framed mirror to add sparkle to the buffet table. Be sure to place the candles so that no one has to reach across them to get food.

1856
A band of 497 Mormons left Iowa City, Iowa, for Salt Lake City, carrying their possessions in two-wheeled handcarts.

1934
Donald Duck made his first film appearance.

1958
The song "Yakety Yak" by the Coasters was released.

—BK

It isn't tying himself to one woman that a man dreads when he thinks of marrying; it's separating himself from all the others.

—*Helen Rowland*

10

1652
The Pine Tree shilling
was minted in the
American colonies
against the wishes of the
British government.

1922
Singer Judy Garland
was born.

1935
Alcoholics Anonymous
was founded.

• • •

**The hardest thing
to raise in my garden
is my knees.**
—*Author Unknown*

Water Garden How-To

WATER CREATES the illusion of space, reflects the sky, invokes tranquillity, and offers an environment for aquatic bog plants and exotic flowers such as lilies and lotuses. Fish add excitement and fun to the pond while eliminating mosquito larvae. Ponds also attract a wonderful array of wildlife, from thirsty birds to dragonflies and frogs.

PRACTICAL PRIMER

Once a water garden is established, it's easy to maintain. Because recirculating pumps reuse water for fountains and waterfalls, water is not wasted. Even the most elaborate water garden requires only about 2 to 3 hours of labor per week, and the maintenance cost is only about $50 per year. Here are a few tips.

❧ Work with whatever space you have. No garden is too small for a fountain or even a tiny pond.

❧ Look for a shaded spot, which will keep algae from forming, but avoid locations directly under large trees, where leaves and debris will be a constant problem.

❧ Before you move any soil or start to dig, be certain you are nowhere near buried electrical and telephone lines. Mistakes can be dangerous and costly.

❧ Make sure the water is at least 50°F before adding water lilies and tender bog plants.

HOME REMEDIES FOR GARDENERS

❖ Garden chores leaving you with blisters? Apply calendula ointment (made from the pot marigold) or make an antiseptic wash with 2 drops of chamomile oil in ½ cup water.

❖ Wrap a strip of flypaper around your hat and fasten it with a paper clip to catch blackflies that swarm around your head. Perhaps you'll start a fashion trend.

❖ For pests, think pesto. Rub basil on the skin as an insect repellent.

❖ If a honeybee stings you, seek the honey plant (*Melissa officinalis*) for relief. Also called lemon balm, it can be crushed into a poultice to ease insect bites, added to your bathwater to soothe frazzled nerves, or made into a tea to ward off insomnia.

❖ Mix together equal parts witch hazel and rubbing alcohol and use it to massage a tired back or sore muscles. This refreshes the skin, too.

*In prosperous fortunes
be modest and wise,
The greatest may fall, and
the lowest may rise.*

—Ben Franklin

For decades, Swiss companies controlled the world market for watches. Then, in 1962, a consortium of Swiss companies funded an effort to develop a new kind of watch, one that would use the minute vibrations from quartz crystals to keep time far more accurately than traditional timepieces. The resulting quartz watch was displayed for the first time at the World Watch Congress in 1967.

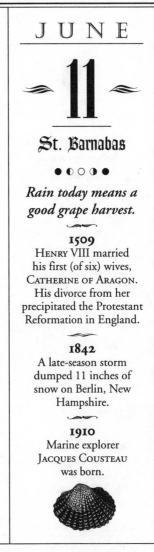

But established Swiss watchmakers weren't convinced that the new watches would sell. After all, they were completely different from regular watches, which used springs and gears to keep time. The Swiss were so indifferent to the new technology that they didn't bother protecting the invention. Japanese companies saw the potential in a technology that was a thousand times more accurate than traditional watches, and they began marketing quartz watches. Within a decade, the Japanese dominated the world market, and Swiss companies held only 10 percent of the market.

Don't let the past hold you back. Always be alert to the possibilities of something new.

A man with a watch knows what time it is. A man with two watches is never sure.

—*Segal's Law*

Rain today means a good grape harvest.

1509
Henry VIII married his first (of six) wives, Catherine of Aragon. His divorce from her precipitated the Protestant Reformation in England.

1842
A late-season storm dumped 11 inches of snow on Berlin, New Hampshire.

1910
Marine explorer Jacques Cousteau was born.

TIME-SAVERS

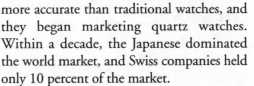

❖ For a quick vegetable dip, add 2 tablespoons salsa to ½ cup sour cream or plain yogurt.

❖ Whenever a messy job rears its ugly head, think about the easiest cleanup. For example, line a bucket with a plastic bag before mixing paint, cement, or glue. Just throw away the liner when you're done.

❖ Buy extra bell peppers and onions and chop more than you need for any given recipe. Freeze them in self-sealing plastic bags or containers to have on hand when you are in a hurry.

JUNE

12

When hornets build their nests high, expect a hot summer.

Birth of JOHANNA SPYRI (1829), Swiss author who wrote *Heidi,* and ANNE FRANK (1920), whose *Diary of a Young Girl* was published on this day in 1952.

1924
Birthday of GEORGE HERBERT WALKER BUSH, 41st president of the United States (1989–1993).

1967
State laws prohibiting interracial marriage were ruled unconstitutional by the U.S. Supreme Court.

∎ ∎ ∎

NATURE WATCH

In the woods and fields of the upland South, watch for the clear rose pink flowers of the mountain phlox *(Phlox ovata),* which grows 12 to 15 inches tall and has a large flower closely resembling that of the cultivated phlox.

Who pleasure gives, shall joy receive.

—BEN FRANKLIN

A WORD TO THE WISE

THE CITIZENS of Zurich, Switzerland, were baffled when posters of a black-and-white Jack Russell terrier began showing up at bus and subway stops around the city. The posters showed the dog in a variety of poses—catching a ball, walking through tall grass, begging on a stool. Although the posters bore no logo or advertising slogan, most people assumed they were being set up for an advertising campaign.

In fact, the posters were a gift to the city's working people from a wealthy businessman, who hired an advertising agency to create them. The donor merely wanted to bring some joy into the lives of city dwellers. When people realized it wasn't an advertising ploy, the agency was swamped with requests for copies of the posters. According to the agency's creative director, "They were extremely happy when they realized the posters were just there for their innocent enjoyment."

THE JOY OF STRAWBERRIES

❖ Strawberries are a great source of vitamin C. For the best-quality berries, don't wash or hull them until just before you are ready to use them. Wash them before removing the caps so that the berries don't get waterlogged.

❖ The size of strawberries is irrelevant to their taste. Both small and large may be sweet.

❖ If you have to keep strawberries longer than a few hours, refrigerate them without washing and cover loosely with waxed paper. Berries mildew quickly, so the best plan is to eat them as soon as possible.

❖ Let small children hull strawberries by pushing a drinking straw through the berry from the bottom. No sharp knives!

Magic Square
(Perfect for a Rainy Day)

JUNE

13

St. Anthony
of Padua

● ○ ○ ●

1967
THURGOOD MARSHALL
became the first African-
American U.S. Supreme
Court justice.

■ ■ ■

BEN FRANKLIN enjoyed astounding his friends by quickly numbering a 64-square grid so that the sum of the numbers in each of the columns and rows (including, amazingly, a series of bent rows) always added up to 260. His "magic square" used plane symmetry and was based on the mathematical formula at left.

$$\frac{n(n^2 + 1)}{2}$$

Do you love trying your hand at puzzles? Here are a few more to make you cudgel your brain.

- S. P. Chandler's 1888 puzzle has 12 unconnected rectangular pieces, each with angular notches, to assemble.
- A block puzzle patented by Allen Dreyer in 1965 has 27 little cubes, all connected by an elastic cord—the trick is to assemble the jumble into a single perfect cube.
- Rubik's Cube, a toy invented by Hungarian Erno Rubik in 1975, uses 2 connected, rotating sets of 8 cubes to stimulate logical thinking.

THE
Inspired
MIND

In 1970, Stewart Coffin of Andover, Massachusetts, began making elegant wooden puzzles with identically shaped symmetrical pieces that can be assembled into interlocking, self-supporting shapes. He reveals how to make many of his 165 or so puzzles in *The Puzzling World of Polyhedral Dissections.* Coffin, like Ben Franklin before him, encourages the free use and application of his inventions.

"Contrariwise,"
continued
Tweedledee, "if it
was so, it might
be; and if it were
so, it would be;
but as it isn't,
it ain't. That's
logic."
—*Lewis Carroll*

Magical (and Logical) Tricks to Remove Stubborn Stains

❆ Saturate an ink stain with milk, or rub it with a cut tomato. Next, soak the whole garment in laundry detergent and cold water, then launder as usual.

❆ To remove pollen, turmeric, or curry stains on washable fabrics, apply a solution of one part hydrogen peroxide and six parts warm water, then launder as usual.

❆ To remove a grease spot from cotton or woolen fabrics, mix cold water and Ivory Liquid, then rub the suds into the spot. Rinse with warm water.

❆ If red wine is spilled, cover the spot with salt. Let stand for a few minutes, then rinse with cold water.

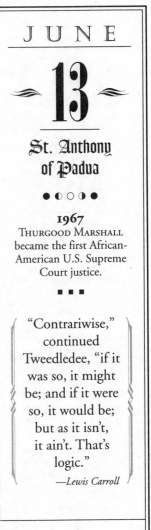

14

Flag Day

● ● ○ ○ ●

1777
The Stars and Stripes became the official U.S. flag.

1811
Birth of HARRIET BEECHER STOWE, author of *Uncle Tom's Cabin.*

1834
ISAAC FISHER was granted a patent for sandpaper.

1921
EVA BEATRICE DYKES became the first African-American woman to receive a Ph.D.

■ ■ ■

FLAG DAY ETIQUETTE

Whenever the flag is to be flown at half-staff, it is always raised to the top of the pole first, then lowered to halfway. Upon bringing it in, first raise it to the top again, then lower it for folding.

He who multiplies riches multiplies cares.

—BEN FRANKLIN

WOULD MORE MONEY make you happier? Most people think so, but the truth is, it might not. Research conducted around the world shows that once basic human needs are met, affluence matters surprisingly little. The correlation between income and personal happiness, notes researcher Ronald Inglehart, "is surprisingly weak." Even lottery winners typically gain only a temporary jolt of joy from their winnings, and their overall happiness usually returns to its prelottery level.

Between 1957 and 1998, real personal wealth in the United States more than doubled. Even so, the percentage of people reporting themselves as "very happy" declined from 35 percent in 1957 to 33 percent in 1998. Once the "basic needs" threshold is crossed, contentment seems to be related to factors other than money: family, friends, community, and health. Even for the very rich, more stuff doesn't equal more happiness.

Not every billionaire believes that, however. Oil magnate Jean Paul Getty was once asked by a reporter if it was true that he was worth more than a billion dollars. "I suppose so," Getty replied. "But remember, a billion dollars doesn't go as far as it used to."

A WORD TO THE WISE

YOU GO, GRILL!

❖ For even browning of meat and poultry, pat the surface with a paper towel to remove moisture before grilling, broiling, or frying.

❖ If your steaks curl on the grill, score the outer layer of fat at 1-inch intervals.

❖ Refrain from pressing hamburger patties on the grill with a spatula. This sacrifices the juices and makes for dry burgers. Similarly, do not puncture sausages while grilling, or the flavorful juices will drip out onto the coals.

❖ Use a sprig of parsley or rosemary for brushing marinade, melted butter, or oil on meat, fish, or vegetables.

Neither trust, nor contend,
nor lay wagers, nor lend;
And you'll have peace to your
Lives end.

—BEN FRANKLIN

IN THE MUSICAL *Guys and Dolls,* Sky Masterson recounts the advice his father gave him about sure bets. One day, the old man said, someone would bet that he could make the jack of spades jump out of a deck of cards and squirt cider in his son's ear. "But son, do not accept this bet, because as sure as you stand there, you're going to wind up with an ear full of cider."

MOZART

Mozart once bet Haydn that he couldn't play a piece Mozart had written that afternoon. Haydn accepted the challenge and got along fine until the end, which required his hands to be at opposite ends of the keyboard while simultaneously playing a note in the middle. Haydn gave up, and Mozart played the piece—by hitting the final note with his nose.

The industrialist John W. Gates once challenged an associate to an odd wager: They each dunked their bread in their coffee, then watched to see which piece attracted more flies. Gates won the $11,000 bet, neglecting to mention that he'd put six spoonfuls of sugar in his coffee first.

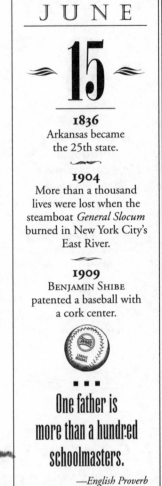

JUNE

15

1836
Arkansas became
the 25th state.

1904
More than a thousand
lives were lost when the
steamboat *General Slocum*
burned in New York City's
East River.

1909
BENJAMIN SHIBE
patented a baseball with
a cork center.

* * *

One father is
more than a hundred
schoolmasters.

—*English Proverb*

Ben's Dear Old Dad

In his *Autobiography,* Ben Franklin wrote affectionately about his father: "He was ingenious, could draw prettily, was skilled a little in music, and had a clear, pleasing voice, so that when he played psalm-tunes on his violin and sung withal, as he sometimes did in an evening after the business of the day was over, it was extremely agreeable to hear."

IN DAD'S BAILIWICK

❧ Keep sheets of sandpaper from curling by storing them between two pieces of plywood cut to size. Wrap the stack with a rubber band.

❧ Keep a package of cupcake liners in your workshop or crafts area and use them, doubled, to hold screws, pins, or other small parts of things you work on.

❧ Put metal shower curtain hooks through keys, tools, and utensils that have holes in the handles so they'll be easy to hang.

16

*When bees
to distance wing
their flight
Days are warm and
skies are bright.*

● ● ○ ○ ●

1806
A total solar eclipse was
observed from California
to Massachusetts.

1963
Soviet cosmonaut
VALENTINA TERESHKOVA
became the first woman
in space.

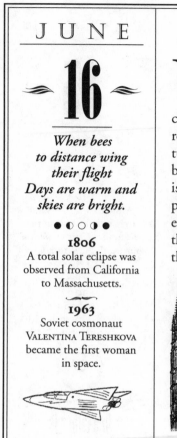

Lore of the Dings

WEATHER LORE about thunder and lightning, based on the experiences of farmers and amateur observers, has been passed down for centuries and included in most almanacs. "If the birds be silent, expect thunder" refers to the peculiar quietness preceding a storm. Watch for fractured flashes: "Forked lightning at night, the next day clear and bright." The idea that thunderstorms aid crops is included in the proverb "Abundance depends on sour milk." Increased atmospheric electricity from lightning oxidizes elements in the air, which can sour standing milk even as the rain helps the crops.

THE
Inspired
MIND

In Europe, people rang church bells during a storm to dissipate thunder and lightning. New bells were often christened with prayers to drive away the demons behind thunderstorms. Although it was well-known that many church spires were struck by lightning and many bell ringers killed, believers were slow to change their ways. A steeple in London, destroyed by lightning in 1750 and again in 1764, was rebuilt in 1768 with no lightning rod, although Ben Franklin had invented the device in 1752.

CONTAINER GARDENING: A MOVABLE FEAST

❖ Soak unglazed clay pots in water for 2 to 3 hours before using. If you don't, they'll soak up the first watering you give your plants.

❖ Use a strawberry jar to hold a compact herb garden. Cover the bottom with potting soil and insert plants in the lower openings. Anchor them with a layer of soil, then continue layering plants and soil to the top, gently tamping down each soil layer.

Thyme (several varieties), marjoram, lemon balm, and trailing mints work well in the side pockets. Put parsley

and chives on top, adding a few nasturtiums for color.

❖ Double-pot your container garden to cut down on the need for watering. Find pots that are at least an inch or two larger than those that hold your plants, make a nest of sphagnum moss inside the larger pots, and nestle the smaller containers into the moss. Soak the moss thoroughly. Double-potting slows evaporation.

A traveler should have a hog's nose, deer's legs, and an ass's back.

—BEN FRANKLIN

SMART TRAVELERS might also want to keep an atlas handy. Two young Brits who planned a vacation to Sydney, Australia, booked their flight on the Internet and took off from London. They realized something was wrong when they changed planes in Halifax, Nova Scotia. Their flight did indeed take them to Sydney—Sydney, Nova Scotia, on the opposite side of the world from Australia. Having come all that way, the misplaced travelers decided to spend a few days vacationing. "We're having fun," Raoul Sebastian told the press at the time. "People are being really nice."

Next time, the couple might want to use a psychic technique called remote viewing, pioneered by a professor at Emory University in Atlanta. (For information, type in "remote viewing" on a Web search engine.) In his book *Cosmic Voyage*, Courtney Brown claims that he used the extrasensory technique to travel to Mars. Of course, he also claims that aliens have visited Earth and are living here among us. Apparently, *they* didn't book their flights on the Internet.

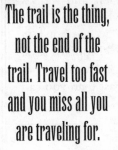

The trail is the thing, not the end of the trail. Travel too fast and you miss all you are traveling for.

—Louis L'Amour

1775
The Battle of Bunker Hill took place in Charlestown, Massachusetts. (It was actually fought on nearby Breed's Hill.) The British won but suffered heavy casualties.

1856
The Republican Party opened its first national convention, held in Philadelphia.

1885
The Statue of Liberty, a gift from the people of France, arrived in New York Harbor in 214 packing cases.

TRUSTY TRAVEL TIPS

❦ On a single sheet of paper, write down the names and addresses of everyone you want to send postcards to on a trip and store the paper in your wallet so it's always handy.

❦ For a quick mileage gauge when traveling, roughly convert miles to kilometers by multiplying by 8, then dividing by 5. To go from kilometers to miles, divide by 8 first, then multiply by 5.

❦ In a notebook or diary, keep track of places you eat and stay while on vacation. Affix business cards or record addresses and phone numbers of special places so you can find your way back.

18

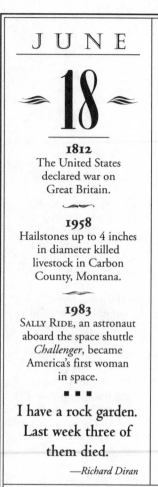

1812
The United States declared war on Great Britain.

1958
Hailstones up to 4 inches in diameter killed livestock in Carbon County, Montana.

1983
SALLY RIDE, an astronaut aboard the space shuttle *Challenger*, became America's first woman in space.

■ ■ ■

I have a rock garden. Last week three of them died.

—*Richard Diran*

The wise and brave dares own that he was wrong.

—BEN FRANKLIN

FILM PRODUCER Samuel Goldwyn, known for his strong opinions, once said, "I am willing to admit that I may not always be right, but I am never wrong."

Daniel Boone, the legendary frontiersman, was asked when he was an old man if he had ever been lost. "No, I can't say I was ever lost," Boone replied. "But I was bewildered once for three days."

Once, at a contentious summit meeting with Nikita Khrushchev, President John F. Kennedy asked the Soviet premier if he ever admitted a mistake. "Certainly I do," Khrushchev said. "In a speech before the Twentieth Party Congress, I admitted all of Stalin's mistakes."

By way of contrast, there's Joe Montana, four-time Super Bowl champion quarterback for the San Francisco 49ers and Kansas City Chiefs, who was willing to take the blame when things went wrong on the field, even if it wasn't his fault. "When you're a leader, you've got to be willing to take the blame," Montana says. "People appreciate when you're not pointing fingers at them, because that just adds to their pressure. If you get past that, you can talk about fixing what went wrong."

LANDSCAPING WITH ROCKS

❖ To encourage plants to cascade from spaces in a stone wall, fill knee-high nylons with rich soil and knot the tops. Force them into the crevices, knotted end first, cut a slit in the end you can see, and tuck a plant inside.

❖ Plant a slope or rock garden with low-growing sedum, candytuft, phlox, thyme, hen and chickens, low-growing campanula, and moss rose.

❖ Around walkways, stepping-stones, and gaps in brick or stone patios, plant

tough, low-growing perennials that can endure some occasional foot traffic without being crushed. Good choices include Roman chamomile, Corsican mint, moss, sedum, thyme, and veronica.

❖ When you need to level heavy stones, use a crowbar to lift them up while a second person replaces the soil underneath.

Skewered Shrimp and Red Rice

Grilled shrimp on red rice makes a festive entrée for Juneteenth.

16 large shrimp, peeled
3 tablespoons olive oil
2 tablespoons chopped fresh
  basil
2 tablespoons butter
1 jar (8 ounces) roasted red
  peppers, drained and
  chopped, or 1 large red
  bell pepper, roasted, peeled,
  and chopped
¼ cup chopped scallions
1 cup long-grain rice
1¾ cups water
Salt and freshly ground black
  pepper

In a large bowl, toss the shrimp with the olive oil and basil and let stand for 30 minutes. Preheat the grill. Meanwhile, melt the butter in a 2-quart saucepan and sauté the peppers and scallions for about 2 minutes. With a slotted spoon, remove the peppers and scallions from the skillet and puree them in a blender; set aside. In the same skillet, sauté the rice until translucent. Add the water, cover, and cook until tender, about 20 minutes. Stir in the pepper puree and add salt and pepper to taste. Thread the shrimp onto 4 skewers and grill for 5 minutes, turning once.

Makes 4 servings

CUTTING BOARD WISDOM

❦ Avoid setting a hot pot on a cutting board. The surface can retain heat, creating a warm environment that encourages bacterial growth.

❦ Rub cutting boards vigorously with lemon juice and salt to clean.

❦ If your cutting board slips while you're chopping, place a damp dish towel on the counter under it. You'll find this technique works especially well with Plexiglas boards.

❦ Keep your cutting board from imparting odors and oils to milder foods by labeling the ends of the board with an indelible marker —"strong" for one end and "mild" for the other.

❦ If chopping onions makes you cry, sprinkle vinegar on the cutting board before chopping.

*Wet June,
dry September.*

● ◐ ○ ◑ ●

1865
By order of the occupying Union army in Galveston, all Texas slaves were freed. The anniversary, known as Juneteenth (a contraction of June 19), is celebrated around the country as African-American Emancipation Day.

❧

1912
The federal government established the 8-hour workday.

1978
The National Weather Service broke with long-standing tradition by assigning a male name—Bud—to a tropical storm.

■ ■ ■

What is patriotism but the love of the good things we ate in our childhood?

—*Lin Yü-t'ang*

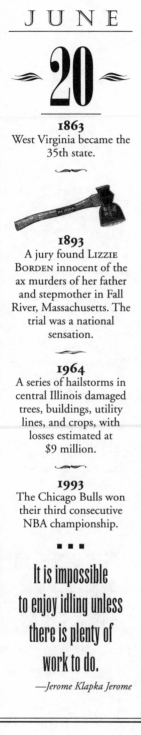

1893
A jury found LIZZIE BORDEN innocent of the ax murders of her father and stepmother in Fall River, Massachusetts. The trial was a national sensation.

1964
A series of hailstorms in central Illinois damaged trees, buildings, utility lines, and crops, with losses estimated at $9 million.

1993
The Chicago Bulls won their third consecutive NBA championship.

• • •

It is impossible to enjoy idling unless there is plenty of work to do.

—*Jerome Klapka Jerome*

Summertime . . . And the Living Could Be Easier

EASY OR NOT, summertime makes its debut with the summer solstice, the time of longest daylight in the Northern Hemisphere (June 20–23, depending on the year). Use that as a cue to hang up your hammock and take stock of what it is you're working for. Perhaps you believe, as did the English dramatist Noel Coward, that "work is much more fun than fun." If so, you're one of the lucky ones. By contrast, the Greek philosopher Aristotle believed that "we work, in order to have leisure."

PRACTICAL PRIMER

With fewer leisure hours these days, it's good to be clear on how you want to spend your free time when you have it. Most important, make sure that your time off is time *off*. Take a break. Ignore the housework. If yard work is leisure for you, go for it; otherwise, let it wait. Go for a bike ride. Have coffee with a friend. See a show. Read a good book (not a trade magazine). Do anything but work, so that when you do return to your job, you'll be refreshed.

FUN TIME FOR KIDS

❧ Let children make a simple bug box and collect ladybugs or other nonstinging insects.

❧ Wishing your child would read more? Consider starting a parent-child book group this summer with other readers at approximately the same level.

❧ Encourage children to hold a cookie sale or open a lemonade stand, then let them choose where to donate the proceeds.

❧ Post a checklist by the door to help kids remember the things they need to take to day camp or sports events.

The second vice is lying; the first is running in debt.

—Ben Franklin

COMEDIAN JACKIE GLEASON was just getting started in his career when he found himself unable to pay the rent at the seaside boardinghouse where he was staying. To sneak out without paying, he lowered his suitcase out his window to a waiting friend, then walked out of the house in his swimsuit as if he were going to the beach. Years later, he returned to pay the debt he owed and nearly gave the landlady a heart attack. "Oh my lord," she exclaimed. "I thought you were drowned!"

A WORD TO THE WISE

Here are a few tips for getting out of debt without having to sneak out on it.

- Pay off high-interest debts first. It's better to pay off a credit card that's charging between 10 and 20 percent interest than to make extra payments on your mortgage, since mortgage interest is generally lower and tax deductible.
- Don't buy a new car as soon as you finish paying for your current car.
- Stop juggling debt. Moving debt around from one credit card to another isn't the same as paying it off.

JUNE

21

A north wind in June foretells a good rye harvest.

● ○ ○ ○ ●

1788
New Hampshire became the ninth state.

1834
Cyrus McCormick received a patent for his reaping machine.

1948
Columbia Records introduced the long-playing (LP) record.

1997
The Women's National Basketball Association played its first game.

Reap It and Weep: Help for Hay Fever

❖ Pollen, ragweed, fungal spores—any of these can bring on the congestion and itchy, runny eyes and nose of hay fever. When you come inside, wash your hands and face and run a damp washcloth over your hair to minimize the pollen you bring along. Change your pillowcase often.

❖ If you have asthma, drink chamomile tea, a natural antihistamine. Or decoct Roman chamomile flowers and inhale the steam. (A decoction is a cooking down, or boiling, of herbal ingredients. Soak the flowers overnight in cool water, then bring them to a boil and simmer for 10 to 20 minutes, inhaling all the while.)

❖ Herbal remedies for hay fever include goldenrod, goldenseal, and ribwort, all considered toners for the respiratory system. Teas of dandelion root, chamomile, hyssop, nettle, or thyme sometimes help.

GOLDENROD

When flowers bloom, I hope you'll not sneeze, And may you always have someone to squeeze!

—*Irish Blessing*

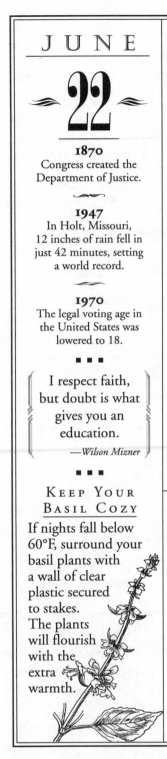

JUNE

22

1870
Congress created the
Department of Justice.

1947
In Holt, Missouri,
12 inches of rain fell in
just 42 minutes, setting
a world record.

1970
The legal voting age in
the United States was
lowered to 18.

• • •

I respect faith,
but doubt is what
gives you an
education.

—*Wilson Mizner*

• • •

KEEP YOUR
BASIL COZY

If nights fall below
60°F, surround your
basil plants with
a wall of clear
plastic secured
to stakes.
The plants
will flourish
with the
extra
warmth.

Making Sense of the Census

THE
Inspired
MIND

BEN FRANKLIN was the first newspaper editor in America to publish lists of burials, keeping track of Philadelphia deaths beginning in 1729. In 1751, he published *Observations Concerning the Increase of Mankind, Peopling of Countries, &c.,* which contained his ideas on demographics. Based on his observations of births, deaths, and marriages, Ben calculated that the American colonies would double in population every 25 years. "There are suppos'd to be now [1751] upwards of One Million English Souls in North-America," he wrote. From there, he projected a population of 2 million in 1776 and 4 million in 1801. The 1790 U.S. census total of 3.9 million proved that he was on track. Ben's prophecy held true roughly until the early 20th century. Whereas his 25-year doubling calculation would have yielded 128 million by 1926, the Census Bureau counted only 123 million Americans in 1930.

Ben also correctly wrote, "The Number of purely white People in the World is proportionably very small." Today the Census Bureau predicts that by 2060, the United States will have a majority of non-Whites—for the first time since Ben's century.

STASH IT IN THE FREEZER

❦ If you store plastic wrap in the freezer or refrigerator, it will not cling to itself.

❦ You can save space by freezing soup in self-sealing plastic bags laid flat to freeze.

❦ Storing popcorn in the freezer makes more kernels pop.

❦ Foods that contain natural oils—oatmeal, whole-grain flours and cornmeal, shelled

nuts, brown rice, coffee—will stay fresh longer if they are stored in the freezer.

❦ When you bring a bag of flour home from the store, seal it in a plastic bag and store it in the freezer for 48 hours to kill any insect eggs.

Pride is said to be the last vice the good man gets clear of.

—Ben Franklin

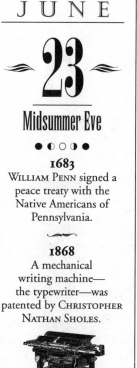

● ○ ○ ● ●

1683
William Penn signed a peace treaty with the Native Americans of Pennsylvania.

1868
A mechanical writing machine—the typewriter—was patented by Christopher Nathan Sholes.

1953
An armistice ending the Korean War was signed.

A WORD TO THE WISE

BEN SHOULD KNOW. When he compiled his list of cardinal virtues (see January 1), there were originally only 12. But when a friend pointed out that Ben was often overbearing and insolent in discussions, Ben got the message. He added humility to the list and determined to expunge the vice of pride from his character. He removed words such as *certainly* and *undoubtedly* from his speech and avoided contradicting his opponents, even if he knew them to be wrong. As a result, he found that people were more receptive to his ideas and more likely to agree with him when he was right. And he was less embarrassed when he was proved wrong.

By his own admission, Ben was never a great public speaker. He often hesitated when trying to choose the right word and occasionally violated the rules of grammar. But he became known for his tact and diplomacy, a characteristic that made him increasingly influential with his peers.

> We must take human nature as we find it; perfection falls not to the share of mortals.
>
> —*George Washington*

THINNING, SNIPPING, AND PINCHING

❖ Thin beets, carrots, parsnips, and onions so you can get three fingers between individual plants.

❖ To harvest mesclun, snip straight across the entire planting every 2 to 3 weeks, when the leaves are no more than 2 to 3 inches tall.

❖ When brussels sprouts begin to form on the stalks, pinch back the tips of the plants to encourage vigorous growth.

❖ When new raspberry shoots are several feet tall, pinch off the tips to encourage side branching.

❖ Pinch off the growing points of chrysanthemum plants until the Fourth of July to make them bushy.

❖ Thin forget-me-not plants to 10 inches apart so their roots have room to develop.

24

St. John the Baptist

Midsummer Day

Rain today brings a wet harvest.

● ● ○ ○ ○ ●

1497
JOHN CABOT sighted the coast of Canada.

1895
Birth of boxing champion JACK DEMPSEY.

1949
The movie features of Hopalong Cassidy, starring WILLIAM BOYD as Hopalong, premiered on TV, edited to 30- and 60-minute versions.

■ ■ ■

Nothing is as obnoxious as other people's luck.

—*F. Scott Fitzgerald*

Fortune is as fickle as she's fair.

—BEN FRANKLIN

THIS SAYING, which comes from a collection of Ben Franklin's precepts about how to get rich, could certainly describe the case of Larry Hatch, who bought a couple of drinks at Burger King during a sweepstakes giveaway. Peeling the stickers off the drinks, he found that one of them contained the winning ticket, worth $1 million. Since the photocopier at the restaurant was broken, he took the ticket to a nearby grocery store to have a copy made. Returning home, he realized that he had the copy but not the original ticket. In a panic, he retraced his steps to the grocery store and found the ticket lying on the floor near the checkout lane, where it had fallen out of his pocket. It had lain on the floor for 3 hours, and one wonders how many people had walked over it without realizing they were stepping over a million dollars.

Celebrate Midsummer Day with a Swimming Party

By tradition, today was the earliest day deemed safe for swimming, because of its connection with St. John the Baptist, who blessed Jesus in the Jordan River. Also, most lakes and swimming holes will have warmed up by now. Here are some ideas for hosting a swimming party today.

☾ Pour some party punch into a ring mold and add a handful

of fresh berries, fresh mint leaves, or edible flower petals, then freeze. When you float the ice ring in the punch bowl, it will look beautiful and won't water down the punch.

☾ For a poolside party, float an assortment of colorful beach balls in the pool or suspend a few in bunches like balloons.

☾ Check fabrics before you use insect repellent. Bathing suits made of stretch fabrics, spandex exercise suits, and synthetic fabrics used for tents and windbreakers may be damaged by the application of bug dope. Test a hidden swatch first.

For a Good Time, Dial C-O-M-P-O-S-T

COMPOSTING is easy, efficient, and fun. It provides a balanced fertilizer for your plants; it's a great way to recycle garden debris and kitchen scraps (no meat, bones, or fats, though—unless you *like* attracting vermin); and you can shake it through a garden sifter to make the world's best potting soil. Just pile up the leaves, grass clippings, and scraps and watch the pile transform itself into rich, crumbly compost. If you prefer a neater look, contain the pile in a bin. Read on for some quick compost tips.

PRACTICAL PRIMER

- To help your compost pile break down faster, water it with an infusion of yarrow or chamomile or add chopped comfrey leaves.
- Turn your compost pile with a pitchfork about once every 2 weeks. When you turn up dark, crumbly, practically odorless stuff that looks like good dirt, congratulations—you've made compost. Apply it to plants as is without fear of burning or overfertilizing.

- Mix one part finished compost with five parts water in a large barrel or trash can, cover, and let sit for a week. Then strain and use the liquid as compost tea for your plants. You can use the spent compost as a side-dressing in the garden.

NEVER TOO LATE

Getting a late start on this year's garden? Go to your local nursery and look for bargains. Leggy petunia, salvia, alyssum, or cosmos plants will thrive in your beds. Pinch them back to a presentable shape, tuck them into your garden to fill in gaps between perennials, and water diligently to coax out the next round of blooms.

26

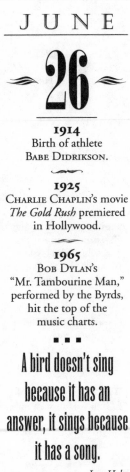

1914
Birth of athlete
BABE DIDRIKSON.

1925
CHARLIE CHAPLIN'S movie
The Gold Rush premiered
in Hollywood.

1965
BOB DYLAN'S
"Mr. Tambourine Man,"
performed by the Byrds,
hit the top of the
music charts.

∎ ∎ ∎

**A bird doesn't sing
because it has an
answer, it sings because
it has a song.**

—*Lou Holtz*

He who buys has need of one hundred eyes, but one's enough for him that sells the stuff.

—BEN FRANKLIN

A FAMOUS OPERA SINGER named Giovanni Martinelli once appeared in a print advertisement in which he claimed that a particular brand of cigarettes never irritated his throat. Later, Martinelli was questioned by an interviewer about his tobacco usage and denied that he smoked. The interviewer reminded him of the cigarette endorsement, and Martinelli replied that it was entirely accurate. "How could they irritate my throat?" he said. "I have never smoked."

A piano maker asked Will Rogers for an endorsement of its pianos, which he had never played. Rogers replied, "Dear sirs, I guess your pianos are about the best I ever leaned against."

A restaurant once put out this sign: The Best Food in Town. Indignant, the restaurant across the street posted another sign: The Best Food in the State. The first establishment responded with The Best Food in the Country, and the competitor came back with The Best Food in the World. Finally, a small restaurant nearby brought the contest to an end with its sign: The Best Food on This Street.

BACKYARD BATHS FOR BIRDS AND BUGS

❖ One way to attract more birds to your yard is by adding a birdbath. Any clean, shallow dish can suffice, as long as the birds can get knee-deep (but no deeper). Keep it clean and filled throughout the  season, and place it where the birds won't be sitting ducks for cats.

❖ In a dry summer, even the beneficial bugs, such as butterflies and predatory wasps, need a source of water. Make a bug-size birdbath by filling a small tray with stones or gravel and keeping them wet but not immersed. Butterflies also enjoy mud puddles, where they can take up minerals from the mud along with water.

❖ Birds need dust baths to ward off parasites. Leave an area of mixed soil and sand, perhaps below the bowl of a birdbath, for this purpose.

Whole Wheat Buttermilk Biscuits

These tender biscuits are irresistible when split, toasted, and buttered like English muffins.

1½ cups whole wheat flour

1½ cups all-purpose flour

1 teaspoon baking powder

1 teaspoon sugar

¼ teaspoon salt

½ teaspoon baking soda

1 cup buttermilk

1 tablespoon canola oil

3 tablespoons sour cream

Preheat the oven to 425°F. Sift together the flours, baking powder, sugar, and salt. Dissolve the baking soda in the buttermilk and combine with the oil and sour cream in a large bowl. Stir the dry ingredients into the liquid mixture with a fork. Knead lightly on a floured surface until uniform in texture, then roll out on a lightly floured board to ½ inch thick. Cut into 3-inch rounds and place on a greased baking sheet. Bake for 8 to 10 minutes, then turn over and bake for 4 to 5 minutes more. Cool on a wire rack. *Makes 12*

TIPS FOR BAKING BETTER BREAD

❖ To prevent sogginess, cool freshly baked breads and muffins on a wire rack so that air circulates around them.

❖ For a soft bread crust, brush loaves lightly with melted butter as soon as they come out of the oven.

❖ For a beautiful crust and even browning, bake bread in a black pan, which will absorb and transmit heat more efficiently than a shiny pan.

Gather Ye Roses

☙ Prune climbing roses after they flower, not before.

☙ To cut down on disease, rake up leaves that fall off your rosebushes and keep the area under them clean.

☙ Sprinkle Epsom salts around the bases of rosebushes to supply needed minerals.

☙ Save banana peels and bury them around your rosebushes to provide potassium.

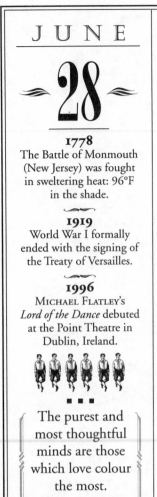

JUNE

28

1778

The Battle of Monmouth (New Jersey) was fought in sweltering heat: 96°F in the shade.

1919

World War I formally ended with the signing of the Treaty of Versailles.

1996

MICHAEL FLATLEY'S *Lord of the Dance* debuted at the Point Theatre in Dublin, Ireland.

■ ■ ■

The purest and most thoughtful minds are those which love colour the most.

—John Ruskin

What Color Shall We Paint the House, Dear?

WHETHER YOU HIRE a crew of college students or decide to paint your house yourself, you still have to pick the color. Here are a few guidelines to help in this momentous decision.

❧ Before picking out an exterior paint color, consider how your house relates to the sun. All colors look lighter under the sun's glare, darker in the shade. Once you narrow down your choice of colors, take your samples outside at different times of the day to see how they look in natural light.

PRACTICAL PRIMER

❧ Don't forget to coordinate with your roof color, or you may be disappointed with the overall effect. Also consider any painted doors, brick accents, landscaping, and porch or step railings you may have and how their colors will work with your chosen shade.

❧ If you're still undecided, choose a few finalists, then test them on an inconspicuous area of your house. Wait several days before making a decision.

❧ Although trims and accents are fun, a small home generally looks better with fewer paint colors. For a larger home, try a main color accented by several other colors.

HOUSE-PAINTING HINTS

❖ Keep bugs away from your paint and paint can by adding a few drops of liquid citronella to the paint.

❖ Dip no more than half of the length of your paintbrush bristles into the paint can to avoid overloading your brush. Then gently tap the brush on the side of the can, rather than wiping it.

❖ Spray hot vinegar on old paint on windowpanes. This softens the paint and makes it easy to scrape off.

❖ If your house needs more than one coat, put on one coat this year, then wait 2 or 3 years for the second coat. The paint will be less likely to peel in the long run.

❖ To paint a set of steps efficiently, start by painting alternating steps one day, then do the remaining steps the next day. That way, you'll be able to use the stairs.

Vainglory flowereth, but beareth no fruit.

—Ben Franklin

W HEN BEN FRANKLIN began signing up contributors for the first subscription library in North America, he wasn't very successful. Eventually, he decided he would present the project as originating with a group of friends rather than being his own pet project, lest he be suspected of self-promotion. Subscriptions to the library promptly took off.

Ben determined to conduct all his future affairs in the same way and encouraged others to do the same. "The present little sacrifice of your vanity will afterwards be amply repaid," he said. What if someone else takes credit for your work? No problem, said Ben. People who are envious of the claim jumpers will eventually expose their pretense, and you'll get the credit you deserve.

When actor Spencer Tracy was starring with Katharine Hepburn, he always insisted on having his name listed first in the credits. A director challenged him, saying it was more gallant to let the lady go first. Tracy replied, "This is a movie, not a lifeboat."

A WORD TO THE WISE

If the English language made any sense, lackadaisical would have something to do with a shortage of flowers.

—Doug Larson

Rain today rots the roots of the rye.

1906
Colorado National Monument, containing ancient cliff dwellings, was dedicated.

1956
CHARLES DUMAS broke the 7-foot barrier in the high jump.

1994
All-time state records for high temperature were set at Lake Havasu City, Arizona (128°F), and Laughlin, Nevada (125°F).

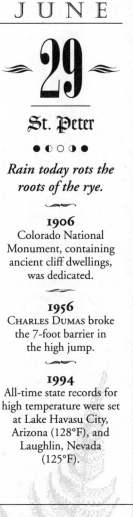

TAKE A HIKE

❖ If you or your boots are new to hiking, include a blister kit in your backpack: premoistened wipes, antiseptic cream, nail scissors, and moleskin.

❖ Control foot odor by sprinkling baking soda into socks before wearing them.

❖ If a long hike gives you hot, tired feet, try putting a few ferns inside your socks.

When June Is Busting Out All Over

☾ If your roses or peonies are in full bloom, consider nesting a tea candle inside one of the extravagant blossoms, then placing the flower in a shallow bowl of water. The warmth of the candle will bring out the flower's fragrance.

☾ Dry pansies and ferns by pressing them between paper towels in a heavy book. Display them in a photo frame.

30

1906
The U.S. Pure Food and Drugs Act and the Meat Inspection Act were passed.

1966
The National Organization for Women was founded.

1972
As a result of catastrophic flooding caused by Hurricane Agnes, the entire state of Pennsylvania was declared a disaster area. Forty-eight people died, and $2.1 billion in damage was sustained.

• • •

NATURE WATCH

The humble spiderwort *(Tradescantia virginiana)* is blooming now. Although it is a native of woods and thickets in the East, you can readily find it in the Great Plains along railroad embankments in full sun. Flowers range from pure white to blue and violet. Enjoy it in the morning, for the flowers fade by midday.

Is It Ripe?

PRACTICAL PRIMER

FORBIDDEN FRUIT is sweet, but luckily so is the vine-ripened summer bounty found at your farmers' market or local fruit and vegetable stand. Let your nose tell you when cantaloupes, honeydew melons, pineapples, peaches, plums, and nectarines are ripe. All should offer a mild perfume but not an overpowering scent.

🍂 A pineapple leaf should yield to a gentle tug.

🍂 When you thump a watermelon, it should go "plunk," not "plink."

🍂 When you shake a honeydew melon, listen for a watery sound and loose seeds.

🍂 Berries should appear plump, not wrinkled. Fruit-stained baskets may indicate overripe fruit.

🍂 Ripe mangoes and papayas should feel heavy for their size and have smooth skin. Both will continue to ripen, softening slightly so they yield to the touch.

FAVORITE FRUIT FACTS

❖ Cover your fruit bowl to avoid fruit flies and accelerate ripening.

❖ Try using peach pits as scrapers for pots and pans.

❖ Too much fruit? Blend it with yogurt for easy fruit smoothies. Or freeze pureed fruit into Popsicles.

❖ To pit cherries in a pinch, wash the cherries and take off the stems. Unfold a sterilized paper clip and push the rounded part into the cherry close to the stem end. Hook the pit and pull it out. You will lose very little juice or flesh.

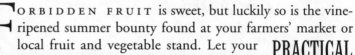

❖ Before you buy red or green grapes, shake the bunch gently. If grapes fall off easily, they are past their prime. Look for grapes that hug the stems.

The ripest peach is highest on the tree.
—James Whitcomb Riley

JULY, *the Seventh Month*

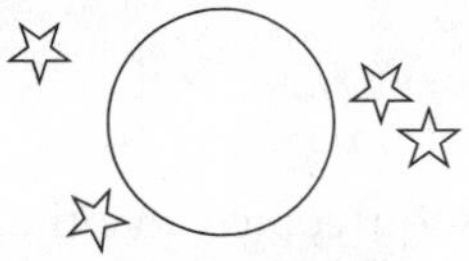

Full Buck Moon

is the Native American name for this month's moon, inspired by the new velvety antlers of male deer.
It's also called the *Full Thunder Moon* for the dramatic weather July brings.

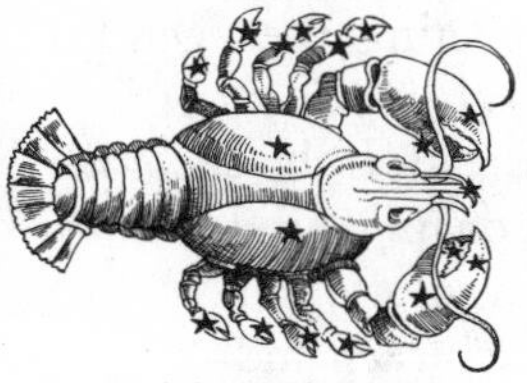

Sign of the Zodiac: Cancer
(June 21–July 22)

Element: Water

Quality: Sensitive

Birthstone: Ruby

Flower: Larkspur

JULIUS CAESAR named July after himself when he reworked the old Roman calendar. (Ironically, the change went into effect in 44 B.C., the year Caesar was assassinated.) Although Earth is at its farthest point (aphelion) from the sun this month, the sunshine comes with enough power to make July the warmest month in most of the country. Sweet corn—knee-high by the Fourth of July, with luck—thrives now, and an attentive gardener literally can hear it growing (just listen for a creaking sound).

Old-timers know that "the gardener's shadow is the best manure," and it's wise this month to concentrate on one task: weeding. Weeds have one goal in life: to survive long enough to go to seed and thus perpetuate themselves. The gardener's job is to keep them from succeeding. Bury them in mulch, dig them up, chop their heads off—whatever it takes to keep the balance of power in favor of the plants you want.

The hot and humid dog days begin on the 3rd. For many of us, this is a sign to start our vacations. July is for sailboats and lemonade, thunderstorms and ripe peaches, haying and fireworks. Traditionalists eat eggs on St. Swithin's Day (the 15th) and oysters on St. James's Day (the 25th). The rest of us fire up our grills or head for the clam shack.

JULY

1

Canada Day

● ○ ○ ○ ●

1731
America's first private lending library was founded by Ben Franklin in Philadelphia.

1819
The Toleration Act, ending a tax levied against citizens for support of their local church minister, was passed in New Hampshire.

■ ■ ■

If you have a garden and a library, you have everything you need.

—*Marcus Tullius Cicero*

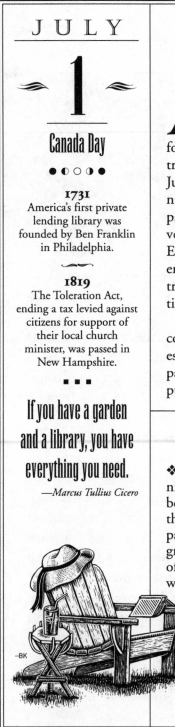

Ben Franklin's Subscription Library

AMERICA'S FIRST lending library grew out of Ben Franklin's suggestion to fellow members of the Junto, a club devoted to intellectual advancement, that their efforts could be aided by a depository of books. Fifty artisans and tradesmen signed the charter to establish a subscription library on July 1, 1731, paying a membership fee and annual dues. Ben's brainchild, the Library Company of Philadelphia, was spectacularly diverse. The first shipment of books from England included books on law, natural science, astronomy, and mathematics; a how-to treatise for tradesmen; *Gulliver's Travels;* Homer's *Iliad;* and a dictionary of gardening.

Although Ben's subscription library was soon copied in other colonies, it wasn't until 1833 that the first free public library was established, in Peterborough, New Hampshire. The Library Company of Philadelphia continues in operation today. It is free to the public, and, just as in Ben's time, anyone may join.

Keep Your Lawn Furniture Spiffy

❖ Plastic or resin outdoor furniture is susceptible to stains because it is porous. To prevent this, apply car wax to all resin parts. When the furniture gets grimy, clean it with a solution of 1 part vinegar and 10 parts water, then reapply the wax.

❖ Steel or cast-iron furniture left outdoors may rust easily. Sand any suspect areas immediately, then apply a rust-resistant touch-up paint designed for exterior use.

❖ Avoid detergents when cleaning the cushions on outdoor furniture. To maintain their protective coating, use a gentle soap such as Ivory Snow or Woolite instead. If the cushions are stained or mildewed, wash them with a solution of ¼ cup nonchlorine bleach and 2½ gallons water, then follow up with an outdoor fabric finish.

❖ Consider how you will store porch, deck, or lawn furniture over the winter before you buy anything.

Trusty Must-Removal Tricks

THOSE MUSTY MAGAZINES and old books you found in the cellar or garage can be made odor-free if the pages aren't stuck together. First, lay the items out in the sun for a day. Next, open them at random and sprinkle the pages with baking soda. Let sit for at least an hour, then brush off. Repeat until the musty smell disappears.

To neutralize musty smells that come with storage, place an open box of baking soda inside a travel trunk, gym bag, or piece of luggage and leave it there overnight.

PRACTICAL
PRIMER

For ongoing must control in a garage or basement, hang grocery bags with handles from the rafters. Put about ½ inch of baking soda in each bag and replace it every 3 months or so. Keep the space ventilated as well as possible. If your cellar is closed and damp, invest in a heavy-duty dehumidifier. It'll cost more than baking soda but less than repairing the damage to your possessions.

> Never interrupt someone doing what you said couldn't be done.
> —*Amelia Earhart*

J U L Y

2

Ne'er trust a July sky.

● ○ ○ ○ ●

1937
Aviator AMELIA EARHART disappeared over the Pacific Ocean.

1964
President LYNDON JOHNSON signed the Civil Rights Act.

2002
STEVE FOSSETT became the first person to make a solo flight around the world in a balloon, accomplishing the feat in 13 days.

FLEA MARKET FINDS

❦ Summer is the time for auctions and flea markets. If you come home with an antique bureau that smells musty inside, make simple pomanders of green apples stuck with whole cloves. Place one in each drawer to restore the clean smell.

❦ If you have just bought a piece of antique wicker furniture and notice that it smells of mildew, eliminate the smell by washing the furniture with a solution of one part vinegar and one part water. Use a toothbrush to get the mixture into all the crevices. Use straight vinegar if the problem persists.

❦ Yard sales are great places to find bargain wineglasses, brandy snifters, or martini glasses, which you can use to hold votive or tea candles. Add a bit of water at the base of the candle to protect the glasses.

JULY

3

*Dog days bright and
clear, indicate a
happy year.*

● ◑ ○ ◑ ●

1775
GEORGE WASHINGTON
took command of the
Continental Army.

1863
The Battle of Gettysburg,
turning point of the Civil
War, ended with the
Confederates' withdrawal.

1890
Idaho became
the 43rd state.

■ ■ ■

LORE & LEGEND

DOG DAYS (July 3–
August 11) were so
named in ancient
Egypt because they
coincided with the
rising at dawn of the
Dog Star, Sirius. If it
rains on the first dog
day, it will rain for 40
days after, according
to the weather lore
for these traditionally
hot and sultry days.

What can be done, with care perform today, dangers unthought-of will attend delay.

—BEN FRANKLIN

CHARLES SCHWAB, the chairman of Bethlehem Steel, once asked a consultant how he could work more efficiently. The consultant followed Schwab around for a day and gave him this simple advice: Make a list of priority items to accomplish each day. Don't move on to the second item until the first is completed.

Schwab didn't think much of this advice but asked the consultant how much he charged. The consultant told him to use the method for 6 months and then send him whatever he thought it was worth. Six months later, Schwab sent him a check for $25,000.

A WORD TO THE WISE

In battle, as in business, delay is often catastrophic. Napoleon lost the Battle of Waterloo because one of his generals delayed in attacking the duke of Wellington. General George Meade's failure to pursue General Robert E. Lee's troops after the Battle of Gettysburg undoubtedly prolonged the Civil War.

Got an unpleasant task to perform? Do it first. Imagine how nice it will be not to have it hanging over your head.

Tackling Those Unpleasant Tasks

❖ To vanquish bathroom soap scum, combine 1 gallon warm water, ¼ cup baking soda, ½ cup vinegar, and 1 cup ammonia. Ventilate the area. Use a sponge mop and apply the mixture to the bathtub or shower. Rinse well.

❖ Remove a dab of tar or another sticky substance from carpeting by rubbing in vegetable oil, then blotting it up. After the stickiness is gone, wash the area with mild soap and water.

❖ For a really messy job, make a disposable dustpan by cutting an aluminum pie plate in half.

❖ At least once a year, take the filter out of your range hood and run it through a normal dishwasher cycle. Wipe the fan blades with all-purpose cleaner to remove grease.

Grilling Up a Great Fourth of July

What's July 4 without a picnic? And what's a picnic without yummy burgers, hot dogs, or steaks hot off the grill? Here are some tips for great grilling.

- Spray the cold grill with nonstick cooking spray.
- Cook thin meat fast over direct heat, turning once. If the meat is thicker on one end, place the thin end away from the highest heat. If the meat is uniformly thick, place it on indirect heat so the inside will cook completely.
- Most sauces contain sugar, which blackens on the grill, so apply barbecue sauce near the end of the cooking time.

PRACTICAL PRIMER

- Cook salmon on a plank. Buy an untreated, construction-grade 1- by 8-foot cedar plank, cut into 1-foot lengths, and soak overnight in water. Place one piece of wood on the grill and cook your salmon on it. The salmon will stay moist and be subtly flavored by the wood.
- Put whole bananas (unpeeled) on the grill. Cook for 8 to 10 minutes, turning frequently. Peel and serve with a little butter and brown sugar.
- To achieve that real steak house flavor, sprinkle brown sugar, garlic powder, and black pepper on steak before grilling.

JULY

4

Independence Day

● ○ ○ ● ●

1826
Thomas Jefferson and John Adams died.

1872
Birthday of Calvin Coolidge, 30th president of the United States (1923–1929).

1911
It was a hot Fourth of July in New England. All-time state records were set in Nashua, New Hampshire (106°F), and Vernon, Vermont (105°F).

Picnics and the Pursuit of Happiness

Where the press is free and every man able to read, all is safe.

—*Thomas Jefferson*

❦ Listen to old-timers, who say that ants won't cross a thick chalk line. If you bring a pie to a picnic, draw a chalk circle around it, and it might be safe—from ants at least.

❦ While the coals are cooling off, use the residual heat to loosen that sticky residue on a cast-iron pan. Place the pan inside the grill, then scrape off the residue.

❦ Use cobalt blue glassware to lend a deliciously cool look to your table. A dozen lemons in a cobalt blue bowl, a dozen sunflowers in a cobalt blue vase, ice-cold fresh lemonade in a cobalt blue pitcher—you get the cobalt blue picture.

❦ To repel houseflies, sprinkle the kitchen tablecloth or window screens with a mixture of 2 tablespoons oil of lavender and 1 cup water or rubbing alcohol (preferably the latter).

5

*Much thunder in
July injures wheat
and barley.*

● ◐ ◑ ○ ●

1891
In Rapid City, South
Dakota, hail killed 16
horses, and many more
had to be put down due to
injuries from the storm.

1975
ARTHUR ASHE defeated
JIMMY CONNORS at
Wimbledon.

1996
Scientists at the Roslin
Institute, near Edinburgh,
Scotland, successfully
cloned a mammal from an
adult cell. The birth of
Dolly, a ewe, was not
made public until
February 22, 1997.

Anger and folly walk cheek-by-jowl; repentance treads on both their heels.

—BEN FRANKLIN

ALEXANDER THE GREAT, probably the greatest military leader of all time, conquered everything except his own temper. Once, while drinking with some companions, he got into an argument with his best friend, Cleitus, who had saved his life at the Battle of Granicus. Alexander jokingly accused Cleitus of cowardice, and Cleitus replied that it was cowards like him who had made Alexander great. The verbal sparring escalated until Alexander angrily threw a spear at Cleitus, killing him. According to the historian Plutarch, the great conqueror was so full of remorse that he cried for a day and a half.

Here are some tips from the American Psychological Association on getting the best of your anger before it gets the best of you.

- Learn how to relax, using techniques such as deep breathing, positive imaging, and yoga.
- Restructure the problem, viewing it in a different way so that it doesn't seem like the end of the world.
- Learn how to communicate better and thus avoid misunderstandings.
- Use humor to defuse your own anger.

Back Off, Burn

❮ To ease a mild sunburn, apply cider vinegar, witch hazel, or cold peppermint tea.

❮ Bathe a sunburned face in buttermilk. It's great for the complexion, too.

❮ Add some black or green tea to your bathwater to soothe sunburned skin. Or pat sunburned skin with wet tea bags.

❮ Always protect a baby's tender scalp and skin with a hat and loose, light-colored outerwear.

❮ Remember that water surfaces double your sun exposure. Wear a hat for protection from the sun and apply sunscreen under your eyes and chin to ward off reflected light.

❮ Keep bottles of sunburn remedies in the refrigerator so they'll feel cool when you apply them.

❮ Check the ultraviolet (UV) ratings of various sunglasses. In general, gray lenses block more damaging rays than brown or green.

Searching for Buried Treasure

"Folly and madness," muttered the Busy-Body (one of Ben Franklin's many pseudonyms) in 1729 to describe the "fruitless search after imaginary hidden treasure" by Philadelphians who hunted with exotic devices like the "Mercurial Wand and Magnet." Ben's spoof of treasure hunters might have been less harsh if he had known about metal detectors.

Simon Newcomb, who had been experimenting with electrically charged wire coils, and Alexander Graham Bell, inventor of the telephone, collaborated on the first metal detector in 1881 in hopes of finding the assassin's bullet lodged in President James Garfield. Their attempt failed (and Garfield died of blood poisoning), but Henri-Georges Doll's 1957 "coil assembly for geophysical prospecting" led to Oliver Akers's 1985 patent for a portable metal detector swung from the waist. In 1996, Joe E. Jones of South Dakota used a metal detector to find a bit of treasure that might have turned Ben's head: 43 silver coins, including a number of Franklin half-dollars.

THE *Inspired* MIND

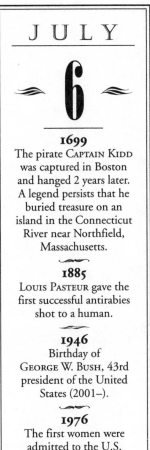

1699
The pirate CAPTAIN KIDD was captured in Boston and hanged 2 years later. A legend persists that he buried treasure on an island in the Connecticut River near Northfield, Massachusetts.

1885
LOUIS PASTEUR gave the first successful antirabies shot to a human.

1946
Birthday of GEORGE W. BUSH, 43rd president of the United States (2001–).

1976
The first women were admitted to the U.S. Naval Academy at Annapolis, Maryland.

> There comes a time in every rightly constructed boy's life when he has a raging desire to go somewhere and dig for hidden treasure.
>
> —*Henry A. Kissinger*

THE SEASONED TRAVELER

❖ If you are bringing your dog or cat on an interstate road trip, remember to pack his vaccination record. Some states require (and check for) proof of vaccination, especially rabies.

❖ To reduce your child's anxieties about going off to summer camp or on other trips, offer an inexpensive instant or disposable camera so that he can record the highlights.

❖ Nothing to do during that long car trip? Find a yard of clothesline and a Boy Scout manual and learn some useful knots. Try the square, bowline, sheet bend, clove hitch, and timber hitch.

❖ If you're on the road and your fan belt starts squealing, dip into your antifreeze and touch a drop or two onto the belt. That should quiet it until you can get it checked.

JULY

7

1969
French and English were designated the official languages of Canada.

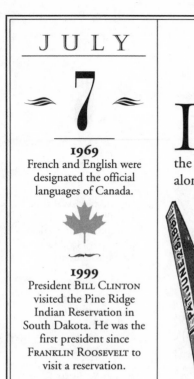

1999
President Bill Clinton visited the Pine Ridge Indian Reservation in South Dakota. He was the first president since Franklin Roosevelt to visit a reservation.

What to Take to a Vacation Rental

PRACTICAL PRIMER

It sounds perfect: a house on the ocean or in the mountains, fully furnished. All you need are a few clothes and something to read. Well, maybe not. To save yourself a trip to the store (if there *is* one within 20 miles) on a hot afternoon, bring along these items in a shoe box or tote bag.

- Duct tape: It does everything from mending torn screens to patching a hole in the kayak.
- First-aid kit: Just in case.
- Good sharp knife: This may sound silly, but most rentals have terrible cutlery.
- Corkscrew: A lot of places don't have one.
- Clock: You might want one in your bedroom or need one with an alarm to get you up that last day.
- Clothespins and a clothesline: How else will you hang up all those wet towels and bathing suits?

SALAD DAYS

❖ To slice tomatoes for a salad, use a sharp serrated knife and slice them vertically (from top to bottom) rather than horizontally. They will lose less juice that way.

❖ No salad spinner? Line a plastic grocery bag with a few layers of paper towels. Put washed lettuce into the bag, close it, and then spin the bag like a lasso until the greens are dry.

❖ If you like raw onion in salads but find yourself with a particularly strong one, dissolve 1 teaspoon sugar in 1 cup lukewarm water and soak the onion slices for about an hour.

❖ Salt does not dissolve well in oil, so when you're making salad dressing, mix the salt

with the vinegar first, then blend in the oil.

❖ For the best salad dressings and fruit salads, add lemon zest, lemon juice, and a bit of sugar for sweetening. Use lemon juice instead of vinegar in your favorite vinaigrette.

❖ For a summer potluck, keep a salad cool and crisp by placing it in a bowl set in a larger bowl filled with ice cubes.

Lettuce is divine, although I'm not sure it's really a food.

—Diana Vreeland

A penny saved is a penny earned.

—BEN FRANKLIN

THE RICHEST PEOPLE often got that way by pinching pennies. Take the wealthy Baron Rothschild, who once gave a cabdriver a miserly tip. The driver complained, "Your lordship's son always gives me a good deal more than this."

"I daresay he does," Rothschild replied. "But then, you see, he has got a rich father. I haven't."

On his birthday, the oil magnate John D. Rockefeller found that his family had bought him one of the newfangled electric cars to help him get around his enormous estate. Rockefeller, who could easily have bought the factory in which the car was made, said, "If it's all the same to you, I'd rather have the money."

Then there was the rich miser whose wife passed away. He went to the newspaper office to insert a paid obituary. When he was told the cost was $1 a word, he filled in the ad form with "Helen Hirkle died." The receptionist explained that there was an eight-word minimum for ads. So the man wrote, "Helen Hirkle died. Pink 1986 Cadillac for sale."

A WORD TO THE WISE

1776
The Declaration of Independence was first read in public, in Philadelphia.

1835
The Liberty Bell cracked as it hung atop Independence Hall in Philadelphia.

1839
Birth of
JOHN D. ROCKEFELLER, industrialist and philanthropist.

■ ■ ■

A rich man is nothing but a poor man with money.

—*W. C. Fields*

TREE CARE

❦ Thin apple trees when the fruit is the size of a dime. Leave one apple per cluster, with apples spaced 8 to 12 inches apart.

❦ To keep mice out of orchards, where they can damage trees, make sure the grass is well mowed and the area cleared of debris and fallen branches.

❦ When you see tent caterpillars building their tents, pull the webby constructions down into buckets of soapy water. Work on a cool, rainy day, when the tents will be full.

❦ Trap flies and moths before they damage your fruit trees by mixing together 1 cup water, ¼ cup cider vinegar, ¼ cup sugar, and 1 tablespoon molasses. Pour it into small containers and hang one or two traps per tree. Clean and refill the traps every few days.

If the wind be hushed with sudden heat, expect heavy rain.

● ● ○ ○ ● ●

1872
JOHN BLONDEL of Maine was granted a patent for the first doughnut cutter.

1958
JOHNNY CASH signed with Columbia Records.

■ ■ ■

The general so likes your music, that he desires you for love's sake to make no more noise with it.
—*William Shakespeare*

Fine music in China gives no pleasure to the nicest ear in Pennsylvania.

—BEN FRANKLIN

SINCE THE INVENTION of subwoofers for car stereos, many young people feel the need to share their music by driving with the volume cranked to the max, rattling the windows of houses and the teeth of passersby. Now innovative judges are fighting back. In one case, a young man was sentenced for drive-by blasting and given the option of paying a stiff fine or purchasing a Wayne Newton compact disc and listening to it for 2 hours straight. Another devotee of ear-splitting music was ordered to listen to 4 hours of the greatest hits of polka king Frankie Yankovic. (Even we must admit that this was cruel and unusual punishment.)

A WORD TO THE WISE

—BK

Elsewhere, music is being used to soothe the savage beast rather than agitate it. In West Palm Beach, Florida, police began playing classical music from an abandoned building in an area known for drug dealing and shootings. According to the police, criminal activity in the area dropped after they began the program.

SUMMER PALATE PLEASERS

❖ Try ICE CREAM PIE for a quick summer dessert. Make the crust for a 9-inch pie from about 1½ cups cookie or graham cracker crumbs mixed with 5 tablespoons melted butter, a dash of pure vanilla extract, and ⅛ teaspoon salt. Press into a pie plate and bake at 350°F for 6 to 8 minutes. (To make one crust, you'll need 50 vanilla wafers, 30 chocolate wafers, 25 gingersnaps, or 15 graham crackers.) Fill the crust with softened ice cream and freeze until firm.

❖ Remember that foods served cold (salads, chilled soups, and pâtés) need extra seasonings, as cold temperatures numb the tastebuds.

❖ Store unripe avocados in a brown paper bag at room temperature, and they will ripen quickly.

❖ Salsa keeps chopped avocado from turning brown.

Cool It

ONE SUMMER DAY in Philadelphia in 1758, when the temperature in the shade reached 100°F, Ben Franklin shed his sweat-drenched shirt. When he put on a dry one, he noticed how much hotter he felt, even though he was sitting in the breeze next to a window. He then experimented with a thermometer by repeatedly wetting the bulb with ether and using a bellows to evaporate it. This produced a 58-degree drop in temperature.

Ben never found a practical application for his insight on evaporative cooling, but it is the principle behind refrigeration machines,  *THE Inspired MIND* which came into use in the 1840s, when Dr. John Gorrie's invention helped cool sickrooms in a Florida hospital. In 1902, Willis Carrier developed the modern air conditioner, first used to regulate the air in a Brooklyn print shop. (Ben would have been proud.) By 1930, 300 theaters used Carrier air conditioners, and by the end of the 20th century, more than 75 percent of American homes were air-conditioned.

This is July of the bountiful heat, Month of wild roses, and berries, and wheat.
—Albert D. Watson

Beat the Heat on the Hottest Day

❧ Open your house to the breeze after sunset and leave it open right up until dawn. Then close everything up and draw the shades before the temperature starts to rise.

❧ If you're expecting a baby, take special care not to get overheated.

❧ Keep a cooler in the back of your car for frozen items, dairy products, and meat. Use it to bring groceries home safely during the hottest months.

❧ To feel cooler, eat cooler. Reduce your protein intake and increase fluids. Avoid hot caffeinated beverages and alcohol, which are dehydrating.

JULY

10

1890
Wyoming became the 44th state.

1893
Dr. DANIEL HALE WILLIAMS performed the first open-heart surgery by removing a knife from the heart of a stabbing victim, who made a successful recovery.

1913
The temperature at Greenland Ranch in Death Valley, California, soared to 134°F, the hottest reading ever recorded in North America.

1989
MEL BLANC, the voice of Bugs Bunny, Daffy Duck, and Porky Pig, died in Los Angeles.

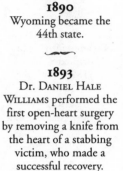

NATURE WATCH

In the western plains, the lovely meadowsweet known as queen of the prairie *(Filipendula rubra)* is blooming now. The blooms reach a height of 3 feet.

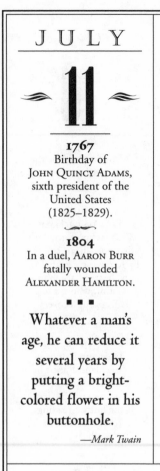

11

1767
Birthday of
JOHN QUINCY ADAMS,
sixth president of the
United States
(1825–1829).

1804
In a duel, AARON BURR
fatally wounded
ALEXANDER HAMILTON.

■ ■ ■

Whatever a man's
age, he can reduce it
several years by
putting a bright-
colored flower in his
buttonhole.

—*Mark Twain*

'Tis more noble to forgive than to revenge an injury.

—BEN FRANKLIN

A WORD TO THE WISE

A QUAKER GENTLEMAN was robbed of some hides from his warehouse. Rather than posting a reward for the capture of the thief, he had a notice inserted in the newspaper stating that he wished to befriend whoever had stolen the hides. If poverty had driven the person to the act, the man would help the thief earn money in an honest fashion. A short time later, the thief came to the man's house to return the stolen hides. The owner forgave him and gave him a job, and the onetime thief remained an honest man.

Dale Carnegie told the story of Bob Hoover, a well-known test pilot who was flying home from an air show when the engine of his World War II plane died. Thanks to his skill, he was able to land safely, whereupon he discovered that the mechanic who had serviced the plane had filled it with jet fuel rather than gasoline. Needless to say, the mechanic expected to be raked over the coals. Instead, Hoover was forgiving. He said to the mechanic, "To show you I'm sure you'll never do this again, I want you to service my F-51 tomorrow."

Harvesting Flowers and Herbs

❖ Gather flowers early in the morning, when the plants are least stressed by heat. Use sharp scissors, for dull blades destroy the water-carrying cells. Get the flowers into a bucket of tepid water immediately.

❖ Cut herbs while the dew is still on them, on the morning of what promises to be a hot day. Herbs that have not yet flowered will be richest in essential oils.

❖ To dry herbs, strip the leaves from the stems and spread the leaves on wire mesh trays in the shade. Stir them once a day for 4 days, then pack into airtight containers.

❖ To have fresh herb flavor available for soups and sauces all year long, rinse fresh

herbs, then puree them in a blender or food processor with a little water or broth. Freeze in ice cube trays, then store the frozen cubes in labeled plastic bags.

Wonders of the Microscope

"JUST ARRIVED from London . . . the Solar or Camera Obscura Microscope," declared Ben Franklin's advertisement in the *Pennsylvania Gazette* on July 12, 1744. A demonstration of the sensational device was held in Philadelphia. People crammed into a darkened room to see blood flowing in a live frog's foot, watch the pulse of a louse's heart, and view bugs projected through a lens onto a screen. The wooden box containing the lens was placed next to a small opening that let in the room's only light. Although the camera obscura had been used for centuries by artists for tracing outlines, the "microscope" version produced enlargements using magnifying lenses.

THE *Inspired* MIND

By the late 1700s, pocket botanical microscopes had been introduced to aid in the popular exploration of nature's miniature world. The microscope was steadily improved during the 19th and 20th centuries. The modulation contrast microscope, which gives transparent objects such as living cells and tissues a three-dimensional appearance, was introduced in 1980.

Today relatively inexpensive light microscopes with adjustable magnification are available for home and school use. They reveal the same wonders that mesmerized audiences in Ben's day and bring out the microbiologist in all of us.

Birth of architect and visionary BUCKMINSTER FULLER (1895) and artist ANDREW WYETH (1917).

1933
The minimum wage—40 cents an hour—was established.

1980
Lightning struck a large broiler establishment in Branford, Florida. The ensuing fire charred 11,000 chickens.

• • •

You've got to think about big things while you're doing small things, so that all the small things go in the right direction.
—*Alvin Toffler*

Small Repairs

❦ Before filling a small crack in a wall, run a razor blade down it to remove any loose particles, then brush out the dust with a clean paintbrush or other soft brush.

❦ To repair a small hole in a leather tabletop, melt a piece of crayon of the same color and smooth it into the hole with your finger.

❦ If a knob or pull on a drawer is loose, detach it and dip the screw end into colorless nail polish or shellac, then screw it back in. The shellac or polish will tighten the screw.

❦ Patch small holes in screens by dabbing them with clear nail polish.

❦ Repair small scratches or chips in white appliances by applying a little white nail polish or white typewriter correction fluid. Cover the repaired spot with clear nail polish.

13

*Whatever July and
August do not boil,
September cannot fry.*

● ○ ○ ● ●

1762
BEN FRANKLIN described
his recent invention of a
musical instrument, the
glass armonica (Italian
for "harmony").

1863
The first U.S. military
draft sparked 4 days of
rioting in New York City.

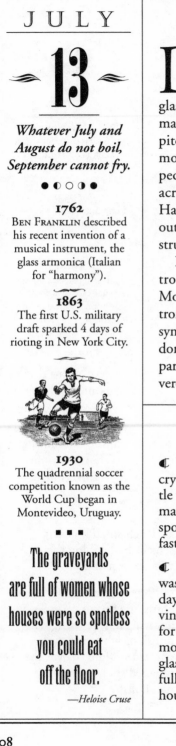

1930
The quadrennial soccer
competition known as the
World Cup began in
Montevideo, Uruguay.

■ ■ ■

The graveyards
are full of women whose
houses were so spotless
you could eat
off the floor.

—*Heloise Cruse*

The Glass Armonica

DIP YOUR FINGER in water, slide it around the rim of a partially filled glass of wine, and a hauntingly sweet tone will give you an idea of the sound of Ben Franklin's glass armonica. He refined the technique of wineglass performance by using different-size glass bowls to create the different pitches, nesting them inside each other and mounting them on a rod turned by a foot pedal. Soon Ben's armonica was so popular across Europe that Mozart, Beethoven, and Haydn composed for it. The armonica went out of fashion in the 1830s when people began to fear that the instrument's penetrating tones caused melancholia.

In 1920, Leon Theremin used vacuum tubes to produce electronic tones on an instrument bearing his last name. Robert Moog's 1969 performance synthesizer launched modern electronic music, and today the glass armonica's ethereal tones can be synthesized. In 1999, Moog and inventor David Van Koevering donated an interactive touch screen piano to the California Department of Mental Health for use in therapy for children with severe emotional disturbances.

THE *Inspired* MIND

Vinegar for Sparkle and Shine

❧ When hand-washing fine crystal and glassware, add a little vinegar to the rinse water to make them sparkle and remove spots. It also helps them dry faster.

❧ If your automatic dishwasher has dulled your everyday glassware, add a cup of vinegar to the final rinse cycle for one load. You can also remove this filmy buildup on glassware by soaking glasses in full-strength vinegar for an hour, then rinsing clean.

❧ Remove coffee and tea stains from fine china by rubbing with a paste of salt and vinegar. Apply with a cloth, let dry, and then rinse off.

❧ When hand-washing pots and pans, add 2 tablespoons vinegar to the dishwater to cut grease.

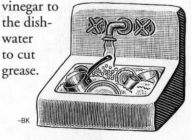

–BK

None but the well-bred man knows how to confess a fault, or acknowledge himself in an error.

—Ben Franklin

THE STORY IS TOLD of a German prince who was visiting one of Louis XVI's arsenals in France. In honor of his visit, the commandant of the arsenal told the prince that he could set free any one of the galley slaves he chose. Wanting to make the best choice, the prince spoke to each man about the circumstances of his imprisonment. Each one explained that he was innocent, that he had been jailed unjustly and deserved to be set free—except for one man, who acknowledged that he deserved his fate, and worse.

"It is a pity you should be placed among so many honest men," the prince said. "By your own confession, you are bad enough to corrupt them all; but you shall not stay with them another day." The prince turned to the commandant and told him the one repentant inmate was the one he wished to have released.

Nobody's perfect, and if we pretend we are, we're only fooling ourselves.

GARDEN INGENUITY

❖ Weed your garden after a rainstorm or watering, when the roots are easier to pull out.

❖ Buy a few bales of mulch hay or straw and use them to weed-proof your vegetables. Don't fluff up the sections of hay, but lay them flat, like carpet tiles, so they can suppress weeds and retain soil moisture.

❖ If your garden hose springs a small leak, insert a toothpick or wooden match into the hole, break it off, and wrap the area securely with duct tape.

❖ Weed your window boxes with a long-handled, two-tined cooking fork.

❖ If you can't bend over easily, you can deliver water and fertilizer to individual plants by pouring it down a 3-foot (or longer) piece of polyvinyl chloride (PVC) pipe.

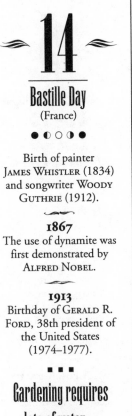

JULY

14

Bastille Day
(France)

● ● ○ ◗ ●

Birth of painter
JAMES WHISTLER (1834)
and songwriter WOODY
GUTHRIE (1912).

1867
The use of dynamite was
first demonstrated by
ALFRED NOBEL.

1913
Birthday of GERALD R.
FORD, 38th president of
the United States
(1974–1977).

▪ ▪ ▪

Gardening requires
lots of water—
most of it in the form
of perspiration.

—Lou Erickson

JULY

15

St. Swithin

● ○ ○ ○ ●

St. Swithin's Day,
if thou dost rain,
For 40 days it will
remain.

1916
Torrential rains
in the southern
Appalachian Mountains
caused flooding and
damaged railroads.
Altapass, North Carolina,
got more than 22 inches
of rain in 24 hours.

1933
WILEY POST began the
first solo airplane flight
around the world.

Simple Rice and Egg Salad

Cool, colorful, and easy to prepare ahead, this summer salad
makes a perfect lunch or light supper.

3 cups cooked long-grain
white rice, cooled
3 hard-boiled eggs, chopped
½ cup mayonnaise
½ cup finely chopped
scallions
1 jar (2 ounces) pimientos,
drained and diced
1 teaspoon Dijon mustard
Salt and freshly ground
black pepper
Romaine lettuce leaves
¼ cup toasted pine nuts

Combine the rice, eggs, mayonnaise, scallions, pimientos,
mustard, and salt and pepper to
taste in a large bowl. Toss to thoroughly combine. Refrigerate and
serve on a bed of lettuce leaves,
garnished with the pine nuts. (To
toast pine nuts, bake in a 300°F
oven for about 5 minutes or heat
gently in a dry skillet.)

Makes 6 servings

KITCHEN POINTERS

❦ Storing rice, flour, pasta,
cornmeal, and the like with a
bay leaf in each canister or jar
will repel bugs.

❦ If you thoroughly wash the
small scoops that come in powdered laundry detergent, you
can use them for sugar, flour,
and rice.

❦ Food cooked with eggs,
meat, fish, or dairy products
should not be left at room
temperature for longer than
2 hours total.

❦ To test whether an egg is
fresh, place it in a pot of salted
cold water. If the egg sinks, it is
fresh. If it floats, it is not.

LORE & LEGEND

ST. SWITHIN, English ecclesiastic and bishop of Win-
chester, died in 862. His final wish was to be buried
outdoors. According to legend, when his remains were
moved to an indoor shrine years later—on July 15—
40 days of rain ensued.

Rain or shine, eggs and apples are the traditional
fare for St. Swithin's Day. The saint was credited with
restoring to wholeness a basket of broken eggs that an
impoverished woman had carried to market.

If It Does Rain Today

Wash the insides of
your windows. You'll
have less trouble with
streaks on rainy days,
since the hot sun won't
dry the window solu-
tion before you have a
chance to wipe it off.

Three Simple Headboards to Spruce Up Your Bedroom

A BED WITHOUT a headboard is like a painting without a frame. If you want a more finished look without spending a bundle, create the illusion with these tricks.

PRACTICAL PRIMER

1. Add a "window" above your bed by attaching a curtain rod to the wall, either at ceiling height or about 2 feet above your pillow. Hang curtains so that they extend down behind your bed. If you don't want to purchase curtains, you can make your own using flat sheets to match your bed linens.

2. Find an old fireplace mantel (try a yard sale or junk shop) that can function as a shelf above your bed. Sand and paint it to coordinate with your bedroom. Cut a piece of plywood the same length as the mantel and wide enough to reach from your bed to the mantel. Cover the plywood with batting, then with a coordinating fabric, tightening and stapling it to the back. Nail the plywood to the back of the mantel, then attach the whole piece to the wall behind your bed.

3. Purchase an inexpensive garden trellis and paint it to match your bedroom decor. Attach the trellis to the wall behind your bed. Leave it plain or decorate it with artwork, photos, fabric, or silk flowers.

JULY

16

1911
Birthday of dancer GINGER ROGERS.

1935
The nation's first parking meter was installed in Oklahoma City.

–BK

1945
The first atomic bomb test explosion occurred.

■ ■ ■

Finish each day before you begin the next, and interpose a solid wall of sleep between the two.

—*Ralph Waldo Emerson*

HIDDEN STORAGE IN THE BEDROOM

❖ Add a towel bar to the inside of your bedroom closet door and use it to hang a blanket or quilt.

❖ To store seldom used bulky items in a bedroom or family room, buy a big plastic trash can and cut a plywood circle a bit bigger than the top. Place the plywood on top of the can and cover it with a round tablecloth that hangs to the floor. Now you have storage and an extra table.

❖ To make more storage space under your bed, invest in bed risers, which will make the bed 1 foot higher.

❖ Store comforters by turning them into pillow stuffing. Sew together big pieces of bright fabric to make seasonal pillow covers and stuff them with the comforters.

JULY

17

1867
The first dental school in the United States was established at Harvard University.

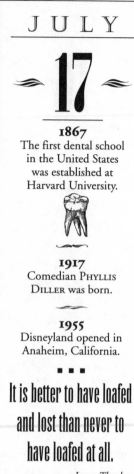

1917
Comedian PHYLLIS DILLER was born.

1955
Disneyland opened in Anaheim, California.

■ ■ ■

It is better to have loafed and lost than never to have loafed at all.

—*James Thurber*

He that can take rest is greater than he that can take cities.

—BEN FRANKLIN

WHEN CRITICIZED for taking a vacation before the start of an important trial, judge Louis Brandeis, associate justice of the Supreme Court, said, "I find that I can do a year's work in eleven months, but I can't do it in twelve."

Contrast that with the emperor Napoleon Bonaparte, who often worked long hours and expected those around him to do the same, a habit that grated on some of the easygoing members of the court. When an admirer commented, "God made Bonaparte and then rested," an émigré count responded, "God should have rested a little earlier."

Not getting enough rest can be dangerous, according to a recent study. The *Journal of Occupational and Environmental Medicine* reports that getting less than 5 hours of sleep a night two or more times per week can double your chances of having a heart attack. The authors of the report recommend working no more than 40 hours a week, getting more sleep, and taking breaks during the workday—advice with which we wholeheartedly agree.

ARE WE THERE YET?

❖ For long car rides or anytime a child needs to sit still for a long stretch, make up a story with her as the hero. The taller the tale and the wilder the adventure, the better.

❖ To save on gasoline, turn off the engine. Idling the engine for more than 15 seconds consumes more fuel than turning off the car and restarting it.

❖ Hang pocket organizers on the backs of the front seats of your car to hold maps, toys, and snacks for long rides.

❖ To stave off motion sickness, try drinking a mixture of ½ teaspoon powdered ginger and 1 cup water before embarking, taking a capsule of powdered ginger (available at health food stores), or sipping on ginger ale made with real ginger. Get plenty of air, and don't try to read. Sit in the front passenger's seat. As a last resort, try closing your eyes.

Whirlwinds and Waterspouts

WHIRLWINDS and waterspouts fascinated Ben Franklin. He once sped off on horseback to track a whirlwind across the Maryland landscape, later writing down detailed observations, such as its width at ground level ("no bigger than a common barrel") and his failed attempt "to break this little whirlwind by striking my whip frequently through it." Two years before, in 1753, Ben had noted the white interior and black edges of a waterspout and quoted Cotton Mather's description of a waterspout as a whirlwind "with a Pillar of Light in it . . . horribly tearing up Trees by the Roots." Ben theo-

THE *Inspired* MIND

rized that the light was caused by the opacity of swirling particles surrounding the inner "vacuum" and suggested that "it is no Wonder now to those who understand Electricity, that Flashes of Lightning should descend by the Spout."

When a waterspout (a whirling column of water and spray) travels onto land, it can turn into a dangerous tornado, as happened in 1878 when 34 people were killed in Wallingford, Connecticut. In 1928, a Kansas farmer had the frightening experience of looking up into the core of a tornado and described the spinning walls being lit by repeated flashes of lightning, accompanied by screeching, hissing noises.

Birth of comedian RED SKELTON (1913) and statesman NELSON MANDELA (1918).

1986
A slow-moving but moderate tornado with winds up to 150 miles per hour touched down in northern Minneapolis, appearing live on local television.

• • •

It is not light that we need, but fire; it is not the gentle shower, but thunder. We need the storm, the whirlwind, and the earthquake.

—*Frederick Douglass*

Remedies for Excessive Wind Emanating from Your Innards

☾ Dietary substances that reduce flatulence include allspice, cloves, caraway, dill, fennel, peppermint, and sage. If the cabbage in coleslaw is a trigger for you, try adding fennel, dill, or caraway seeds.

☾ Too much stress and worry in your life may lead to flatulence. Find a way to release tension through exercise, yoga, or meditation instead.

☾ Gas can signal lactose intolerance. If you can't digest a big glass of milk, you may still be able to tolerate dairy products such as hard cheese (aged cheddar, Swiss, or Jarlsberg), sour cream, and buttermilk. Yogurt with active cultures is a good bet as well.

19

1848
The first women's rights convention was held at Seneca Falls, New York.

1865
Birth of surgeon CHARLES HORACE MAYO, one of the founders of the Mayo Clinic.

Santa Fe Summer Turkey Kabobs

Chunks of turkey marinated in the flavors of the Southwest cook in less than 15 minutes. Serve with warm tortillas and salsa, if desired.

¼ cup finely chopped scallions
⅓ cup fresh lime juice
2 tablespoons olive oil
2 cloves garlic, minced
2 teaspoons chili powder
1 teaspoon Tabasco sauce
1 teaspoon cumin
1 teaspoon dried oregano
1 tablespoon finely chopped
    fresh cilantro
2 pounds turkey tenderloin

The day before cooking, prepare the marinade by thoroughly mixing together all the ingredients except the turkey. Cut the turkey into cubes and marinate overnight in the refrigerator. Remove from the marinade and thread onto skewers. Grill over medium heat until cooked through, 10 to 15 minutes.

Makes 4 servings

Success with Kabobs and Marinades

❦ Always use nonreactive containers—glass or ceramic bowls or self-sealing plastic bags—for marinades. The acid in marinades can react with metal containers, affecting the taste.

❦ If the marinade does not completely cover the food, stir occasionally so that the food marinates evenly. If you're using a self-sealing plastic bag, simply turn the bag every so often.

❦ When grilling, presoak wooden skewers for 30 minutes to prevent them from burning.

❦ Roll a lemon or lime on the counter a few times before juicing. You'll get more juice that way.

USING GARLIC

❖ Don't peel garlic cloves before pressing. Pressing unpeeled cloves saves time and, because the husk remains behind, makes cleaning the garlic press easier.

❖ Cut off any green on a garlic clove before pressing—it's bitter.

❖ Store garlic at room temperature and away from light, in a container with air holes. Don't refrigerate.

❖ If you grow your own garlic, snip a few inches of the green tops and add to salads and salad dressings for a subtle garlic flavor.

❖ To roast garlic, place an entire head on a square of aluminum foil, drizzle with a little olive oil, wrap up, and bake at 350°F for 1 hour, until soft. Squeeze the softened cloves onto crackers or bread. It's also delicious on a roast beef sandwich.

There's no sauce in the world like hunger.

—Miguel de Cervantes

> *A change of fortune hurts*
> *a wise man no more than*
> *a change of the moon.*
>
> —BEN FRANKLIN

SOMETIMES ALL IT TAKES is a keen eye and an open mind to turn bad luck to good. Take the case of Robert Chesebrough, an out-of-work chemist who in 1859 traveled to Titusville, Pennsylvania, to see a new oil-drilling operation. His attention turned to the rod wax that built up on the pistons, literally gumming up the works. The riggers scraped the stuff off, discarding it. But occasionally, Chesebrough noted, they used the gooey substance on burns and scrapes. He tested a sample and discovered that it contained petroleum jelly, an odorless, colorless gel that allowed wounds to heal by sealing out infections. He named his gel Vaseline and never looked back.

A scientist at 3M Company was disappointed with the new adhesive he had created because it didn't stick very well. But another employee came up with a novel use for it. As a member of his church choir, he was frustrated that the little slips of paper he used to mark the pages of his hymnal kept falling out. He decided to coat the slips with the not-so-sticky adhesive. Thus the Post-it note, now found in every modern office, was born.

1933
Author CORMAC MCCARTHY was born.

1968
The first Special Olympics were held in Chicago.

1969
NEIL ARMSTRONG and EDWIN "BUZZ" ALDRIN walked on the moon.

FROM GARDEN TO TABLE

❖ Swish spinach and lettuce gently in tepid water to remove all the dirt and grit.

❖ Before cooking cabbage or broccoli, soak it in 1 gallon water mixed with 1 teaspoon salt to make sure any worms or bugs float out.

❖ To retain the highest vitamin content, always bring water to a boil for 2 minutes before cooking vegetables.

Midsummer Vegetable Harvest

☾ Pick beans every 2 or 3 days to encourage continued production. They'll have the best flavor if you harvest them in the morning.

☾ Use two hands to pick peas. Hold the vine with one hand and pull off the pods with the other.

☾ After you finish harvesting a crop, pull up the plants, compost them, and put something else in the garden. Lettuce, spinach, and Swiss chard are good late-season crops.

21

*Fireflies in great
numbers indicate
fair weather.*

● ● ○ ◐ ●

According to the ancient
Egyptians, the world was
created on this day.

1856
Birth of LOUISE
BLANCHARD BETHUNE,
the first professional
woman architect in the
United States. She
designed the Hotel
Lafayette in Buffalo.

1987
Thunderstorms in
North Dakota produced
baseball-size hail,
and high winds toppled
two 80-foot towers,
cutting off electricity to
the town of Blanchard.

Lightning on the Wing

BEN FRANKLIN, interested in both lightning and insects, would be intrigued by our knowledge of the lightning bug. (He would agree with its other name, the firefly, since he often described lightning as "electrical fire.") Technically neither bug nor fly, the four-winged beetles are most often found in

THE
Inspired
MIND

warm, humid areas. But curiously in the United States, the glowing kinds are usually seen only east of central Kansas. Lightning bug larvae feed on worms, snails, and slugs, while adults drink nectar.

In 1951, William D. McElroy discovered that fireflies produce light by a chemical reaction involving enzymes, organic compounds, and oxygen. Unlike a flash of lightning, the firefly produces cold light, with little wasted energy. Males and females of each species use their own distinctive flashing patterns—a continuous glow, single flashes, or pulsing dots—to attract members of the opposite sex. In fact, the females of some species mimic the behavior of other fireflies to attract—and devour—males, like sirens luring sailors onto the rocks.

–BK

What is life?
It is the flash of a firefly
in the night.

—Crowfoot

Create Your Own Twilight Glow

❖ To add special elegance to a summertime gathering in the evening, hang lanterns in the trees near your patio, deck, or gathering place. To make your own lanterns, gather canning jars and other decorative glass jars. Wrap a thin copper wire in the groove below the lip of the jar and attach a second, longer wire as a handle. Put a layer of sand in the bottom and care-fully set tea lights or votive candles inside. Hang the jars from trees, porch railings, or plant hangers attached to your house.

❖ String tiny Christmas lights along porches, among tree limbs, and around bushes for a festive flare without the glare.

❖ Use citronella candles to deter those few remaining mosquitoes from spoiling your party.

A Basic Kit for Cleaning

YOU NEED NOT buy another commercial cleaning product if you keep these basic ingredients on hand for household chores.

- Ammonia*
- Bleach*
- Baking soda
- Lemon juice
- Vinegar
- Salt

PRACTICAL PRIMER

Among them, you have strong cleaning power, mild abrasive power, and the acidic qualities that can handle tough jobs. Ammonia can cut through anything greasy, strip wax, remove dirt, clean an oven, and clean glass without streaks. Bleach is essential for killing household mold and mildew on walls and in the laundry, and it's a wonderful spot remover and disinfectant. Baking soda acts as a mild abrasive and a mild bleach, and it can deodorize just about anything without leaving a chemical or perfume smell. Lemon juice is a good cleaner and deodorizer. Vinegar also has deodorizing properties, softens laundry, and is an excellent stain remover. Salt is a mild abrasive and can absorb liquid stains when they are fresh.

* Never mix ammonia and bleach. If you use either ingredient in a cleaning solution, always add it after you've added water.

JULY

22

1844
Birth of Rev. WILLIAM ARCHIBALD SPOONER, whose frequent slips of the tongue ("half-wormed fish" and "Beeping Sleauty," for example) resulted in the term *spoonerism.*

1898
Poet STEPHEN VINCENT BENÉT was born.

1944
The *Ziegfeld Follies* had its 553rd and final performance, after opening in New York City in 1907.

BATTLING BATHROOM MILDEW

❖ Paint bathroom ceilings with a mildew-resistant paint.

❖ Stop mildew buildup on your shower doors by wiping them with a damp sponge sprinkled with baking soda. Rinse well.

❖ Remove mildew from shower curtains by tossing them in the washing machine with ½ cup baking soda and washing in warm water.

❖ Wash plastic mats, curtains, and liners in the washing machine along with several bath towels. Add laundry detergent and a little bleach.

❖ Use packaged baby wipes to give your bathtub or shower walls a quick cleanup that will help control mildew.

❖ To lighten grout and kill mold and mildew, mix one part chlorine bleach and nine parts water in a spray bottle. Spray onto grout and scrub. Then apply silicone water repellent with a small brush to prevent further mildew.

We thought, because we had power, we had wisdom.

—Stephen Vincent Benét

23

*When the perfume
of flowers is
unusually perceptible,
expect rain.*

● ○ ○ ● ●

1846
HENRY DAVID THOREAU
was arrested for refusing
to pay a poll tax.

1971
Birth of singer
ALISON KRAUSS.

2000
At 24, TIGER WOODS
became the youngest
golfer to win the
Grand Slam.

■ ■ ■

NATURE WATCH

Campers in the East might be awakened at any hour by the whoops and hoots of a barred owl, also known as the hoot owl. The large, dark, round-headed owl will respond to nearly any mimicked hoot, so feel free to converse.

—BK

Distrust and caution are the parents of security.

—BEN FRANKLIN

PERHAPS, BUT SOMETIMES security experts can take things a bit too far. When Canada's prime minister Jean Chretien went to Vancouver for a handshaking tour, police were warned to be on the lookout for someone who was planning to "pie" the prime minister. (He had been hit by a custard pie 2 years earlier.)

A WORD TO THE WISE

Bystander William Christiansen was carrying an iced bun when a police officer stopped him and asked what he was going to do with it. "I told her I was going to eat it," Christiansen said, but when he refused to eat it on the spot, he was arrested.

Another man, Cameron Ward, was arrested and his car was towed because he matched the description of a known pie tosser and police suspected that the trunk of his car was full of baked goods. "I can assure you I have not visited a bakery within the last forty-eight hours," Ward said. Both men were later released.

There is no truth to the rumor that Canadian police will begin to require bakery patrons to register their purchases.

GOING CAMPING?

❦ For the best-burning campfires, choose dry oak, ash, beech, birch, or maple. Pine and other resinous softwoods tend to spit. Fires made with alder, chestnut, poplar, and willow tend to smoke and smolder.

❦ Kindle seaside campfires with dried seaweed, if necessary.

❦ What's a campfire without s'mores? Be sure to pack graham crackers, chocolate bars, and marshmallows for your trip.

❦ Bring a gallon-size self-sealing plastic bag on your next camping trip, fill it loosely with air, zip it shut, and voilà!— your pillow.

Paddle Tale

BEN FRANKLIN loved to swim, and as a boy he experimented with two wooden oval paddles for his hands, each with a thumb hole, to help him swim faster. He also developed paddles for the feet, but it wasn't until 1933 that a Frenchman named Louis de Corlieu patented swim fins, which he called swimming propellers. The fins gained immediate popularity with recreational skin divers and sport fishermen.

THE
Inspired
MIND

Ben's paddle-style fins, the model for today's swim fins, underwent a startling improvement in 1998, the year of physicist Pete McCarthy's patent for a more flexible flipper. His fin is split down the middle to take into account the principles of aerodynamics, increasing the fin's lift while decreasing drag. The split fin gives a swimmer greater speed than the paddle fin for the same exertion, something Ben would surely applaud.

By the Sea, the Beautiful Sea

❖ To prevent those after-swim earaches, combine equal parts white vinegar and rubbing alcohol and put one or two drops in each ear three times a day as an antiseptic.

❖ If you're prone to swimmer's ear, try using Silly Putty for earplugs. It easily conforms to the ear's shape, is waterproof, and can be reused many times.

❖ To relieve a nosebleed, try a good cold swim in a pond, ocean, or stream.

❖ To minimize a bout of seasickness once it comes on, stay on deck and near the center of the boat. Avoid exhaust fumes. Don't try to read or scan charts. Focus on the horizon or close your eyes. Sip ginger ale and nibble a few dry crackers.

JULY

24

Now the state of the crops is known.

● ◐ ○ ○ ●

1725
Birth of JOHN NEWTON, who captained a slave ship, had a religious conversion at age 22, and wrote the hymn "Amazing Grace."

1850
The clipper ship *Sea Witch* sailed from New York City to San Francisco in 97 days.

1987
HULDA CROOKS, age 91, climbed Mt. Fuji.

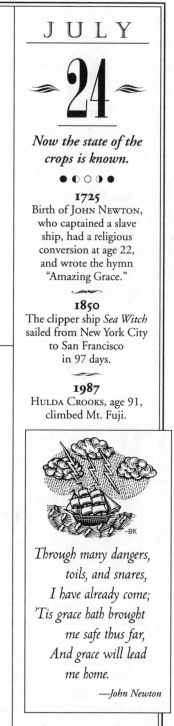

Through many dangers, toils, and snares, I have already come; 'Tis grace hath brought me safe thus far, And grace will lead me home.

—*John Newton*

JULY

25

St. James

● ○ ○ ○ ●

1941
Boston Red Sox pitcher
LEFTY GROVE won his
300th game. It would be
his last career victory.

1954
Birth of NFL running
back WALTER PAYTON.

1979
Alvin, Texas, was deluged
with 43 inches of rain,
the state's all-time record
for a 24-hour period.

---

*O lazy-bones! Dost thou think God
would have given thee arms and legs,
if he had not design'd
thou should'st use them?*

—BEN FRANKLIN

A WORD TO THE WISE

SCIENTISTS HAVE KNOWN for some time that modern Americans are taller than their forebears, but it turns out that may not be such a good thing. Apparently, our bones are longer but not as strong as those of our ancestors. What caused the change? Forensic anthropologists at the University of Tennessee—who were looking for an easy way to date skeletons—stumbled on the realization that we actually have less bone mass than our ancestors. The researchers suspect it's due to too little exercise and too much food, or overnutrition, as they call it. Early Americans got lots of exercise—most people walked wherever they went—to stimulate healthy bone growth. But the early American diet wasn't as good as ours. Better nutrition causes us to grow faster than our ancestors, and that makes our bones develop differently. We always suspected our ancestors were tough, and now we know one reason why.

The athlete
does not
embark upon a
sport but upon
a way of life.

—*W. R. Loader*

TOP TIPS FOR ATHLETES

❖ Try running or walking 3 to 5 days a week instead of 7 to give limbs and joints more time to heal. You'll experience fewer shinsplints, heel problems, and other common ailments.

❖ Remember the RICE technique for sprained ankles or muscle strains. Rest, ice, compression, and elevation are the keywords. Ice should be 10 minutes on, 10 minutes off. Compression is best accomplished with a not-too-tight elastic bandage.

❖ Use a few drops of lavender oil in warm water to make a natural deodorant wash. Or try eating more raw vegetables—their chlorophyll reduces perspiration odor.

❖ To cure athlete's foot, a fungal infection, soak your feet in cider vinegar, apply aloe vera, and change your socks frequently.

❖ To get dingy athletic socks white again, boil them in a large kettle with a slice of lemon. Or wash them in your washing machine with 2 teaspoons dishwasher detergent.

The First Postmaster General

WHEN BEN FRANKLIN lobbied for an appointment as deputy postmaster general of North America in 1751, he was hoping his placement would facilitate intercolony communication "among [the] ingenious men" who belonged to the American Philosophical Society. Two years later, he was appointed to the post. He immediately visited all the post offices in the northern colonies, helped survey and select roads and ferries, added more frequent mail service, and reorganized the entire accounting system. In 1775, he was elected the first postmaster general by the Continental Congress.

THE *Inspired* MIND

The country grew fast, and its citizenry spread far and wide. The U.S. Post Office used every form of transportation available to deliver the mail. In 1860, ads appeared in newspapers recruiting Pony Express riders: "Wanted: Young, skinny, wiry fellows not over 18. Must be expert riders willing to risk death daily. Orphans preferred."

Railway mail service was in place by then, and mail was sorted in transit. By 1863, the Post Office had set uniform rates regardless of distance. One hundred years later, in 1963, the zip (zoning improvement plan) code was introduced, streamlining the delivery process and opening the door to automation.

–BK

Letters are expectation packaged in an envelope.

—*Shana Alexander*

BE A WOOD STAIN MASTER

❦ To get stain into tight corners without drips, work from the corner out and remove any excess stain immediately by dabbing it with a small, dry paintbrush.

❦ To prevent the porous cut ends of a piece of wood from absorbing too much stain, sand them with a higher-grit sandpaper.

❦ When staining a vertical surface, first brush across the surface horizontally. This will keep the finish from running. Then work vertically from the bottom up.

❦ To stain a dowel, cut a V shape into an inexpensive foam brush and use it to apply the stain evenly around the dowel.

1775
The U.S. Post Office was established and BEN FRANKLIN was made postmaster general.

1788
New York became the 11th state.

Birthday of writer PEARL BUCK (1892) and rock musician MICK JAGGER (1943).

1917
New York City's last horse-drawn trolley made its final run on Bleeker Street.

27

Bells are heard at greater distances before a rain.

● ○ ○ ○ ●

1905
Birth of baseball player and manager LEO DUROCHER.

1931
Grasshoppers plagued Iowa, Nebraska, and South Dakota.

1940
Bugs Bunny made his animated film debut in *A Wild Hare*.

● ● ●

I did not become a vegetarian for my health, I did it for the health of the chickens.

—*Isaac Bashevis Singer*

Ben Franklin, Occasional Vegetarian

BEN FRANKLIN became a vegetarian at the age of 16, believing that killing animals for food was "unprovoked murder." He had just read Thomas Tryon's *The Way to Health* (1691), an influential book advocating temperance and vegetarianism. Although Ben gave up vegetarianism after a year, he occasionally returned to it later in life.

THE *Inspired* MIND

The 6th-century B.C. philosopher Pythagoras may have been the father of vegetarianism. He developed a code of ethics that included a strict rule against eating meat. Some well-known vegetarians, past and present, include Leonardo da Vinci, Leo Tolstoy, George Bernard Shaw, Henry David Thoreau, Albert Schweitzer, Mahatma Gandhi, Isaac Bashevis Singer, Fred "Mister" Rogers, Clara Barton, and Paul McCartney.

The North American Vegetarian Society, founded in 1974, counts an estimated 13 million to 24 million vegetarians in the United States who abstain from meat, fish, and fowl, with varying degrees of commitment. Ovo-lactovegetarians eat dairy products and eggs. Vegans, or pure vegetarians, confine their diets strictly to the vegetable kingdom. Vegetarians are usually motivated by ethical, environmental, or health issues.

Banishing Bugs and Beetles

❧ Pick ripening raspberries every day so Japanese beetles don't set up housekeeping on overripe berries.

❧ Remove Japanese beetles and potato bugs from plants by hand (wear gloves if you're squeamish) and drop them into buckets of soapy water.

❧ Experiment with your own organic pest control spray by mixing together 1 teaspoon dishwashing liquid, 1 cup vegetable oil, and 1 gallon warm water in a watering can or sprayer. Test it on a few plants before spraying it on the entire garden.

❧ Loosely tie brown paper lunch bags around bunches of ripening grapes to protect them from birds, hail, and insects.

Blueberry Peach Cobbler

Ripe fruit in a heavenly combination make this dessert fit for the gods. Serve it warm, perhaps with ginger ice cream.

2 pints blueberries

5 peaches, peeled, pitted, and sliced

2 cups flour

2 teaspoons baking powder

1 teaspoon salt

1¼ cups sugar

2 eggs

10 tablespoons butter, melted

1 teaspoon cinnamon

Preheat the oven to 350°F. Spread the blueberries and peaches in a lightly greased 9- by 13-inch baking pan. Combine the flour, baking powder, salt, and sugar in a bowl. Add the eggs and mix with a fork until crumbly (allow some mix to remain dry). Spread over the fruit. Drizzle the butter on top and sprinkle with the cinnamon. Bake for 45 minutes, or until golden brown and bubbly.

Makes 8 servings

How to Handle Berries and Peaches

❖ Do not pick berries that are wet from dew or rain; you can spread mildew and other diseases.

❖ Store fragile berries such as raspberries in a single layer in the refrigerator. Do not wash them before storing. Better yet, eat them as soon as possible.

❖ To freeze fresh blueberries and raspberries, place them on cookie sheets in a single layer and pop them into the freezer. As soon as they are frozen solid, transfer them to plastic bags and use as desired in muffins, pancakes, and cobblers.

❖ Pick 4 cups berries for a 9-inch pie.

❖ Choose tree-ripened peaches and buy only as many as you can use within a few days. Unripe peaches will not sweeten after they are picked.

❖ To peel peaches easily, blanch them first: Cut an X into the skin of each peach at the pointed end. Submerge in boiling water for a minute or two, until the skin loosens. Quickly transfer from the boiling water to a bowl of very cold water. When cool, peel with a paring knife.

JULY

28

When the rooster goes crowing to bed He will rise with watery head.

● ● ○ ○ ●

1866
Peter Rabbit creator
BEATRIX POTTER
was born.

1933
The first singing telegram
was delivered.

1952
A severe hailstorm broke
windows, damaged roofs,
and stripped trees of
their leaves near Benson,
Arizona. The hail
accumulated to 3 inches,
with drifts nearly
4 feet deep.

■ ■ ■

**Thank goodness
I was never sent to
school; it would have
rubbed off
some of the
originality.**

—Beatrix Potter

29

St. Martha

● ○ ○ ○ ●

*Wind in the east,
the fish bite the least.
Wind in the west,
the fish bite the best.*

1899

The first motorcycle race
was held at Manhattan
Beach, New York.

1954

*The Fellowship of the Ring:
Being the First Part of
"The Lord of the Rings"*
by J. R. R. Tolkien
was published.

Toleration

IN A 1743 LETTER to his sister Jane Mecom of Boston, Ben Franklin responded to her concerns about his unorthodox religious convictions. He gently explained his beliefs and concluded, "There are some things in your New England doctrines and worship, which I do not agree with, but I do not therefore condemn them, or desire to shake your belief or practice of them." The 37-year-old Ben was ahead of his time in embracing religious toleration, although the Maryland toleration act of 1649 protected anyone from being compelled to follow a religion without his or her consent.

THE *Inspired* MIND

In 1791, the First Amendment to the U.S. Constitution forbade laws "respecting an establishment of religion, or prohibiting the free exercise thereof." In pursuit of upholding the Constitution and interpreting laws, the Supreme Court has ruled that religious liberty demands the "widest toleration of conflicting views," protecting Americans against trials for heresy (1944); that religious instruction in public schools (1948) and religious tests for public officeholders (1961) violate the establishment clause; and that giving tax dollars to parents to send their children to religious schools does not violate the Constitution (2002).

SETTING A LOVELY SUMMER TABLE

❖ Strew fresh herbs, trailing vines (ivy or bittersweet), or fresh flowers over a plain tablecloth to dress up a banquet table. Place large grape leaves under wine bottles, or use them to line a fruit tray.

❖ Tuck fresh herbs or flowers into folded napkins to dress up a table setting. Or tie napkins with fresh chives,

raffia, ribbon, or even long-stemmed flowers.

❖ Float flower petals in water around the base of a candle to spruce up your table.

❖ To make casual place mats, cut painted oilcloth into summer shapes

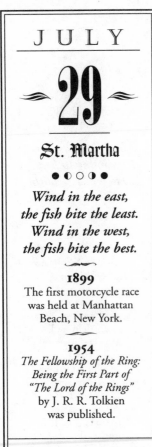

such as flowers and butterflies. Buy inexpensive oilcloth tablecloths or buy oilcloth by the roll at a fabric store.

❖ Use two large terracotta pots, even plastic ones, to make an occasional table for a porch or garden room. Set them an appropriate width apart and add a glass tabletop.

It will not do to leave a live dragon out of your plans if you live near one.

—*J. R. R. Tolkien*

If Life Brings You Lemons

PLINY THE ELDER, the 1st-century Roman historian, prescribed lemons as a precaution against snakebite. In 1493, Christopher Columbus took on supplies in the Canary Islands, including the pips (seeds) of lemons. And by 1565, the Florida citrus empire had begun in St. Augustine.

According to the 17th-century herbalist Nicholas Culpeper, lemon juice "cools the blood, strengthens the heart, [and] mitigates the violent heat of fevers." The superbly opinionated Mrs. Beeton, author of *The Book of Household Management* (1861), considered lemons suspect, but she endorsed the Roman use of them as a moth repellent. Even today, the lemon's nonculinary uses are numerous. Here are a few favorites.

PRACTICAL PRIMER

- Lemon juice soothes insect stings, cleans piano keys and copper pots, brightens porcelain and marble, absorbs odors, and removes lipstick and wine stains.
- Half a lemon, from which most of the juice has been squeezed, makes a fresh cleaning pad for faucets and sinks. Use it with a little salt as an abrasive.
- Equal parts lemon juice and beaten egg white can be boiled briefly and scented with rose water to make a natural face lotion.
- Undiluted fresh lemon juice is just the thing to clean water spots and stains from your automobile chrome.

When cats sneeze, it is a sign of rain.

● ○ ○ ○ ●

1715
A Spanish fleet loaded with gold and silver disappeared near the St. Lucie Inlet, off the coast of Florida.

1890
Birth of baseball player and manager CASEY STENGEL.

■ ■ ■

I want to thank my parents for letting me play baseball. I'm thankful I had baseball knuckles and couldn't become a dentist.

—*Casey Stengel*

Pure and Simple Lemonade

Try this unadulterated lemonade, fit to quench any thirst. Add fresh mint sprigs, if you have them, along with the lemon slices.

8 lemons, rolled between your palm and a tabletop, then squeezed (strain out the seeds)
1 cup sugar
3 cups cold water
1 lemon, sliced as thinly as possible, for garnish

Combine the lemon juice, sugar, and water in a glass pitcher. Refrigerate until well-chilled. Serve over ice in the tallest glasses you can find, garnished with the lemon slices.

Makes 4 servings

31

1790
The U.S. Patent Office issued its first patent, to Samuel Hopkins for a method of making potash and pearl ash.

1971
DAVID SCOTT and JAMES IRWIN drove the Lunar Roving Vehicle on the moon.

1976
Intense rain from a thunderstorm in northeastern Colorado created a flash flood that took more than 150 lives.

Diligence is the mother of good luck.

—BEN FRANKLIN

WHEN BEN FRANKLIN was a child, his father often repeated to him this proverb of King Solomon: "Seest thou a man diligent in his calling, he shall stand before kings, he shall not stand before mean men." (*Mean* in this case would translate as petty or small.)

As a young businessman and father, Ben had reason to be diligent in his calling. He was in debt for his printing business, he was raising a young family, and he was competing against two other printers who had been in business before he even started. The only way to succeed was to work harder than his competitors, and although he was confident of success, he never expected to actually stand before kings. By the end of his life, however, he had stood before five kings and even sat down to dinner with one, the king of Denmark.

Still, not everyone agreed with King Solomon. The eminent lawyer Clarence Darrow told of being brought up on a farm, where one of his jobs was to stack hay as it was being cut. It was hot, miserable work, and one day Darrow decided he'd had enough. "That afternoon I left the farm, never to return," he told an interviewer. "And I haven't done a day of hard work since."

> Gardens are not made by singing "Oh, how beautiful," and sitting in the shade.
>
> —*Rudyard Kipling*

Deadheading, Pinching Back, and Performing Other Garden Tasks

❖ Routinely pinch off faded petunia blossoms to keep plants flowering.

❖ When deadheading roses, cut faded blooms back to a healthy outside bud with five leaflets.

❖ To keep alyssum and ageratum plants blooming all season, snip the tops off as soon as seedheads appear.

❖ Transplant oriental poppies when they're dormant, usually sometime in July. The foliage will be brown and dry, but the plants are not dead.

❖ In the North, stop pruning boxwood after mid-July to prevent tender new growth from being damaged by frost.

❖ Get a group of friends together and order spring-flowering bulbs in bulk by midsummer. Buying in large quantities will significantly lower the price per bulb and let you enjoy more variety.

AUGUST, *the Eighth Month*

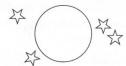

Full Sturgeon Moon

is the name given by
the Native American
tribes of the Great Lakes,
who fished for this large
quarry during August,
smoking and drying
some of their catch.
It was also known as the
Full Green Corn Moon.

Sign of the Zodiac: Leo
(July 23–August 22)

Element: Fire

Quality: Dramatic

Birthstone: Peridot

Flower: Poppy

NAMED FOR Augustus Caesar, the month of August once had the Anglo-Saxon label of Weod-monath, or "weed month." If for some reason (no doubt a good one) you haven't been weeding your garden all along, now's the time to plunge in—if you can still find the plants you want. Everything is flourishing now, and gardeners are playing the zucchini game, stashing overgrown squash in their neighbors' cars and mailboxes or on their front porches in the dead of night.

One of the finest pleasures of August is this: On a clear night between the 11th and 13th, put a blanket on the lawn, invite someone you like to join you, and lie back to watch the sparkling Perseid meteors streak across the sky.

Soon after, along about the middle of the month, summer often seems to run out of steam. A subtle change—a few cool nights, a shift in the quality of the light, the scritch of crickets instead of the trill of songbirds—is all it takes to remind us not to take these summer days for granted. The orb weavers know the season is shifting, and every morning the woodshed is festooned with their work. We duck under the webs and grab a few sticks of firewood, just in case the evening is cool.

1

Lammas Day

● ○ ○ ○ ●

1771
BEN FRANKLIN began
writing his *Autobiography*
at the age of 65.

1819
Writer HERMAN MELVILLE
was born.

—BK

1876
Colorado became
the 38th state.

Lefties

BEN FRANKLIN, Queen Victoria, Albert Einstein, Charlie Chaplin, and Marilyn Monroe were all left-handed. So are Gerald Ford, Ronald Reagan, George H. W. Bush, and Bill Clinton. In fact, about 10 percent of the population is hardwired this way. On the one hand, left-handers struggle with scissors, can openers, three-ring binders, school desks that wrap around from the right, and guitars and baseball gloves designed for use by right-handers.

PRACTICAL PRIMER

On the other hand, lefties have the advantage at drive-up windows at banks, automatic teller machines (ATMs), and fast-food restaurants. Most lefties become at least somewhat ambidextrous to accommodate to a right-handed world.

Immanuel Kant called hands "the visible part of the brain." Since we know that the left side of the body is controlled by the right side of the brain, may we conclude that lefties are the only ones who are in their right minds?

LORE & LEGEND

LAMMAS DAY, halfway between the summer solstice and fall equinox, was celebrated in old England by eating oatcakes. The first ripe grains of the season—usually oats—were baked into unleavened bread and consecrated at a loaf Mass, or Lammas (from the Old English *hlaf,* or "loaf"). In Ireland, grain and berry puddings thickened with Irish moss (carrageen, a nutritious seaweed) were favorite fare for Lammas Day. Baskets of fresh berries, signifying fertility, were often exchanged by sweethearts.

LEFT-HANDED LIVING

❖ Replace an annoying three-ring binder with a clipboard, used with the clip at the bottom. Instead of using a conventional spiral notebook, try a stenographer's notebook, wired at the top.

❖ For checkbooks, registers, or other record books with a bulky stub on the left, remove the check or paper first, then fill it out.

❖ At a crowded dining table, try to sit at a left end so that you don't bump elbows (or forks) with a right-hander sitting next to you.

❖ Avoid erasable ink, which smudges just as easily as soft lead pencil.

Remember, Ginger Rogers did everything Fred Astaire did, but backwards and in high heels.

—*Faith Whittlesey*

Well done is better than well said.

—BEN FRANKLIN

THE LATE Peter Marshall, chaplain of the U.S. Senate, often told the story of the keeper of the spring, an old man who lived above the hills of an Austrian town. Quietly, without fanfare or acclaim, the old man kept the pools above the town free from leaves, branches, and debris that would otherwise have choked off the flow of water providing refreshment and power to the town. One year, however, the town officials decided to eliminate the keeper's pay from the budget, figuring that no one had heard from him for a long time and his work was probably unnecessary anyway.

A WORD TO THE WISE

For a while, the springs bubbled as before, but eventually the water turned stagnant and the flow was reduced to a trickle. The leaders of the town quickly realized their error and hired back the keeper of the springs, and the water began to flow freely again.

"Whatsoever thy hand findeth to do," the author of Ecclesiastes wrote, "do it with thy might."

> Hard work spotlights the character of people: some turn up their sleeves, some turn up their noses, and some don't turn up at all.
>
> —*Sam Ewing*

After Lammas, corn ripens as much by night as by day.

● ◐ ○ ◑ ●

1858
The first street mailboxes were set up in Boston and New York City.

1909
The U.S. government bought its first airplane.

1938
The Brooklyn Dodgers and St. Louis Cardinals tried using a yellow baseball for better visibility.

■ ■ ■

NATURE WATCH

Tree crickets, not surprisingly, often live in trees (sometimes in weedy fields), where they lay their eggs in twigs and stems. Male tree crickets are the musical stars of the insect world. If you add 40 to the number of chirps a tree cricket makes in 14 seconds, the total will tell you the temperature in degrees Fahrenheit. Try it!

GROWING GREAT PRODUCE

❦ Once the fruit forms, water squash and pumpkins diligently to coax them to the largest size.

❦ Suspend melons in nylon mesh, secured to a tepee or trellis, to save garden space and keep the fruit from rotting in contact with the soil.

❦ If bean plants look scraggly as they start to flower, fertilize them with fish emulsion. Avoid high-nitrogen fertilizer, or you'll have bushy plants and no beans.

❦ Faithfully snip off flowers that form on basil and lemon verbena plants. This will keep them bushy and flavorful.

AUGUST

3

1880
The American Canoe
Association was founded.

1900
Birth of journalist
ERNIE PYLE.

1921
JOHN MACCREADY
of Troy, Ohio, was the first
to use an airplane
for crop dusting.

1949
The National Basketball
Association was formed.

The Problem of Perspiration

PERSPIRATION stains on collars and underarm areas may be caused by undissolved deodorant or soap particles. Softer water may prevent this problem from developing, so if you think your water is hard, always use a fabric softener in the rinse cycle of your wash.

PRACTICAL PRIMER

& Before washing a new garment for the first time, pretreat the areas where stains usually appear—the collar and underarms—by rubbing them with warm water and Fels Naptha soap. This will help prevent staining.

& For fresh perspiration stains, prepare a mixture of equal parts ammonia and water. Sponge it onto the stains, then rinse with clear water and wash as usual.

& If the yellow stains have been around for a while, dissolve 1 tablespoon baking soda in 1 cup water and work this into the stains with a brush. Let stand for an hour, then wash as usual.

& For stubborn perspiration stains, make a paste of equal parts baking soda and water. Rub the paste into the stains, then sprinkle with ½ cup white vinegar and launder.

Sweat is
the cologne of
accomplishment.
—*Heywood Hale Broun*

THE STAINS OF SUMMER

❖ Remove yellow stains from white linen and cotton by soaking for 30 minutes in warm water, laundry detergent, and nonchlorine bleach. Then wash as usual. Or spray the stains with hot white vinegar, then work in borax and launder.

❖ Saturate grass stains on cotton garments with rubbing alcohol, let stand for 10 minutes, and launder as usual.

❖ To remove berry stains, apply a paste of salt and lemon juice. Rinse after 5 minutes and launder as usual. If this doesn't work, stretch the stained material

over a large bowl and pour boiling water through the stains. If they remain, bleach the area with hydrogen peroxide or chlorine bleach.

❖ For a washable fabric with bloodstains, cover the stains with meat tenderizer. Apply warm water to make a paste, wait 20 minutes, and sponge with cool water. Soak using a presoak product, then wash as usual.

Solar Heat

IN A 1761 LETTER to his friend Polly Stevenson, Ben Franklin mentioned the experiment he once made with colored squares of cloth taken from a tailor's swatch book. Laying the squares—which included one black square and one white square, among others—on a patch of snow one bright winter morning, Ben waited several hours, then observed that the darker the cloth, the more heat it absorbed and the deeper it sank into the snow. The black square sank deepest, and the white cloth didn't sink at all. Ben concluded that white clothes, being more reflective, would be cooler than dark ones in a sunny, hot climate.

THE *Inspired* MIND

Today we use white roofing to reflect solar rays and keep our houses cooler in warm regions. (In cold regions, black shingles are obviously more useful.) Athletes competing on sun-drenched fields use eye black—a mixture of petroleum jelly, lanolin, and wax—under their eyes to reduce glare. Or they might use Curtis Mueller's 2001 invention—a combined antiglare, sunscreening adhesive strip placed under the eyes and across the nose. Ben Franklin anticipated such aids when he told Polly that folks should wear summer hats of white fabric "lined with Black, as not reverberating on their Faces those Rays which are reflected upward."

If the first week in August is unusually warm, the winter will be white and long.

● ● ○ ○ ● ●

1901
Musician LOUIS ARMSTRONG was born.

1917
The United States finalized the purchase of the Virgin Islands from Denmark for $25 million.

1922
Telephones across the United States—some 13 million—were silenced for 1 minute on the day of ALEXANDER GRAHAM BELL's funeral.

My advice to you is not to inquire why or whither, but just enjoy your ice cream while it's on your plate.

—*Thornton Wilder*

ICE CREAM INGENUITY

❦ On hot summer days, prevent ice cream drips from a sugar cone by first putting a mini-marshmallow in the bottom of the cone to act as an edible cork.

❦ Double-wrap ice cream containers with plastic wrap or aluminum foil to prevent freezer burn.

❦ To minimize the formation of ice crystals in ice cream, return it to the freezer immediately after serving.

❦ Heat your ice cream scoop in boiling water for easier scooping, but be sure to dry it well before using.

❦ To check the freezer temperature, stick a meat thermometer into a carton of ice cream. It should read between 0° and 6°F.

AUGUST

5

1861
Congress abolished
punishment by flogging
in the military.

1961
Washington's
all-time state record for
highest temperature
(118°F) was registered at
Ice Harbor Dam.

1972
JAMES BROWN's song
"Get on the Good Foot,"
considered the inspiration
for the origin of break
dancing, entered the
musical charts.

. . .

**Some people
can stay longer
in an hour than others
can in a week.**
—*William Dean Howells*

Fish and visitors stink in three days.

—BEN FRANKLIN

THE FAMED children's author Hans Christian Andersen once visited with the family of Charles Dickens in England. Apparently, Andersen overstayed his visit, because after he left, Dickens stuck a card in the bedroom in which he had slept: "Hans Andersen slept in this room for five weeks—which seemed to the family ages."

A WORD TO THE WISE

Oscar Levant, the noted pianist and humorist, was a frequent guest at the home of playwright George Kaufman. After one particularly long visit, Mrs. Kaufman told Levant that the servants expected to be tipped, but since she knew he didn't have any money, she had given them each $3 and told them it was from him. "You should have given them five," Levant protested. "Now they'll think I'm stingy."

Then there was the uninvited "visitor" to the magnificent Prado art museum in Madrid. The guest was a painting that had been superglued to a wall by an unknown painter (one Victor Ruiz Roizo), who later said that he wanted to be displayed "with Rembrandt and all those guys." The painting remained in place until a museum patron asked about it 4 days later—1 day more than Ben Franklin would have given it.

Make a Fine Fish Chowder

❖ When making chowder, if you don't have time to make fish stock, substitute bottled clam juice.

❖ Use a firm white fish such as haddock, cod, or pollack for chowder; the flesh flakes naturally when cooked. To make sure your chowder has good-size chunks of fish, add the whole fillet to the chowder, then gently break it into big chunks when it is cooked.

❖ When choosing fresh fish, let your nose be your guide. The fish should smell briny but not fishy or of chlorine, and the eyes should be bright. And don't let 3 days go by before using fresh fish. If you are not going to cook fish within 24 hours, freeze it to preserve its freshness.

Ben's Magic Cane

BEN FRANKLIN enjoyed a trick that made him appear to possess magical powers. While walking with friends on a windy day next to a stream with wind-whipped waves, he would state that he had the power to calm the water. Walking alone a short distance upstream, he would extend his arms out over the water and wave his cane three times in the air. Soon the waves disappeared, and the stream became as smooth as glass. Ben explained to his astonished companions that he

THE *Inspired* MIND

kept oil in a secret compartment in his cane and had flung the oil over the water. Oil reduces friction between wind and water, thus eliminating the waves.

In 1773, Ben tried calming ocean breakers with oil, hoping it "might possibly be of use to Men in Situations of Distress," but the experiment failed. Today we know that oil on water is harmful to nature. In 1975, Johann Rafael of Austria patented a floating device to clean ocean water polluted by oil. It collects oily water in a domed holding tank and siphons off the oil, which, as Ben well knew, floats on top.

My brain is the key that sets me free.

—*Harry Houdini*

When it rains in August, it rains honey and wine.

● ◐ ○ ◑ ●

1911
Comedian LUCILLE BALL was born.

1926
HARRY HOUDINI stayed underwater for 91 minutes in an airtight case in which an ordinary person could have survived for only a few minutes.

1962
Jamaica became an independent country.

GARAGE CLEANUP

❦ Apply cat litter or wood shavings to an oil spill in the driveway or garage, then sweep up the mess.

❦ Put an old bookcase in your garage or toolshed and use it for storing flowerpots, gardening tools, work gloves, sunscreen, and insect repellent.

❦ To save garage space, screw a large hook into a beam and hang your bike from the back wheel.

❦ Sort all hardware, nails, screws, and other items according to size. Put all odd or mismatched pieces in a separate box. Do-it-yourselfers, schoolchildren, and artists often find inspiration and utility in a "junk" box.

Terrible Tar

Use vegetable oil to remove fresh tar from your automobile. Rub it on, using a lot of elbow grease, let it sit for a few seconds, and then wipe away both oil and tar.

7

Crickets chirping louder than usual warn of a coming storm.

● ● ○ ○ ● ●

1721
The *New England Courant,* first American newspaper to feature literary articles and humorous essays, began publication.

1959
Explorer VI transmitted the first photograph of Earth from space.

Silence Dogood

THE
Inspired
MIND

IN THE 1720S, readers in Massachusetts could open their newspapers to find letters to the editor commenting on topics such as smallpox inoculation and the infringement of Englishmen's rights by meddling politicians. Timothy Turnstone, Hugo Grim, Obadiah Plainman, and Anthony Afterwit offered sharp opinions, as did Betty Diligent, Celia Single, Fanny Mournful, and Alice Addertongue. We know now that all of these personas were inventions of Ben Franklin, the author of their "letters."

Ben's most famous alter ego was Silence Dogood, a widowed housewife, under whose name he wrote a series of arresting essays in Boston's *New England Courant* on personal freedom, education, and morals. Ben fabricated the name to make fun of two books written by the puritanical Boston minister Cotton Mather—*Silentarius* and *Essays to Do Good.* Ben lampooned Mather's stifling piety, but in his *Autobiography* he wrote that reading *Essays* when young "gave me a turn of thinking that had an influence on some of the principal future events of my life."

> What dreadful hot weather we have! It keeps me in a continual state of inelegance.
>
> —*Jane Austen*

YARD WORK REMINDERS

❖ During dry spells, mow your lawn less frequently and raise the blades on your mower so you don't clip the grass too short.

❖ Cut dahlias as often as you can to encourage more flowers to form. For longer stems and spectacular single blooms, clip off the side buds.

❖ To dry the smaller, ornamental sunflowers, cut them in midmorning, leaving lots of stem. Hang them upside down in a dark, well-ventilated area for about 3 weeks.

❖ Shake the seeds out of dried hollyhock pods and plant them in pots. As soon as the shoots emerge, move them to a permanent location.

❖ Cut phlox to the ground when it stops flowering to prevent the spread of powdery mildew.

To err is human, to repent divine, to persist devilish.

—Ben Franklin

● ○ ○ ○ ●

An evangelist named J. John had a big impact on his audience in Norfolk, England, on May 15, 2001. He preached a simple message: Thou shalt not steal. John explained that stealing is stealing, whether it's a few paper clips from work or evading taxes. He concluded his lecture with an admonishment to repent of past thefts and directed the audience to an "amnesty bin," where they could turn in items they might have stolen.

The results were surprising. By the end of his series of lectures, attendees had placed about 90 items in the bin, including an oil painting and a gold watch. The Norfolk police checked the items and returned what they could to the rightful owners. The rest were auctioned off, and the money was given to charity.

True repentance isn't just regret; it also requires changed behavior.

1829
America's first locomotive, the *Stourbridge Lion,* was tested in Honesdale, Pennsylvania.

1963
In England, robbers made off with 2.6 million pounds in the Great Train Robbery.

1974
Richard Nixon announced his resignation from the presidency.

1976
The Chicago White Sox baseball team suited up in shorts.

■ ■ ■

Suspicion always haunts the guilty mind; The thief doth fear each bush an officer.

—*William Shakespeare*

Pasta with Pesto

For a quick summer supper, put the water on to boil for pasta while you make an easy pesto sauce. Serve with sliced ripe tomatoes or a tossed salad. Supper can be on the table in 20 minutes.

4 cups fresh basil leaves
5 or 6 cloves garlic, peeled
1 pound pasta
½ cup extra-virgin olive oil
2 to 3 ounces good-quality Parmesan or Asiago cheese, cut into chunks
¼ cup pine nuts (optional)

Bring a pot of salted water to a boil while you rinse the basil and peel the garlic. When the water is boiling, add the pasta. Place the basil leaves, garlic, olive oil, cheese, and pine nuts in the bowl of a blender or food processor. Just before draining the pasta, process the pesto until fairly smooth. Add a ladleful of the pasta cooking water (about ½ cup) and process briefly. Drain the pasta and pour the pesto on top. Toss and serve.

Makes 4 to 6 servings

AUGUST

9

*Dry August,
arid, warm,
Doth harvest
no harm.*

● ◯ ◯ ● ●

1842

After lengthy negotiations, the Webster-Ashburton Treaty set the U.S.-Canada border from Maine to Lake of the Woods (northern Minnesota). The United States gained the Mesabi Range, later found to be rich in iron ore.

1936

JESSE OWENS won his fourth Olympic gold medal.

The magistrate should obey the laws, the people should obey the magistrate.

—BEN FRANKLIN

WOODROW WILSON was a stickler for rules, even the rules of the road. He and his wife, Edith, loved to be driven around in the Rolls-Royce that Congress had purchased for their use, but he always insisted that the chauffeur drive at the speed limit—at the time, 22 miles per hour. Once, the car was stopped by a policeman on a bicycle. When Wilson asked what the problem was, the officer said, "It's all right, Mr. President. I didn't know it was you."

"On the contrary," Wilson replied. "I of all people must obey the laws."

To make drivers in Vilnius, Lithuania, obey traffic regulations, authorities came up with a novel solution: cardboard cops. In 2002, local officials, faced with a shortage of traffic officers and one of the highest rates of traffic fatalities in Europe, placed lifelike replicas of traffic police on busy streets to fool drivers into slowing down. Initial reports suggested that drivers were indeed hitting the brakes for the ersatz officers. Woodrow Wilson would have approved.

A WORD TO THE WISE

RULES FOR SUCCESSFUL CANNING

❦ Different foods require different processing methods, so consult a reliable canning guide before you start.

❦ Assemble clean canning jars and new lids (do not reuse lids). Sterilize jars in boiling water. Do not rely on the microwave for this, because the heat may be uneven.

❦ It will take at least 30 minutes to bring a canning kettle full of water to a boil, so start your water while you prepare foods and fill the jars.

❦ It's a myth that adding aspirin to canned foods will prevent spoilage. Only the proper heat treatment ensures preservation.

❦ Salt is not necessary for safe processing. Add salt only for taste, if at all. For pickles, use only kosher or pickling salt. (Iodized salt can cloud your pickles.)

❦ When removing jars from a boiling-water bath, handle them gently with tongs so you don't break the seal.

Garden Tomato Bake

Simplicity itself, this combination of tomatoes and buttered bread crumbs depends on perfectly ripe tomatoes for its success.

3 pounds large ripe tomatoes, halved and thickly sliced
Salt
4 slices white bread, quartered
¼ cup + 3 tablespoons cold unsalted butter, cut into small pieces
Freshly ground black pepper

Preheat oven to 400°F. Butter a 9- by 11-inch baking dish. Layer the tomatoes in the dish, overlapping them as necessary. Sprinkle with salt. Process the bread and ¼ cup butter in a blender or food processor until crumbly. Sprinkle over the tomatoes and dot with the remaining

3 tablespoons butter. Season with salt and pepper to taste. Bake for 35 to 40 minutes, or until golden and bubbly.

Makes 6 to 8 servings

Totally Tomatoes

❖ Four or 5 medium tomatoes weigh about 1 pound. Peeled and seeded, this yields about 1½ cups tomato pulp.

❖ If you are troubled by diarrhea or indigestion, try eating tomatoes.

❖ The speediest way to ripen tomatoes is to place them in a brown paper bag with an apple or pear. (These fruits emit ethylene gas, which hastens ripening.) Do not put them on a sunny windowsill to ripen; they may rot before they are ripe.

❖ To store ripe tomatoes, place them in a cool spot in a single layer with the stem ends up. Never refrigerate tomatoes. Always serve at room temperature for maximum flavor.

❖ Instead of a tossed salad, offer a simple platter of sliced tomatoes sprinkled with chopped fresh basil leaves and coarse salt and drizzled with extra-virgin olive oil.

❖ To help your body beat the heat, drink plenty of fluids and minimize your intake of protein-rich foods. Try a ripe tomato, right out of the garden, instead.

❖ To prevent tomato sauce from staining a plastic storage container, spray the container lightly with nonstick cooking spray before filling.

● ○ ○ ○ ◐

Fine weather today means a good wine harvest.

1821
Missouri became the 24th state.

1874
Birthday of HERBERT HOOVER, 31st president of the United States (1929–1933).

1921
At his summer home on Campobello Island in New Brunswick, Canada, FRANKLIN DELANO ROOSEVELT was stricken with polio.

▪ ▪ ▪

The greatest service which can be rendered any country is to add a useful plant to its culture.

—Thomas Jefferson

AUGUST

11

Dog days end.

● ○ ○ ● ●

1896
HARVEY HUBBELL
patented an electric
lightbulb socket with
a pull chain.

1921
Birthday of writer
ALEX HALEY.

1992
The Mall of America,
largest of its kind
in the United States,
opened in Bloomington,
Minnesota.

Playing with Fire

THE Inspired MIND

THE 18TH-CENTURY fascination with experiments attempting to prove that lightning was electrical carried great risks. Ben Franklin's parlor studies to elicit sparks from the discharge of static electricity taught him how to devise safe experiments in the field, and he shared that knowledge openly. He was very careful to incorporate grounded rods or insulated devices when experimenting with lightning and was never injured, much to the amazement of his nonscientific peers.

German professor Georg Wilhelm Richmann was not so fortunate. He was electrocuted while conducting a lightning experiment in Russia on August 6, 1753. The experiment had been devised by Ben, but Richmann ignored Ben's stipulation to ground the iron rod.

For those who believed that lightning was the weapon of a wrathful God, Richmann's death was proof that the Almighty disliked these "philosophical" investigations. But Ben was determined to ignore superstition. He freely gave the lightning rod, the device that safely channels nature's terrifying force, to the world.

HOW TO MAKE FLEAS FLEE

The dog days—the traditional time of hot, humid weather that began on July 3—might be over, but flea season is not.

❖ To test your pets for fleas, have them stand on a white sheet while you brush them. If small black flecks drop on the cloth, dissolve them in a drop of water. If the flecks turn red, they're flea droppings, not dirt. Get the flea shampoo!

❖ If you must bathe your dog but aren't prepared to get wet yourself, try holding the dog's snout as you work. For many breeds, this will prevent the dreaded canine shake that can soak anything nearby.

❖ To rid the house of fleas, fill a shallow plate with water and a squirt of dishwashing liquid. Place it on the floor with a gooseneck lamp about 6 inches overhead. Leave the light on at night while the rest of the house is dark. The fleas will be attracted to the light, jump into the dish, and drown.

❖ To repel fleas, rub a drop of lemon oil or rosemary oil into your dog's or cat's regular collar. Adding 1 tablespoon brewer's yeast or 1 tablespoon vinegar to your pet's food or drinking water also can help.

A professor must have a theory as a dog must have fleas.

—*H. L. Mencken*

A Simple Utensil Rack for Your Kitchen

IF YOU HAVE TO DIG around in your kitchen drawers for utensils as the bouillabaisse boils over and the soufflé scorches, here is a quick and inexpensive system for organizing the jumble.

1. Purchase seven 3-foot lengths of 1- by 3-inch pine. If they're rough, sand them smooth.
2. Place two of the sections 2 feet apart and arrange the other sections perpendicularly on top of them, evenly spaced (like railroad tracks).
3. Nail or screw the five top sections to the two bottom pieces.
4. Paint or stain the unit to complement your kitchen's decor.
5. Attach decorative hangers, cup hooks, and L-shaped hooks to hold your whisks, spatulas, measuring spoons, and so on.
6. Securely fasten the unit to a bare wall by screwing the two supporting sections to studs in the wall. Arrange your favorite utensils on the unit and start cooking.

-JS

UTENSIL TIPS AND TRICKS

❦ Before using a grater, coat it with nonstick cooking spray to prevent foods from sticking.

❦ Keep a toothbrush near the kitchen sink for cleaning your colander, strainer, grater, blender and food processor blades, and other hard-to-clean items.

❦ Wash your can opener after every use. The blade (encrusted with bits of leftover food) is one of the most common sources of bacterial contamination in the kitchen.

❦ To test the thickness of sauces and gravies, dip in a wooden spoon. If the sauce coats the spoon, it is the right consistency.

❦ To extend the life of your sieve, always use a rounded utensil, such as a ladle, to push food through.

❦ Never put wooden tools in a dishwasher or allow them to soak in your sink.

❦ To crush berries for pies and jams, use a potato masher.

AUGUST

12

If you wet your feet with dew in the morning, you may keep them dry for the rest of the day.

● ● ○ ◐ ●

1865
JOSEPH LISTER became the first surgeon to use a disinfectant during an operation.

1955
The minimum wage per hour was raised from 75 cents to $1.

1981
IBM introduced its personal computer and operating system, PC-DOS version 1.0.

▪ ▪ ▪

I was 32 when I started cooking; up until then, I just ate.

—*Julia Child*

A double husk on corn indicates a severe winter.

● ○ ○ ● ●

1934
Al Capp's comic strip "Li'l Abner" made its debut.

1985
Road graders were called out to clear 3-foot drifts of hail from Highway 9 near Logan, Kansas.

■ ■ ■

NATURE WATCH

Do not blame goldenrod (*Solidago* spp.) for your hay fever. Ragweed (*Ambrosia* spp.) is the culprit. Both wildflowers bloom in late summer. Goldenrod flowers are one-sided in arcing racemes; ragweed flowers are sparse and clustered. Goldenrod leaves are oval or lance-shaped; ragweed leaves are segmented or lobed.

RAGWEED

If you would have guests merry with your cheer, be so yourself, or so at least appear.

—BEN FRANKLIN

NOT ONLY WILL a cheerful outlook make your parties more fun, but it could lengthen your life. In the 1960s, researchers at the Mayo Clinic in Rochester, Minnesota, gave personality tests to 447 people to identify optimists and pessimists. Thirty years later, they examined the health of those people and found that the optimists had lived longer, suffered fewer ailments, and generally enjoyed life more than those with a dour outlook on life.

Here are a few ways to gain a better perspective on life.

A WORD TO THE WISE

🖐 Squash perfectionism. Accept that you can't do everything perfectly. Give yourself a break and accept your own failings.

🖐 Let go of little annoyances. Life is too short.

🖐 Forgive those who have wronged you. Remember that bitterness is a poison you swallow, hoping that it will kill the other person.

🖐 Live in the moment. Too many of us live for the day we'll be grown-up, find the perfect spouse, have children, own a great house, or retire. By then, life is over. Live now.

Good Medicine for Body and Soul

❖ Keep a pepper grinder on the kitchen table. Black pepper *(Piper nigrum)* contains natural compounds that help fight off osteoporosis.

❖ Eat seasonally whenever you can. As Henry David Thoreau said, "Live in each season as it passes; breathe air, drink the drink, taste the fruit, and resign yourself to the influences of each."

❖ If genes are not your strong point when it comes to health, try laughter. It's a great stress buster and elevates the immune system.

The public is like a piano. You just have to know what keys to poke.
—*Al Capp*

How to Enjoy Your Own (Big) Dinner Party

ONCE YOU'VE INVITED everyone, it's easy to become overwhelmed when planning food and drinks for a crowd. Relax! Parties are meant to be fun for everyone, even the host. Just get organized before your guests walk through the door.

- Lay out a simple buffet meal. Rely on foods such as smoked fish, ham, spreads served on bread, or fancy sandwiches that taste fine at room temperature.

PRACTICAL PRIMER

- Think through the menu, shop a day ahead, and devote several hours during the day of the party to preparing the table.
- Use salad plates rather than dinner plates to make servings look generous. Also, they take up less room on the dinner table.
- Designate a bed or back room for coats.
- When guests ask if they can help, say yes. Suggest that they bring specific dishes, or put them to work at the party. Ask them to check that everyone has a beverage or to replenish items that are disappearing.
- If it's too warm to appreciate a fire, light candles in your fireplace for a festive look.
- Establish a place to put dirty dishes. Or assign a helpful teenager the job of gathering them up and washing them.

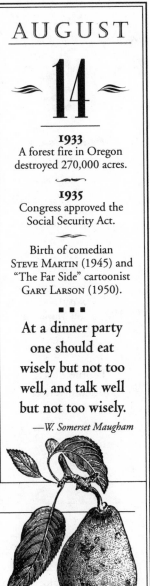

CHOOSING RIPE FRUIT

- When choosing a cantaloupe, look for a golden color (although green melons will ripen in a couple of days at room temperature), a nice round shape, and a sweet aroma (no mold) at the stem end.

- Pineapples don't ripen after picking, so select one that is already ripe. Turn the pineapple over and smell the bottom: the stronger the pineapple aroma, the riper the fruit. Dark spots indicate an overripe pineapple.

- A ripe watermelon has a yellow patch on the bottom, and its rind can be pierced with your fingernail. Give it a thump: A ripe watermelon should feel and sound more like a human head than a human chest.

- A pear advertised as "tree-ripened" may be mealy. Choose (or harvest) pears that still show a bit of green, with just a faint yellowish blush. They will ripen in 3 to 5 days.

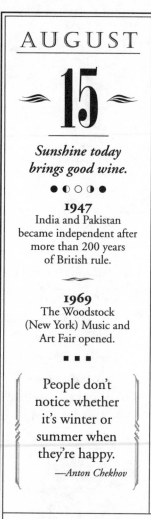

15

Sunshine today brings good wine.

● ◐ ○ ◑ ●

1947
India and Pakistan became independent after more than 200 years of British rule.

1969
The Woodstock (New York) Music and Art Fair opened.

■ ■ ■

People don't notice whether it's winter or summer when they're happy.
—*Anton Chekhov*

Ben's Spin on His Sister's Engagement

WHEN BEN FRANKLIN heard of his 14-year-old sister Jane's engagement, he wrote to her: "You know you were ever my peculiar favourite. . . . I hear you are grown a celebrated beauty." As for a present, he wrote, "I had almost determined on a tea table, but when I considered that the character of a good house-wife was far preferable to that of being only a pretty gentlewoman, I concluded to send you a spinning wheel."

THE *Inspired* MIND

Ben doesn't reveal whether his practical gift was a "great wheel" (one with a large drive wheel, with the spinner walking to and fro while the wool twisted) or a small "treadle wheel" (operated by foot, which left both hands free to work with the fibers). Franz Voegtli's improved cast-iron treadle spinning wheel, patented in 1874, had the spindle directly above the wheel. In 1876, Julia Snapp patented a clever fiber-spinning attachment for foot-treadle sewing machines. During the 1970s revival of hand-spinning, Jan Louet Feisser of Holland invented the Louet wheel, a handsome wooden upright wheel that is still popular today.

THE FRUGAL COOK

❖ If you find yourself with overripe bananas and haven't the time to make banana bread or muffins, peel the bananas and freeze them whole in plastic bags for use in smoothies or baked goods.

❖ For best energy efficiency, choose a chest freezer rather than an upright model. Cold air, being heavier than warm air, does not escape upward as quickly as it does outward when you open the door.

❖ If you are overflowing with ripe peaches, pears, berries, and other fruits that will spoil before you can eat them, take a few minutes to peel and puree them. Freeze the puree in self-sealing plastic bags or ice cube trays (covered with plastic wrap). Use the frozen puree in smoothies to give them a thick and creamy consistency.

❖ If your bag of sugar is full of hard lumps, put it in the refrigerator for a day, and the lumps will disappear.

Beauty and folly are old companions.

—BEN FRANKLIN

"VANITY OF VANITIES," wrote the author of Ecclesiastes. "All is vanity." And that was before the advent of face-lifts, tummy tucks, body sculpting, and injections of lethal toxins that deaden nerves to prevent wrinkles. Originally developed to assist soldiers disfigured in combat, plastic surgery soon evolved into cosmetic surgery, providing people with the opportunity to change what God (or simply too much good living) had given them.

One suspects that Ben Franklin would roll his eyes at our modern preoccupation with washboard abs, perfect noses, and full heads of hair on 90-year-old men. Ben wasn't much for ostentation in other areas either. In his will, he left his daughter a diamond-studded painting of the king of France, with explicit instructions that she was not to "form any of those diamonds into ornaments either for herself or daughters, and thereby introduce or countenance the expensive, vain, and useless fashion of wearing jewels in this country."

FOUND ART

❧ Save attractive paper seed packets, buy them at yard sales, or pick them up on sale at your garden center. (Store any viable seeds in labeled envelopes.) Arrange the packets in a frame for garden-inspired art.

❧ Collect pinecones and heap them in decorative baskets or bowls, or throw a few on the fire for the scent of evergreen.

❧ Use empty compact disc cases to make little frames for photos, pressed flowers, artwork, or memorabilia. Create a background with decorative fabric or wrapping paper, if desired.

1777
American militia defeated the British under General JOHN BURGOYNE at the Battle of Bennington, Vermont.

1829
The original "Siamese" (conjoined) twins, CHANG and ENG, arrived in the United States for their first Western exhibition.

1977
ELVIS PRESLEY died at Graceland at age 42.

■ ■ ■

NATURE WATCH

In late summer, lobsters and crabs shed their shells and begin the slow process of growing new, bigger ones. It takes at least 2 months for the new exoskeletons to become hard enough to protect the creatures from predators. Meanwhile, soft-shell crustaceans go on the menu at coastal seafood shanties. Connoisseurs will tell you that the meat of soft shells is exceptionally sweet.

AUGUST

17

Cat nights begin.

● ○ ○ ○ ●

1790
The capital of the United States was moved from New York City to Philadelphia.

1835
SOLYMAN MERRICK patented the wrench.

1978
The first successful transatlantic balloon trip was completed.

■ ■ ■

LORE & LEGEND

CAT NIGHTS originate in an Irish legend about a witch that could turn herself into a cat and back again eight nights in a row, but on the ninth night—August 17— she had to remain a cat. This may be the origin of the idea that a cat has nine lives. It also helps explain why cats are particularly "yowly" in August.

Ben's Watery Legacy

WHEN BEN FRANKLIN died in 1790, his will included a generous 1,000-pound fund for both Boston and Philadelphia. The money was to be loaned out at 5 percent interest. Ben calculated that at the end of 100 years, each fund would be worth 131,000 pounds. Each city was then to spend 100,000 pounds (about $2 million in today's terms) on public works. A priority for Philadelphia, Ben suggested, would be to pipe in spring water.

But Philadelphia, then America's largest city, couldn't wait 100 years. The 1790s saw repeated and deadly outbreaks of yellow fever attributed to foul water supplies. In response to citizen petitions, the city finally established its first waterworks in 1801. Then in 1815, it opened the Fairmount Water Works on the Schuylkill River, the country's first large-scale public water service.

Today the Philadelphia Water Department operates three drinking water treatment plants to clean more than 300 million gallons of water per day.

WATERING THE GARDEN

❖ Stick your finger an inch into the garden soil. If it feels dry, the garden needs water.

❖ Water your plants early in the morning, when moisture evaporates more slowly than during the heat of the day.

❖ To keep your hose from kinking as you round tight corners, anchor it in a gentle arc with croquet wickets or strategically placed stakes or stones.

❖ Roll up your garden hose and put it away after every use. Direct sunlight will weaken it.

❖ When you buy a watering can, choose one that holds at least 2 quarts, fits under your faucet, and has an angled spout so water won't spill out.

If the rain spoils our picnic, but saves a farmer's crop,
who are we to say it shouldn't rain?

—Tom Barrett

Doing an injury puts you below your enemy; revenging one makes you but even with him; forgiving it sets you above him.

—Ben Franklin

AUGUST

18

When hornets build their nests near the ground, expect a cold and early winter.

● ◐ ○ ◑ ●

1587
Virginia Dare became the first English child born in the New World.

1920
The 19th Amendment to the Constitution, giving women the right to vote, was ratified by the states.

1960
G. D. Searle & Company began marketing the first birth control pills in the United States.

CLARA BARTON, humanitarian and founder of the American Red Cross, never held a grudge. Once, a friend reminded her of a wrong that had been done to her many years before. "Don't you remember?" the friend asked.

"No," Barton replied. "I distinctly remember forgetting that."

A WORD TO THE WISE

Edith Cavell was a British nurse who was executed by German authorities in 1915 for helping Allied soldiers escape from Belgium to the Netherlands, a neutral country. Before her execution, Cavell declared that she harbored no bitterness toward her enemies. "Patriotism is not enough. I must have no hatred or bitterness toward anyone."

When a honeybee stings, its barbed stinger becomes anchored in the flesh of its victim. The only way the bee can escape is to literally tear itself away, leaving part of its abdomen behind. The bee dies a short time later. Bitterness, resentment, and the desire for revenge may wound our enemies, but in the end revenge will hurt us even more.

Whoever is out of patience is out of possession of his soul. Men must not turn into bees, and kill themselves in stinging others.

—*Sir Francis Bacon*

The Things That Sting

❰ Know your stinging insects. Paper wasps, which are slender in shape and colored brown or reddish, typically build nests of paper "cells" attached to the eaves of buildings by a short stem. These wasps are not highly aggressive, although they can have a strong sting. In contrast, hornets (black, with a chunky shape) and yellow jackets (black with yellow bands) build solid nests near buildings or in the ground and are very aggressive. Their painful stings are more likely to cause allergic reactions.

❰ Relieve the pain of a sting by applying cider vinegar, lemon juice, or a slice of raw onion.

19

Ringing in the ear at night indicates a change of wind.

● ○ ◐ ○ ●

1812
The USS *Constitution* defeated the British frigate *Guerrière* off the coast of Nova Scotia.

1856
GAIL BORDEN patented his process for condensing milk. During the Civil War, condensed milk became a staple for soldiers.

1871
ORVILLE WRIGHT was born in Dayton, Ohio.

1946
Birthday of WILLIAM JEFFERSON "BILL" CLINTON, 42nd president of the United States (1993–2001).

The Roar of the Cloud

THE *Inspired* MIND

IN ONE OF Ben Franklin's experiments on electricity, he brought two electrically charged gun barrels to within 2 inches of each other, creating a loud snap. If lightning is electrical, he hypothesized, and a large thunderhead approaches near enough to release its charge, "how loud must be that crack?"

Lightning heats up the air around it, causing the air to expand rapidly, and the heated air molecules bump into cooler ones, causing the waves of air pressure we hear as thunder. The more forcefully the air molecules collide, the louder the thunderclap.

Sound—those fluctuating waves of air pressure—can be measured in decibels (dB), starting at 0 dB, the threshold of hearing. Normal conversation is 60 dB; a vacuum cleaner registers 80 dB. Excess exposure to noises above 90 dB can cause hearing loss. A loud motorcycle may register 100 dB, but a clap of thunder at 120 dB is right up there with the noise of a jackhammer or a front row seat at a rock concert.

The Purr of the Cat

A purring cat is, generally speaking, a relaxed, content cat. Recent studies suggest that the more your cat purrs, the greater its chances of a long and healthy life.

To figure your cat's age in equivalent human years, assign 16 human years to the cat's 1st year, 6 human years to the cat's 2nd year, and 4 human years to each succeeding cat year.

The exhilaration of flying is too keen, the pleasure too great, for it to be neglected as a sport.

—*Orville Wright*

APPLIANCE ADVICE

❦ Never install a dishwasher next to a refrigerator. They both emit heat and will run more efficiently if separated.

❦ To reduce the noise of appliances, especially the refrigerator, dishwasher, washing machine, and dryer, consider placing them on rubber or cork pads.

❦ Vacuum behind your refrigerator—especially the coils and condenser—at least once a year. To clean underneath, place an old nylon stocking or long sock over a yardstick and slide it around.

❦ Clean the rubber gaskets of your refrigerator using cotton swabs dipped in diluted ammonia.

Eat to please thyself,
but dress to please others.

—BEN FRANKLIN

FROM THE DAY he went into business for himself, Ben Franklin determined that he would not only *be* industrious but also would *appear* industrious to the watching world. He dressed plainly, never went fishing or hunting, and avoided "places of idle diversion." To demonstrate how hardworking he was, he would carry the paper he'd purchased back to his shop in a wheelbarrow he pushed himself. Meanwhile, Ben's chief competitor dressed like a dandy, lived expensively, frequented "places of idle diversion," and generally neglected his business. "Upon which," Ben said, "all business left him."

Of course, there are those who take plainness of dress to an extreme. On her way to work one day, social activist Dorothy Day passed some homeless men, one of whom approached her. He told he'd heard of some legal difficulties she was having and handed her a check, saying, "Here's two-fifty." She didn't look at the check until later, when she realized it wasn't for $2.50 but for $250. It was signed by W. H. Auden, the well-known poet.

1833
Birthday of BENJAMIN HARRISON, 23rd president of the United States (1889–1893).

1910
Birth of Finnish-American architect EERO SAARINEN, designer of the St. Louis Gateway Arch and Lincoln Center.

1940
British prime minister WINSTON CHURCHILL commended the Royal Air Force: "Never in the field of human conflict was so much owed by so many to so few."

THE EGG AND YOU

❖ For tender scrambled eggs, add 1 to 2 teaspoons water, milk, or cream for each egg when beating. The fluid produces steam, which lightens the eggs.

❖ To keep eggs fresh longer, store them in the carton (not uncovered in the refrigerator

egg compartment) in the coldest part of the refrigerator.

❖ The night before boiling eggs for deviled eggs, tape the carton shut and turn it on its side in the refrigerator. This centers the yolks for a nice presentation.

❖ For easy deviled eggs, put the yolks from hard-boiled eggs in a self-sealing plastic bag

and add the other ingredients (mayonnaise, salt, black pepper, cayenne pepper or Tabasco sauce, and perhaps minced celery or herbs). Knead the bag to mix. Snip off a corner of the bag and pipe the filling into the egg whites. Garnish as desired.

❖ Use a sturdy egg slicer for slicing strawberries, mushrooms, and peeled kiwifruit as well as hard-boiled eggs.

AUGUST

21

Guitar strings shorten before rain.

● ○ ○ ● ●

1841
JOHN HAMPSON of New Orleans patented an improved version of venetian blinds.

1959
Hawaii became the 50th state.

■ ■ ■

Let my words,
like vegetables, be
tender and sweet,
for tomorrow I may
have to eat them.

—*Author Unknown*

Garden Ratatouille

This classic summer dish can be made ahead and served warm or cold. Use any leftovers to fill omelettes and tortillas.

1 medium eggplant, about
   1 pound, peeled and cut
   into 1-inch cubes
2 medium zucchini, cut into
   ¼-inch-thick slices
2 teaspoons kosher salt
3 tablespoons olive oil
1 large onion, chopped
2 green bell peppers, seeded
   and cut into strips
2 cloves garlic, minced
2 tablespoons chopped fresh
   basil
1 tablespoon chopped fresh
   oregano
3 medium ripe tomatoes,
   coarsely chopped
1 teaspoon salt
Freshly ground black pepper
¼ cup imported black olives,
   pitted

Place the eggplant and zucchini in a colander and sprinkle with the kosher salt. Let drain for 30 minutes. Rinse and dry the vegetables and set aside. Heat the oil in a 12-inch skillet over medium heat and cook the onion, peppers, and garlic until tender, stirring often. Add the eggplant, zucchini, basil, and oregano. Cover and cook, stirring often, for about 10 minutes, or until the vegetables are soft. Add the tomatoes, cover, and cook for about 5 minutes, until the tomatoes are soft. Add the salt and season with pepper to taste. Garnish with the olives. Serve hot or cold.

Makes 4 servings

Harvesting Hints for Vegetables

◖ When you pull carrots, wash them off with the hose and cut off the green tops. (Leaving the tops on will make the carrots limp.) Store in plastic bags in the refrigerator.

◖ Patrol your zucchini patch daily and pick the squash when they're about 8 inches long. Feed your compost— or your chickens—those baseball bat–size zucchini and feel no guilt.

◖ Harvest onions for storage when the tops have turned brown and keeled over. Let the onions sit on top of the dirt (as long as it is dry) for a day before storing.

◖ If you wait until a hard frost to dig your potatoes, be sure to mark the rows now, before the foliage dies back.

Before You Paint

I F Y O U W E R E N ' T responsible for painting something the first time, always make sure you know what you're about to paint over. To test whether a painted finish is oil- or latex-based, apply a small drop of nail polish remover to a hidden section. If it is latex paint, the remover will soften it and make it easy to rub off. If it is oil paint, the remover will dull the finish. As a rule, do not apply latex paint over oil. If it's safe to proceed, follow these steps.

PRACTICAL

PRIMER

1. Scrape off any loose paint.
2. Fill any holes or cracks.
3. Sand the filled areas.
4. Wipe with a damp cloth. If the surface is heavily soiled or has a glossy finish, clean with a commercial cleaner such as trisodium phosphate (TSP).
5. Remove all switch plates, electrical socket plates, and window hardware and store them, with their screws, in a coffee can. Or put each item and its hardware in individual plastic sandwich bags.
6. Apply a primer base coat, if necessary. Cover water-stained areas with a commercial stain-killing product.
7. Remove any dust or particles again with a damp cloth.
8. Use masking tape to cover adjacent windows and door sash.
9. When you begin painting, place a paper plate under your paint can to protect against paint rings.

NATURE WATCH

Anyone who has tried to help a child catch a dragonfly for a science project knows how fast these winged creatures fly. If you see a pair hovering near the edge of a pond, it's probably a male hovering above a female. She is looking for a place to lay her eggs; he is protecting his genetic interests. Her fertilized eggs will be laid in the water, unless the female is so harassed by competing males that she flies off in disgust.

AUGUST

22

So many fogs in August we see, So many snows that year will be.

● ◐ ○ ◐ ●

1485
King RICHARD III was killed at the Battle of Bosworth Field, England.

1762
ANN FRANKLIN, sister-in-law of BEN FRANKLIN, became the editor of the *Newport (R.I.) Mercury.*

1902
THEODORE ROOSEVELT became the first president to ride in an automobile.

■ ■ ■

What may be done at any time will be done at no time.

—*Scottish Proverb*

23

1912
Birthday of dancer
GENE KELLY.

1933
A hurricane hit Norfolk,
Virginia, producing a tide
7 feet above normal.

1966
Lunar Orbiter 1 took the
first photograph of Earth
from the moon.

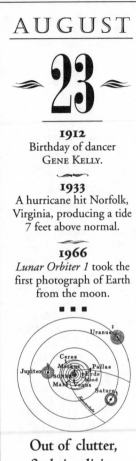

Out of clutter,
find simplicity.
—*Albert Einstein*

Let all your things have their places; let each part of your business have its time.

—BEN FRANKLIN

OF ALL THE VIRTUES Ben Franklin attempted to practice, he found orderliness the most difficult to achieve. "In truth, I found myself incorrigible with respect to order," he wrote.

But when it comes to clutter, Ben had nothing on the infamous Collyer brothers. The sons of well-to-do Manhattanites, Homer and Langley Collyer lived most of their lives in the family's three-story mansion, becoming more and more reclusive as they grew older. When the brothers died in 1947, authorities removed more than 100 tons of junk from

their home, including mountains of newspapers, broken furniture, old phone books, rusted machinery, toys, medical equipment (including an x-ray machine), and much, much more. Junk was fashioned into elaborate booby traps to keep anyone from entering the house, which prevented police from even finding the brothers for several days.

In 1875, Samuel Smiles wrote a book titled *Thrift*, which contains the now famous prescription for those of us who are order-challenged: "A place for everything, and everything in its place."

Getting Organized and Staying That Way

◖ Keep a canvas bag in the car to hold all those items you pick up while running everyday errands.

◖ Subdivide big dresser drawers with shoe boxes or several plastic storage boxes to help little kids put away and find their clothing. This is also helpful for "big kids"

who need to separate their underwear from their socks or their running clothes from their pj's.

◖ Sort your mail next to a recycling bin, which can immediately receive junk mail, duplicate catalogs, envelope stuffers, and anything else you don't want. Separate bills

from personal mail and put them where you will have to handle them only once.

◖ Send your child off to college with a two-drawer filing cabinet with a locking bottom drawer. He can use it as a bedside table, for school files, and as a place to keep valuables.

String Too Short to Be Saved

LEST YOU BE DEEMED a pack rat, consider carefully what you choose to stockpile. Twist ties come in handy and are easy to store, but newspapers and empty boxes pile up quickly and can take over the house. In general, do not stockpile what you can recycle or someone else can use. Value your free space and time as much as you value your stuff. "Waste not, want not" is all well and good, within limits, but if you haven't found a use for something within a year, pass it on.

PRACTICAL PRIMER

- If an item of clothing or pair of shoes doesn't fit or you haven't worn it in a year, get rid of it. Pass it on to the Salvation Army or another secondhand shop.
- Go through the medicine cabinet twice a year and throw out any expired prescriptions or anything you've forgotten how to use.
- Sort through your photos and discard duplicates or any poor shots. Throw away negatives unless you need them for copies.
- Keep only the current issue of mail-order catalogs. When a new issue arrives, recycle the previous one.

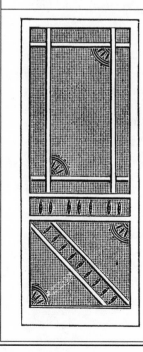

HANDYPERSON PROJECTS

❖ If your screen window or door has sustained a puncture or tear, clip a square of metal screening a little larger than the ripped area. Bend the wires at the edges so they are perpendicular to the flat mesh, then press the patch over the tear. Reaching from the opposite side of the torn screen, press the edge wires flat so that they hook around the original screening.

❖ Make an instant root cellar by burying an old metal school locker in the dirt floor of a shed or garage, with the door facing up. Store root crops in it, cushioned in straw, and cover it with a piece of carpet.

25

Hang up a snakeskin, and it will bring rain.

● ○ ○ ● ●

1875
MATTHEW WEBB became the first person to swim the English Channel.

1916
The National Park Service was established.

1944
Paris was liberated by U.S. and French troops during World War II.

■ ■ ■

So live that your memories will be part of your happiness.

—Author Unknown

Learning to Swim

IN 1726, while in England, 20-year-old Ben Franklin taught two friends "to swim in a few hours," he wrote in his *Autobiography*. Then just before embarking for home, Ben was asked by an Englishman to teach his sons how to swim, promising to reward him handsomely. Time did not permit it, but if he "were to remain in England and open a swimming-school," Ben mused, he could make a good living at it. He went on to write *The Art of Swimming* (1768), but the first swimming school in America didn't open until 1827, when Francis Leiber founded one in Boston. Students practiced their strokes while being suspended by a rope from a pole.

THE *Inspired* MIND

J. Arthur Trudgen, learning from Native American swimmers, popularized a thrusting style in the 1870s. By 1920 Hawaiian swimmer Duke Kahanamoku (like Ben, self-taught) used a crawl stroke, passed down from generations of island swimmers, to become a champion competitor. In 1962, a 2-year-old swimmer became the youngest person ever to complete the beginner's test of the American Red Cross, and the child's teacher, Virginia Newman, wrote a book that Ben would have appreciated, *Teaching an Infant to Swim*.

KEEPING SUMMER MEMORIES

❦ Collect plain, inexpensive picture frames. Paint each one, then attach a trinket that relates to the photo to be framed —a fishing lure, a baby's safety pin, a small souvenir.

❦ Encircle a plain frame with glued-on buttons, beach glass, coins, or other memorabilia.

❦ Cover frames with fabric to match your decor. Cut fabric 2 inches larger than the frame on all sides. Snip off the corners of the fabric. Brush the frame

with a thin coat of glue, then fold the fabric around, gluing the excess to the back. Cut a large **X** in the front of the fabric (where the opening is), with the "arms" extending from opposite corner to opposite corner. Draw the fabric smoothly to the back, gluing and trimming as needed.

—JS

Courage would fight, but discretion won't let him.

—Ben Franklin

D URING THE French and Indian War (1754–1763), relations between regular British troops and their American counterparts were often strained. One American commander named Israel Putnam ran afoul of a British major, who challenged him to a duel. Realizing that he was unlikely to survive such an encounter, Putnam invited the major to his tent to discuss an alternative test of honor. The men were seated on gunpowder kegs into which Putnam had inserted fuses. He suggested that they light the fuses, and the first one to move would be the loser.

The major accepted the challenge. The fuses were lit, and Putnam calmly began smoking his pipe. As the

fuses burned down, the major grew more and more nervous, but Putnam didn't flinch. Finally, as the others in the tent ran to escape the impending explosion, the major decided he'd had enough. He leaped up and ran, admitting defeat. Only then did the truth come out—the kegs were full of onions, not gunpowder, unlikely to hurt even the bravest soldier.

1883
The Krakatoa volcano erupted in the East Indies, an explosion that was heard 2,500 miles away. Volcanic ash drifted around the globe and caused the sun to appear blue or green.

1935
Birth of
GERALDINE FERRARO, the first woman to be nominated for vice president by a major U.S. political party.

WOMANLY WISDOM

❖ If pre- or postmenstrual cramps give you trouble, avoid alcohol, caffeine, sugar, chocolate, cola, and tobacco. Increase your consumption of calcium.

❖ For *le moment de la lune* (the moon change, or menstruation), add vitamin B_6–rich foods to your diet: sunflower seeds, lentils, lima beans, pinto beans, black-eyed peas, rice bran, broccoli, and asparagus.

❖ For yeast infections, reduce your sugar intake, drink cranberry juice, and add garlic to your diet.

❖ Apply a compress of mint leaves to your forehead to relieve tension headaches. Or soak a cloth in a tea made from chamomile or dill and apply it to your forehead or eyes.

❖ To identify herbal remedies that are especially helpful to women, consider the common name of the plant. Motherwort, birthwort, lady's-mantle, and mother's-heart were all traditional cures used by midwives.

27

1908
Folsom, New Mexico,
telephone operator
SARAH ROOKE managed
to warn most of the
townspeople of rising
floodwaters but perished
when the building she was
in was swept away.

1908
Birthday of
LYNDON B. JOHNSON,
36th president of the
United States
(1963–1969).

1910
MOTHER TERESA
was born.

1912
EDGAR RICE BURROUGHS's
book *Tarzan of the Apes*
was published.

Fresh Corn Chowder

*This sweet and buttery chowder takes advantage of
the bountiful sweet corn crop of late August.*

6 ears sweet corn, shucked
3 medium red potatoes, cut
   into ½-inch cubes
3 tablespoons unsalted butter
1 medium onion, diced
¼ cup finely chopped red bell
   pepper
1 tablespoon flour
3 cups milk
1 bay leaf
Salt and freshly ground
   black pepper

Stand an ear of corn on its
stem end in a large bowl and
slice down the rows of kernels (a
serrated knife works well), taking
care not to dig into the cob. Repeat for the remaining ears. Set
the kernels aside.

Place the cobs and potatoes in
a large pot of salted water and
bring to a boil. Simmer for 10
minutes, or until the potatoes are
cooked but still firm. Drain, re-
serving 1 cup of the cooking
water. Discard the cobs. Toss the potatoes with the corn kernels.

In a large saucepan, heat the butter over medium heat. Add the
onion and bell pepper and cook until soft. Do not let brown. Add
the flour and stir until the mixture foams. Add the reserved cooking water and bring to a boil, stirring until the mixture thickens.
Slowly add the milk, stirring well. Add the corn-potato mixture
and bay leaf. Cover and heat gently (do not
boil) for about 5 minutes, just until the corn is
tender. Remove the bay leaf and season with
salt and pepper to taste.   *Makes 4 to 6 servings*

SWEET CORN SUCCESS

❖ Pick corn when the silks feel
slightly dry and a kernel pierced
with your fingernail squirts white
milk. Eat as soon as possible.

❖ Cook sweet corn in a steamer
basket over boiling water for about
5 minutes. Or grill it on a gas or
charcoal grill. To grill, carefully
pull back the husks, remove the
silks, rub the corn with butter or

olive oil, and rewrap the husks
around the cob. Grill for about 10
minutes, turning frequently.

❖ Never boil sweet corn for more
than 5 minutes, and always cook it
in unsalted boiling water. To keep
sweet corn yellow, add a drop of
lemon juice to the cooking water
after the corn has cooked and before you remove the ears.

*August brings the
ears of corn,
Then the harvest
home is born.*
—*Sarah Loleridge*

Corn and Blackbirds

FARMERS AND GARDENERS put up scarecrows and hang shiny mirrors to scare blackbirds out of the corn patch, but do you know that blackbirds prey on the insects that do great damage to corn? Although blackbirds have an undeniable appetite for ripening corn, legions of corn earworms, European corn borers, and fall armyworms also attack sweet corn. Predatory insects such as the 12-spotted ladybug and the insidious flower bug can help control these pests. Other biocontrol stars, such as the parasitic *Trichogramma* wasp and the Mexican free-tailed bat, also have amazing appetites for corn pests.

In a 1753 letter to a friend in England, Ben Franklin pointed out the wisdom of allowing nature to regulate itself:

In New England they once thought Black-birds useless and mischievous to their corn, they made Laws to destroy them, the consequence was, the Black-birds were diminished but a kind of Worms which devoured their Grass, and which the Black-birds had been used to feed on, increased prodigiously; Then finding their Loss in Grass much greater than their saving in corn they wished again for their Black-birds.

Summer's End

St. Augustine of Hippo (born in North Africa in A.D. 354), was known for his profound understanding of theology and insights into human nature. Perhaps memories of his wild youth in Carthage, filled with carousing and what we would now consider "risky behavior," helped to deepen his compassion as an adult.

Summer, like youth, is fleeting. We "welcome the coming, speed the parting guest," but few of us like to see summer end. If it's any comfort, time moves a little slower in the summer, or at least the grandfather clocks do. It turns out that metal pendulums expand with the heat, making them slightly longer and slightly slower. So enjoy your extra bit of summer and extended youth, ethereal though they may be. After that, "It is time to be old, / To take in sail," as Ralph Waldo Emerson advised.

1609
HENRY HUDSON, sailing for the Dutch East India Company, began exploring Delaware Bay.

1908
Ornithologist ROGER TORY PETERSON was born.

1963
MARTIN LUTHER KING JR. delivered his "I Have a Dream" speech in Washington, D.C.

■ ■ ■

Youth is the gift of nature, but age is a work of art.

—*Stanislaw J. Lec*

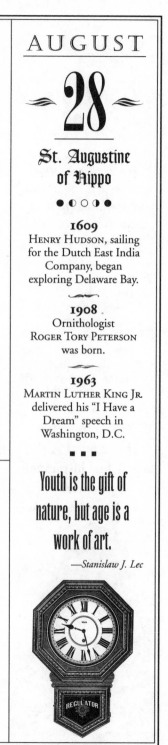

29

If crows fly in pairs, expect fine weather. A crow flying alone indicates foul weather to come.

● ○ ○ ◐ ●

1894
BILLY "POP" SCHRIVER caught a ball dropped from the Washington Monument.

1915
Actress INGRID BERGMAN was born. She died on her birthday in 1982.

■ ■ ■

You don't get tired of muffins, but you don't find inspiration in them.

—*George Bernard Shaw*

Sausage and Corn Breakfast Muffins

Practically a meal in themselves, these savory muffins make a hearty back-to-school breakfast for kids or a fine contribution to a Sunday brunch.

1 pound lean bulk sausage
1¼ cups flour
¾ cup cornmeal
¼ cup sugar
1 scant tablespoon baking powder
1 teaspoon baking soda
½ teaspoon salt
2 eggs
1 cup buttermilk
¼ cup vegetable oil
1 cup grated cheddar cheese
1 cup fresh corn kernels (2 to 3 ears corn)
¼ cup minced red bell pepper
1 tablespoon minced fresh parsley

Preheat the oven to 400°F. Grease a 12-cup muffin tin. In a skillet, cook the sausage over medium heat until done; drain well on paper towels. In a large bowl, combine the flour, cornmeal, sugar, baking powder, baking soda, and salt. In another bowl, beat together the eggs, buttermilk, and oil. Add the liquid mixture to the flour mixture and stir until moistened but still lumpy. Fold in the cheese, corn kernels, bell pepper, parsley, and sausage. Spoon into the prepared tin and bake for 20 minutes, or until a toothpick inserted in a muffin comes out clean. Let sit for 5 minutes, then transfer to a wire rack to cool. *Makes 12*

MUFFIN MAGIC

☾ For ease in removing muffins and cakes from pans after cooking, take the hot pan out of the oven and place it on a wet towel for a couple of minutes.

☾ If you are unable to serve your freshly baked muffins right out of the oven, don't let them sit in the tin until serving, or they will get soggy. To rewarm muffins, place them in a paper bag in a low oven (200°F) for 5 to10 minutes.

☾ If you don't have enough batter to fill the muffin tin, fill the empty cups partway with water to keep the heat evenly distributed. This will help the muffins bake without scorching.

☾ Use an ice cream scoop as a dipper for muffin batter and cookie dough.

> *Do good to thy friend to keep him, to thy enemy to gain him.*
>
> —BEN FRANKLIN

WHEN AVERELL HARRIMAN was ambassador to Russia, he was under constant surveillance by the KGB. He knew it, and they knew he knew it.

One winter weekend, Harriman drove to the country to visit a friend, a long and arduous journey even in his four-wheel-drive jeep. He warned the police that it would be a tortuous drive, but an officer was assigned to tail him anyway. Sure enough, the police sedan got stuck on the way, and the officer had no choice but to follow Harriman on foot. The ambassador obligingly slowed his vehicle so the policeman could keep up, but he began to worry that the policeman would freeze to death (and, no doubt, he wanted to get to his engagement sooner rather than later). He invited the policeman into his jeep, promising not to tell anyone, and the officer and the ambassador rode together for the remainder of the journey.

A WORD TO THE WISE

> My interest is in the future because I am going to spend the rest of my life there.
>
> —*Charles Franklin Kettering*

AUGUST

30

1830
The B&O Railroad discontinued horse-powered locomotives.

1908
Actor FRED MACMURRAY was born.

1963
A telephone hotline was established between the White House and the Kremlin.

Indoor Traffic: Cleaning Underfoot

❖ Clean a bathroom tile or no-wax floor with a mixture of ½ cup baking soda and 1 gallon warm water. Mop, then rinse.

❖ Sprinkle baking soda on a damp sponge and use to remove black heel marks or rust spots on vinyl or linoleum floors. Or use a pencil eraser to rub out black scuff marks on light-colored linoleum floors.

❖ Wash a wood or tile floor with an orange cut in half. Put one half in each hand, get down on your knees, and work in circles to remove grease and dirt. Rinse with a damp rag.

❖ To absorb grease stains on carpets, sprinkle the stains with cornmeal. Let sit for 1 hour, then vacuum. Repeat, if necessary.

❖ Remove greasy spills by sponging with a solution of four parts rubbing alcohol and one part salt.

~31~

1870

Birthday of educator
MARIA MONTESSORI
(1870) and violinist
ITZHAK PERLMAN (1945).

1964

The U.S. Census Bureau
reported that
California had surpassed
New York as the most
populous state.

∎ ∎ ∎

**Try as we may to make
a silence, we cannot.**

—*John Cage*

---

*As we must account for
every idle word, so we must for
every idle silence.*

—BEN FRANKLIN

AN ENGLISH COMPOSER found out that silence may indeed be golden when he released a piece that consisted entirely of, well, silence. Mike Batt, formerly with a group called the Wombles, released a song called "A One-Minute Silence" with his new group, the Planets. Unfortunately, the late American composer John Cage had already "composed" a song of silence called "4:33," which consists of 4 minutes, 33 seconds of silence (except for patrons coughing and shuffling their programs) recorded at a concert hall. The company that owns the copyright to Cage's recording sued Batt for copyright infringement, seeking thousands of dollars in royalties. Batt, who denied that he copied Cage's composition, said he'd rather go to prison than pay the royalties. "Mine is a much better silent piece," he said. "I have been able to say in one minute what Cage could only say in four minutes and thirty-three seconds."

A WORD TO THE WISE

Animal Meteorologists

You can expect:

❖ Rain when dogs eat grass, cats wash behind their ears, or donkeys bray.

❖ A mild winter when chipmunks stay active after October.

❖ A storm when foxes bark at night.

❖ An early winter when horses' coats are rough and thick.

NATURE WATCH

Tiger moths, active at night, are among the most beautiful winged creatures, with their bright gold and black markings. But did you know that the caterpillar form of the Isabella tiger moth is the beloved, bristly woolly bear? These caterpillars, which curl up into a ball if you bother them, are thought to predict the weather during the coming winter: the wider the black band on the brown caterpillar, the more severe the winter. Check out your local woolly bears and make a note.

TIGER MOTH

SEPTEMBER, *the Ninth Month*

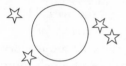

Full Harvest Moon

is the full moon closest to the autumnal equinox. If September's moon turns full early in the month, it is usually called the *Full Barley Moon* instead, and the harvest moon moves to October.

Sign of the Zodiac:
Virgo (August 23–September 22)

Element: Earth

Quality: Logical

Birthstone: Sapphire

Flower: Aster

SEPTEMBER WAS the seventh (*septem*) month in the old Roman calendar. When Julius Caesar decided to start the year with January instead of March, September kept its name but not its position. We love it right where it is. As Henry Wadsworth Longfellow wrote,

> *The morrow was a bright September morn;*
> *The earth was beautiful as if new-born;*
> *There was that nameless splendor everywhere*
> *That wild exhilaration in the air.*

Perhaps the only thing prettier than a September morn is the sight of the Full Harvest Moon rising, bathing our gardens and fields in golden light. In medieval Europe, harvest festivals made this a gala month, and the greatest of them was Michaelmas, on the 29th. Everyone feasted on the fat Michaelmas goose, fresh oatcakes and barley cakes, and new wine.

Amid the hustle and bustle of school bus schedules, backpacks, and lunch boxes, we take the first Monday in September off to honor American workers. We buy freshly harvested cranberries and crisp apples and scan the trees for autumn tints. We throw a sweater around our shoulders after sunset, worry about frost, and, just as our ancestors did, wait for that big old harvest moon to rise.

SEPTEMBER

1

1730
BEN FRANKLIN and
DEBORAH READ became
husband and wife in a
common-law union.
Deborah's first husband,
a scoundrel named
ROGERS, had fled
Philadelphia after
stealing a slave.

1849
A photograph of the full
moon was taken by
SAMUEL HUMPHREY at
Canandaigua, New York.
It is the earliest surviving
photo of Earth's satellite.

1878
The first female
telephone operator was
employed, in Boston.

• • •

Describing her
first day back in
grade school after
a long absence,
a teacher said,
"It was like trying
to hold 35 corks
under water at the
same time."

—*Mark Twain*

A man without a wife, is but half a man.

—BEN FRANKLIN

—BK

EN FRANKLIN'S WIFE, Deborah, was a helpmate to him, recognized for her work ethic and many skills. Others of Ben's generation also readily acknowledged how much they relied on their wives. Abigail Adams, for example, was more than a helpmate to her husband, John; she was his political advisor, sounding board, and soul mate.

Women's roles have changed since the days of Ben Franklin and John Adams, and divorce rates have gone through the roof, but the marital bond remains strong, at least for some. Consider the experience of Mark Wayne Clark, the American general who was supreme commander of United Nations forces in Korea. Clark was once asked what was the best advice ever given to him. He replied, "To marry the girl I did." When asked who gave him that advice, Clark said, "She did."

How to Ease Into the New School Year

❖ Offer a yo-yo to a child who is nervous while waiting for the school bus. Playing with a yo-yo—and learning new tricks to show her friends—is an excellent stress buster.

❖ Include chopsticks in a meal or lunch box to add fun and encourage the sampling of new foods. Even young children can manage the tweezer-type "cheaters."

❖ At the end of the day, treat your child to a calming cup of tea (chamomile is a good choice) or some soothing music. Avoid soda, caffeine, or sugary snacks that provide a quick surge of energy but then a crash.

❖ Start a file for each child with the "best of the best" in school papers and artwork. Present their portfolios to them at the end of the school year as keepsakes.

The King's cheese is half wasted in parings: But no matter, 'tis made of the people's milk.

—Ben Franklin

Each month from 1975 to 1988, Wisconsin senator William Proxmire gave the Golden Fleece Award to a government agency that demonstrated what he called "wasteful, ridiculous, or ironic use of the taxpayers' money." Following are some of the winners of the not-so-coveted award.

- Department of Agriculture, which spent nearly $46,000 to find out how long it takes to cook breakfast
- Law Enforcement Assistance Administration, for a $27,000 study that examined why inmates want to escape from prison
- Department of the Army, which spent $6,000 to create a 17-page document explaining how to buy a bottle of Worcestershire sauce
- Department of Education, for its expenditure of $219,592 on a curriculum designed to teach college students how to watch television
- Environmental Protection Agency, which spent more than $1 million in 1980 to preserve a sewer in Trenton, New Jersey, as a historical monument

A WORD TO THE WISE

Enjoying the King's Cheese

For a wheel of hard cheese, cut wedges from the center out, then slice the wedges crosswise. For a wheel of soft cheese, such as Brie, also cut triangular wedges, but slice the wedges lengthwise into thin pieces.

Bring cheese to room temperature before serving. Always leave it wrapped while it is warming up.

Simply cut or scrape off mold on the outside of cheese. It is not harmful.

Do not overcook cheese. When it is melted, it is cooked. High temperatures and long cooking toughen cheese.

Serve cheese with a sturdy bread rather than with crackers. The yeast in the bread "marries" the cheese with wine or beer.

SEPTEMBER

2

When seagulls fly inland, expect a storm.

● ◐ ○ ◐ ●

1789
The U.S. Department of the Treasury was established.

1935
A Labor Day hurricane in the Florida Keys took 400 lives.

1945
Japan formally surrendered to the United States aboard the battleship *Missouri*.

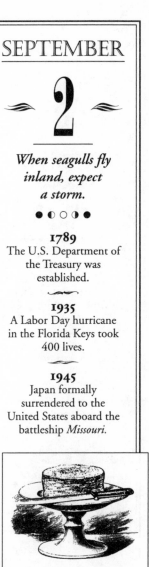

Only peril can bring the French together. One can't impose unity out of the blue on a country that has 265 different kinds of cheese.

—*Charles de Gaulle*

3

St. Gregory the Great

● ○ ○ ○ ●

1714

BEN FRANKLIN was enrolled in a Boston grammar school at the age of 8. His family later switched him to a school for writing and arithmetic. The school's founder, GEORGE BROWNELL, also taught dancing, music, and fancy embroidery.

1783

The Treaty of Paris was signed, ending the Revolutionary War.

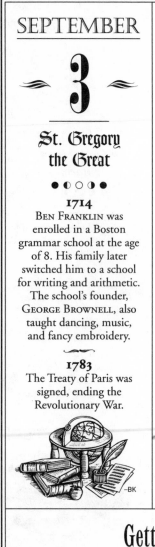

—BK

A cypher [zero] and humility make the other figures and virtues of ten-fold value.

—BEN FRANKLIN

THE IRISH POET Thomas Moore described it this way: "Humility, that low, sweet root, from which all heavenly virtues shoot."

Take the case of the college that was in dire financial straits. A visitor to the campus was considering donating some money but wanted to make sure it would be used well. He came to the campus and asked a man who was whitewashing a wall where he might find the president of the college. "I think you can see him at his house at twelve," the man said.

A WORD TO THE WISE

The visitor went to the house at noon and met the president—the same man who had been whitewashing the wall. The visitor was so impressed by the president's humble dedication that he wrote the college a check for $50,000 the next day.

St. Francis of Assisi renounced his earthly wealth, privilege, and prestige, but he still achieved greatness. When asked to explain this, Francis said that God had looked for the littlest, most insignificant man on the face of the earth and, finding Francis, had said, "I will work through him. He won't be proud of it."

> If I only had a little humility, I'd be perfect.
>
> —*Ted Turner*

Getting Organized for School and Work

◖ Buy a three-hole punch and a three-ring binder and keep them near your phone and household calendar. Organize all those schedules and notices regarding school, sports, and community events. Buy plastic sleeves with prepunched holes for schedules you refer to often.

◖ If you work the night shift and find that it disrupts your sleep habits, try keeping your work lights brighter than usual, then wearing very dark sunglasses for the hour or so before you plan to sleep. Also darken your bedroom or wear an eye mask while you sleep.

◖ Has Labor Day prompted you to ask for a raise? Consider how your timing fits into the fiscal year. Never compare yourself directly with other employees, but know the pay range and the local market. Mention skills you've recently added or unusual productivity.

The Newsboy

THE FIRST TO ANSWER the *New York Sun*'s ad seeking a vendor and offering a "liberal discount . . . to those who buy to sell again" was 10-year-old Barney Flaherty, who became the nation's first paperboy on September 4, 1833. Newspaper Carrier Day commemorates that date.

In Great Barrington, Massachusetts, a statue of a newsboy, dedicated in 1895, was

THE *Inspired* MIND

the gift of a grateful publisher whose success depended on his youthful hawkers. Yet hundreds of young "newsies" in New York City went on strike in 1899 for better pay, revealing that children were being exploited by powerful newspaper publishers. After 2 weeks, seeing sales plummet, publishers Joseph Pulitzer and William Randolph Hearst made concessions to the newsboys.

But was Barney Flaherty *really* the first paperboy? Fifteen-year-old Ben Franklin, apprenticed to his brother James, publisher of the *New England Courant* in Boston, printed the newspaper beginning in 1721. In addition, Ben reports in his *Autobiography,* "I was employed to carry the papers thro' the streets to the customers."

A warm autumn, a long winter.

● ● ○ ○ ●

1888
GEORGE EASTMAN patented a camera that used rolls of film.

1972
Swimmer MARK SPITZ became the first Olympic competitor to win seven gold medals in one Olympic Games.

1988
Red Bluff, California, was the nation's hot spot with a reading of 118°F, while Los Angeles equaled its all-time high of 110°F.

■ ■ ■

WHAT MICE REALLY HATE

If you store furniture for a season or close up a summer cottage, spread newspapers on mattresses and furniture. Mice don't like running across noisy papers.

A good newspaper, I suppose, is a nation talking to itself.

—*Arthur Miller*

7 Ingenious Ways to Use a Fabric Softener Sheet

Use it:
1. To rub soap scum off your shower doors
2. To polish the chrome fixtures in your bathroom
3. To give a quick shine to your shoes
4. In your suitcase to keep clothes smelling fresh
5. In your underwear drawer for a fresh scent
6. To dust your computer or television screen
7. To dust the leaves of houseplants

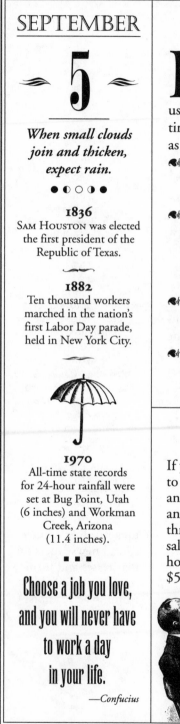

5

When small clouds join and thicken, expect rain.

● ● ○ ◐ ●

1836
Sam Houston was elected the first president of the Republic of Texas.

1882
Ten thousand workers marched in the nation's first Labor Day parade, held in New York City.

1970
All-time state records for 24-hour rainfall were set at Bug Point, Utah (6 inches) and Workman Creek, Arizona (11.4 inches).

■ ■ ■

Choose a job you love, and you will never have to work a day in your life.

—*Confucius*

Work, Work, Work

B Y WORKING faithfully 8 hours a day, you may eventually get to be a boss and work 12 hours a day," quipped poet Robert Frost, who preferred to be his own boss. For most of us, work is a necessity and, if we are lucky, a pleasure. For those times when your job is stressful or tedious, perhaps the remedy is as close as your teacup or lunch box.

PRACTICAL PRIMER

- Choose chamomile tea to help you relax on stressful workdays. For clearer thinking, choose ginkgo.
- Do you get headaches on weekend mornings, just when you have the chance to sleep in? Consider whether caffeine withdrawal may be the reason. If you ordinarily drink two or more cups of coffee early in the day, you may get a headache when you don't.
- Job review coming up? To reduce tension, eat a calcium-rich snack, such as a cup of yogurt, a honey sesame granola bar, or a glass of milk or fortified orange juice.
- If you are in the habit of leaving for work without your lunch box, try this: Pack your lunch, then put your car keys on top. You won't get far without them.

Should You Take That New Job?

If you are offered a new job at a certain hourly wage, here's how to compute the annual salary quickly. Double the hourly wage and add three zeros. For example, if a job pays $8 an hour, double that to get $16, then add three zeros to get $16,000 a year in salary. Go in reverse to figure the hourly wage from the salary: $50,000 is $25 an hour.

Rush Hour Pasta and Peas

Prepare the vegetables while the pasta is cooking, and this colorful and satisfying supper will be on the table in about 20 minutes.

3 tablespoons olive oil or butter

2 cloves garlic, finely chopped

3 ripe tomatoes, coarsely chopped

2 stalks celery, finely chopped

1 cup fresh peas or frozen petite peas

8 ounces pasta, cooked and drained

Freshly grated Parmesan cheese

1 tablespoon chopped fresh parsley

Heat the oil or butter in a skillet over medium heat. Add the garlic and sauté until tender. Do not brown. Add the tomatoes, celery, and peas. Cook for 5 minutes, stirring occasionally. Serve over the hot pasta, sprinkled with the Parmesan cheese and garnished with the parsley.

Makes 4 servings

Cooking with Peas

❧ One pound medium peas in the pod yields about 1 cup cooked shelled peas (2 or 3 servings). When buying fresh peas, look for plump, bright green pods. Avoid pale or yellowish pods, because the peas inside will be starchy.

❧ Peas should always be undercooked—they will taste sweeter. When cooking fresh peas, wash a few of the empty pods and add them to the peas during cooking to intensify the flavor.

❧ One pound dried split peas yields about 5 cups cooked split peas. For a 6-serving batch of soup, 8 ounces of split peas is usually enough.

NATURE WATCH

Along the Atlantic, Mississippi, and Pacific Flyways of North America, migratory birds are beginning their long journeys from as far north as the Arctic Circle to their wintering grounds thousands of miles to the south. This is an exciting time of year for bird-watchers, since unusual avian visitors may stop for a rest. Invest in a good field guide so you can identify local and migrant birds.

6

1620
The Pilgrims left England for America.

1757
Birthday of the marquis de LAFAYETTE, French soldier who fought in the American Revolution.

1989
The ROLLING STONES held a rehearsal at Three Rivers Stadium for their upcoming concert, bumping the Pittsburgh Steelers football team from a practice on their own field.

• • •

The greatest lesson we can learn from the past . . . is that freedom is at the core of every successful nation in the world.

—*Frederick Chiluba*

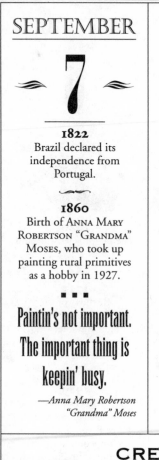

SEPTEMBER

7

1822
Brazil declared its independence from Portugal.

1860
Birth of ANNA MARY ROBERTSON "GRANDMA" MOSES, who took up painting rural primitives as a hobby in 1927.

■ ■ ■

Paintin's not important. The important thing is keepin' busy.

—Anna Mary Robertson "Grandma" Moses

There are lazy minds as well as lazy bodies.

—BEN FRANKLIN

WHEN YOUNG Ben Franklin moved to Philadelphia, his first employer was a printer named Keimer. Once, Ben accompanied Keimer on a trip to New Jersey to print an order of paper money for the colony. Several local men had been appointed to watch the process and ensure that only the requested amount of money was printed.

The locals were impressed by Ben's wit and breadth of knowledge, which he credited to his habit of constantly reading and trying to improve himself. As a result, the citizens treated him very kindly, inviting him to their homes and introducing him to other members of the community. Ben's boss, however, didn't fare so well. "In truth, he was an odd fish," Ben said. Ignorant of everyday life, argumentative, slovenly, and somewhat dishonest, old man Keimer was largely ignored by the locals. Eventually, Keimer went out of business, and the tireless and charming Ben became one of the most prosperous businessmen in the colonies.

CREATING A COUNTRY LOOK

❖ To re-create the intricate pattern in a vintage lace handkerchief or doily, make a color photocopy of it. Cut the copy into decorative paper edges for shelves or china cabinets.

❖ Spray-paint a collection of old, dented flatware using the colors of your kitchen or breakfast nook. Then use pliers to bend the forks, knives, and spoons into hooks that can be nailed up to hold towels, aprons, and brooms. Or nail the hooks to a board to make an unusual rack for coats and hats.

❖ Use an old cradle, maple syrup bucket, or cranberry scoop as a magazine rack.

❖ Make your own cloth napkins from colorful cotton fabric. One yard of 36-inch-wide cotton makes nine 12-inch squares, which you can hem or bind to finish the napkins. Buy some additional fabric for a coordinating tablecloth or runner.

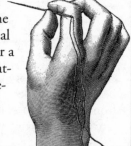

How Sweet It Is

CHALLAH IS DIPPED in honey on Rosh Hashanah eve to bring a new year of sweetness. Folklore lists honey under remedies for arthritis, asthma, bed-wetting, constipation, coughs, sore throats, and weight control. The nutritional powers of honey are well-documented, although children under the age of 1 should avoid it until their digestive systems are more well-developed. "Too much honey cloys the stomach," so moderation is key. Luckily, it takes only a teaspoon of honey in a hot drink to promote relaxation and sleep. Steaming bishop, wassail, ales, mead, and other age-old warming beverages all contained honey.

PRACTICAL PRIMER

- Chew a bit of honeycomb to help your body beat the heat in summer.
- Use a touch of honey on chapped lips as a healing balm.
- If you're dieting, mix 1 tablespoon cider vinegar and 2 tablespoons honey into a glass of unsweetened grapefruit juice and drink before meals. It may help diminish your appetite.

COOKING WITH HONEY

❧ Store honey at room temperature. If it crystallizes, stand the jar in a pot of hot water until it liquefies again.

❧ Before you measure honey for cooking, oil the measuring cup, and the honey will pour out easily.

❧ Substitute ¾ cup honey for 1 cup granulated or brown sugar in a recipe, but reduce the liquid in the recipe by ¼ cup for every ¾ cup of honey you use. Cookies and cakes made with honey keep much longer than those made with sugar.

❧ Because honey caramelizes at a lower temperature than sugar, reduce the oven temperature by 25°F when baking with honey.

❧ To glaze cooked sliced carrots, stir in 2 tablespoons each honey and butter and heat briefly.

❧ Slowly heat 1 cup honey with ½ teaspoon cinnamon or ground cloves. Cool and serve over waffles or ice cream.

SEPTEMBER

8

1565
St. Augustine, Florida, was founded.

1900
A hurricane struck Galveston, Texas, claiming the lives of more than 6,000 people.

1930
New York City schools began teaching Hebrew.

▪ ▪ ▪

Where your pleasure is, there is your treasure; where your treasure, there your heart; where your heart, there your happiness.

—*St. Augustine*

▪ ▪ ▪

LORE & LEGEND

Dreaming about bees foretells riches or success in business. To encourage those dreams and prevent insomnia, stir 2 teaspoons honey into a cup of warm milk and drink just before bedtime.

SEPTEMBER

9

1762
WILLIAM FRANKLIN, BEN'S son, was commissioned royal governor of New Jersey.

1850
California became the 31st state.

1954
MARILYN BELL swam across Lake Ontario.

∎ ∎ ∎

Never argue at the dinner table, for the one who is not hungry gets the best of the argument.

—Voltaire

Disputing, contradicting, and confuting people are generally unfortunate in their affairs.

—BEN FRANKLIN

IN 1754, the governor of Pennsylvania resigned, tired of the disputes his office entailed. The new governor, Robert Morris, met with Ben Franklin and asked if he should expect to have as much trouble. Ben explained that the governor would get along fine if he avoided fighting with the assembly. "My dear friend," Morris said, "how can you advise my avoiding disputes? You know I love disputing; it is one of my greatest pleasures."

Morris was an eloquent speaker and loved nothing better than a good argument, having been taught the art of debating from childhood. His father had even encouraged his children to argue various topics around the dinner table as a pastime. Ben, who had learned the art of gaining friends and influencing people, didn't think that was a particularly wise way to raise children and was likely to produce argumentative, unsuccessful adults. "They get victory sometimes," he noted, "but they never get good will, which would be of more use to them."

A WORD TO THE WISE

SEASONAL GARDENING TASKS

❖ Plant new perennials a month before the date of your usual first hard freeze. Identify each plant with a stake (permanent marker on a Popsicle stick works fine) so you can find its emerging leaves in the spring.

❖ Divide spring-flowering perennials such as Siberian irises, bleeding hearts, and daylilies and water well. To divide peonies, cut back the foliage and divide each plant into at least four clumps. Plant in full sun and well-turned soil, making sure the buds face upward and are no deeper than 1½ inches below the surface.

❖ Withhold fertilizer from ornamental plants until spring. Feeding now will stimulate tender new growth that could be winter-killed.

❖ Shell sunflower seeds by rubbing the flower heads on a washboard. Cut huge flowers into quarters first.

❖ Let a few radishes go to seed and pick the mild seed-pods for stir-fries and salads.

Consumer Advocates

IN THE 1700S, no universal standards of weights and measures existed. A bushel of Connecticut oats might weigh 28 pounds, but in New Jersey a bushel was defined as 32 pounds. In 1836, Congress finally acted, establishing the Office of Weights and Measures, the first step toward standardization. In 1901, the National Bureau of Standards was charged with establishing accurate measures for all weights and volumes. In 1914, the Federal Trade Commission (FTC) was created by Congress to enforce consumer protection laws.

THE *Inspired* MIND

Consumers need all the help they can get. Recently, for example, the FTC found that 4 out of 10 times, consumers get less milk than advertised on cartons. Consumer advocate Ralph Nader and other activists have launched private watchdog groups such as Public Citizen to help protect the public interest.

Ben Franklin would appreciate these efforts by government and private citizens. In 1751, when the colonies were in danger of attack, he wrote that the best way to secure the friendship of the Native Americans was "to regulate the Indian trade, so as to convince them, by experience, that they may have the best and cheapest goods, and the fairest dealing from the English."

You hit home runs not by chance but by preparation.

—*Roger Maris*

SPORTS EQUIPMENT SANITY

❡ If your family is involved in sports, buy a set of large plastic tubs and make sure each sport's equipment—baseball, lacrosse, skiing, and so on—stays together.

❡ If your children outgrow their soccer shoes faster than you can buy them, organize an annual sports swap in your neighborhood or town to recycle kids' sports equipment. It can mean a substantial saving for every family and will keep outgrown equipment from moldering in your cellar.

❡ Wondering what to do with worn-out tennis balls? Suspend one from the ceiling of the garage so that it touches your windshield when the car is perfectly parked.

SEPTEMBER

11

1743
Birth of SARAH FRANKLIN, the only daughter of BEN and DEBORAH.

⌇

1814
The U.S. Navy decisively defeated the British in the Battle of Lake Champlain near Plattsburgh, New York.

⌇

1936
Boulder Dam, now known as Hoover Dam, was dedicated.

⌇

2001
Three hijacked airplanes crashed into the World Trade Center towers and the Pentagon. A fourth plane went down in Pennsylvania before reaching its intended target.

. . .

If we were logical, the future would be bleak indeed. But we are more than logical. We are human beings, and we have faith, and we have hope.

—*Jacques Cousteau*

The first degree of folly, is to conceit one's self wise; the second to profess it; the third to despise counsel.

—BEN FRANKLIN

IN 1755, during the French and Indian War, General Edward Braddock was made commander in chief of British forces in the American colonies. He was a brave soldier, according to Ben Franklin, but was too self-confident. As Braddock prepared to battle the French at Fort Duquesne in Pennsylvania, Ben warned him to be on the alert for attacks by Native Americans, who were skilled in the art of ambush.

GEN. BRADDOCK

The general was unconcerned. "These savages may, indeed, be a formidable enemy to your raw American militia," he said, "but upon the king's regular and disciplined troops, sir, it is impossible they should make any impression."

Braddock and his troops headed off, but before they reached Fort Duquesne, they were ambushed by French troops and their Native American allies. Half of Braddock's soldiers were killed, including two-thirds of the officers. The rest fled in confusion, and Braddock himself was mortally wounded. According to Ben, "This whole transaction gave us Americans the first suspicion that our exalted ideas of the prowess of British regulars had not been well founded."

PLANTING FOR POSTERITY

❧ Plant hardy trees and shrubs while the ground is still easy to dig, and keep them well-watered. You will be rewarded next spring and for decades to come.

❧ Choose easy-to-grow shrubs, such as forsythia, rhododendron, lilac, or hydrangea.

Plant forsythia and lilac in full sun, rhododendron and hydrangea in sun to partial shade.

❧ Or select shrubs that add character in the winter: American holly, crab apple, Henry Lauder's walking stick (contorted filbert), red twig dogwood, or winterberry.

BEN FRANKLIN'S ALMANAC

Lightning Bells

BEN FRANKLIN invited lightning into his house in 1752 by attaching a rod to his chimney and running a ground wire through a glass tube installed in the roof. The wire ran to the cellar but was severed near his bedroom door in the stairwell of the house. Ben attached bells to the two ends of the wire and fixed them to the staircase 6 inches apart. Between the bells he suspended a brass ball on a silk thread so that when lightning struck the rod, passed down the wire, and jumped the 6-inch gap, the agitated ball rang the bells, alerting Ben. "I was one night awaked by loud cracks on the staircase," he wrote, when the lightning charge was so great that a white stream arcing between the bells lit the stairwell "as with sunshine."

THE
Inspired
MIND

Nikola Tesla, born in 1856 in Croatia and later a U.S. citizen, invented an air-core transformer that produced high-voltage energy in spectacular, colorful effects. Tesla's coils used alternating current that could arc 5 to 20 feet. His electromagnetic system illuminated the Chicago World's Columbian Exposition in 1893, and he was the first to transmit electricity without wires—unless we count Ben's lightning bells.

All power corrupts, but we need electricity.

—Haythum R. Khalid

SEPTEMBER

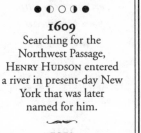

12

Spring rain dampens, autumn rain soaks.

● ○ ◐ ◑ ●

1609
Searching for the Northwest Passage, HENRY HUDSON entered a river in present-day New York that was later named for him.

1913
Sprinter JESSE OWENS was born.

1977
Twice during the day thunderstorms deluged Kansas City, Missouri, with torrential rain.

LAUNDRY SOLUTIONS

❖ To get rid of a mothball smell in stored clothes and woolen blankets, toss them in the dryer with a fabric softener sheet, but hold the heat.

❖ Wash feather pillows in the washing machine two at a time, adding a small amount of laundry detergent and using warm water and the delicate cycle. Tumble dry along with a clean sneaker or a child's stuffed animal, which will help fluff the feathers.

❖ To clean delicate silk or wool items, soak them in cool water with a teaspoonful of liquid laundry detergent. Rinse in cool water and roll up in a towel, then air-dry.

❖ Brighten delicate hand-washables with a mild whitener made by adding ¼ cup baking soda and ¼ cup lemon juice to a bucket or sink filled with lukewarm water. Soak and rinse.

SEPTEMBER

13

When the bubbles of coffee collect in the center of the cup, expect fair weather.

● ● ○ ◐ ● ●

1788
New York City was established as the capital of the United States.

1911
Birth of BILL MONROE, the father of bluegrass music.

1922
The thermometer at El Azizia, Libya, reached 136.4°F, the highest surface temperature ever recorded on our planet.

Be not niggardly of what costs thee nothing, as courtesy, counsel, & countenance.

—BEN FRANKLIN

A WORD TO THE WISE

CECIL RHODES, South African businessman and benefactor of the Rhodes scholarship, once hosted a formal dinner party at his home. A guest who had come by train arrived wearing an old suit that bore the grime of travel. He was dismayed to find that he had no time to change into the formal attire the other guests were already wearing. Embarrassed, he waited with the others for their host to arrive. When Rhodes appeared, he was wearing an old suit, which he had changed into purposely to make his guest feel comfortable.

At another dinner party, given by the great actress Ethel Barrymore, an invited guest failed to appear or send her regrets. Later, the young woman ran into the great actress and said, "I think I was invited to your house to dinner last Thursday."

"Oh yes," Barrymore replied. "Did you come?"

Finally, someone once complained to painter James Whistler that although the French made a great deal about courtesy, it was mostly on the surface. Whistler replied, "That is a very good place for it."

A Perfect Cup of Coffee, Part 1

Humans have been drinking a brew made from the roasted beans of the coffee shrub for at least 3,000 years. Here's what we know about making a truly good cup of coffee.

❖ Never boil coffee or let it sit over high heat. This disperses the classic aromas and intensifies the acids and bitterness.

❖ Always start with good-quality roasted beans. Arabica beans are known for their full flavor. The cheaper robusta beans are more bitter and are usually made into instant coffee.

❖ Grind your beans at the last minute, if possible. Use 1½ to 2 tablespoons ground coffee for each cup.

If this is coffee, please bring me some tea; but if this is tea, please bring me some coffee.

—*Abraham Lincoln*

Putting Your Roses to Bed

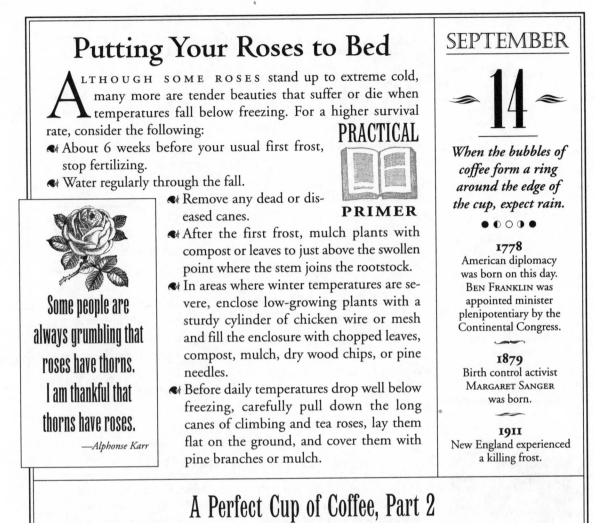

ALTHOUGH SOME ROSES stand up to extreme cold, many more are tender beauties that suffer or die when temperatures fall below freezing. For a higher survival rate, consider the following:

- About 6 weeks before your usual first frost, stop fertilizing.
- Water regularly through the fall.
- Remove any dead or diseased canes.
- After the first frost, mulch plants with compost or leaves to just above the swollen point where the stem joins the rootstock.
- In areas where winter temperatures are severe, enclose low-growing plants with a sturdy cylinder of chicken wire or mesh and fill the enclosure with chopped leaves, compost, mulch, dry wood chips, or pine needles.
- Before daily temperatures drop well below freezing, carefully pull down the long canes of climbing and tea roses, lay them flat on the ground, and cover them with pine branches or mulch.

PRACTICAL PRIMER

Some people are always grumbling that roses have thorns. I am thankful that thorns have roses.

—*Alphonse Karr*

SEPTEMBER

14

When the bubbles of coffee form a ring around the edge of the cup, expect rain.

● ● ○ ◗ ●

1778
American diplomacy was born on this day. BEN FRANKLIN was appointed minister plenipotentiary by the Continental Congress.

1879
Birth control activist MARGARET SANGER was born.

1911
New England experienced a killing frost.

A Perfect Cup of Coffee, Part 2

Coffee originated in the Ethiopian highlands and spread to Europe during the Middle Ages. Today it is the most popular beverage in the world (after water), with 400 billion cups consumed annually. It is the second most valuable international trade commodity after petroleum.

❦ For filtered coffee, heat fresh cold water to just below boiling, then pour it over the grounds in the filter. Let the grounds absorb the water for a minute, then pour on additional water.

❦ If you use an automatic coffeemaker, keep it immaculately clean so that the oils from old pots of coffee don't taint the new. Serve immediately or pour into a thermos to keep hot.

❦ Don't follow the old practice of throwing eggshells or a glob of raw egg white into a pot of coffee to "settle" the grounds. It isn't necessary.

15

*This day is fine
6 years out of 7.*

● ○ ○ ● ●

1857
Birthday of
WILLIAM HOWARD TAFT,
27th president of the
United States
(1909–1913).

1890
Mystery writer
AGATHA CHRISTIE
was born.

1971
Greenpeace was founded.

■ ■ ■

**The best time
to plan a book is
while you're doing
the dishes.**

—*Agatha Christie*

Beware the Cully Mully Puff

BETWEEN 1739 and 1763, 483 different almanacs were published in the colonies, according to Arthur Berthold in *American Colonial Printing* (1970), making stiff competition for Ben Franklin's *Poor Richard's Almanack*. To avoid taking himself too seriously while at the same time attempting to bolster his own standing, Ben poked fun at authors of almanacs.

"Upon the Talents Requisite in an Almanack-Writer" (1737) offered the public three keys for identifying talent. First, a writer "should be descended of a great Family" and ostentatiously exhibit his coat of arms on the title page—or copy one from *The Peerage of England* if he is "meanly descended." Second, in order to write almanac doggerel, a writer "shou'd not be a finish'd Poet, but a Piece of one." Finally, a "compleat Almanack-Writer" should appear grave, since gravity is often equated with wisdom, and the marks of this trait are "sentences that neither himself, nor any Body else can understand." To wit:

THE
Inspired
MIND

January 23. Beware, the Design is suspected.
April 10. Cully Mully puff appears.
June 7. The Cat eat the Candle.

DISHWASHING 101

❖ Hand-wash dishes from the cleanest to the dirtiest: glasses, silverware, plates and bowls, serving dishes, pots and pans.

❖ Use scissors to cut squares of steel wool soap pads or scouring pads into halves or even quarters to stretch their usefulness.

❖ Sprinkle a broiling or roasting pan with salt and dishwashing liquid as soon as you remove

the meat. Cover the bottom of the pan with wet paper towels and leave them in place until you're ready to wash the pan.

❖ Before washing heavy pots and large platters, drape a folded towel or a rubber sink liner across the top edge of one side of your sink. Rest the pot or platter on this to prevent slipping while you wash it.

Humility makes great men twice honourable.

—Ben Franklin

SEPTEMBER

16

1853
Henry Steinway
sold his first
American-made piano.

1924
Birth of actress
Lauren Bacall.

1976
The Episcopal Church in
the United States
approved the ordination
of women priests.

• • •

I think your
whole life shows
in your face
and you should be
proud of that.

—*Lauren Bacall*

WHEN OLIVER CROMWELL sat for a portrait by a painter who was known for his beautiful paintings of nobility, he cautioned the artist to paint him "as you see me," warts and all. "Otherwise I will never pay a farthing for it."

On her deathbed, Queen Elizabeth I interrupted the archbishop of Canterbury, who was praising the virtues and achievements of her reign. "My lord," she said, "the crown which I have borne so long has given enough of vanity in my time. I beseech you not to augment it in this hour when I am so near my death."

A young woman visited the Beethoven museum, which houses the piano on which the master wrote many of his great compositions. She asked the guard if she could play the piano, accompanying her request with some cash. The guard agreed, and after the woman played a bit, she asked him if all the great pianists who came there wanted to play the piano. "Well," he replied, "Paderewski was here a few years ago and he said he wasn't worthy to touch it."

SECRETS OF STACKING FIREWOOD

❰ If wood is stacked in a freestanding row, make crisscross stacks at the ends to hold the pile together. The crisscross pillars must be tightly fit from angular sticks so the wood won't roll.

❰ If two rows of wood are stacked together, start several inches apart at the bottom and gradually lean the rows toward each other so the gap is closed at the top. This will ensure that the woodpile leans toward the center from every direction and won't fall.

❰ Stack firewood at least 10 feet from your house to prevent wood-nibbling insects from working their way into your siding.

❰ For best drying, stack firewood with the ends toward the prevailing wind.

Pick up inexpensive wood pallets to use as a base and provide air circulation from the bottom.

17

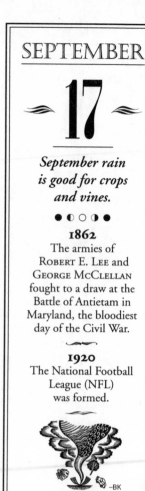

*September rain
is good for crops
and vines.*

● ○ ◐ ◑ ●

1862
The armies of
ROBERT E. LEE and
GEORGE McCLELLAN
fought to a draw at the
Battle of Antietam in
Maryland, the bloodiest
day of the Civil War.

1920
The National Football
League (NFL)
was formed.

—BK

1988
A tornado hit Kelly Air
Force Base in San
Antonio, Texas.

■ ■ ■

NATURE WATCH

Whenever you are
outside, look up—
there's a good chance
you will see migrating
hawks. The peregrine
falcon, for example,
travels 5,000 miles
from Alaska to Argen-
tina every autumn.

---

*Be civil to all; serviceable
to many; familiar with few; friend
to one; enemy to none.*

—BEN FRANKLIN

PETER MILLER was a Baptist minister who lived in
Pennsylvania at the time of the Revolution. Miller had an
adversary who persistently vilified him. The man was later
charged with treason and sentenced to death by hanging. Hearing
this, Miller set out for Philadelphia, a walk of
nearly 70 miles, to plead for clemency for the
man. But his plea was rebuffed by George Washington, who said, "Your plea for your friend cannot be granted."

"My friend!" Miller exclaimed. "He is the
worst enemy I have." Washington was astonished
that Miller had walked 70 miles to save the life of
an enemy and decided to pardon the traitor.

During the Civil War, Abraham Lincoln was
criticized for being too lenient with the rebel-
lious states. An elderly woman chastised him,
saying that he should want to destroy his enemies rather than be so kind to them. "Why
madam," Lincoln replied, "do I not destroy my
enemies when I make them my friends?"

Both sides forget
that we are all
Americans.

—*Robert E. Lee*

Rooting for Your Root Crops

❧ Plant next year's garlic crop
now by separating a head into
cloves. Dig a trench 4 inches
deep, space the cloves 5 to 6
inches apart, and set them so
the tops are 2 inches below the
soil surface. Cover with soil
and mulch well. The garlicky
greens will be a treat in the
early spring, and you can harvest the heads next summer.

❧ Store onions and potatoes
separately. Onions give off a
gas that can spoil potatoes.

❧ Whether you dig your own
potatoes or buy them at a farm
stand or grocery store, don't
wash them until right before
you use them. Washing potatoes shortens their storage life.

❧ Dig potatoes on a dry day.

The Science of Government

To prepare himself and other delegates for the Constitutional Convention to be held in Philadelphia, where America's new form of government would be finalized, Ben Franklin organized the Society for Political Inquiries early in 1787. At the weekly meetings in Ben's home, members (including Thomas Paine and George Washington) discussed the "science of government" and how best to codify their ideas for the government's structure.

Similar inquiries form the course of study in undergraduate departments of government at many colleges today. At the graduate level, the School of Public Administration was established at Harvard University in Massachusetts in 1936, evolving into the John F. Kennedy School of Government in 1978.

Since 1964, White House Fellowships have been awarded to young people who assist cabinet members and presidential advisors and who participate in educational programs in governance. The Congressional Intern Program for students and the Congressional Senior Citizen Intern Program offer young and old the opportunity to understand firsthand the workings of government on Capitol Hill.

THE *Inspired* MIND

> There seems to be a law that governs all our actions, so I never make plans.
>
> —*Greta Garbo*

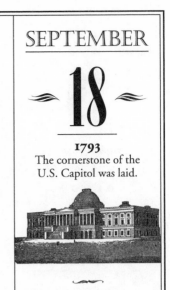

1793
The cornerstone of the U.S. Capitol was laid.

1830
The *Tom Thumb,* the first American-built steam locomotive, raced a horse on a 9-mile course and lost.

1905
Actress Greta Garbo and choreographer Agnes de Mille were born.

When Food Sticks to the Pan
(and How to Prevent It)

If your roasted vegetables hopelessly adhere to the roasting pan, your lasagna seems bonded to its dish, or scorched pudding has formed an impermeable layer in your saucepan, there's hope.

❖ Sprinkle baking soda in the bottom of a burned pan, cover with water, and boil gently for 10 minutes. Let

cool, then pour off the charred residue.

❖ Use fabric softener sheets to loosen the bond between food and pan. Soak the pan with one sheet overnight, and cleanup should be easy.

❖ When heating milk to scald it, first chill the pan in cold water. The milk will be less likely to stick.

<table>
<tr><td>

SEPTEMBER

19

*Rain before 7,
Clear before 11.*

● ● ○ ● ●

1819
Poet JOHN KEATS
wrote "To Autumn."

1898
The Cornell University
College of Forestry was
established.

1905
Birth of Watergate lawyer
LEON JAWORSKI.

■ ■ ■

**He that sups upon salad,
goes not to bed fasting.**

—*Thomas Fuller*

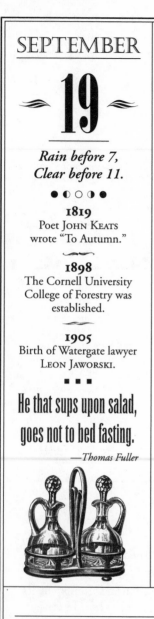

</td><td>

Antipasto for a Crowd

*This traditional Italian appetizer platter features meat, cheese, fish,
eggs, vegetables, and pickles, artfully arranged. Bring it to a tailgating
party or an open house at your child's school.*

APPETIZERS:

2 jars (7 ounces each) roasted red peppers, drained and sliced lengthwise

24 miniature fresh mozzarella balls (about 8 ounces), or 8 ounces thinly sliced provolone cheese

1 cup each cauliflower and broccoli florets, blanched for 30 seconds and rinsed in cold water, or 1 jar (24 ounces) *giardiniera* (Italian pickled vegetables), drained

1 jar (7 ounces) marinated mushrooms, drained

1 jar (7 ounces) pickled cocktail onions, drained

1 jar (7 ounces) *peperoncini* (Italian pickled peppers), drained

2 cans (14 ounces each) artichoke hearts, drained and quartered

8 ounces kalamata or other oil-cured black olives

8 ounces thinly sliced prosciutto or pepperoni, or 2 cans (6 ounces each) solid white tuna, drained

6 hard-boiled eggs, quartered

1 small can anchovies, drained and blotted dry

2 tablespoons extra-virgin olive oil

Freshly ground black pepper

Bread sticks or garlic bread

Arrange the appetizers artistically on a large serving platter, sprinkle with the oil, and season with pepper to taste. Serve the bread sticks or garlic bread alongside in a basket.

Makes 12 servings

</td></tr>
</table>

VERSATILE VINEGAR

Distilled white vinegar is the handiest ingredient in the kitchen. Here are just a few ways you can use it.

❖ Combine vinegar and salt and use to clean cutting boards and remove white residue from crystal glassware.

❖ Add a spoonful when cooking red cabbage, beets, or red potatoes to help them keep their bright red color.

❖ Add a spoonful when cooking potatoes for salad to help them hold a firm shape.

❖ Swish ¼ cup vinegar in the cavity of a chicken to retard bacterial growth.

Internal Waves

WHILE ON BOARD a ship off the coast of Spain in 1762, Ben Franklin was annoyed with the light in his cabin: The cross breeze through the portholes made his candle flicker. He poured equal parts water and whale oil into a glass tumbler and floated a wick on the surface, reporting excellent lighting as the glass shielded the burning wick. As the glass lamp swayed back and forth, Ben noted, the oil stayed perfectly calm, but "the water under the oil was in great commotion, rising and falling in irregular waves." He could not explain the phenomenon.

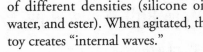

THE *Inspired* MIND

Like oil and water, salt water and fresh water have different densities and do not readily blend. In 1898, Norwegians Vilhelm Bjerknes and Walfrid Ekman, using a tank containing dyed salt water and clear fresh water, determined that when a ship generates internal waves at the intersection of fresh and salt water, the underwater agitation impedes the ship's progress. We can see these effects in Alfred Ewald's toy, patented in 1978, that contains dyed liquids of different densities (silicone oil, water, and ester). When agitated, the toy creates "internal waves."

SEPTEMBER

20

Much fog in autumn, much snow in winter.

● ● ○ ○ ●

1797
The USS *Constitution* was launched.

1873
The New York Stock Exchange closed to halt a panic.

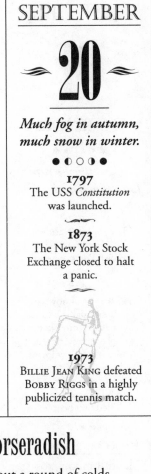

1973
BILLIE JEAN KING defeated BOBBY RIGGS in a highly publicized tennis match.

Look when the clouds are blowing
And all the winds are free:
In fury of their going
They fall upon the sea.
But though the blast is frantic,
And though the tempest raves,
The deep immense Atlantic
Is still beneath the waves.

—*Frederick William Henry Myers*

The Glories of Horseradish

❦ A new school year always brings out a round of colds. To fight back, make a sandwich of whole wheat bread, raw onion, cheddar cheese, brown mustard, and a good half inch of horseradish. This old Vermont remedy will definitely clear out the sinuses.

❦ To grind fresh horseradish without tears, put it in a blender, add a little vinegar, and cover. If you use a hand grinder, put a plastic bag over the top.

❦ Keep a jar of horseradish in the refrigerator and add a judicious teaspoonful to tuna salad, ham salad, coleslaw, and applesauce (for a delicious meat condiment). Add to ketchup along with a spoonful of fresh lemon juice to make cocktail sauce for shrimp.

21

St. Matthew

● ○ ○ ○ ●

*St. Matthew's rain
fattens pigs and goats.*

1792
The French National
Convention voted to
abolish the monarchy.

1938
A hurricane known as
the Long Island Express
smashed into New
England, resulting in
widespread blowdowns
and flooding. The storm
destroyed a quarter of
a billion trees and
killed 600 people.

● ● ●

LORE & LEGEND

The full moon closest
to the autumnal
equinox is known as
the harvest moon
because it is bright
enough to enable
farmers to work in the
fields by moonlight.
If it rises red, it is
thought to predict
wind. If it rises pale,
expect rain. If the full
moon shines on you
while you are sleeping,
you are moonstruck.

Don't Forget to Plant Your Bulbs

FALL IS a busy time around the house, and it may seem impossible to find the time to plant bulbs. But the rewards in spring make a little effort now well worthwhile.

PRACTICAL PRIMER

- Plant bulbs at least 6 weeks before the ground freezes.
- Avoid areas where water collects, such as the foot of a hill.
- Prepare the planting bed by digging the soil so that it's loose and workable. If it's not an established garden, add some organic matter such as compost or peat moss.
- Plant big bulbs (tulips and narcissuses) about 6 inches deep and small bulbs (crocuses and grape hyacinths) about 3 inches deep.
- Plant bulbs in clusters for the greatest impact. Don't plant one bulb alone or make a long, thin line along the walk.

More Bulb Know-How

❦ Plant a clove of garlic with each spring-flowering bulb to deter rodents. Or try setting the bulbs in a ring of gravel. For really pesky pests, bury chicken wire around the bulbs.

❦ Put peanuts out for the squirrels to keep them away from newly planted bulbs.

❦ Fertilize bulbs in early fall if your spring is short and the weather heats up fast.

❦ For the longest display of color in the spring, plant a range of tulips that includes early-, middle-, and late-flowering varieties.

An optimistic gardener is one
who believes that whatever
goes down must come up.

—*Leslie Hall*

Prayers and provender hinder no journey.

—Ben Franklin

AFTER ESCAPING from slavery, Harriet Tubman returned to the South 19 times to rescue others from bondage. As the chief conductor on the Underground Railroad, she depended on God and a network of friendly supporters to provide food and hiding places.

One time, she knocked at the door of a safe house, only to find that the owner had been run out of town for harboring runaways. Tubman knew that their presence in town was revealed and said a speedy prayer. Then she remembered a nearby swamp and took the refugees there. They spent a miserable day hiding in the cold, wet grass. After dusk, they saw a man walking along the edge of the swamp, talking in a stage whisper about a horse and wagon that stood waiting at a nearby farm. The fugitives found the wagon, loaded with provisions.

In all, Tubman freed more than 300 people from slavery and always counted her faith as the most important item she carried with her along the way.

I never ran my train off the track, and I never lost a passenger.

—*Harriet Tubman*

When beechnuts are plenty, expect a mild winter.

● ● ○ ○ ●

1776
Schoolmaster-turned-spy NATHAN HALE was executed by the British in New York City.

1862
President ABRAHAM LINCOLN announced the Emancipation Proclamation, to take effect January 1, 1863.

1964
Fiddler on the Roof opened on Broadway, followed by 3,241 performances.

Making Blemished Wood Look as Good as New

❖ If gum is stuck to wood, hold an ice cube on the gum until it hardens, then use an old credit card or plastic dough scraper to crack it off the surface. Polish lightly.

❖ For white marks on wooden tables caused by hot dishes or water, use a thin paste of salt and salad oil to remove the blemish. Or rub the mark gently with a paste made of equal parts baking soda and toothpaste, then polish lightly.

❖ If paper is stuck to wood, remove it by soaking it with vegetable oil or olive oil. Let the oil sit for a few minutes, then rub along the grain with a coarse towel or cheesecloth. Dry and finish with polish.

23

1642
Harvard College held its
first commencement.

1879
The first hearing aid
was patented.

1939
A time capsule was
buried at the New York
World's Fair. It contained,
among other items,
the Lord's Prayer in
300 languages, rules for
poker and football,
and sheet music for
"The Flat Foot Floogie."

A Useful Education

THE
Inspired
MIND

ALTHOUGH BEN FRANKLIN had just 2 years of formal education and never attended college, he had radical ideas about public education that he proposed in a 1749 pamphlet. Instead of training students for religious ministry and mandating the study of Latin and Greek, as did all existing universities, Ben's proposed institution would allow students to "learn those things that are likely to be most useful and most ornamental, regard being had to the several professions for which they are intended." This practical application to learning did not include the compulsory study of ancient languages.

Ben's ideas stimulated the founding of the Academy of Pennsylvania, which became the College of Philadelphia in 1755 and had evolved into the University of Pennsylvania by 1791. The nation's first medical school (1765) and business school (1881) were established at Penn. Currently, the university has about 10,000 undergraduates in 4 schools and a library containing 5 million books. The separate College for Women merged with its male counterpart in 1974. With a 2002 budget of $3.2 billion and a payroll of $1.3 billion, Penn is also Philadelphia's largest private employer.

> Education is not the filling of a pail, but the lighting of a fire.
> —*William Butler Yeats*

Foundation Plantings: A Cautionary Word

First, the caution:

❖ The soil near the foundation of your house is most likely poor-quality backfill, not intended to support life.

❖ Little trees and shrubs become big trees and shrubs, blocking windows –BK

and causing moisture problems for your siding.

❖ Tree roots can grow into the foundation and cause cracking.

If you have your heart set on them:

❖ Choose plant varieties that will stay fairly small.

❖ Position plants at least 4 feet out from the foundation.

❖ Dig a hole 3 feet deep, remove all the soil, and replace it with good topsoil. Then plant the shrub.

❖ Consider fragrant shrubs such as lilacs and summer sweet (*Clethra* species), which will waft lovely scents when in bloom.

Diligence overcomes difficulties, sloth makes them.

—BEN FRANKLIN

WHEN THE CIVIL WAR destroyed Edmund McIlhenny's sugar plantation in Louisiana, he was wiped out, except for some Mexican peppers that had reseeded in the garden. McIlhenny crushed the peppers and mixed them with vinegar and salt to make a sauce to spice up his meager diet. His neighbors loved the sauce, especially with seafood. Today his descendants still run the company that produces Tabasco sauce for sale around the world.

A WORD TO THE WISE

Just after 1900, a young boy from Decatur, Illinois, dreamed of being a photographer. He sent away for an instruction book. When the publisher sent him a book on ventriloquism by mistake, he began reading the book and practicing the techniques. Eventually, the boy, named Edgar Bergen, mastered the art and went on to become one of the most famous ventriloquists of all time—thanks to a dummy named Charlie McCarthy, a publisher's mistake, and a conquering spirit.

There is music in the meadows,
in the air—
Autumn is here;
Skies are gray, but hearts are mellow.

—*William Stanley Braithwaite*

You Do the Math

Misspend 15 minutes a day, and by year's end, you'll have wasted nearly 9 days of 10 hours each. Or if you work for 50 weeks at 40 hours a week and waste just 15 minutes each workday, you'll have been paid for more than 1½ weeks' work that you didn't do.

Milkweed closing at night indicates rain.

● ● ○ ◐ ●

1869
Robber barons trying to corner the gold market caused America's first Wall Street crash.

1936
Muppet creator JIM HENSON was born.

1968
The television program *60 Minutes* made its debut.

■ ■ ■

NATURE WATCH
Monarch butterflies migrate north from central Mexico each spring, heading for the northern United States and southern Canada and their favorite food, the milkweed. At about the time of the autumnal equinox, decreasing daylength and chilly temperatures tell the butterflies to begin the long trek south.

25

When cockleburs turn brown, expect frost.

● ○ ○ ◐ ●

1723
Seventeen-year-old
BEN FRANKLIN left home,
sailing from Boston to
New York City to look for
work as a printer.

1926
Ford Motor Company
established an
8-hour workday and a
5-day workweek.

1932
Birth of pianist
GLENN GOULD.

■ ■ ■

For disappearing
acts, it's hard
to beat what
happens to
the eight hours
supposedly
left after eight
of sleep and
eight of work.

—Doug Larson

The First Spelling Checker

AS A PRINTER assembling and disassembling words, Ben Franklin knew intimately the variations of sound the English alphabet had acquired. For example, the different sounds of *c* in *piece* and *crate* challenged spellers. Believing that writing derived from speech, Ben invented a phonetic alphabet wherein each letter would always have the same sound. But his new alphabet never overcame the inertia of commonly accepted (if inconsistent) grammatical practice.

George Bernard Shaw, disgusted with the Latin alphabet, set up a competition to create a phonetic English alphabet. The winning entry, created by Kingsley Read in 1958, is known as the Shavian alphabet, but it hasn't taken hold.

THE *Inspired* MIND

The Linguistic Society of America has recognized Ebonics, or African-American English, as a natural speech variety, but no phonetic alphabet has been developed. We're still stuck with remembering "*i* before *e* except after *c*" or, depending on our computers' spelling checkers, knowing the difference between *Geronimo* and *geranium*.

TONGUE TIDE

Swamped by vocabulary words when learning a new language? You need only about 2,000 words to be considered fluent in any tongue. The English language contains a whopping 600,000 words, but most of us use only a small fraction of them. Even professional writers use only about 50,000 words, not even one-tenth of the possible choices.

Brightening the Yard

When you shop for colorful chrysanthemums to add color to your yard and deck, add a couple of pots of winter pansies. These beauties will bloom all fall and even into the winter (from Zone 5 south) and will revive again next spring.

Eat to live, and not live to eat.

—BEN FRANKLIN

BEN FRANKLIN, who also famously said, "To lengthen thy life, lessen thy meals," knew from experience that too much of the good life might mean an attack of gout. These days, the average American's diet is loaded with sugar, salt, and fat, and 60 percent of the U.S. population is overweight. For many, a dependence on fast food is the culprit, especially with the recent trend of supersizing meals. According to the Food Policy Institute, the burger, fries, and soft drink you bought at McDonald's in the 1950s contained about 590 calories. Today a typical Extra Value Meal can contain three times that many calories—enough to sustain a person for an entire day.

A WORD TO THE WISE

> Square meals, not adventurous ones, are what you should seek.
>
> —*Bryan Miller*

What's the solution? The next time a clerk at a fast-food restaurant asks if you want the super special, do yourself a favor and say, "No, thanks."

1774
Birth of JOHN CHAPMAN, better known as JOHNNY APPLESEED.

1953
Sugar rationing ended in Great Britain, 8 years after the end of World War II.

1969
Abbey Road, the BEATLES' last album, was released.

A TOAST TO HEALTHY EATING

❖ Mash leftover cooked beans or canned pinto beans with minced garlic, vinaigrette, salsa, or yogurt to make a wonderful low-calorie dip for tortilla chips.

❖ Depend on herbs and spices rather than salt to add flavor to your food. Store jars of herbs and spices in a shallow kitchen drawer, with the labels facing up. They're easier to find and will stay fresher away from light and heat.

❖ For dessert, choose angel food cake over butter-based cakes and single-crust over double-crust pies. Every little bit helps.

❖ Drink six to eight glasses of water a day for beautiful skin as well as appetite control. Sometimes we think we are hungry when we are actually thirsty.

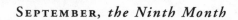

27

*Spiderwebs floating
at autumn sunset,
Bring frost that night,
on this you may bet.*

● ◐ ○ ○ ●

1722
Birthday of Revolutionary
War hero SAMUEL ADAMS.

1936
A storm lasting 60 hours
dumped 21.3 inches of
snow at the Denver airport.

1937
In Albion, New York,
the first Santa Claus
school opened.

You may talk too much on the best of subjects.

—BEN FRANKLIN

LITERARY CRITIC Charles Lamb was a lifelong friend of poet Samuel Coleridge, who was known for his talkativeness. Generally, Lamb put up with Coleridge's incessant monologues, but once Coleridge interrupted his own dissertation to ask, "Charles, have you ever heard me preach?"

With a weary sigh, Lamb replied, "I've never heard you do anything else."

George Bernard Shaw was once seated at a dinner party next to a young man who talked nonstop about an endless variety of subjects. Finally, Shaw interrupted him to say that between the two of them, they knew everything there was to know in the world. When the young man asked how that could be, Shaw said, "Well, you seem to know everything except that you are a bore. And I know that."

So what do you do when you're trapped by an incessant chatterer? You could do what the British politician F. E. Smith did when he found himself stuck with a fellow who wouldn't shut up. Smith hailed a waiter and said, "Would you mind listening to the end of this gentleman's story?"

How to Find North without a Compass

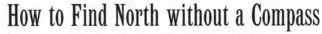

❖ In the desert, the giant barrel cactus always leans to the south.

❖ In the woods, moss often grows on more than the north sides of trees. However, trees often grow fuller on the south sides.

❖ In the Great Plains, pilotweed aligns its leaves along a north-south axis.

Pioneers relied on it to show them the way west.

❖ On a clear night, if you connect the two stars (called the Pointers) marking the end of the bowl of the Big Dipper and extend the line upward to the next bright star, you will find Polaris, the North Star. It lies directly over the North Pole.

How to Predict a Frost

MANY GARDENERS swear by the belief that a frost is most likely around the full moon, next most likely around the new moon. But gardening, like politics, is local, even personal, and a chilly night under a full moon may nip a neighbor's garden but spare yours—or vice versa. Consider these factors when the radio and TV reports say "frost tonight."

- How warm was it during the day? If the temperature reached 75°F (in the East or North) or 80°F (in the desert Southwest), the chance of the mercury falling below 32°F is slim.
- Is it windy? A still night allows cold air to pool near the ground; a breeze keeps things stirred up.
- Is it cloudy? If the sun sets through a layer of thickening clouds, the clouds will slow radiational cooling and help stave off a frost.
- What is the dew point? As a rule of thumb, don't worry about a frost if the dew point (the temperature at which water vapor condenses) is above 45°F on the evening weather report.
- How is your garden sited? Gardens on slopes or high ground often survive when the coldest air puddles down in the valleys and hollows.

PRACTICAL PRIMER

SEPTEMBER

28

1839
Educator and feminist
FRANCES E. WILLARD
was born.

1892
The first night football
game was played in
Mansfield, Pennsylvania.

■ ■ ■

The world is
wide, and I will
not waste my life
in friction when it
could be turned
into momentum.

—*Frances E. Willard*

BETTER SAFE THAN SORRY

When nights get cold, protect tomato, eggplant, and pepper plants with old sheets, paper bags, or plastic at night and remove the coverings in the morning.

Pot up cannas before a frost and bring them indoors to a sunny location. Fertilize periodically and be careful not to overwater.

Bring geraniums indoors before the first frost arrives. Keep them in a sunny window in a relatively moist room; the kitchen is often best.

Harvest basil and other tender herbs before a frost. Even if they survive the frost, they don't do well in cold temperatures. The same is true for summer squash, peppers, and most annuals.

If your houseplants spent the summer outdoors, gradually get them used to being indoors. Several weeks before you expect a frost, bring them in at night and move them back outside on warm days.

Harvest all tomatoes and let them ripen indoors on tabletops or counters out of the sun.

29

St. Michael

● ○ ○ ● ●

On St. Michael's day, the devil puts his foot on the blackberries.

~

1950
Bell Laboratories announced the development of the telephone answering machine.

~

1990
The National Cathedral in Washington, D.C., begun on this day in 1907, was finally completed.

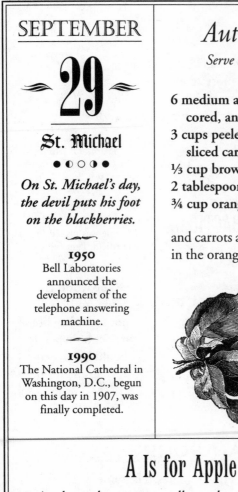

Autumn Apple Carrot Casserole

Serve this tasty side dish with pork chops and fresh cider for a real harvest feast.

6 medium apples, peeled, cored, and thinly sliced
3 cups peeled and thinly sliced carrots
⅓ cup brown sugar
2 tablespoons flour
¾ cup orange juice

Preheat the oven to 350°F. Lightly grease a 3-quart casserole with olive oil. Arrange half the apple slices in the casserole and add half the carrot slices. In a small bowl, combine the brown sugar and flour; sprinkle half this mixture over the carrots. Add a second layer each of apples and carrots and top with the remaining brown sugar mixture. Pour in the orange juice and bake for 45 minutes. *Makes 6 servings*

A Is for Apple

◖ Apples and carrots go well together in cooking, but don't store them in the same vegetable crisper. The ethylene gas from ripening apples can make carrots bitter.

◖ If you're cutting and peeling a lot of apples and want to prevent them from discoloring, toss them with lemon juice or vinegar diluted with a little ice water.

◖ Use tart, firm apples (Granny Smith, Northern Spy, and the like) for pie. If you love the taste of McIntosh, cut the slices thicker than you would with a firmer apple.

When the apple is ripe, it will fall.
—*Irish Proverb*

LORE & LEGEND

MICHAELMAS marked the end of the growing season and was traditionally a day for arranging rents and leases, paying farmworkers, and hiring new help. People gathered in the market squares for commerce, feasting, and revelry, often driving flocks of fat geese before them to sell. Roast goose, originally a sacrifice to St. Michael, is the traditional fare for the day. Eating it was considered a good luck charm to forestall hunger for another year.

No man e'er was glorious, who was not laborious.

—BEN FRANKLIN

AS A SOPHOMORE in high school, Michael Jordan tried out for the varsity basketball team but didn't make it. A taller boy got the spot, but Jordan took it in stride. "He didn't sulk or threaten to quit," said Fred Lynch, Jordan's high school coach. "He just started working harder and improving his game. If anything, it made him even more determined." And the other player? He never made it to the NBA.

After Nolan Ryan threw his seventh no-hitter in 1991 (a major league record), reporters pressed him for the secret to his success. "The secret is that there is no secret," Ryan said, and went on to explain that it was all about hard work. Tom House, pitching coach for the team, explained Ryan's success this way: "He does three hours of preparation for every one that anyone else does."

That's an attitude summed up by another Ben Franklin aphorism, one that has changed little in more than 2 centuries and has become a byword in sports: "No gains without pains."

SEPTEMBER

30

1882
The first hydroelectric plant began operation in Appleton, Wisconsin.

1902
Rayon was patented.

1927
BABE RUTH hit his 60th home run of the season.

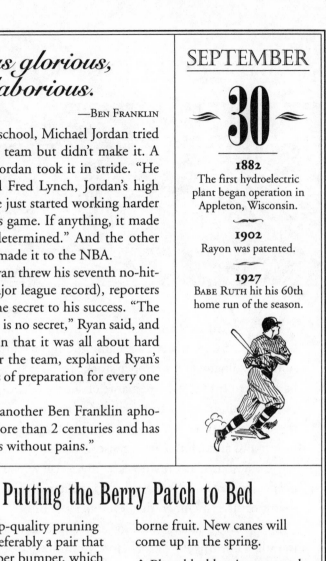

I've always believed that if you put in the work, the results will come. I don't do things half-heartedly. Because I know if I do, then I can expect half-hearted results.

—Michael Jordan

Putting the Berry Patch to Bed

❖ Buy top-quality pruning shears, preferably a pair that has a rubber bumper, which lessens the shock of closing and is kinder to your hands.

❖ Prune summer-bearing raspberries carefully, leaving six of the strongest brown canes for every 1 foot of your row.

❖ Prune fall-bearing raspberries ruthlessly, mowing them to the ground after they have borne fruit. New canes will come up in the spring.

❖ Plant blackberries now and mound up the soil around the canes to prevent hard frosts from heaving them out of the ground.

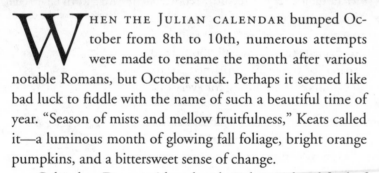

WHEN THE JULIAN CALENDAR bumped October from 8th to 10th, numerous attempts were made to rename the month after various notable Romans, but October stuck. Perhaps it seemed like bad luck to fiddle with the name of such a beautiful time of year. "Season of mists and mellow fruitfulness," Keats called it—a luminous month of glowing fall foliage, bright orange pumpkins, and a bittersweet sense of change.

Columbus Day provides a handy 3-day weekend for leaf peepers to gawk at New England's fabulous colors, but how many of us remember that October 9 honors a different "leaf"—Leif Eriksson, the Norseman who landed in Newfoundland nearly 500 years before Columbus?

This month, tune in to natural signs that foretell winter weather. If autumn leaves are slow to fall, a cold winter is in store. Onion and apple skins, cornhusks, and nutshells are traditional indicators: the thicker the exterior, the harsher the winter. And be sure to notice migrating hawks:

> *Hawks flying high means a clear sky.*
> *When they fly low, prepare for a blow.*

The garden tasks for this month are clear: Harvest before the first hard frost; clean up the garden before the first snow.

Full Hunter's Moon

marked the time when fallen leaves and fattened deer meant good hunting for Native Americans, as it still does.
The alternative name, *Full Dying Grass Moon*, evokes the coming of winter.

Sign of the Zodiac: Libra (September 23– October 22)

Element: Air

Quality: Friendly

Birthstone: Opal

Flower: Calendula

I have never seen the Philosopher's Stone that turns lead into gold, but I have known the pursuit of it turn a man's gold into lead.

—BEN FRANKLIN

GET-RICH-QUICK SCHEMES are nothing new, but hucksters occasionally come up with a new spin that manages to take in gullible people. Take the swindlers in Hungary who convinced small investors that earthworms were the key to financial success. All the participants had to do was invest their life savings (or borrow money at interest rates of up to 30 percent) and purchase hundreds of thousands of earthworms. According to the promoters, the earth-worms would transform ordinary manure into rich soil, which could then be sold overseas at a huge profit. Large numbers of people signed on to the scheme, motivated in part by Hungary's depressed economy. Unfortunately, the naive worm breeders soon learned that although there was plenty of manure involved in the scheme, there was no profit.

A WORD TO THE WISE

Unless you win the lottery, the phrase "get rich quick" is an oxymoron (like "jumbo shrimp" or "serious joke"). As Ben Franklin said elsewhere, "Content and riches seldom meet together. Riches take thou, contentment I had rather."

Many go out for wool, and come home shorn themselves.

—Miguel de Cervantes

October always has exactly 19 fine days.

● ● ○ ○ ●

1880
JOHN PHILIP SOUSA was named director of the U.S. Marine Corps Band.

1896
Rural free delivery (RFD) of mail began.

1920
CHARLES PONZI, originator of the investment swindle known as the Ponzi scheme, was indicted.

1924
Birthday of JAMES EARL "JIMMY" CARTER, 39th president of the United States (1977–1981).

TAKING CARE OF YOUR FRUIT TREES

This month, spend an hour or two tending to your fruit trees.

❖ Pick up any dropped fruit to keep insects and diseases from overwintering nearby.

❖ If you're planting apple trees, space them at a distance equal to their mature height. Stake newly planted trees for at least a year, until their roots are well-established.

❖ Keep grass and weedy growth mowed around fruit trees. Pull back any mulch from around the trunks to deter voles and mice.

❖ To keep young fruit trees from splitting in freezing temperatures and winter sun, apply white latex paint to the bottom 2 feet of the trunks.

OCTOBER

2

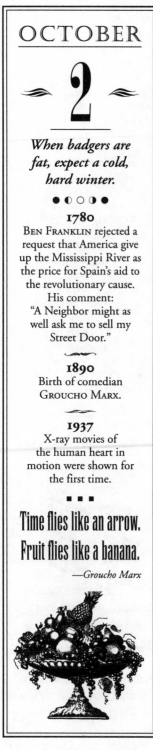

When badgers are fat, expect a cold, hard winter.

● ◐ ○ ○ ●

1780
BEN FRANKLIN rejected a request that America give up the Mississippi River as the price for Spain's aid to the revolutionary cause. His comment: "A Neighbor might as well ask me to sell my Street Door."

1890
Birth of comedian GROUCHO MARX.

1937
X-ray movies of the human heart in motion were shown for the first time.

● ● ●

Time flies like an arrow. Fruit flies like a banana.

—*Groucho Marx*

Seared with a Kiss

THE *Inspired* MIND

A LITTLE SHOWMANSHIP can be just the thing to spark people's interest in science. Wouldn't you attend a lecture on electricity to see experiments like these?

- An artificial spider animated by "electric fire" so as to appear alive
- Fire darting from a woman's lips to repulse anyone bold enough to kiss them
- A hole drilled through a ream of paper by a spark
- An instrument of eight musical bells that plays tunes using "electric fire"
- Eleven guns discharged by a spark after it has passed through 10 feet of water

These were some of the amazing experiments demonstrated by Ebenezer Kinnersley, a friend of Ben Franklin's, in the 1750s, when the study of static electricity formed the beginnings of electrical science. Ben designed most of the experiments, which used silk rubbed on glass tubes to produce the charges, and Kinnersley delivered the lectures. The "Philadelphia experiments," as they came to be known, were popular in America and astounded the learned of Europe. Kinnersley was the first to show that water was an electrical conductor. He also built an orrery (model of our planetary system) propelled by electricity and suggested that the solar system might operate in the same way.

Storing Pumpkins under the Bed
(and Other Good Ideas)

- Store a bumper crop of pumpkins and winter squash under the bed in an unheated guest room.

- File leftover seed packets in metal recipe card boxes.

- Store your spuds in a cool, dark, dry place with good airflow. Never store potatoes in the refrigerator—the starch will turn to sugar.

- Roll up your summer clothes and store them under a bed in a zippered snowboard bag.

- Toss an apple into the potato bin to keep the potatoes from sprouting too quickly.

> *Lend money to an enemy,*
> *and thou'lt gain him, to a friend*
> *and thou'lt lose him.*
>
> —BEN FRANKLIN

W HEN BEN FRANKLIN first arrived in Philadelphia, he traveled with a friend who borrowed a substantial sum of money from him. Later, the two fell out, and the friend left the city without paying him back. Ben never heard from him again.

On his first trip in England, Ben lent money to another friend who was unable to find work. The friend took a job in the country, leaving behind a mistress, who also borrowed money from Ben. Misreading her attentions, he "attempted familiarities" with her, which she reported to the friend. The friend was outraged and told Ben he considered all of his debts to Ben canceled.

The English author Joseph Addison once lent money to a friend with whom he had enjoyed many intense debates. After borrowing the money, however, the friend began yielding to every opinion Addison put forth. Eventually, Addison decided he'd had enough. When the friend agreed with something Addison knew he'd previously opposed, Addison demanded, "Either contradict me, sir, or pay me my money!"

COOKING FRESH SAUSAGES

❖ Always cook beef, lamb, or pork sausages to an internal temperature of 160°F.

❖ Use this test for doneness: A cooked fresh sausage link will be firm to the touch and hot all the way through.

❖ Cook 1-inch-diameter pork or beef sausages for about 20 minutes. For larger sausages, cook for 5 to 10 minutes more, then cut off a slice and check for doneness.

❖ To panfry sausages, start them in a cold skillet with about ½ inch water and cook until the water evaporates and the sausages are browned.

❖ When grilling sausages outdoors, don't prick the skins before grilling, or you will lose flavor and moisture.

OCTOBER

3

In October dung
your field,
And your land its
wealth shall yield.

● ● ○ ○ ●

1776
The United States went into debt for the first time when Congress authorized the government to borrow $5 million to cover wartime expenses.

1912
A drought that would last for 767 days began in Bagdad, California.

1990
East and West Germany were reunited.

■ ■ ■

Laws are like
sausages; it is better
not to see them
being made.

—*Otto von Bismarck*

OCTOBER

4

**St. Francis
of Assisi**

● ● ○ ○ ◐

*Onion skins very thin,
Mild winter
coming in.*

1822
Birthday of
RUTHERFORD B. HAYES,
19th president of the
United States
(1877–1881).

1957
The Soviet Union
launched the
22-inch-diameter *Sputnik,*
the first manmade
satellite, into orbit.

▪ ▪ ▪

Start by doing what's
necessary; then do
what's possible; and
suddenly you are doing
the impossible.

—*St. Francis of Assisi*

Northern Lights and Sunspots

IN OCTOBER 1730, "there was seen throughout this Province . . . a very bright Appearance of the Aurora Borealis, or Northern Twilight," reported the *Pennsylvania Gazette,* "but a sufficient Number of Observations have not yet been made by the Curious, to enable them to assign the Cause of this Phaenomenon." In 1733, Frenchman Jean Jacques d'Ortous de Mairan wrote about the correlation between solar activity and auroral activity, and in 1749 Ben Franklin theorized that the northern lights were an electrical phenomenon.

THE *Inspired* MIND

It was not until 1900 that the Norwegian physicist Kristian Birkeland demonstrated the electromagnetic nature of the aurora borealis. Charged electrons, exploding from sunspots, are carried by solar wind through space, intersecting Earth's magnetic field. The electrons collide with oxygen molecules, whose agitation generates the electrical waves we see as the northern lights.

Auroral activity peaks around the time of sunspot maxima, which occur about every 11 years. Records compiled by the National Climatic Data Center show that shortly before 1730, sunspot numbers peaked at 122, up from a minimum of 11 in 1723. Spectacular, far-reaching northern lights were seen in North America in 1989 during a sunspot maximum, when 158 sunspots were recorded.

SEEING SPOTS?

It might be your cleaning technique. Here are some tips to improve.

❰ To clean ivory piano keys, wipe gently with denatured alcohol. Rub with half a lemon dipped in salt or with a damp cloth dipped in baking soda.

❰ Treat rusty or yellow stains on old porcelain tubs with a paste of hydrogen peroxide and baking soda. Paint the paste on with a paintbrush, then cover the area with damp paper towels. Let sit for 30 minutes, remove the towels, and scrub the stained areas.

❰ To clean chrome fixtures, apply a paste of baking soda and water with a soft rag, then buff dry.

How few there are who have courage enough to own their faults, or resolution enough to mend them!

—Ben Franklin

And for those of us who can admit our faults, there are some modern aids and incentives. A German organization, the Lazarus Society, released a CD-ROM that lists 200 of the most popular sins, allows you to customize the list to match your particular temptations, and includes suggested penances and links to online priests.

Then there's the Franciscan friar in Somerville, Massachusetts, who gave his parishioners coupons for 50 percent off the sin of their choice. A thrifty sinner could redeem the coupon so that, for example, a 10-novena sin would cost him only 5.

A WORD TO THE WISE

Finally, there was the exhibit at an Italian trade show that featured a high-tech confessional to which people could fax their confessions. Apparently, as Oscar Wilde wrote, "it is the confession, not the priest, that gives us absolution."

Illuminating Tips for a Lower Electric Bill

❖ Remove every lightbulb in the house and garage (the barn, too, if you have one) and wash it to remove dust. A dusty lightbulb can be 40 percent less efficient than a clean one.

❖ Don't let computers, printers, and other equipment run overnight.

❖ Make sure your freezer is defrosted. Ideally, keep it as full as possible for efficient operation.

❖ Check the gaskets on your refrigerator and freezer for a good seal. You should not be able to pull a dollar bill through a closed door.

❖ If you have an electric water heater, ask your plumber to replace the "sacrificial rods" (anticorrosion anode rods) at the top of the heater every 5 years for greater efficiency. (A gas water heater also will benefit from this change.)

Onion skins thick and tough, Coming winter cold and rough.

1737
Ben Franklin began his duties as postmaster of Philadelphia, promptly setting up the post office in his home.

1829
Birthday of Chester A. Arthur, 21st president of the United States (1881–1885).

1921
A World Series baseball game was broadcast on radio for the first time.

• • •

—BK

I will love the light for it shows me the way, yet I will endure the darkness because it shows me the stars.

—*Og Mandino*

OCTOBER

6

1820
Soprano JENNY LIND, the Swedish Nightingale, was born.

1847
CHARLOTTE BRONTË's *Jane Eyre* was published under the pseudonym CURRER BELL.

1876
The American Library Association was founded.

■ ■ ■

NATURE WATCH

Moles are highly specialized burrowers that can easily drill through 15 yards of soil in a day, tunneling with their powerful front limbs in a motion like a breaststroke. Because moles eat insect grubs, they would be considered beneficial if it were not for the damage they do to plants and lawns with their digging. In the fall, moles move into their underground burrows, where in the North they will hibernate until spring.

Poverty, poetry, and new titles of honour, make men ridiculous.

—BEN FRANKLIN

TELL THAT to William Topaz McGonagall, who died in 1902 after 25 years of creating poetry that earned him the title World's Worst Poet in his hometown of Dundee, Scotland. McGonagall, who worked in the textile industry, was bitten by the poetry bug at the age of 47 and pursued his art with a passion, although the muse never rewarded his devotion with success. During his lifetime, the people of Dundee loved to hear him read his poetry just so they could make fun of it. McGonagall was also the butt of practical jokes, such as the fraudulent letter he received dubbing him the Knight of the White Elephant (a title he claimed until the day he died).

In 2002, 100 years after McGonagall's death, Dundee decided to honor his memory by inscribing one of his verses on a walkway by the river Tay. Was it because they finally realized how good he was? No. According to a member of the McGonagall Appreciation Society, "No one can surpass him for being the worst poet."

> Always be a poet, even in prose.
>
> —*Charles Baudelaire*

Keeping Things Green

❦ If you put lime on your lawn, spread half of it as you walk north to south, the other half as you walk east to west, to ensure complete coverage.

❦ Don't give up on your watering yet. Your perennials and shrubs will thank you for it this winter.

❦ To maximize the southern exposure of a freestanding greenhouse, orient it with the ridge running east to west.

Foil Foliage

BEN FRANKLIN, who printed money for colonial governments, developed the technique of "nature printing" to protect the paper currency from counterfeiting. On one side of the bills were images of real leaves showing their outlines and veins, printed from metal blocks. These he made by pouring molten type into a plaster mold that had been cast from a leaf. He laboriously leaf-printed each bill.

THE **Inspired** MIND

Ben would be fascinated to learn about innovative anticounterfeiting measures adopted by the Treasury Department to protect the new Franklin $100 bill released in 1996. The features designed to foil bogus bill makers (who use improved copy machines, scanners, and printers) include the following:

- A larger, more detailed engraving of Ben placed off center, away from the area of greatest wear
- A second portrait of Ben in the form of a faint watermark embedded in the paper
- Ink in the lower right-hand corner numeral that changes from green to black when viewed from different angles
- A security thread in the bill that glows red under ultraviolet light and contains the barely visible number 100 in a miniature American flag
- "The United States of America" microprinted on the lapel of Ben's coat

Warm October, cold February.

● ○ ○ ◐ ●

1930
The first glider license was awarded to L. A. WIGGINS of Akron, Ohio.

1988
A morning low of 28°F in Rockford, Illinois, set a record there, and fog in other locations reduced visibility to near zero.

■ ■ ■

The sun, down the long mountain valley rolled,
A sudden swinging avalanche of gold.

—Archibald Lampman

Put a Leaf in the Table and Throw a Fall Foliage Party

❖ For harvest season parties, hollow out a pumpkin or other gourd to use as a vase. An orange pumpkin filled with bright purple asters will make your table glow.

❖ Brush brightly colored leaves with melted beeswax and use them in centerpieces and bouquets.

❖ Use fresh artichokes to make attractive place card holders that will dress up individual place settings.

❖ Declare your party a harvest potluck and ask a few attendees to bring their favorite variations on apple crisp. Whether it's a grunt, cobbler, crisp, brown Betty, buckle, slump, or even a pandowdy, it's bound to be good.

OCTOBER

8

Tight cornhusks mean a cold winter.

● ● ○ ◑ ●

1755
The Acadians were expelled from Nova Scotia.

1871
The Great Chicago Fire leveled 3½ square miles of the city.

1890
American fighter pilot EDDIE RICKENBACKER was born.

By diligence and patience, the mouse bit in two the cable.

—BEN FRANKLIN

ROBERT FLAHERTY was a young adventurer who traveled Alaska in search of iron ore and fish during the early 1900s. Along the way, he shot thousands of feet of film of the northern wilderness and its people. Movies were still a fairly new technology, and a wealthy financier convinced Flaherty that he could salvage something from his travels by making a film out of the footage.

Flaherty worked for weeks editing the film. When he finished it, he lit a cigarette to celebrate. Unfortunately, he dropped the match on the floor, sparking the highly flammable cuttings and starting a conflagration that destroyed the film and almost killed him. Undaunted, he returned to Alaska, determined to make an even better film about Eskimo life. The result was *Nanook of the North* (1922), the first major film documentary, still critically acclaimed today.

Recently, when executives from the largest U.S. companies were asked what made people successful, the top responses were hard work and determination. Robert Flaherty knew that.

Tricks for Quitting Smoking

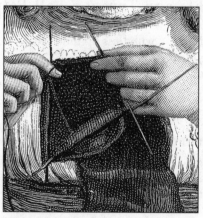

❦ Chew chamomile flowers or cardamom pods.

❦ Try fruit chews, gum, hard candy, or Cheerios (eat them one at a time).

❦ If you always drank coffee when you smoked, switch to cocoa or tea.

❦ Use acupuncture, hypnosis, or deep breathing to change your psyche.

❦ Find a buddy who also wants to quit.

❦ Buy yourself a big fish tank and stock it. Watch the fish when you get the urge to smoke.

❦ Post your decision on your refrigerator.

❦ Learn to knit. Knit an afghan—then knit another. Then learn to knit socks.

Forcing Bulbs
for Winter Bloom

IT'S EASY TO TRICK a number of spring-flowering bulbs to bloom indoors in winter. Hyacinths, tulips, crocuses, and daffodils, among others, simply need to spend 10 to 15 weeks in a cool, dark spot. An old refrigerator or unheated basement is ideal.

PRACTICAL **PRIMER**

1. Fill flowerpots or other containers with potting soil to within 2 inches of the rim.
2. Set the bulbs on top of the soil, as many as will fit, and fill in with more soil. Leave the tops of the bulbs just visible above the soil line.
3. Water well, let sit for 24 hours, and water again. Label with the date, using a piece of tape or a wooden marker in the soil.
4. Cover each pot with a brown paper bag and set in a cool, dark place (between 40° and 50°F) for 8 to 10 weeks for hyacinths, 12 to 16 weeks for tulips, 8 to 12 weeks for crocuses, or 10 to 12 weeks for daffodils. Keep the soil barely moist.
5. When you can see roots sticking out of the bottom of the pots, remove the bags and move the pots to a warmer spot for a week or two. Then transfer them to a cool, sunny location, where they will flower in several weeks.

BEAUTIFUL, BOUNTIFUL BULBS

❖ When choosing bulbs and corms for indoor forcing, think beyond the ubiquitous paperwhites. Lilies of the valley, tulips, crocuses, squills, and chasmanthes (a favorite of Thomas Jefferson at Monticello) will dress up your windowsills for months.

❖ The Victorians loved to force hyacinths in pinched-waist vases made especially for the job. You can use any container with an opening just large enough to support a hyacinth bulb. Put some small stones in the bottom for ballast and add water to just below the bulb.

Place in a cool (50°F), dark spot until you see roots emerge (change the water twice a week), then move to a sunny spot as the flower spike grows.

–BK

OCTOBER

9

Circle around the moon, rain or snow soon.

● ● ○ ● ●

1855
JOSHUA STODDARD patented the first calliope, or steam piano.

1903
Central Park in New York City was deluged with 11.2 inches of rain, the state of New York's all-time record for a 24-hour period.

1940
Singer and songwriter JOHN LENNON was born.

1977
President JIMMY CARTER proclaimed LEIF ERIKSSON Day in honor of the Norse explorer, son of ERIK THE RED.

■ ■ ■

I perhaps owe having become a painter to flowers.

—*Claude Monet*

OCTOBER

~ 10 ~

1865
JOHN WESLEY HYATT
patented the billiard ball.

1900
Actress HELEN HAYES
was born.

1987
TOM MCCLEAN arrived in
England after rowing
across the Atlantic Ocean
from Canada in a
record-setting 54 days.

. . .

**Curiosity may have
killed the cat,
but it did all right
by me.**

—*Helen Hayes*

*Bad commentators spoil
the best of books,
So God sends meat (they say)
the devil cooks.*

—BEN FRANKLIN

HELEN HAYES was one of America's great actresses, but her family didn't trust her cooking. One night before bringing the food out of the kitchen, she announced, "This is the first turkey I've ever cooked. If it isn't right, I don't want anybody to say a word. We'll just get up from the table, without comment, and go down to the hotel for dinner." When she came back from the kitchen with the turkey, she found the family members seated around the table—wearing their coats and hats.

Louis Pasteur realized that making great scientific discoveries in microbiology had its drawbacks. Extensive experiments with bacteria—how they grow on foods that aren't properly cooked or preserved—made eating out worrisome for Pasteur. To allay his fears when served food at restaurants and friends' houses, he would discreetly examine samples of his meal with a portable microscope, checking for signs of contamination.

THAT GOURMET TOUCH

❦ Add candles, cloth napkins, and cool jazz (not too loud, please) to make even the plainest meal special.

❦ Chop fresh parsley to make ½ cup. Add 2 teaspoons minced garlic and the minced zest of ½ lemon. Cover and store in the refrigerator. Use this mixture—known as **PERSILLADE**—as a flavoring or garnish for soup,

meat, and seafood, adding it a pinch or two at a time just

before cooking is complete. It also gives salad dressings a boost.

❦ Cut acorn squash in half, remove the seeds, place the squash in a baking pan, and brush with melted butter and honey. Sprinkle with nutmeg and allspice, or a dash of powdered mustard, then bake at 350°F until soft, about 45 minutes.

Sour Cream Apple Pie

This single-crust pie with a crumb topping celebrates the apple harvest.

2 tablespoons flour
⅛ teaspoon salt
¾ cup sugar
1 egg
1 cup sour cream
1 teaspoon pure vanilla
　extract
¼ teaspoon nutmeg
4 cups peeled, cored, and
　sliced apples
9-inch pastry shell

CRUMB TOPPING:
⅓ cup sugar
⅓ cup flour
1 teaspoon cinnamon
¼ cup butter

Preheat the oven to 400°F. In a large bowl, sift together the flour, salt, and sugar. Add the egg, sour cream, vanilla, and nutmeg. Beat to a smooth, thin batter. Stir in the apples. Pour into the pastry shell and bake for 15 minutes. Reduce the oven temperature to 350°F and bake for 30 minutes.

Meanwhile, prepare the topping. In a small bowl, cut the sugar, flour, and cinnamon into the butter. Sprinkle over the pie, increase the oven temperature to 400°F, and bake for about 10 minutes, or until golden brown.

Makes 8 servings

PERFCT PIE CRUST

❖ Try substituting cold milk for water in your favorite piecrust recipe. The crust will brown evenly and remain flaky.

❖ For the flakiest piecrust, chill a bowl and pastry cutter, then combine all the ingredients, working the dough as little as possible. The most tender crusts are made by hand, without a mixer or food processor.

❖ If you are making your own pie pastry, double or triple the recipe

and freeze the excess. To freeze pastry dough, shape it into a ball and wrap in plastic. Thaw at room temperature before unwrapping and rolling.

❖ Use up leftover pastry scraps with this recipe. Reroll the dough, spread with butter, and sprinkle with a mixture of equal parts brown sugar, granulated sugar, and cinnamon. Cut into squares, roll loosely into little tubes, and bake for about 10 minutes.

-BK

OCTOBER

11

1884
Birthday of First Lady
ELEANOR ROOSEVELT.

1925
An early-season snowstorm left up to 2 feet of snow in parts of New Hampshire and Vermont, blocking traffic and canceling football games.

1983
The last hand-cranked telephones in the United States were replaced by dial phones in Bryant Pond, Maine.

· · ·

To handle yourself,
use your head;
to handle others,
use your heart.

—Eleanor Roosevelt

12

Twinkling stars, a sprinkling of frost.

● ○ ○ ○ ●

1492
COLUMBUS landed in the central Bahamas, probably on San Salvador.

1935
Operatic tenor
LUCIANO PAVAROTTI
was born.

■ ■ ■

Even if something is left undone, everyone must take time to sit and watch the leaves turn.

—*Elizabeth Lawrence*

Shipshape

As a youngster living in the port of Boston, Ben Franklin yearned to go to sea. His dream of being a sailor never came true, but he became the first to publish news about the shipping trade. In a 1731 issue of his *Pennsylvania Gazette,* Ben published information on ships visiting the largest colonial ports in order to account for each colony's share in trade. He would no doubt appreciate some present-day statistics.

THE *Inspired* MIND

- In 2000, according to the Army Corps of Engineers, the Port of South Louisiana led the nation in total shipping trade with 217 million short tons (Houston was 2nd, while Philadelphia was 19th).

- The U.S. port industry consists of more than 100 public port authorities located along the Atlantic, Pacific, Gulf, and Great Lakes coasts, employing 1.4 million Americans.

- In 1999, domestic waterborne shipping handled 1.1 billion short tons of cargo, about one-quarter of all domestic surface transportation traffic.

LESSONS IN LEAF PEEPING

❧ Immerse yourself in color. Instead of fighting the traffic in your car, take to the trails, streams, or skies for your leaf peeping. Even those who are less than fit can sit on a train or in a small plane or hot-air balloon. People who are more athletic can hike, canoe, or bike.

❧ If you're rubbernecking while leaf peeping by automobile, pull over from time to time. Some folks have to get to work!

❧ If you bring the children with you on your fall foliage tours, seek out apple orchards that make their own doughnuts and pies, offer wagon rides, or allow you to pick your own.

❧ For the best colors during foliage season, get up early, when the morning dew is still on the leaves. The best photos are usually taken when the sun is at a slant—morning or late afternoon.

BEN FRANKLIN'S ALMANAC

> ### *If you would be revenged of your enemy, govern yourself.*
> —BEN FRANKLIN

SOMEONE SHOULD have told that to an Austrian woman who was sick of hearing her neighbor's music blaring from the apartment next door. She tried pounding on the walls and shoving notes under the neighbor's door, but the cacophony went on. Finally, the woman confronted her neighbor, who claimed the music wasn't coming from her apartment. When the noise continued, the irate woman went to a market and bought 20 pounds of herring, which she proceeded to shove— one fish at a time—through her neighbor's letter box. (Apparently, she thought the neighbor was hard of herring.)

A WORD TO THE WISE

The neighbor returned home to find something fishy going on and called the police. While interviewing the original accuser, they found that the music was coming from a radio that she herself had left on beneath her bed.

> ### Autumn is a second spring when every leaf is a flower.
> —*Albert Camus*

When pigs gather leaves and straw in fall, expect a cold winter.

● ○ ◐ ○ ●

1792
The cornerstone of the White House was laid.

1884
Greenwich, England, was adopted as the universal time meridian of longitude.

1942
Birth of singer-songwriter PAUL SIMON.

What to Do with Your Parsley, Sage, Rosemary, and Thyme (and Chives)

❖ Parsley, a biennial, will withstand a light frost. In Zone 5 or colder, cover it on cold nights. It has a long taproot and does not transplant well.

❖ Thyme is fairly indestructible. A perennial, it will go dormant in the fall, then revive in the spring.

❖ Sage is a perennial in most areas and does not need special treatment for the winter.

Before frost stops its growth, cut a branch or two to dry and use in turkey stuffing at Thanksgiving.

❖ Rosemary is a tender evergreen perennial that should be sheltered outside (Zone 6) or potted up and brought inside (Zone 5 and colder) for the winter.

❖ Chives are hardy perennials. Dig up a clump and pot it, then let the foliage die down and freeze for several weeks. Bring the pot indoors to a sunny, cool spot. Water well and harvest chives throughout the winter.

14

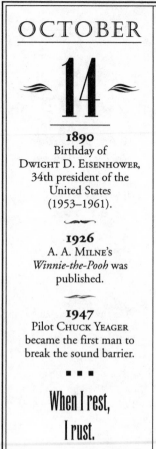

1890
Birthday of
DWIGHT D. EISENHOWER,
34th president of the
United States
(1953–1961).

1926
A. A. MILNE'S
Winnie-the-Pooh was
published.

1947
Pilot CHUCK YEAGER
became the first man to
break the sound barrier.

■ ■ ■

When I rest,

I rust.

—*German Proverb*

Putting the Vegetable Garden to Bed

Y OU CAN POSTPONE the inevitable (that is, winter) for a while by covering your vegetables with old sheets or bedspreads on cold nights, but the declining light and chilly daytime temperatures will naturally bring plant growth to a halt. If you do a good job cleaning up in the fall, it will be that much easier to start again in the spring.

PRACTICAL PRIMER

- Leave carrots, garlic, horseradish, leeks, parsnips, radishes, and turnips in the garden for harvesting through early winter. Mark the rows with tall stakes so you can find them in a heavy snow, and cover them with a thick layer of mulch to keep the ground from thawing.

- Pull up tomato, squash, pea, and bean plants. If they're disease-free, compost them. If they're diseased, either burn them or discard separately. Pull up all the stalks, put away the stakes, and remove weeds and debris.

- Once most of the garden soil is exposed, add a layer of compost, leaves, manure (if you have it), and lime (if you need it). Till it all into the soil.

- If some areas have hopelessly gone to weeds, cover them with black plastic and leave it in place over the winter and into the spring to kill sprouting seeds.

GET THE RUST OUT

❖ Remove rust from garden tools with a steel wool soap pad dipped in turpentine. (Do this outdoors to dissipate the fumes.)

❖ Remove rust stains from delicate fabrics by covering the spots with cream of tartar, then twisting the cloth to hold it in. Put the fabric in a kettle of cold water and heat the water gradually to a boil. Remove the fabric and launder as usual.

❖ To remove rust from tinware, rub with a peeled potato dipped in baking soda or salt.

❖ Rub a rust stain on clothing with lemon juice, then sprinkle with salt. Place the clothing in the sun for several hours, then launder as usual.

❖ Scrub rust spots on your car with a piece of crumpled aluminum foil, shiny side out. This also works on the chrome shafts of golf clubs.

Many dishes many diseases, Many medicines few cures.

—BEN FRANKLIN

IN HIS LATER YEARS, Mark Twain suffered from bronchitis and asthma. Well-wishers often sent him patent remedies, miracle cures, and homemade elixirs guaranteed to make him well. Responding to these cure-alls began taking so much time that Twain composed a form letter to acknowledge them.

Dear Madam,

I try every remedy sent to me. I am now on number 87. Yours is 2,653. I am looking forward to its beneficial results.

Few people at the beginning of the nineteenth century needed an adman to tell them what they wanted.

—*John Kenneth Galbraith*

For odd cures, it's hard to beat that of Menelik II, the Ethiopian emperor who was convinced that eating a few pages of the Bible would help when he wasn't feeling well. After a stroke, he felt very ill and decided to eat the entire Book of Kings. He died before he got to the end.

These days, you can't turn on the TV or read a magazine without seeing some new miracle prescription drug. That makes us wonder: If these drugs are so great, why all the advertising? They say, "Ask your doctor if Nostroquack is right for you." No thanks. Drug companies can do their own advertising.

OCTOBER

15

St. Teresa of Avila

● ○ ◐ ●

1858
U.S. Senate candidates ABRAHAM LINCOLN and STEPHEN DOUGLAS engaged in their final debate.

1908
Economist JOHN KENNETH GALBRAITH was born.

1918
The Spanish influenza, a pandemic, struck Philadelphia, where 4,500 people died during the 3rd week of October.

Drying, Storing, and Using Wood Products

❧ Store green lumber outdoors for drying. Place sticks between boards so they will dry evenly, and cover the pile loosely with a tarp.

❧ Store building materials that come in sheets, such as plywood and drywall, flat. If that is impossible, build a rack to hold them upright.

❧ When storing building materials—such as plywood—flat, make sure each end is weighted down to prevent warping.

❧ When storing items in a cellar or basement, particularly a potentially damp one, place them on wooden pallets or shelves.

❧ Use plywood to make excellent, inexpensive shelves. Cut it to fit and coat with clear, high-gloss polyurethane to which you've added dry painter's pigment (found at art stores). Apply the polyurethane until the grain is obscured, sanding between each coat.

16

St. Gallus

● ○ ○ ○ ●

*No rain on
St. Gallus's Day,
expect a dry spring.*

1758
Birthday of lexicographer
NOAH WEBSTER.

1925
The Texas State
Textbook Board banned
information about
evolution in textbooks
used in public schools.

Benjamin Banneker, Almanac Maker

THE *Inspired* MIND

AN ALMANAC PUBLISHED between 1792 and 1797 in Philadelphia earned its author fame and fortune. Before publishing it, the printers asked America's most famous scientist and astronomer, David Rittenhouse, to review the astronomical predictions. Rittenhouse, a great friend of Ben Franklin's, pronounced Benjamin Banneker's calculations "extraordinary."

Banneker was a Maryland farmer and self-taught astronomer. Like Ben Franklin, he grew up poor and had little if any formal schooling. His maternal grandmother was English—a convicted felon banished to the colonies, who bought a slave, freed him, and married him. Banneker's parents, freed slaves, were farmers who passed down their knowledge of agriculture and weather to him. A child prodigy in mathematics, he once disassembled a borrowed watch, mapped its inner workings, and fashioned a standing clock of wood that worked perfectly for decades.

In 1792, Banneker theorized (ahead of his time) that "every star is . . . the centre of a magnificent system" resembling our own solar system. And like Ben Franklin, he used his almanacs to promote morality, especially the antislavery cause. On the day of his funeral in 1806, a suspicious fire destroyed Banneker's cabin, journals, and papers. What a loss to posterity.

> The almanac writer makes the almanac, but God makes the weather.
> —*Danish Proverb*

WORKING WITH THE WEATHER

Housekeeping and maintenance chores are best accomplished in concert with the weather. For example:

❖ For exterior painting, pick a day above 40°F for best paint flow. Never paint after a long wet spell or if the day is too windy.

❖ Save nasty jobs such as cleaning the oven or scrubbing the bathroom with bleach for a breezy day when you can open the windows for good ventilation.

❖ For interior painting, choose a dry day with temperatures from 50° to 60°F

and a light breeze at most. Keep the windows open for drying and venting of fumes.

❖ Wash windows on a mild, cloudy day. Too much cold air or sunshine can cause streaking.

❖ On a dull, rainy day, dust.

Your Annual House Inspection

EVERY FALL, before wintry weather sets in, take advantage of a pleasant day to do a thorough inspection of your house. To make sure your home is ready to face the rigors of winter, work your way through this checklist of maintenance tasks.

PRACTICAL PRIMER

- ❧ Clean gutters and drainpipes to remove leaves and other debris. If your driveway passes over a culvert, be sure leaves have not clogged the pipe.
- ❧ Make an appointment to have your furnace cleaned and your chimney swept. If you have a woodstove, be sure the stovepipe leading into the chimney is cleaned and any creosote is removed.
- ❧ Install or replace weather stripping around exterior doors. A 1/16-inch crack around a door is like having a 4-inch hole. Swap your screen doors for storm doors and your window screens for storm windows.
- ❧ Repair or caulk any windows that leak. Windows are the biggest culprits in heat loss.
- ❧ Once window air conditioners are no longer needed, cover them with plastic or remove and store them.
- ❧ Check roof shingles to be sure none have blown off or worn out. If repairs are needed, call a roofer—today.

FOUR EASY WAYS TO MAKE ORDER

1. Hang a three-tiered mesh vegetable basket in the bathroom and use it to keep track of hairbrushes, combs, cosmetics, and vitamin bottles.

2. Store clipped recipes, letters, or photos in an old-fashioned hinge-top bread box.

3. If you see old-fashioned leather suitcases with beautiful fabric lining at yard sales, buy them. They may be too heavy to take traveling, but you can use them to store important papers, linens, or other household items. Stack several in a corner or slide them under the bed.

4. Keep a magnet in your sewing box to gather up loose pins and needles.

–BK

OCTOBER

1829
Sam Patch, the Yankee Leaper, jumped 120 feet from a platform atop Niagara Falls into the river below. He survived.

1888
The first issue of *National Geographic* magazine went on sale.

1933
Albert Einstein arrived in the United States from Germany.

● ● ●

NATURE WATCH

The fall aster blooms throughout the eastern United States, starting near the Canadian border in September and progressing southward, flowering in the Middle Atlantic states as late as December. The lovely daisylike flowers are usually purple or lavender but can be white or pink. The aster is usually the last plant to bloom in most locations, making it all the more precious.

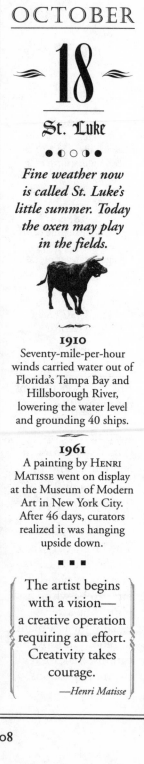

18

St. Luke

● ○ ○ ● ●

*Fine weather now
is called St. Luke's
little summer. Today
the oxen may play
in the fields.*

1910

Seventy-mile-per-hour
winds carried water out of
Florida's Tampa Bay and
Hillsborough River,
lowering the water level
and grounding 40 ships.

1961

A painting by HENRI
MATISSE went on display
at the Museum of Modern
Art in New York City.
After 46 days, curators
realized it was hanging
upside down.

■ ■ ■

The artist begins
with a vision—
a creative operation
requiring an effort.
Creativity takes
courage.

—*Henri Matisse*

A Glass Act

BEN FRANKLIN is sometimes credited with introducing streetlights to the city of Philadelphia. But it was actually John Clifton who set up a lamp by his front door, which convinced townsfolk to light the streets in 1757. Ben did figure out a way to improve the glass globes imported from London, which became sooty soon after the wicks were lit. His idea was to use four flat panes of glass, allowing smoke out through a funnel in the top.

THE
Inspired
MIND

The flat panes in Ben's lamps may have been made in New Jersey, where America's first large-scale glassworks was set up in 1739. During manufacture, the stretching of the molten glass resulted in the distorted, wavy panes prized today in old houses.

In 1902, William Heal of Indiana patented a process for making distortion-free glass by floating molten glass on molten tin. Heal failed to commercialize his idea, which lay dormant until an Englishman, Alastair Pilkington, patented his own float glass and oversaw a worldwide revolution in glassmaking beginning in 1957.

What to Do with All Those Leaves

❦ Rake up leaves into loose piles and run the lawn mower over them. Use them to mulch perennial and bulb beds or till them into the garden.

❦ Add leaves to the compost bin in thin layers to keep them

from getting compacted. Throw in old hay, dry garden rakings, and other fluffy material, as well as coffee grounds and other kitchen-generated material. (No fat or meat, please.)

❦ Instead of filling plastic leaf bags or garbage cans, rake leaves onto a large sheet or tarp, then drag it to your compost pile.

❦ Don't leave fallen leaves on the lawn. (But isn't that why they're called leaves?) You might be sorry in the spring when you try to rake up a matted layer of half-rotted debris.

For age and want save while you may; no morning sun lasts a whole day.

—Ben Franklin

WHAT WILL your standard of living be after retirement? According to the Consumer Federation of America (CFA), a majority of Americans expect it to be lower than it is currently—and they're probably right. A study conducted by the CFA indicated that 56 percent of Americans are behind in saving for their retirement.

What's the key to making sure you will have enough money for your retirement? Here are some tips from the CFA.

◆ Save money regularly. Even small amounts saved regularly can add up to a nest egg.

◆ Have a plan. People who have a financial plan generally save twice as much money as those who don't.

◆ Save at work. If your employer offers a retirement plan or a pre-tax savings plan, be sure to take advantage of it.

Of course, Ben Franklin advised thrift. In his 1756 almanac, Ben wrote, "Remember, a patch on your coat, and money in your pocket, is better and more creditable than a writ on your back, and no money to take it off."

Tips from Real-Life Millionaires

In their book The Millionaire Next Door, *Thomas J. Stanley and William D. Danko reveal some surprising facts about rich Americans: Most of them do not live high on the hog, and most of them did not inherit their wealth. Want to be a millionaire? If so:*

❖ Spend less than you earn.

❖ Invest 15 to 20 percent of your income every year.

❖ Live below your means: no new car every 2 or 3 years.

❖ Choose Russian, Hungarian, or Scottish ancestors (the leading ethnic backgrounds of American millionaires).

Following these simple rules can turn a little into a lot. As Ben Franklin once wrote, "Save and have. Every little makes a mickle [a great amount]."

OCTOBER

19

The old moon seen in the new moon's arms is a sign of fair weather.

● ○ ○ ○ ●

1781
CORNWALLIS surrendered to Washington at Yorktown, Virginia, ending the American Revolution.

1987
The stock market crashed as the Dow-Jones average plunged 508 points, or 22.6 percent, the largest percentage drop ever.

■ ■ ■

October. This is one of the peculiarly dangerous months to speculate in stocks. The others are July, January, September, April, November, May, March, June, December, August, and February.

—Mark Twain

OCTOBER

20

1732

Birth of FRANCIS FOLGER FRANKLIN, son of BEN and DEBORAH, who died of smallpox at the age of 4. "I long regretted bitterly, and still regret, that I had not given [smallpox] to him by inoculation," Ben wrote years later.

1955

The Return of the King: Being the Third Part of "The Lord of the Rings" by J. R. R. TOLKIEN was published.

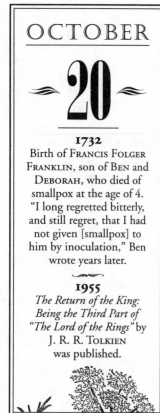

Lamb and Pear Curry

Chunks of lamb simmer in a spicy pear sauce to make a warming supper for family or friends. Serve this with white rice.

3 tablespoons olive oil
1 medium Vidalia onion, chopped
2 cloves garlic, crushed
1½ pounds boneless lamb, cut into 1-inch cubes
2 tablespoons tomato paste
2 tablespoons flour
1 tablespoon curry powder
1 teaspoon paprika

¼ teaspoon chili powder
1 teaspoon sugar
2 cups chicken broth
2 Bosc or Anjou pears, cored and sliced
Indian condiments such as chutney, toasted coconut, and roasted peanuts (optional)

Heat the oil in a large pot or Dutch oven over medium heat. Add the onion and garlic and sauté until tender. Add the lamb and brown. Stir in the tomato paste, flour, curry powder, paprika, chili powder, and sugar. Slowly pour in the broth, stirring to blend. Cover and simmer for 30 minutes. Add the pears and cook for about 10 minutes, or until the pears are tender. Serve with a selection of Indian condiments, if desired. *Makes 4 servings*

CURRYING FAVOR IN THE KITCHEN

❖ Cooks in India grind their own fresh curry powder every day, using as many as 20 different spices, herbs, and seeds. If you'd like to mix your own, the most common components are cardamom, cayenne pepper, chili powder, coriander, cumin, fenugreek, ginger, and turmeric.

❖ Curry powder stays fresh for only about 3 months, so it's best to buy it in small quantities.

❖ You can transform plain leftovers—perhaps some roast chicken and rice—by making a sauce with gravy, broth, or plain yogurt flavored with curry powder or paste. Add pieces of chopped apple or mango, sautéed onion, sliced almonds, coconut, or other ingredients, if you wish.

❖ The flavor of curried dishes tends to intensify with time, so go easy on the hot spices if you are cooking these dishes ahead.

❖ You can give deviled eggs, fruit salad, fried potatoes, or spice cake a special lift with a pinch of curry powder.

❖ Sautéing curry powder with vegetables and meat mellows the flavor of the spices.

All hobbits, of course, can cook, for they begin to learn the art before their letters.

—*J. R. R. Tolkien*

BEN FRANKLIN'S ALMANAC

Take counsel in wine, but resolve afterwards in water.

—BEN FRANKLIN

DURING KING GEORGE'S WAR in the 1740s, Ben Franklin and other leading citizens of Philadelphia were concerned that Pennsylvania was defenseless against an attack by the French. He proposed a voluntary militia (the Quaker-controlled assembly having declined to enact a compulsory militia) and soon had a force of 10,000 men organized. However, providing the militia with artillery to defend the city was another matter. A few old cannons were brought from Boston, and more were requested from England.

In the meantime, the leaders of the militia visited the governor of New York and asked to borrow some cannons. The governor refused their request but did invite them to stay for dinner. At dinner, the wine flowed freely, and the governor began to soften. He could, he decided, see fit to lend the Philadelphians 6 cannons. After a few more glasses of wine, the governor  increased his offer to 18. The cannons were transported to Philadelphia, where Ben took his turn with the rest of the guard on the battery below the town.

1805
LORD NELSON won a great victory over France and Spain at the Battle of Trafalgar.

1917
Jazz trumpeter DIZZY GILLESPIE was born.

1967
Vietnam War protesters stormed the Pentagon.

• • •

Men have died for this music. You can't get more serious than that.

—*Dizzy Gillespie*

Thoughts of Pumpkins and Gourds

☾ Only 10 days until Halloween! Pick out your pumpkin while the picking is good. Field pumpkins are generally large and a lighter shade of orange. They are best for jack-o'-lanterns. Sugar pumpkins are usually smaller and darker orange. They are best for cooking. Store all pumpkins in a cool, dry spot.

☾ Eating pumpkin may encourage sleepiness.

☾ Harvest gourds when their rinds are too hard to pierce with a fingernail. Gently wash them in a mixture of 1 part bleach and 10 parts water to remove all the dirt, then store them in a warm (50° to 70°F), dry place.

☾ For a pumpkin-colored addition to floral arrangements and centerpieces, look for the dried orange flowers of the Chinese lantern plant, often found along wooded roadsides, and bittersweet, a vine that likes to climb trees and stone walls. Keep them in a vase without water and enjoy their bright colors.

-BK

Rain in October means wind in December.

● ◐ ○ ◑ ●

1844
WILLIAM MILLER'S prophecy that Christ would return to earth on this day proved false, disillusioning some 100,000 Millerites.

1882
Birth of painter N. C. WYETH.

1987
The first volume of the Gutenberg Bible was sold at auction for $5.39 million.

■ ■ ■

God writes the gospel not in the Bible alone, but on trees, and flowers, and clouds, and stars.

—*Martin Luther*

Making New of the Old

PUBLISHED IN 1611, the King James Version (KJV) of the Bible has been the standard English translation for 400 years. Biblical scholars and linguists began translating the Old and New Testaments from the original Hebrew and Greek in 1604, duly consulting previous translations from the 1500s, such as those by William Tyndale and Miles Coverdale. (The established church had fought the translation of the Bible into common English for fear of losing the power to define scripture to its advantage.)

THE *Inspired* MIND

An important revision of the KJV was Benjamin Blayney's 1769 Oxford edition, which may have inspired Ben Franklin to rewrite the Lord's Prayer. Also composed in 1769, while he was residing in London, Ben's version uses simpler language derived from his own historical, literary, and theological investigations. The opening phrase, "Our Father which art in Heaven, hallowed be thy name," was transformed by Ben into "Heavenly Father, may all revere thee."

The New Revised Standard Version of the Bible (NRSV), published in 1989, is based on advances made in accurately translating the Bible's original documents (including the Dead Sea Scrolls) and eliminates archaic pronouns and male-oriented language.

Make Your Heating System More Efficient

❧ Use your vacuum cleaner's dust brush and crevice tool to clean around and under radiators and baseboard heaters. For more thorough cleaning, combine 1 gallon hot water, ½ cup vinegar, ½ cup ammonia, and ¼ cup baking soda in a pail. Wear rubber gloves for scrubbing and ventilate the area. Follow with a clear water rinse.

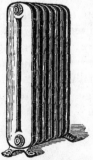

❧ Each month, vacuum the exterior of your furnace to reduce the dust load. Clean the vents you can easily reach.

❧ If you're planning to repaint your household radiators, forget the designer colors and stick to silver. The aluminum-derived paint radiates more heat and is less apt to chip or peel.

*A man in a passion
rides a mad horse.*

—BEN FRANKLIN

WHAT IS IT about getting behind the wheel of a car that makes us leave our common sense and patience behind? According to the American Automobile Association (AAA), incidents of road rage have increased 7 percent a year since 1990. In a AAA survey, 60 percent of drivers admitted to losing their tempers while driving, and 41 percent said they purposely punish other drivers when crossed. Here are some tips to keep you from becoming a victim of another driver's fury.

A WORD TO THE WISE

• Dim your headlights for oncoming cars.
• Lay off your horn.
• Signal your turns.
• Don't cut people off.
• Don't tailgate.
• Don't block the fast lane.

Of course, you don't have to be in a vehicle to behave irresponsibly. Police at European ski resorts have noted an increase in incidents of ski rage.

The best advice for avoiding other people's rage? Chill out.

Patience is something you admire in the driver behind you and scorn in the one ahead.

—*Mac McLeary*

OCTOBER

23

The swallows depart from San Juan Capistrano today.

● ○ ○ ● ●

1826
JAMES SMITHSON wrote his will, bequeathing his fortune to the United States for the establishment of a museum in Washington, D.C., to be named the Smithsonian Institution.

1915
The first U.S. championship horseshoe tournament was held in Kellerton, Iowa.

CAR TRAVEL MADE EASY

❖ Keep a clean chalkboard eraser in your glove compartment for wiping steam or condensation off the inside of the windshield. It works much better than your hand.

❖ Use your car trunk for seasonal storage. In anticipation of winter, fill a canvas bag with winter driving aids: a jug of windshield wash, an ice scraper, jumper cables, a tow chain, and a bag of dry cat litter for traction.

❖ Word games are a great way to break up the tedium of a car trip. Play the geography game, where the first player says the name of a place and the second player thinks of a place that begins with the last letter of the first player's choice. (Example: If the first player chooses Spain, the second player must choose a place that starts with the letter *n*.)

313

24

1901

Annie Edson Taylor was the first person to go over Niagara Falls in a barrel. She did it on her 63rd birthday.

1945

The United Nations was founded.

• • •

There is something in October sets the gypsy blood astir: we must rise and follow her.

—*Bliss Carman*

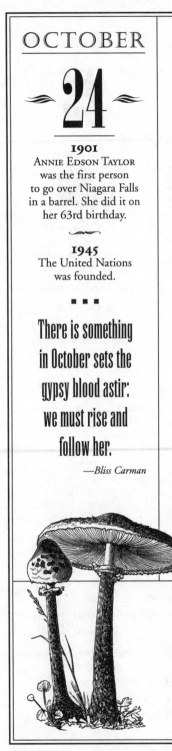

The Great Semiannual Clothes and Gear Swap

UNLESS YOU LIVE in San Diego, where the climate is virtually the same year-round, every spring and fall you switch your wardrobe to adapt to warmer or cooler weather. You take out and put away (or not) seasonal clothing, footwear, and sports equipment. Here are a few ideas to keep some sense of order in this exchange.

PRACTICAL PRIMER

- If possible, designate the closet or hallway closest to the entrance door for current outerwear and gear only. Soon it will be winter jackets and coats, warm gloves and hats, boots, perhaps ice skates and snow pants. Raincoats and light jackets that can be worn during any season stay there all the time. Add a few hooks for umbrellas, baseball hats, and other items.

- If you can, designate a second closet in the house as the home for off-season clothes and equipment. Before putting away your summer things, make sure they are clean and repaired.

- Use big plastic storage bins to hold baseball gloves, flip-flops, bathing suits, beach towels, and other items you won't need until next spring. The bins are waterproof, mouseproof, mothproof, and stackable.

- If you have growing children, use these semiannual swaps as a time to set aside outgrown clothes and other things you can't use. Give them away, consign them, sell them—do anything but keep them, or you will be awash in useless stuff before you know it.

NATURE WATCH

Autumn is a prime time to search for edible mushrooms in meadows and woods. Fungi feed off decaying leaves and other organic matter, and if you identify them correctly, you can feed off the fungi. Favorite edible mushrooms include the beefsteak fungus (found on oak trees), common puffball (grassy places), parasol mushroom (clearings), blewits (woods), and chanterelle (woods). Get a good field guide and go on a treasure hunt.

All would live long, but none would be old.

—BEN FRANKLIN

GOOD HUMOR may be the best way to deal with growing older. On Sir Winston Churchill's 80th birthday, while he was being photographed, the photographer commented that he hoped to be able to photograph the great statesman at age 100. "I don't see why not, young man," Churchill replied. "You look reasonably fit to me."

At the age of 85, comedian George Burns said that he had been raised to respect his elders. Then he added, "I've now reached the age when I don't have anybody to respect."

Supreme Court justice Oliver Wendell Holmes Jr. was 87 when he passed a pretty girl on the street and remarked to a friend, "Oh to be seventy again."

Agatha Christie, queen of the mystery novel, was married to a noted archaeologist. When asked what it was like being married to an archaeologist, she replied that that was the best kind of husband a woman could have. "The older she gets, the more interested he is in her," she quipped.

Upon turning 100, jazz pianist Eubie Blake—a lifelong smoker and drinker—commented, "If I'd known I was going to live this long, I'd have taken better care of myself."

1923
The Senate began investigating the Teapot Dome oil reserve scandals.

1981
A tornado caused $2 million in damages to Blountstown, Florida, in less than 5 minutes.

• • •

Thank God for tea! What would the world do without tea?— how did it exist? I am glad I was not born before tea.

—*Sydney Smith*

Polly, Put the Kettle On

❖ Always start with fresh water in your teakettle and bring it to a boil. Meanwhile, preheat your teapot or mug by filling it with hot water.

❖ Store tea in an airtight tin or jar to prevent it from absorbing moisture and odors.

❖ Take your favorite tea bags along when you're on the road. Making a cup of tea is much less of a rigmarole than brewing a cup of coffee when you need a quick pick-me-up.

❖ To make your own flavored tea, pour loose tea into a jar with a tight-fitting lid and add small amounts of appealing flavorings: minced vanilla bean, whole cloves, cinnamon sticks, crystallized ginger, dried citrus rind, or cardamom pods.

❖ For a sweet-smelling, stain-free teapot, rub the inside with a paste of baking soda and water, then wash and rinse well.

OCTOBER

26

*A good October and
a good blast,
To blow the hay,
acorn, and mast.*

● ◐ ○ ◑ ●

1825
The Erie Canal opened in
upstate New York, linking
the Midwest to the
Atlantic Coast.

1881
The gunfight at the
O.K. Corral occurred near
Tombstone, Arizona.

■ ■ ■

REMEMBER
TO FALL BACK

☾ Daylight saving
time ends on the last
Sunday in October.
Let the change of the
clocks remind you to
buy new watch bat-
teries each year.

☾ As in the spring,
be extra careful while
driving during the
week after the time
change. Traffic acci-
dents increase every
year at this time as
people reset their
inner clocks as well.

Coping with Insomnia

BEN FRANKLIN recommended "due exercise and great temperance" and "a constant supply of fresh air in your bed chamber" as guarantors of a good night's sleep. But what about those nights when you lie awake, mind spinning, tired but not sleepy, dreading the next day, hating every tick of the clock?

❧ Bring on a yawn—and then another. Yawning makes you feel sleepy.

❧ Use all-cotton sheets. Some polyester-cotton blends are treated with formaldehyde, which can keep you awake.

❧ If you find the sound of the ocean relaxing, get a tape recording of waves breaking on the shore.

PRACTICAL
PRIMER

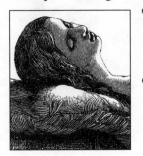

❧ Make a 2- by 5-inch eye pillow out of silk or cotton fabric and fill it with dried lavender. Drape it over your eyes to induce sleep.

❧ Slowly recite something you know by heart—the 23rd Psalm, the Pledge of Allegiance, the Boy Scout Law—and be mindful of your breathing, which should be slow and deep.

How to Stay Awake While Driving

You'll wish for insomnia if you are ever attacked by an overwhelming urge to sleep while driving. Don't let yourself catch even one tiny wink, but instead pull over immediately. And try these tips, gathered from long-distance truck drivers.

❖ Buy a bag of sunflower seeds, a cup of coffee, and a soda. Drink the coffee. One by one, crack open the sunflower seeds with your teeth. Put the shells in the empty coffee cup.

When you are thirsty, drink the soda. This will get you many miles down the road.

❖ Take a ginseng capsule with a spoonful of honey.

❖ Try sipping cold water. Caffeine helps up to a point, but it is dehydrating, which in turn leads to fatigue.

❖ Pull over for a short nap— no longer than 20 minutes, or you will feel groggy.

Kite Buggies, Kite Skis, Kite Sails, and Ben

PLACES LIKE El Mirage Dry Lake in California and Alvord Dry Lake in Oregon are inhospitable flatlands to most of us, but to buggy riders, they're paradise—especially if it's a breezy day. That's when kite-powered buggies rumble across the "playa" at speeds approaching 20 miles per hour or more. When a buggy rider encounters standing water, it's an opportunity to spray some "roostertail," but for purely aquatic thrills, there are kite skis and kite-sail boats.

THE *Inspired* MIND

For snow skiing, German Dieter Strasilla invented a parachute-like sail connected to a harness (1978), and recently a kite-venting system with control lines was developed to help skiers tack uphill.

All of these kite-propelled activities were predated by Ben Franklin's exploits. Ben used to fly a kite while swimming to pull himself through the water.

If you want creative workers, give them enough time to play.

—*John Cleese*

OCTOBER

27

1858
Birthday of
THEODORE ROOSEVELT,
26th president of the
United States
(1901–1909).

1925
FRED WALLER received a
patent for water skis.

1939
Actor JOHN CLEESE
was born.

1978
ANWAR EL-SADAT and
MENACHEM BEGIN won
the Nobel Peace Prize.

TIPS FOR NEW DRIVERS

Young road warriors need rules of the road. Here are three suggestions.

1. Discuss the perils of drinking and driving with your child and agree on a "no questions asked" ride home in the event of trouble.

2. Help new drivers minimize distractions by advising them to turn off the music, ignore the cell phone, and limit passengers (especially in the backseat).

3. Ask them to stick to driving during the daytime and in good weather until they get some experience. Some states enforce this policy with legal restrictions on new drivers.

NATURE WATCH

That beautiful red plant you see climbing over stone walls or entwined in a hedge may not be your best choice for a dried arrangement or bouquet if it is poison ivy. Although many species of birds feed on the berries and leaves, most humans have a severe allergic reaction to all parts of the plant. In practical terms, poison ivy is perhaps the most useful plant you can learn to identify.

POISON IVY

28

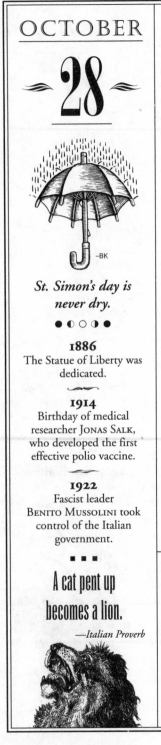

—BK

*St. Simon's day is
never dry.*

● ◐ ○ ◑ ●

1886
The Statue of Liberty was
dedicated.

1914
Birthday of medical
researcher JONAS SALK,
who developed the first
effective polio vaccine.

1922
Fascist leader
BENITO MUSSOLINI took
control of the Italian
government.

■ ■ ■

A cat pent up becomes a lion.

—Italian Proverb

Pizza Bread (Focaccia) with Rosemary

*Serve this bread cut into wedges with soup or stew,
or use the dough to make two 12-inch pizzas.*

1 teaspoon salt
1 teaspoon brown sugar
1 package (1 scant tablespoon)
  active dry yeast
2 cups lukewarm water (105°
  to 115°F)
5 tablespoons olive oil
5 cups flour (approximately)
1 tablespoon minced fresh
  rosemary
Coarse salt and freshly ground
  black pepper

In a large mixing bowl, dissolve the salt, brown sugar, and yeast in the water. Add 2 tablespoons of the oil and stir in the flour 1 cup at a time until a soft dough forms. Turn the dough out onto a lightly floured board and knead by hand until smooth. Roll into a ball and transfer to a lightly oiled bowl, turning to coat all sides. Cover with plastic wrap or a dry linen cloth and let rise for 1 hour, or until doubled in bulk.

Preheat the oven to 425°F. Gently deflate the dough and press it evenly into a generously oiled 10- by 15-inch baking pan. (It should be slightly thicker than pizza dough.) Make indentations in the dough with your index finger at 1-inch intervals and drizzle with the remaining 3 tablespoons oil. Scatter the rosemary over the surface. Season generously with coarse salt and pepper. Bake for 20 to 25 minutes until golden; don't let the rosemary burn.

To make pizzas, prepare the dough in the morning, cover, and let rise in the refrigerator. In the evening, punch it down, let rest for about 10 minutes, divide in half, and roll out to fit two 12-inch pizza pans.

Makes 1 flat bread or two 12-inch pizzas

PIZZA NIGHT

❖ If each family member wants a different topping on pizza night, cut off chunks of dough about the size of an apple and fit them into round cake pans or aluminum pie plates. Let everybody fix his or her own personal pan pizza. Add toppings and bake.

❖ For two 12-inch pizzas, you need 12 to 16 ounces grated cheese, about 1½ cups pizza sauce, and whatever toppings you like.

*If your riches are yours,
why don't you take them with you
to the t'other world?*

—BEN FRANKLIN

A WEALTHY MAN was determined to refute the old expression "You can't take it with you." On his deathbed, he called his three best friends together and gave each of them an envelope containing $10,000 in cash. "At my funeral, I want each of you to throw the money into the casket before they close it."

The friends agreed, and a short time later the man died. At the funeral, the friends did as he had instructed, but afterward one of them had a guilty conscience. "I feel terrible," he confessed to his friends. "I needed money, so I threw in only $5,000."

That prompted the second friend to admit that he had kept some money also. "I put in only $2,000," he said contritely.

The third friend shook his head and said, "You know, I'm really ashamed of you guys. How could you do such a thing?"

"You mean you didn't keep any?" the friends asked.

"Of course not. I put in a check for the full amount."

A WORD TO THE WISE

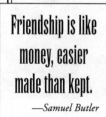

Friendship is like money, easier made than kept.

—*Samuel Butler*

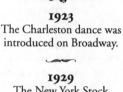

1923
The Charleston dance was introduced on Broadway.

1929
The New York Stock Exchange crashed, and the Great Depression began.

1947
A forest fire in Concord, New Hampshire, was drenched by manmade rain.

LATE-SEASON YARD WORK

❦ Hang a bucket over a hook in your toolshed or garage and use it to store hose nozzles and sprinkler attachments.

❦ When a frost blackens the leaves of dahlias, gladioli, and cannas, carefully dig them up and let them dry indoors on newspaper for a few days. Then pack them in Styrofoam peanuts, dry peat moss, or shredded newspaper and store in a dark, humid spot at 40° to 50°F until spring.

❦ On a mild day, run your garden hose up over a railing or over the shed to remove all the water. Then roll it up and put it away.

❦ To prolong the life of window boxes, take them down, scrub them with a solution of water and bleach, and store them until next season.

❦ Mow your lawn as late into the fall as the grass grows. Grass left too long when deep snow arrives can develop brown patches in the spring.

1735
Birthday of JOHN ADAMS,
second president of the
United States
(1797–1801).

1938
"The War of the Worlds,"
a famous hoax, was
broadcast on radio by
ORSON WELLES.

1945
Wartime shoe rationing
in the United States came
to an end.

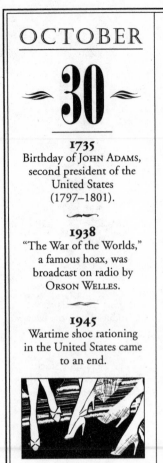

The Fearsome Beastie

IN 1736, Ben Franklin reported in the *Pennsylvania Gazette*, "A Sea Monster has been lately seen, the upper part of whose Body was in the Shape and about the Bigness of a Boy of 12 Years old . . . the lower Part resembled a Fish." Ben's hoax may have fooled some people, just as today some of us believe there is a sea monster lurking in the depths of Scotland's Loch Ness.

THE *Inspired* MIND

In the 1960s, high-tech scientific devices were brought to bear on proving (or disproving) the existence of this "fearsome beastie" after numerous photographs and eyewitness accounts dating to the 1930s seemed to establish its existence. Underwater sonar signals picked up large moving objects in 1968, and hydrophone recordings detected the "calls" of unknown aquatic creatures in 1970.

The most famous photograph of the Loch Ness Monster, taken in 1934, was exposed as a hoax when one of the conspirators made a 1994 deathbed confession. But some people claim that the confession itself was a hoax. Until skeletal remains are found or an actual creature is captured, speculation will continue that the real Nessie is a plesiosaur, a thick-bodied eel, a giant sea slug, or a 12-year-old boy.

Quick Leaveners: Baking Powder and Baking Soda

❖ Baking powder contains a combination of baking soda, an acid, and a moisture absorber (cornstarch). When mixed with a liquid, baking powder releases carbon dioxide bubbles. If you run out of baking powder, 1 teaspoon baking soda mixed with 2 teaspoons cream of tartar (the acid) is the equivalent of 1 tablespoon baking powder.

❖ Baking powder will retain its potency for about 18 months. To test whether yours is still active, add ¼ teaspoon baking powder to 1 tablespoon warm water. If it bubbles, it's usable.

❖ Baking soda, or bicarbonate of soda, is an alkali that produces carbon dioxide bubbles when it is combined with an acid, such as buttermilk or molasses. There's no simple substitute for baking soda. It will keep longer in a glass jar with a screw-on lid than in its original cardboard box.

❖ If your box of baking soda looks somewhat elderly, here's how to see if it still has some oomph: Pour 1 tablespoon lemon juice or vinegar over 1 teaspoon baking soda. If it fizzes, you're in business.

Witchcraft

BOSTON CLERGYMAN Cotton Mather, in *Memorable Providences, Relating to Witchcrafts and Possessions* (1689), tried to prove the reality of witches. The year before, Mather had taken a "possessed" child into his house and "cured" her, then oversaw the trial and hanging of Goody Glover, an elderly Irish washerwoman accused of bewitching the child.

THE *Inspired* MIND

Mather helped lay the groundwork for the Salem witch trials of 1692, which resulted in the execution of 20 innocent people. He never condemned the proceedings or regretted his role in prejudicing the populace.

Ben Franklin, who as a youth knew Mather, wrote a satirical account of a witch trial published 2 years after Mather died in 1728. In it, two accusers agreed to undergo the same tests for bewitchment as

—BK

the two accused witches (charged with causing sheep to dance and pigs to sing psalms). In one test, a witch would be outweighed by a Bible if both were placed on a scale. In the other, a bound witch thrown into a pond would float. In Ben's biting spoof, all four persons failed the tests, implying that anyone could be proved a witch.

Birth of Dutch painter JAN VERMEER (1632) and blues singer ETHEL WATERS (1900).

1864
Nevada became the 36th state.

1950
Playing for the Washington Capitols, EARL LLOYD became the first African-American to play in an NBA game.

■ ■ ■

LORE & LEGEND

Before **HALLOWEEN** was associated with Christianity—the eve of Allhallows, or All Saints' Day—October 31 was a day of ghoulish ghosts and scary spirits. For the pagan Celts, this day was the eve of Samhain, a turning point that marked the end of summer (life and light) and the beginning of winter (death and darkness).

TIPS FOR LITTLE GOBLINS

❦ Add some reflective tape to Halloween costumes for extra safety at night.

❦ Put a slip of paper in your child's treat bag with her name, address, and telephone number in case you get separated in the dark.

❦ Make sure trick-or-treaters eat supper before going out. Otherwise, they might be tempted to dine on sugary treats and suffer the consequences of a bellyache.

❦ If you expect trick-or-treaters on Halloween night, make sure that your path is well-lighted and clear of obstacles that might make the going tough for masked visitors.

❦ Consider offering nonedible Halloween treats. Trick-or-treaters will be delighted to find stickers, erasers, or a few coins in their bags.

❦ Besides pumpkins, try hollowing out turnips, squash, or gourds to make lanterns.

NOVEMBER, *the Eleventh Month*

WE'VE MADE this month, named for the old ninth (*novem*) month in the Roman calendar, into a highly social time of community suppers, feasts of thanksgiving, and general elections. In an earlier time, it was a gloomier season, one that the Saxons called Windmonath, the month in which furious windstorms raked the oceans and land. Their neighbors, the ancient Celts, began this month with Samhain, Gaelic for "summer's end," a day to bid goodbye to warmth and light.

We fight the darkness with our candles and luminarias, lay birch logs to blaze in fireplaces, and put on our woollies. We could follow the example of many of nature's creatures, such as the toad and the groundhog, and go into hibernation—but then we'd miss Thanksgiving dinner, easily the most anticipated meal of the year.

Most of the gardener's outdoor tasks are over now, but there's still time to rake leaves and heap them on the beds along with this year's compost. You can till them into the soil next spring, around the time you put all of November's candles and winter flannels away for the season. Meanwhile, there are indoor skills to master, from peeling chestnuts to pulling the lever in the voting booth.

Full Beaver Moon

is the name the Native Americans of the North used for the time to set beaver traps before the swamps froze.

Full Frost Moon, another traditional name, commemorates the season of icy mornings rimed with frost.

Sign of the Zodiac: Scorpio (October 23– November 22)

Element: Water

Quality: Resolute

Birthstone: Topaz

Flower: Chrysanthemum

Eclipsed by a Hurricane

BEN FRANKLIN was eager to view a total eclipse of the full moon on Friday, November 1, 1743. Unluckily, a storm blew into Philadelphia from the northeast, obscuring the eclipse. Later, Ben read in a Boston newspaper that the eclipse had been observed in Boston, with the storm hitting there on Saturday.

THE *Inspired* MIND

This puzzled Ben, because he assumed (like others in his day) that major storms blanketed large areas simultaneously. After reading reports from other locales along the coast, he proposed the idea that storms move from place to place. He hypothesized that hurricanes originate from atmospheric heat in or near the Gulf of Mexico and move across the continent.

Ben's weather studies helped create the foundation of the science of meteorology. The U.S. Weather Bureau, precursor of the National Weather Service (NWS), was founded in 1891. Today the NWS, assisted in the daily gathering of meteorological data by 11,000 volunteer observers, provides forecasts and storm warnings. The Benjamin Franklin Award is given to observers who complete 55 years of service.

How to Peel a Chestnut
(without Cutting Off Your Thumb)

Chestnuts add a sweet, meaty taste to stuffing and stews.

1. Make an **X** on the flat side of the shells with a sharp knife. Wear leather gloves, because the nuts are slippery.

2. Place the nuts in a single layer in a glass baking dish, cover with waxed paper, and microwave on High for about 6 minutes, until the shells begin to peel back.

3. While the nuts are still warm, use a small, sharp knife to peel off the shells and as much of the inner brown skins as you can. Work patiently to avoid bloodshed (your own).

–BK

4. Before adding the nuts to stuffing or other dishes, sauté them in 1 tablespoon butter until golden brown.

NOVEMBER

1

All Saints' Day

● ● ○ ○ ●

If All Saints' brings out winter, St. Martin's brings out Indian summer.

1861
A hurricane near Cape Hatteras, North Carolina, battered Union boats attacking coastal ports during the Civil War.

1959
Montreal Canadiens goalie JACQUES PLANTE became the first player to wear a face mask regularly.

■ ■ ■

LORE & LEGEND

Traditionally, **ALL SAINTS' DAY** features chestnuts, oatcakes, gingerbread, and doughnuts on the menu. The round shape of doughnuts was said to symbolize eternity, a nod to the saints whose lives are celebrated.

NOVEMBER

All Souls' Day

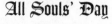

Birthday of
JAMES KNOX POLK (1795),
11th president of the
United States
(1845–1849), and
WARREN G. HARDING
(1865), 29th president of
the United States
(1921–1923).

1889
North Dakota and South
Dakota became the 39th
and 40th states.

1983
RONALD REAGAN signed a
bill designating the third
Monday in January as a
federal holiday to honor
MARTIN LUTHER KING JR.

■ ■ ■

LORE & LEGEND
Regretting the dough-
nuts you enjoyed
yesterday? The tradi-
tional foods for ALL
SOULS' DAY, honor-
ing all those who have
died (besides the
saints), are beans,
peas, and lentils.

Promises may get thee friends, but nonperformance will turn them into enemies.

—BEN FRANKLIN

JESUS TOLD a parable about two sons whose father asked them to work in the vineyard. The first son refused but later thought better of it and went off to work. The second son said he would do the work but never showed up. "Which of his two did what the father wanted?" Jesus asked.

The answer seems obvious, but discerning good intentions from mere talk isn't always easy. A man named George Jelinek ran for the Kansas House of Representatives with the slogan "I will work for you." Jelinek won the election. A short time later, he received a call from a constituent, a farmer who was getting ready to harvest his alfalfa and needed some help. "I voted for you," the farmer said, "and I'm taking you up on your offer."

A WORD TO THE WISE

A man of his word, Jelinek went to the man's farm and helped out, although he learned a lesson: "From now on I'm going to have to watch what I say."

Lentils: Loveliest of Legumes

❖ Lentils, unlike dried beans, do not need soaking.

❖ Brown lentils keep for at least a year in an airtight container and cook to softness in water or broth in about 30 minutes. Throw in a handful of white or brown rice to make a complete protein.

❖ Here's how to make a simple, hearty LENTIL SOUP. Chop 2 onions and 4 carrots. In a soup kettle, combine the onions, carrots, 1 can (15 ounces) diced tomatoes, about 7 cups water or broth, and 1½ cups dried brown lentils. Cover and simmer for about 45 minutes, until it's soup. Season with salt and freshly ground black pepper to taste. Makes 6 servings.

In Praise of Lighthouses

BEN FRANKLIN, in his *Autobiography*, tells a harrowing tale of near disaster off the coast of England in 1775. At midnight, he sighted a light "as big as a cartwheel." The alarm was raised, and by instantaneous action, "we escaped shipwreck, for we were running right upon the rocks on which the lighthouse was erected." Ben was so impressed with the usefulness of lighthouses that he resolved to encourage building more of them in America. Between about 1780 and 1820, some 40 lighthouses were built, the majority perched along the North Atlantic coast.

THE
Inspired
MIND

Nineteenth-century beacons burned whale, rapeseed, and mineral oils, as well as lard. Bright, single-beam lights were achieved in the 1850s with a glass prism lens invented earlier by Augustin Fresnel, and electric lights had become widespread by the 1940s.

In 1939, the Coast Guard took over responsibility for all navigational aids.

Today lighthouses that have not been abandoned are automated and unmanned. Organizations such as the Lighthouse Preservation Society of Newburyport, Massachusetts, help restore them.

SHINING THE SILVER AND BRASS

❦ Pass the ketchup and polish the brass. Rub ketchup on those stained candlesticks, wipe it off, and buff.

❦ Clean brass by using the water in which white beans have been boiled.

❦ Rub brass items with olive oil to prevent tarnishing.

❦ Use a bit of toothpaste (not the gel type) on an old toothbrush to get tarnish out of the crevices of fancy silverware.

❦ Soak tarnished silver in sour milk for 30 minutes, then buff dry.

❦ Place tarnished silver in a large pan of boiling water along with 2 teaspoons salt, 2 teaspoons baking soda, and a piece of aluminum foil. Simmer for 3 minutes. Rinse well and buff.

❦ Store your fine silverware in self-sealing plastic bags to slow tarnishing.

NOVEMBER

3

1718
The Boston Harbor lighthouse keeper was drowned along with his wife and daughter when their boat capsized. Twelve-year-old BEN FRANKLIN penned a memorial ballad, "The Lighthouse Tragedy."

1900
The first National Automobile Show featured the work of 31 carmakers.

1903
Photographer WALKER EVANS was born.

1992
CAROL MOSELEY-BRAUN became the first African-American woman elected to the U.S. Senate.

▪ ▪ ▪

They are ill discoverers that think there is no land, when they can see nothing but sea.

—Sir Francis Bacon

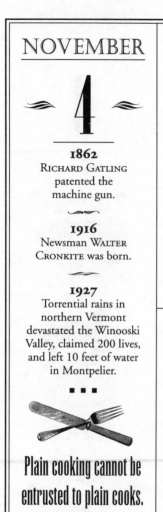

4

1862
RICHARD GATLING
patented the
machine gun.

1916
Newsman WALTER
CRONKITE was born.

1927
Torrential rains in
northern Vermont
devastated the Winooski
Valley, claimed 200 lives,
and left 10 feet of water
in Montpelier.

• • •

Plain cooking cannot be
entrusted to plain cooks.

—*Countess Morphy*

Fine Words Butter No Parsnips

AUTUMN AND SPRING are both harvesttimes for the lowly parsnip, shunned by the unknowing but prized by those who have ever tried them in lamb stew. The sweetest parsnips have gone through one hard frost and are about 2 inches in diameter at the fat end. Many people overwinter their parsnips in the garden for an early-spring harvest, but some cooks say it's best to keep them in moist sand in the root cellar, so they won't turn woody. It may be true that "fine words butter no parsnips," but buttery parsnips will bring many a compliment to your table.

PRACTICAL **PRIMER**

PARSNIP PRACTICALITIES

❖ Add a pinch of nutmeg to bring out a parsnip's best flavor.

❖ Roast parsnips, along with potatoes, carrots, onions, and bell peppers, in the pan beneath any meat.

❖ Add parsnips to your diet if you're battling kidney or bladder prob-

lems. They are considered detoxifying.

❖ For healthier hair, eat parsnips. Because they contain sulfur, parsnips (like cabbages, kale, brussels sprouts, turnips, and raspberries) help nourish the follicles in your scalp.

BEFORE THE GROUND FREEZES

☾ If you're planning to buy a live Christmas tree next month, dig the hole where you'll plant it. Store the soil you remove in the garage or basement, where it won't freeze. Place a board over the hole and mark the location so you can find it in the snow.

☾ If you use a tiller, run it through the vegetable garden in late fall to turn over the soil, chop up leaves, and help expose overwintering insects to freezing temperatures.

☾ Remove water lilies from a pond before the water freezes. Store the tubers in damp peat moss, sand, or gravel in a cool location.

Cobb Salad with Buttermilk Blue Cheese Dressing

This delicious winter salad was made famous at Hollywood's Brown Derby restaurant, where finely chopped chicken or turkey was sometimes added.

1 cup buttermilk
¼ cup sour cream
½ cup crumbled blue cheese
1 large head romaine lettuce, torn into bite-size pieces
8 ounces bacon, cooked crisp and crumbled
4 hard-boiled eggs, sliced into rounds
2 ripe avocados, cut into thin slivers
2 large tomatoes, cut into wedges
1 small red onion, diced
Salt and freshly ground black pepper

In a small bowl, whisk together the buttermilk and sour cream. Gently stir in the blue cheese, cover, and refrigerate until chilled. In a salad bowl, toss the lettuce with ½ cup of the dressing. Add the bacon, eggs, avocados, and tomatoes and gently toss with the remaining dressing. Garnish with the onion and season with salt and pepper to taste.

Makes 4 to 6 servings

Buttermilk: The Magic Ingredient

Good cooks know that buttermilk adds tenderness to baked goods and pancakes, tang to salad dressings, and a low-calorie protein boost to shakes and soups. Buttermilk is simply the liquid left after butter is churned (thus the name), although today it's usually made by adding special bacterial cultures to skim or low-fat milk to thicken and sour it.

❖ Substitute buttermilk for sour milk in any recipe.

❖ Substitute buttermilk for sweet milk in cake or pancake recipes. Add ½ teaspoon baking soda for every 1 cup buttermilk.

❖ To have a steady supply of cultured buttermilk, add 1 cup buttermilk to 3 cups lukewarm skim milk. Stir in ¼ teaspoon salt. Cover and let stand for 24 hours at room temperature, then refrigerate.

1857
Journalist IDA TARBELL was born.

1872
SUSAN B. ANTHONY was arrested for attempting to vote.

1895
GEORGE B. SELDEN of Rochester, New York, was granted the first U.S. patent for an automobile.

∎ ∎ ∎

Suffrage is the pivotal right.
—*Susan B. Anthony*

∎ ∎ ∎

IN THE VOTING BOOTH

☾ Bring a child with you to the voting booth and explain why you vote.

☾ Study a printed ballot ahead of time so you won't feel confused when faced with the real thing.

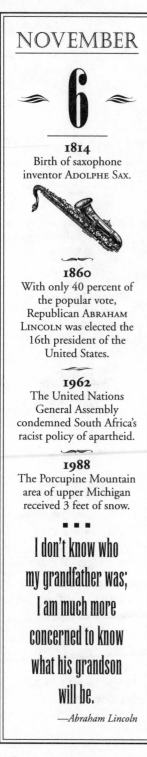

NOVEMBER

6

1814
Birth of saxophone inventor ADOLPHE SAX.

1860
With only 40 percent of the popular vote, Republican ABRAHAM LINCOLN was elected the 16th president of the United States.

1962
The United Nations General Assembly condemned South Africa's racist policy of apartheid.

1988
The Porcupine Mountain area of upper Michigan received 3 feet of snow.

* * *

I don't know who my grandfather was; I am much more concerned to know what his grandson will be.

—*Abraham Lincoln*

Glass, china, and reputation are easily cracked, and never well mended.

—BEN FRANKLIN

JOHN QUINCY ADAMS, sixth president of the United States, was a man of high ethical standards. But his political enemies did everything they could to make his life miserable, including refusing to make repairs to the White House, which had fallen into terrible disrepair.

In 1826, the meticulous Adams presented Congress with an inventory of White House furnishings and included mention of a  billiard table, which he had purchased himself for $61. It was a fatal mistake. Adams's enemies jumped on this detail, accusing him of wasting government money on "gaming tables" (even though it was his own money) and corrupting the nation's youth. Such opposition plagued Adams the entire time he was in office. In the next election, he was trounced by Andrew Jackson, after which Congress immediately authorized necessary renovations to the White House.

JOHN QUINCY ADAMS

Meanwhile, Adams moved into a rented house a few miles away. Among the furnishings he took with him was "the offensive billiard table" that had caused him so much trouble.

Hints for Home Comfort

❦ Turn your heat down to 68°F and humidify your house during the winter months. If you humidify with a pan of water on the stove, add cinnamon and cloves to the water and replenish it regularly.

❦ If you suffer from lower back pain, choose a good rocking chair with a curved back to support your spine and start rocking. Because the body stays in motion, there's less compression and strain on your back, and you get a gentle massage while you rest.

Search for the Northwest Passage

IN 1509, Sebastian Cabot sailed in search of the Northwest Passage, the supposed shortcut to Asia that traders and merchants would seek in vain for 400 years. In 1745, Parliament offered a reward of 20,000 pounds to the discoverer of the Northwest Passage, an offer Ben Franklin could not ignore. He was the chief sponsor of Captain Charles Swaine, who sailed from Philadelphia in 1753. Ben felt that Swaine's effort would be laudable whatever the outcome. If he failed, Ben wrote, *"magnis tamen excidit ausis"* (he fell, however, in a great enterprise). Swaine returned in November after his ship was

THE *Inspired* MIND

blocked by ice chunks in Hudson Bay, but he mapped the coast of Labrador and discovered a rich fishing bank.

Ben's motto for Swaine would have made a good epitaph for John Franklin (not related to Ben). His 1845 voyage to find the Northwest Passage ended in mystery, and he and his men were never found. A series of rescue parties searched futilely for him until 1859, with the unintended outcome that the territory north of Canada was mapped. In 1906, Norwegian Roald Amundsen completed the first navigation of the Northwest Passage.

As many days old as the moon is at the first snow, there will be as many snowstorms before crop-planting time.

● ● ○ ○ ● ●

1885
Canada's transcontinental railway was completed, 6 years ahead of schedule.

1943
Birthday of singer JONI MITCHELL.

1974
New Jersey became the first state to allow girls to play Little League baseball.

A Harvest Project

Teach youngsters to make a cornhusk doll, in celebration of the season. Check your local library for craft books and instructions. It's a fun activity for a child's birthday party, and the dolls make charming keepsakes for the kids.

NATURE WATCH

The winterberry bush, also known as dogberry, lights up the edges of marshes and bogs as far south as New Jersey and Ohio with its bright red berries. If you want to cut a few branches to add color to a basket of greens or a wreath, don't worry that you are robbing the birds. Winterberries are considered low-quality fruits because of their relatively low fat content, and migrating birds usually spurn them in favor of high-fat berries, such as dogwood or spicebush, that also ripen in the fall.

NOVEMBER

8

1656
Astronomer EDMOND HALLEY was born.

1805
LEWIS and CLARK reached the Pacific Ocean near the mouth of the Columbia River and settled in for the winter.

1837
Mount Holyoke, the first college for women in the United States, opened.

1889
Montana became the 41st state.

∎∎∎

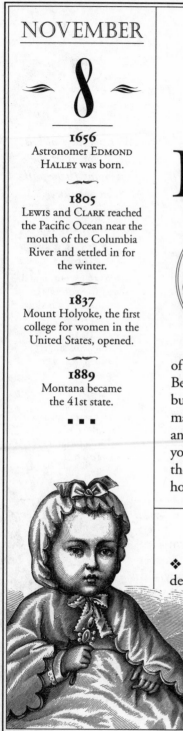

Useful attainments in your minority will procure riches in maturity, of which writing and accounts are not the meanest.

—BEN FRANKLIN

A WORD TO THE WISE

IN 1733, Ben Franklin sent one of his journeyman printers to Charleston, South Carolina, and set him up in business there. In exchange for a press and letters of reference, the young printer was to pay Ben a third of his profits. The printer was honest but no good at accounting, and although Ben received occasional payments, he never got a clear statement of where the business stood financially.

Then the printer died, and his widow took over the business. She was from Holland, where young women were taught accounting as part of their education. Not only did she provide Ben with a clear statement of past transactions, but she never missed a quarterly payment and managed the business well. Ben was impressed and recommended a similar education for all young women "as likely to be of more use to them and their children, in case of widowhood, than either music or dancing."

> This will be an era in female education. The work will not stop with this institution.
>
> —Mary Lyon, founder of Mount Holyoke Female Seminary

Baby Powder: Not Just for Babies

❖ Sprinkle a bit of baby powder on a creaky window shade or door hinge to silence the squeak.

❖ If your gold or silver chain gets hopelessly tangled, sprinkle it with baby powder to make the links slippery. Shake gently to untangle, using a hat pin to tease apart the knots.

❖ Shake baby powder into hiking boots, ice skates, in-line skates, or other stiff footgear to make it easier to slide your foot inside. The powder will help prevent smelly socks, too.

What Is Happiness?

B EN FRANKLIN made a serious attempt in his twenties to write down his beliefs about God: "I believe there is one Supreme most perfect Being," powerful but wise and "infinitely good," who "loves such of his Creatures as love and do good to others." In contrast to the prevailing 18th-century belief that God was powerful but wrathful, demanded obedience, and visited harsh punishments on unfaithful followers, Ben's ideas resemble a natural religion based on reasoning and moral living.

THE
Inspired
MIND

> *Question: Wherein consists the Happiness of a rational Creature?*
> *Answer: In having a Sound Mind and a healthy Body, a Sufficiency of the Necessaries and Conveniencies of Life, together with the Favour of God, and the Love of Mankind.*

Ben, author of these lines, seemed to cultivate the "Favour of God" with his inventive mind and public service. Active and healthy as a young man, he wrote about boating with friends on the Thames River in London. Jumping into the water on a dare, he swam "from near Chelsea to Blackfriars, performing on the way many feats of activity, both upon and under water," bringing happiness to himself and others.

> Happiness makes up in height for what it lacks in length.
> —*Robert Frost*

NOVEMBER

9

—BK

Auspicious day for travel.

● ● ○ ○ ●

1857
The first issue of the *Atlantic Monthly* was published.

1965
A power failure caused a blackout in New York City and along the eastern seaboard.

WHEN THE POWER GOES OUT

❆ If you live where ice storms and other weather events frequently cause the power to go out and you rely on well water, fill the bathtub with water before a storm. You can flush the toilet with bucketfuls of this water. For drinking and cooking water, fill clean jugs with tap water.

❆ Remember that a loaded freezer located in a cool spot and not opened will keep food frozen for at least 3 days, 2 days in warm weather. If the freezer is only half-loaded, the contents may thaw in 1 day. Freeze jugs of water if you need to fill space. An added bonus is that a freezer is cheaper to operate when it is full.

❆ If you anticipate a power outage, try to acquire some dry ice. Place the dry ice on boards or cardboard to separate it from the food and never handle it without gloves.

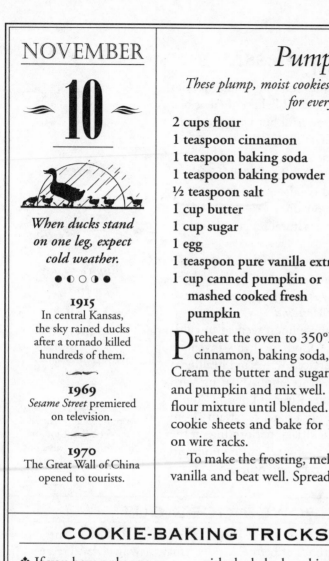

NOVEMBER

10

When ducks stand on one leg, expect cold weather.

● ● ◐ ○ ●

1915
In central Kansas, the sky rained ducks after a tornado killed hundreds of them.

1969
Sesame Street premiered on television.

1970
The Great Wall of China opened to tourists.

Pumpkin Cookies

These plump, moist cookies will be snack and lunch box favorites for everyone in the family.

2 cups flour
1 teaspoon cinnamon
1 teaspoon baking soda
1 teaspoon baking powder
½ teaspoon salt
1 cup butter
1 cup sugar
1 egg
1 teaspoon pure vanilla extract
1 cup canned pumpkin or mashed cooked fresh pumpkin

½ cup raisins
½ cup walnuts or pecans, chopped

FROSTING:
3 tablespoons butter
½ cup brown sugar, packed
1 cup confectioners' sugar
3 tablespoons milk
¾ teaspoon pure vanilla extract

Preheat the oven to 350°F. In a bowl, whisk together the flour, cinnamon, baking soda, baking powder, and salt and set aside. Cream the butter and sugar in a large bowl. Add the egg, vanilla, and pumpkin and mix well. Stir in the raisins and nuts. Fold in the flour mixture until blended. Drop by teaspoonfuls onto ungreased cookie sheets and bake for 12 to 15 minutes, until golden. Cool on wire racks.

To make the frosting, melt the butter. Add the sugars, milk, and vanilla and beat well. Spread on the cooled cookies.

Makes 3 to 4 dozen

COOKIE-BAKING TRICKS

❖ If you have only one or two cookie sheets and are deep into holiday cookie production, line a pan with parchment paper and drop the cookie batter on the paper. While the cookies are baking, drop more cookie batter onto another sheet of parchment. When one batch is done, slide the parchment with the baked cookies off the sheet and slip the next batch on.

❖ To keep cookies moist, add a slice of bread to the cookie jar. Change it every day.

❖ Always cool cookie sheets between batches so the dough doesn't melt from the warmth and lose its shape.

–BK

*We have pumpkin at morning and pumpkin at noon,
If it were not for pumpkin we should be undone.*

—*17th-Century American Folksong*

As often as we do good, we sacrifice.

—BEN FRANKLIN

IN NOVEMBER 1989, an Israeli soldier named Zeev Traum, was killed by Palestinian gunmen outside Gaza City. The soldier's widow chose to donate his heart to a patient awaiting a transplant. The recipient was Hanna Khader, a 54-year-old Palestinian. Why would a woman give her husband's heart to a political enemy? Because, Mrs. Traum said, "If it's possible to save a man's life, I think it's a mitzvah"—a commandment of Jewish law.

Centuries earlier, Louis XII, known as the Father of the People, suffered greatly at the hands of his enemies before being crowned king of France. After his succession, his followers urged him to seek vengeance on those who had wronged him. The king made a list of the malefactors and placed a red cross next to each of their names. Hearing of this, the guilty parties panicked and began to flee the country—until Louis explained that the red cross was a symbol of forgiveness, a reminder of Christ, "who upon his cross forgave all his enemies."

Sometimes doing the right thing involves a sacrifice.

> Peace hath higher tests
> of manhood
> Than battle ever knew.
> —John Greenleaf Whittier

NOVEMBER

11

St. Martin

● ● ○ ○ ●

Veterans Day

1889
Washington became the 42nd state.

1918
The armistice ending World War I was signed; hostilities ceased at 11:00 A.M.

1954
The Two Towers: Being the Second Part of "The Lord of the Rings" by J. R. R. TOLKIEN was published.

KEEP MICE FROM MOVING IN

As the weather gets colder and wild food becomes scarcer, field mice are looking for a warm, well-provisioned place to spend the winter. Do what you can to make your house as unappealing as possible to them. As long as you don't give them a reason to stay, they won't.

❦ Be particularly careful not to leave food lying around. Keep cookies, crackers, bread, and cereal well sealed and put away.

❦ Mice love pet food, grass and vegetable seeds, and birdseed. Keep these items in plastic containers with tight-fitting lids.

❦ Store food that comes packaged in chewable cardboard boxes in metal, plastic, or glass containers.

❦ If mice do take up residence, evict them immediately—before they multiply. You don't have to use poison; humane traps are inexpensive, reusable, and very effective.

12

1815

Birth of social reformer ELIZABETH CADY STANTON.

1954

The immigration station on Ellis Island in New York Harbor closed. Since it opened in 1892, 20 million immigrants registered there.

• • •

American women expect to find in their husbands a perfection that English women only hope to find in their butlers.

—*W. Somerset Maugham*

One good husband is worth two good wives; for the scarcer things are the more they're valued.

—BEN FRANKLIN

THE OFTEN MARRIED Zsa Zsa Gabor was asked how many husbands she'd had. "You mean my own?" she replied coyly.

Another actress, British stage performer Sybil Thorndike, was married to a fellow actor, Sir Lewis Casson. They were married for many years and often toured together giving dramatic presentations. When her husband died, Thorndike was asked if she had ever considered divorce during the time they were married. "Never," she replied. "But murder, often."

In 1985, Elizabeth Dole was appointed secretary of transportation by President Ronald Reagan. Her husband, Bob Dole, was a powerful member of the U.S. Senate. One magazine ran a photo that showed the couple making their bed together, which prompted a man to write to Senator Dole. He complained that the senator had to stop doing housework, because he was making it hard for men across the country.

"You don't know the half of it," Dole wrote back to the man. "The only reason she was helping was because they were taking pictures."

IF LIFE GIVES YOU A LEMON

❖ Add lemon juice to your dishwater to help cut grease.

❖ Apply lemon juice to soften your hands after washing dishes.

❖ Add a splash of lemon- or lime-flavored soft drink to the water in a vase to extend the life of a bouquet.

❖ Whenever a recipe calls for the juice and zest of a lemon, lime, orange, or grapefruit, grate the zest first

(removing only the colored rind, not the white pith, which is bitter), then juice the fruit.

❖ To get more juice from citrus fruits, warm them in the microwave for 20 seconds or submerge them in hot water for 5 minutes before juicing.

Making the Most of Indian Summer

IF IT IS UNSEASONABLY COLD on All Saints' Day (November 1), weather lore predicts a period of unseasonably warm weather, known as Indian summer, from St. Martin's Day (November 11) until about November 20. Use these balmy days to make last-minute winter preparations.

PRACTICAL

PRIMER

- Call the chimney sweep to get your chimney in working order.
- Winterize your car and add an emergency kit to the trunk.
- Finish splitting firewood and stockpile some kindling. If you're left with an unsplittable chunk, save it for the holiday Yule log.
- Clean your woodstove with a rag dampened with white vinegar. Apply stove black during an Indian summer day so that you can light a small fire and open the windows or doors until that first oily smell burns off.
- Remove window screens, wash the windows until they sparkle, and let the sun shine in.

–BK

NOVEMBER

13

1850
Writer ROBERT LOUIS STEVENSON was born.

1927
The Holland Tunnel opened, connecting New York City and Jersey City, New Jersey.

1982
The Vietnam Veterans Memorial was dedicated in Washington, D.C.

• • •

The hound of the autumn wind is slow; he loves to bask in the heat and sleep.

—*Peter MacArthur*

GARDEN ODDS AND ENDS

- Empty all your outdoor containers to keep them from cracking during the winter. Store them upside down.

- Once the ground has frozen hard, cut perennials back to 3 inches and mulch them with a thick layer of leaves or straw. Cover strawberry beds with straw or hay.

- Move potted chrysanthemums to a sheltered spot when their flowers fade. Water well and cover with a thick layer of straw to overwinter them.

- Drain the fuel tank on your lawn mower or any other power equipment. Consult the owner's manual for other winter maintenance.

- Before a heavy snowfall, cover pachysandra with a mulch of pine needles several inches deep.

- If you plan to put in a new flowerbed next spring, cover the area now with heavy plastic or mulch to discourage emergent growth when the ground warms up in the spring.

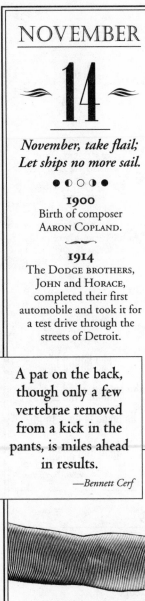

14

November, take flail;
Let ships no more sail.

● ◐ ○ ◑ ●

1900
Birth of composer
Aaron Copland.

1914
The Dodge brothers,
John and Horace,
completed their first
automobile and took it for
a test drive through the
streets of Detroit.

A pat on the back,
though only a few
vertebrae removed
from a kick in the
pants, is miles ahead
in results.

—*Bennett Cerf*

God gives all things to industry.

—Ben Franklin

When the American edition of James Joyce's groundbreaking novel *Ulysses* was published by Random House, one of the company's founders, Bennett Cerf, met with a large distributor about purchasing copies. "I told him I thought we had a big book for him," Cerf said.

"Oh, I suppose it's that dirty book, *Ulysses,*" the spokesman for the distributor said. "I don't think it's for us."

Astonished, Cerf defended the book's artistic merits, and the distributor finally agreed to take 250 copies to "help you out a bit."

That wasn't nearly enough for the whole country, Cerf complained loudly, and the distributor increased his order to 500. Cerf continued his arm-twisting, eventually bringing the order up to 5,000 copies.

By this time, Cerf was sweating profusely, but he was proud of his salesmanship. Then the distributor opened his desk drawer and pulled out an order blank already made out for 5,000 copies. "I thought I'd make you work for it," he said.

If you give up too early, you will never know what you might have been able to achieve.

A WORD TO THE WISE

Five Quick Ways to Measure
(When You Don't Have a Ruler)

1. It's useful to know what your handspan is, from outstretched thumb to tip of little finger. Sometime when you do have a ruler, measure it and remember the number, usually anywhere from 8 to 10 inches. Also measure your foot (which will be 12 inches long only by coincidence) and remember that number.

2. Use your body as a yardstick. Your arm span, fingertip to fingertip, is close to your height in inches, a number you presumably know.

3. A standard-size check from your checkbook is 6 inches long.

4. A stick of chewing gum is 3 inches long.

5. A dollar bill is exactly 6⅛ inches by 2⅝ inches.

The Franklin Stove

I N A L E N G T H Y 1744 booklet that included scientific explanations, a detailed illustration, instructions for installation, and a celebratory poem, Ben Franklin launched his newly invented Pennsylvania Fireplace. Whereas an open fireplace might require 4 cords of wood per season, his fireplace stove, Ben claimed, needed only 1. The freestanding stove warmed the air with its six cast-iron sides and had an interior baffle system to isolate smoke from special air-warming chambers.

THE *Inspired* MIND

For all its innovation, Ben's stove had a fatal flaw: It required the smoke to *descend* into the masonry hearth below the stove before escaping up the chimney. With a poor draft, Ben's original stove would have been smoky and difficult to light. His friend David Rittenhouse devised a more direct vent to Ben's stove, and it became a popular heating device by the 1790s.

Vermonter Duncan Syme's 1978 fireplace stove had a sophisticated baffle arrangement that moved hot, smoky air through a convoluted internal pathway resembling Ben's original system. Today Syme's company, Vermont Castings, produces the world's largest variety of cast-iron stoves, fireplaces, and fireplace inserts.

FIREPLACE REMINDERS

❧ Keep that fireplace broom away from the front of the fireplace, where it might catch stray sparks.

❧ Wait to clean out the fireplace until the ashes are cold—at least 12 hours after having a fire.

❧ Never douse a fire in a fireplace with water unless it is an emergency. Water makes ash residue extremely difficult to clean up, and the steam can crack the bricks.

❧ Remove smoke stains from the inside of your glass fireplace doors with a mixture of ½ cup vinegar, 1 tablespoon ammonia, and 1 gallon warm water. Spray or wipe on, then rinse with warm water and dry with a clean cloth.

❧ Remove soot and ashes from exterior bricks by rubbing with a stiff brush dipped in a mixture of baking soda and water.

1744
BEN FRANKLIN published *An Account of the New-Invented Pennsylvania Fireplaces.* He turned down an offer for a patent.

1887
Painter GEORGIA O'KEEFFE was born.

1937
Debut of Sadie Hawkins Day in AL CAPP's "L'il Abner" comic strip.

∙ ∙ ∙

—BK

I only like two kinds of men, domestic and imported.

—*Mae West*

1733
Superfine Crown Soap,
made by the FRANKLINS,
was advertised in the
Pennsylvania Gazette.

1907
Oklahoma became the
46th state.

■ ■ ■

Childhood is that
wonderful time of life
when all you need to do
to lose weight is
take a bath.

—Richard Zera

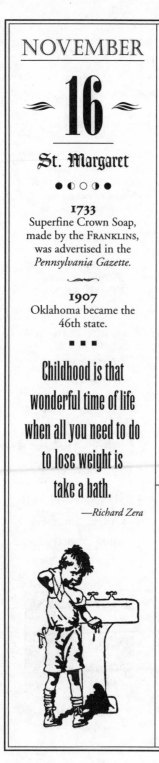

Lard and Lye

AT THE AGE OF 10, Ben Franklin was put to work in the family's soap-making business. Fat from beef was combined with homemade lye to make soap. A barrel was filled with wood ashes, water was poured into the barrel to make a caustic soda, and then the lye water was drawn off at the bottom of the barrel. Boiling the soda ash and fat together created soft soap, but the hard soap needed for laundry and bathing came from re-boiling the batch with salt.

THE *Inspired* MIND

By 1750, the demand for soda ash in the American colonies outstripped the supply, confining soap manufacture to households. In 1783, Frenchman Nicolas Leblanc figured out how to make soda ash from sea salt and sulfuric acid, but

it wasn't until the 1820s that the process became commercially widespread. Around 1830, William Colgate was the first to sell single bars of soap, and in 1879 soap makers Procter & Gamble found that extra mixing blended the lye and fat into a nearly pure soap. They called their product Ivory and successfully marketed it as an inexpensive alternative to the imported castile soaps (made with olive oil) of the day.

SPLENDOR IN THE TUB

℄ To make potpourri "tea bags" for your bathwater, combine equal parts dried chamomile, mint, and lavender and place a spoonful of the mixture in the center of a 6-inch square of muslin. For the scent of roses, use dried rosebuds. If you love citrus, use dried orange or lemon peel. Tie the muslin securely around the aromatics and toss the bag into a tub of warm water.

℄ In a hurry? Just add a couple of store-bought chamomile or peppermint tea bags to your warm bath, light some candles, sit back, and relax.

℄ For simple homemade bath salts, combine equal parts Epsom salts and rock salt in a jar with a lid. Add 20 drops of essential oil or fragrance and shake well. Add a spoonful of the scented salts to your bathwater.

Bargaining has neither friends nor relations.

—Ben Franklin

A SHANGHAI OFFICE WORKER named Han Bin didn't make any friends with the online auction service that sold him a used Volkswagen Passat, but he did get a bargain. Han bid just 16 yuan (about $14) for the car, which was worth about $12,000. When no one else bid on it, he won the auction. Han was overjoyed, although the company that put the car up for auction wasn't so thrilled. "It's unbe-lievable," said a market-ing executive for Yongda Automobile Sales. The company tried to talk its way out of the situation, but Han went to court to make the company hand over the car.

Another tough bargainer was Georges Clemenceau, premier of France during World War I. Browsing in an art gallery, he found a statue that he liked and asked the art dealer the price. The dealer told him 75 ru-pees. Clemenceau offered him 45.

"Impossible!" the dealer exclaimed. "I'd rather give it to you."

"Done," Clemenceau said. He took the statue and gave the dealer a gracious "gift" in return: 45 rupees.

A WORD TO THE WISE

—BK

Sunshine is delicious, rain is refreshing, wind braces us up, snow is exhilarating; there is really no such thing as bad weather, only different kinds of good weather.

—*John Ruskin*

NOVEMBER

17

If ice in November will bear a duck, There's nothing thereafter but sleet and muck.

● ○ ○ ○ ●

1869
The Suez Canal opened in Egypt, connecting the Mediterranean and Red Seas.

1889
Daily railroad service linked Chicago and Portland, Oregon.

Birthday of theater director LEE STRASBERG (1901), movie directors MARTIN SCORSESE (1942) and ROLAND JOFFE (1945), and human rights activist YOLANDA KING (1955).

Cake-Baking Hints

❖ For a light cake, be sure to cream the butter and sugar thoroughly. This blends bub-bles of air into the fat. Bak-ing powder and baking soda enlarge the bubbles, making the cake rise.

❖ For best results, don't let cake pans touch each other or the sides of the oven while baking.

❖ To frost a layer cake, place the first layer upside down, add a layer of frosting or fill-ing, and place the second layer on top, right side up.

Frost the sides, then the top, making a nice swirl around the top edge.

❖ When covering a frosted cake with plastic wrap, lightly coat the plastic with vegetable oil—cooking spray works well—so the icing doesn't cling to it.

18

Thunder this month means a fertile year.

● ◐ ○ ○ ●

1861
JULIA WARD HOWE wrote the lyrics to "The Battle Hymn of the Republic."

~

Birth of comedian
IMOGENE COCA (1908) and astronaut ALAN B. SHEPARD JR. (1923).

1988
Thunderstorms drenched Little Rock, Arkansas, with 7.01 inches of rain, besting the previous record of 1.91 inches for the date.

▪ ▪ ▪

It [Earth] is, in fact, very finite, very fragile . . . so incredibly fragile.

—*Alan B. Shepard Jr.*

Quick as Lightning

LIGHTNING IS a fast and furious force of nature. A flash of lightning typically travels 3 kilometers (about 1.9 miles) between cloud and ground at speeds approaching or surpassing 140,000 kilometers (87,000 miles) per second, roughly half the speed of light. The entire flash lasts about one-fifth of a second, but it is usually made up of several shorter repeating discharges that occur too quickly for the eye to make them out individually. When these single strokes are separated just enough in time to be seen by the eye, we notice it as flickering.

THE
Inspired
MIND

The temperature of the air in the channel of a lightning flash may reach an estimated 54,000°F, nearly six times as hot as the surface of the sun. Lightning can be charged with millions of volts of electricity. (By contrast, the standard American household wiring design uses a 240-volt circuit.) Measurements of lightning current were first made in 1897 in Germany by F. Pockels, who analyzed the magnetic field induced by lightning to estimate the current. Ben Franklin would not be surprised to learn that no one has yet invented a capacitor capable of storing the energy in lightning.

LAUNDRY LESSONS

℃ When taking damp clothes out of the washing machine, take each piece out separately and give it a snap before putting it in the dryer. This reduces wrinkling.

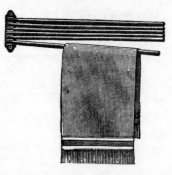

℃ For quicker drying, add one or two dry towels to the load.

℃ After ironing a tablecloth, drape it over a padded hanger and store it in a closet.

℃ Make your own air freshener for the laundry basket by adding baking soda to a paper coffee filter. Tape the filter shut and put it in the bottom of your laundry basket. Replace it every 3 months.

℃ Use an empty hanging plant pot (with drainage holes) for outdoor clothespin storage.

Here comes the orator! with his flood of words, and his drop of reason.

—BEN FRANKLIN

THE GREAT ORATORS of the past were known for giving long, flowery speeches, often going on for a couple of hours. In contrast, the politician Henry Clay was known for short, powerful speeches. He was once criticized by a garrulous rival who stated that Clay was aiming at a contemporary audience, while *he* was speaking for posterity. Clay responded, "And it seems, sir, that you are resolved to speak until the arrival of your audience."

A WORD TO THE WISE

At 270 words, Lincoln's Gettysburg Address is among the shortest speeches ever given. Newspapers of the day gave it poor reviews, calling it a lightweight effort compared to the 2-hour dissertation that Edward Everett gave just before Lincoln spoke. But in a note to Lincoln the next day, Everett wrote, "I wish that I could flatter myself that I had come as near to the central idea of the occasion in two hours as you did in two minutes."

> Words are often seen hunting for an idea, but ideas are never seen hunting for words.
>
> —*Josh Billings*

● ○ ○ ○ ●

1831
Birthday of
JAMES A. GARFIELD,
20th president of the
United States (1881).

1863
ABRAHAM LINCOLN
delivered an address
dedicating a military
cemetery at the
Gettysburg battlefield.

1996
Port Orford, Oregon,
was deluged with 11.7
inches of rain, the state's
all-time record for a
24-hour period.

CARING FOR FANCY FABRICS

❖ **Chiffon:** Hand-wash in lukewarm soapy water and rinse well in cool water. Shape the garment on a large towel, cover with another towel, and roll up. Press with a warm iron while still damp.

❖ **Down comforters and clothing:** Do not dry-clean. Wash in a commercial washer (for large comforters) or home machine. Tumble dry, adding a clean sneaker or stuffed animal to the dryer to help fluff the down. Shake vigorously when dry.

❖ **Lace:** Wash in a mild laundry detergent such as Ivory Snow dissolved in hot water. Squeeze lace; do not rub. Rinse in cool water and roll in a towel. Iron with a damp pressing cloth while still damp.

❖ **Satin:** Add ½ tablespoon kerosene to 1 quart warm soapy water and swish the garment in the solution until clean. Rinse in warm water to which you've added a little borax. Roll in a towel, then iron on the dull side while still damp.

20

1820

The whaling ship *Essex,* out of Nantucket, Massachusetts, was attacked and sunk by an 80-ton sperm whale. HERMAN MELVILLE based his novel *Moby Dick* in part on the incident.

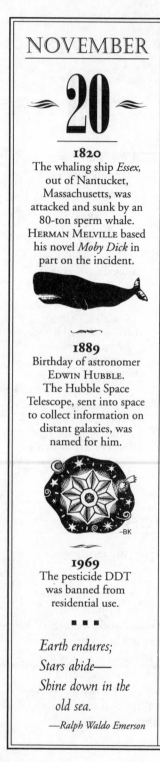

1889

Birthday of astronomer EDWIN HUBBLE. The Hubble Space Telescope, sent into space to collect information on distant galaxies, was named for him.

—BK

1969

The pesticide DDT was banned from residential use.

∎ ∎ ∎

Earth endures;
Stars abide—
Shine down in the
old sea.

—*Ralph Waldo Emerson*

Stargazing

You DON'T NEED a fancy telescope or a doctorate in astronomy to be a stargazer. All you need is darkness, a clear sky, an almanac or star chart to help you interpret what you are seeing, and your own curiosity about the order and beauty of the cosmos.

PRACTICAL PRIMER

- **Darkness:** City dwellers are at a disadvantage because of light pollution. For best viewing, head away from the bright lights.
- **Clear sky:** You need not only good weather but also a moonless night. The best stargazing occurs when the moon is between the last and first quarter.
- **Almanac or star chart:** These sources provide precise information on the constellations, the rising and setting of the visible planets, and periodic events such as the Leonid meteor showers, which are visible every year in mid-November.

Pest Control Strategy for the Vegetable Garden

This month, during a natural lull in the gardening year, is a good time to plan your pest control strategy for next spring.

❧ Read up on integrated pest management, which combines prevention and carefully targeted, nontoxic controls. For information, contact your local extension office or search the Internet for resources.

❧ Lay out next year's garden, using crop rotation to stop the spread of soilborne diseases and insects. Alternating "heavy feeders" such as corn and tomatoes with cover crops or nitrogen-fixing legumes also replenishes the soil.

❧ Order seeds of disease- and pest-resistant varieties of vegetables.

❧ Plan to use companion planting to discourage insects. Tansy, for example, deters Japanese beetles and makes a fine companion to roses and raspberries. Marigolds, the workhorses of companion plants, are thought to deter a wide range of insects. If aphids are a problem, plant nasturtiums nearby.

Tell a miser he's rich,
and a woman she's old, you'll get
no money of one, nor kindness
of t'other.

—BEN FRANKLIN

NOVEMBER

21

1620
The Mayflower Compact
was signed.

1789
North Carolina became
the 12th state.

1835
Heiress HETTY GREEN
was born.

■ ■ ■

AT THE BEGINNING of the 20th century, the richest woman in America—and perhaps the world—was an eccentric heiress named Hetty Green. After inheriting $10 million from her father and aunt, Green began investing, amassing an even larger fortune. Her business acumen was surpassed only by her legendary cheapness. She wore the same plain black dress until it was practically in tatters—an outfit that earned her the nickname the Witch of Wall Street. She lived in cheap boardinghouses, sought medical care at free clinics, and once spent an entire night searching for a 2-cent stamp. When she died, she left more than $100 million to her two children, who promptly began spending it and making generous contributions to charities.

Among other legendary misers, it's hard to ignore the great Jack Benny. Once, on Benny's radio show, a robber held him up at gunpoint, demanding, "Your money or your life." When Benny hesitated, the thief repeated his demand. As the studio audience's snickers grew to a roar, Benny said, "I'm thinking, I'm thinking!"

Every man serves a
useful purpose: A miser,
for example, makes a
wonderful ancestor.

—*Laurence J. Peter*

"I'm Not Cheap; I'm Frugal!"

❖ Don't buy a snazzy Plexiglas cookbook holder. Instead, place a 9- by 13-inch glass baking dish on your open book to hold the pages flat. You will be able to read the recipe through the glass.

❖ Don't toss out those stale crackers. Place them in a preheated 300°F oven on a cookie sheet (not touching) for 5 minutes to crisp them up.

❖ In the winter, let heavy clothes such as jeans, sweatshirts, and towels dry on a rack rather than in the clothes dryer. They'll add humidity to the air and help you save on electricity or gas for the dryer.

NOVEMBER

22

1718
Edward Teach, better known as Blackbeard the pirate, died in a naval fight off the coast of North Carolina.

Birthday of French president Charles de Gaulle (1890) and comedian Rodney Dangerfield (1921).

1963
President John F. Kennedy was assassinated in Dallas at the age of 46.

• • •

For in the final analysis, our most basic common link, is that we all inhabit this small planet, we all breathe the same air, we all cherish our children's futures, and we are all mortal.

—*John F. Kennedy*

He that would live in peace & at ease, must not speak all he knows, nor judge all he sees.

—Ben Franklin

A YOUNG MAN wearing overalls and rubber boots walked into a car dealership in the city of Bodø, Norway, and said he wanted to buy 16 cars. Annoyed, the salesman told him to buzz off, as he didn't have time for jokes. The young man then went across the street to another dealership and made the same announcement. The dealer there took him at his word. It turned out that the man was part of a 16-man fishing crew that had just been given large bonuses for bringing in a record catch. The crew had authorized him to go car shopping for them, figuring they'd get a better price if they bought all the cars at the same place. The second dealer sold him 16 cars at the equivalent of $160,000, a deal the first salesman could have had if he hadn't been so quick to judge.

One person who made a habit of not judging too quickly was President Herbert Hoover. Once, Hoover was riding on a train that passed a flock of sheep, and a fellow traveler mentioned that they had just been sheared. "Well," the cautious Hoover replied, "on this side anyway."

HOLIDAY SAVVY

❖ Don't buy poinsettias if the bracts are covered with yellow pollen. When you get plants home, protect them from chills and drafts, and never put them on top of the TV, which is too warm.

❖ Forget saying "cheese" when you're taking group photos. Instead, tell everyone to smile on the count of three. Smiles will look less wooden that way.

❖ For a holiday party, make simple place cards and let guests decorate each other's cards with humorous verses, quotations, or cartoons. Put out a rhyming dictionary and a copy of *Bartlett's Familiar Quotations* to bolster creativity.

Indian Pudding

Serve this New England favorite warm with cream or vanilla or coffee ice cream.

3½ cups milk
¼ cup molasses
3 tablespoons yellow
    cornmeal
1 egg
½ cup sugar
½ teaspoon salt
1 teaspoon ginger
½ teaspoon cinnamon
Butter the size of an egg,
    about ¼ cup, cut into
    small pieces

Preheat the oven to 325°F. Scald 3 cups of the milk in a medium saucepan, then add the molasses and cornmeal and cook until thickened. Remove from the heat. In a small bowl, blend together the egg, sugar, salt, ginger, and cinnamon and add to the milk mixture. Pour into a greased casserole and bake for 30 minutes. Pour the remaining ½ cup milk around the edges and dot with the butter. Bake for about 45 minutes, until set.   *Makes 6 servings*

The Pilgrims' Favorite Fruit

The Pilgrims learned from the local Native Americans that the tart red berries growing in bogs and beside the ocean were eminently edible. The Native Americans used the berries to make pemmican, poultices, and cold remedies. They were correct in doing so: Cranberries are an excellent source of vitamin C and other nutrients.

☙ To tell if a berry is fresh, bounce it on the counter. Fresh berries have an inner air pocket that results in a jaunty hop.

☙ Buy an extra bag or two of cranberries and pop them into the freezer. They will keep for at least a year.

☙ For a simple **FRESH RELISH**, grind 3 cups fresh cranberries with 1 unpeeled navel orange, cut into quarters. Add sugar to taste and chopped pecans, if desired.

☙ To make **CRANBERRY GINGER SAUCE**, place 4 cups fresh cranberries and ½ cup water in a heavy saucepan. Cover and cook over low heat until the berries burst and are soft. Stir in 1 cup maple syrup and 1 tablespoon grated fresh ginger and heat through. Spoon into jars and store in the refrigerator. This sauce is delicious with turkey, chicken, or pork. Makes 2 cups.

1804
Birthday of
FRANKLIN PIERCE, 14th
president of the United
States (1853–1857).

1835
HENRY BURDEN of Troy,
New York, was granted a
patent for a machine to
make horseshoes.

1889
The first jukebox was
installed, in San Francisco.

• • •

Frequently the more trifling the subject, the more animated and protracted the discussion.

—*Franklin Pierce*

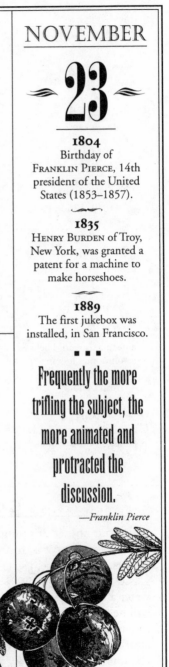

NOVEMBER

24

1784
Birthday of
ZACHARY TAYLOR,
12th president of the
United States
(1849–1850).

1874
JOSEPH GLIDDEN
patented barbed wire.

1904
BENJAMIN HOLT
demonstrated the
track-type tractor in
California. It would help
revolutionize logging,
construction, and
road building.

1993
Congress passed the Brady
handgun control bill.

Buy what thou hast no need of; and e'er long thou shalt sell thy necessaries.

—BEN FRANKLIN

THE DISTINCTION BETWEEN needs and wants seems largely lost in our affluent, advertising-driven society. Television, radio, and print ads assure us that we will be happier, handsomer, and more fulfilled as soon as we acquire the latest model car, the newest antiwrinkle cream, or a complete digital entertainment system.

But materialism is nothing new. The Greek philosopher Sophocles, well-known for his simple lifestyle, was at the market one day, closely examining the many goods for sale. A friend asked him why he came to the market at all, since he never purchased anything. Sophocles explained, "I am always amazed to see how many things there are that I don't need."

It is said that the way to catch a monkey is to drill a hole in a dried coconut and put some rice inside. Upon finding the coconut, the monkey will stick its hand into the hole and grab the rice. Unable to remove its hand and unwilling to let go of its prize, the monkey will hang on, trapped, and can be easily captured. Sometimes we are similarly ensnared by material things.

CURING WHAT AILS YOU

❧ If your nose is dripping, be sure your faucet is, too. At least six glasses of water a day will help thin the mucus and clear up your respiratory ills.

❧ If you must travel by air when your nose is congested, try taking a nasal decongestant or antihistamine an hour or so before takeoff and landing. Suck on a slippery elm or other lozenge to keep you swallowing, which will help unblock the eustachian tubes.

❧ Use garlic, onions, thyme, sage, and vitamin C regularly to help prevent colds and infections. Do not be fooled into thinking that the simplest remedies are the least beneficial. Many people swear by a bowl of hot chicken soup.

All my possessions for a moment of time.

—*Elizabeth I*

Deck Your Halls

GIVE YOUR HOME a natural look this season by bringing some greens indoors. Make evergreen roping for the porch, doorway, staircase, or mantel. Harvest what you like from your own land or shop at a seasonal garden center. The following plants provide long-lasting greens and are the most versatile.

PRACTICAL PRIMER

- Boxwood works well in wreaths and for roping. Save any clippings and tuck them into flower arrangements.
- Holly dries out quickly but gives a traditional accent to arrangements, wreaths, and decorations. The leaves turn black outdoors where temperatures fall below freezing.
- Pachysandra is good for roping and decorations that need bunches of greens.
- Ivy looks lovely trailing from mantels and baskets or tucked into wreaths.
- Firs such as balsam and Douglas have soft needles and hold up well indoors. Use them to adorn staircases or drape across mantels.
- White pine is graceful and soft, with a lovely fragrance. Use branches in centerpieces, on mantels, and to form swags over windows.

NATURE WATCH

The creatures of the forest thrive during a year when trees produce a bumper crop of seeds—known as a good mast year. When white pines, firs, spruces, oaks, beeches, hickories, and other mast producers are carpeting the forest floor with pinecones, acorns, beechnuts, and other high-protein goodies, the seed eaters of the woods are everywhere, eating and caching the harvest. The populations of squirrels, chipmunks, blue jays, and other seed lovers rise and fall depending on the mast.

-BK

1689
JOSIAH FRANKLIN and ABIAH FOLGER, the parents of BEN FRANKLIN, were married. They were the ninth (and last) children born to their respective families.

1846
Social reformer CARRY NATION was born.

1864
A Confederate plan to burn the city of Manhattan was thwarted.

■ ■ ■

I prefer winter and fall, when you feel the bone structure in the landscape.

—*Andrew Wyeth*

NOVEMBER

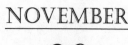

26

1922
Birth of cartoonist
CHARLES SCHULZ.

1942
Casablanca, starring
HUMPHREY BOGART and
INGRID BERGMAN,
premiered in
New York City.

• • •

If law school is
so hard to get
through . . . how
come there are so
many lawyers?

—Calvin Trillin

*A countryman between
two lawyers, is like a fish
between two cats.*

—BEN FRANKLIN

LAWYERS CAME IN for frequent ribbing in *Poor Richard's Almanack.* Maybe it's because Ben Franklin hung out with lawyers. Among the signers of the Declaration of Independence, there were more lawyers (14) than any other profession. (Judges ran a close second, at 13.) Ben was the only publisher, and in the course of doing business he had occasion to run into lawyers more often than he cared to.

In his rhyming parable "The Benefit of Going to Law," Ben told of two beggars who argued over the ownership of an oyster. They went to a lawyer, who resolved the issue fairly: Each of the beggars got one half of the oyster shell, and the lawyer got what was in the middle.

Lawyer and statesman Daniel Webster was good friends with Jeremiah Mason, another lawyer, and the two often found themselves on opposite sides of a case. One day, they met in court, and the clerk asked them which parties they were representing. Mason turned to Webster and asked which side he was on. "I don't know," Webster replied. "Take your choice."

ROOT CELLARS

Most houses no longer come with root cellars, sad to say, but you can improvise a root cellar to store those beautiful potatoes, carrots, apples, and other crops you grew last summer.

❖ Most root crops and tree fruits are best stored at temperatures between 32° and 40°F. If you have a cold basement, build a simple closet with shelves and an insulated door in a back corner. Use a thermometer to monitor the temperature.

❖ A second refrigerator in the basement can mimic the conditions of a root cellar for storing carrots, apples, parsnips, leeks, and other crops. It also will come in handy during the holidays, when you need a place to stash that 20-pound turkey the night before Thanksgiving or Christmas.

❖ If your basement is warm but you have a window on the north side, you can build your root closet around the window, opening the window as needed to regulate the temperature.

Mesmerizing

THE AUSTRIAN PHYSICIAN Franz Anton Mesmer, who studied planetary influences on humans, was influenced himself by Ben Franklin's electrical experiments. In the 1770s, Mesmer began using electricity and magnetism in the medical treatment of nervous disorders, but he eventually dispensed with these aids, resorting instead to his own "animal magnetism" to mesmerize patients and effect cures.

In 1778, Mesmer moved to Paris, where he led group therapy sessions, using Ben's glass armonica for background music. His sessions, popular with royalty and the upper classes, often became raucous. In fact, Mesmer's clients often succumbed to hysteria.

The medical establishment was worried about Mesmer's growing popularity, and in 1784 Ben was appointed to serve on a commission to investigate mesmerism. The commission reported that Mesmer's claims were unproven, causing him to be denounced as a charlatan and seducer of women. His follower, Chastenet de Puysegur, soon discovered how to induce "magnetic sleep," which led to the development of hypnosis in psychological healing.

> Imagination is the key to my lyrics. The rest is painted with a little science fiction.
>
> —*Jimi Hendrix*

1883
An intensely red sunset resulting from Krakatoa's volcanic ash caused fire engines to be called out in New York City and New Haven, Connecticut.

1926
Work began on the restoration of Colonial Williamsburg, Virginia.

1942
Musician JIMI HENDRIX was born.

How to Build a Blazing Fire in a Woodstove

1. If your woodstove still has some hot coals, rake them forward, toward the air supply.

2. If there are no hot coals, ball up three large sheets of newspaper and place them in the firebox near the door.

3. Take several dry sticks of kindling the size of your finger and crisscross them over the hot coals or paper.

4. Add three pieces of dry firewood no bigger around than your wrist. A good fire requires three pieces of wood; it is unlikely to start with fewer. Arrange them so there will be good air circulation.

5. Open any dampers or airholes and light the newspaper. Shut the door of the stove.

6. Let the kindling and firewood burn for about 5 minutes, then add one or two larger pieces of wood. Sit back and soak up the heat.

28

Wolves howl more before a storm.

● ◐ ○ ◑ ●

1863
Americans observed a national holiday of Thanksgiving following a proclamation by President ABRAHAM LINCOLN.

1989
Strong Santa Ana winds with gusts up to 70 miles per hour overturned several tractor-trailers near Los Angeles.

Talking Turkey

YOUR THANKSGIVING TURKEY is likely to be the biggest single food item you buy all year, so the bird you choose merits careful consideration. When shopping for a turkey, a quick rule of thumb is to allow 1 pound of raw turkey for each person. This will provide plenty for the holiday meal plus one serving of leftovers. Always err on the side of a heavier bird, which will have a higher proportion of meat to bones. (One word of caution: Most roasting pans and standard ovens will not accommodate a bird much larger than 30 pounds.)

PRACTICAL PRIMER

If possible, brine the bird overnight in a large, clean container filled with cold water and 2 cups kosher salt. (Remove the neck, gizzard, and organs first.) In the morning, rinse the bird, stuff it lightly, and set it on a rack in the roasting pan. Figure 15 minutes per pound at 350°F for a bird under 16

pounds; 12 minutes per pound for a larger bird. Test for doneness when the bird is roasted to a rich golden brown by inserting a sharp knife into the meaty part of the thigh. When the juices run clear and the leg wiggles easily, the bird is done. Transfer the turkey to a large platter and keep it warm while you make the gravy.

THANKSGIVING DAY TIPS

❖ After the meal, remove all the stuffing from the turkey and put it in a separate container. Keep it in the refrigerator.

❖ For the fluffiest mashed potatoes, do not let them sit covered, or condensation will make them tough. Place a few layers of paper towels under the lid to absorb moisture.

❖ For the lightest whipped cream on your pumpkin pie, chill heavy cream, the beaters, and a stainless steel bowl for several hours before whipping.

If the only prayer you said in your whole life was, "thank you," that would suffice.

—*Meister Eckhart*

He who cannot be happy in any state, can be so in no state.

—BEN FRANKLIN

JOSEPH P. KENNEDY, the wealthy founder of the Kennedy dynasty, was once asked what it was he really wanted. After reflecting for a moment, Kennedy replied, "Everything."

Was he happy? Perhaps. But as Ben Franklin wrote in his 1757 almanac, "Happiness depends more on the inward disposition of mind than on outward circumstances." Ben noted that philosophers have always said that happiness depends on contentment, but they haven't told us how to be content. So he provided this simple rule: "To be content, look backward on those who possess less than yourself, not forward on those who possess more. If this does not make you content, you don't deserve to be happy."

A WORD TO THE WISE

It doesn't take a great philosopher to attain contentment. Bertrand Russell, philosopher and Nobel laureate, once made an odd discovery: "Every time I talk to a savant I feel quite sure that happiness is no longer a possibility. Yet when I talk with my gardener, I'm convinced of the opposite."

1814
In London, a steam-operated press for printing newspapers was used for the first time, replacing the hand press.

1832
Birthday of writer LOUISA MAY ALCOTT.

1890
The first Army-Navy football game was played. Navy won 24–0.

TRICKS FOR TIDYING UP

❆ If your new glassware has a gummy residue where you removed the price tag, just rub vegetable oil on the gunk with a paper towel, then wash in warm soapy water.

❆ If a holiday meal has left grease or wine stains on your wooden table, mix baking soda with mineral, linseed, or lemon oil and rub it gently into the stains. After rubbing, wipe the entire surface with plain linseed oil.

❆ If your couch or your coat is covered with dog hair, use a wet sponge or fabric softener sheet to pick up the hair. Rub in a circular direction.

Have regular hours for work and play; make each day both useful and pleasant, and prove that you understand the worth of time by employing it well. Then youth will be delightful, old age will bring few regrets, and life will become a beautiful success.

—*Louisa May Alcott*

1753
For his work in electricity, BEN FRANKLIN was awarded the Copley Medal by the Royal Society of London.

1991
The U.S. women's soccer team won the first Women's World Cup, outscoring opponents by a combined 25–5 in six tournament games.

● ● ●

Though a good deal is too strange to be believed, nothing is too strange to have happened.

—*Thomas Hardy*

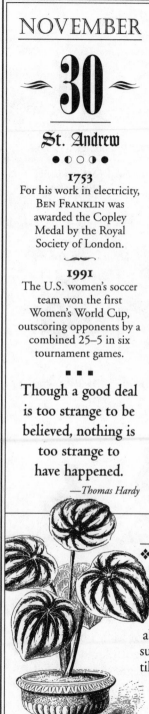

The Ghosts of the Franklin House

AFTER BRITAIN'S Royal Society of Arts conferred membership on Ben Franklin in 1756 for his work with electricity, Ben sailed for England as ambassador for several of the American colonies. Beginning in 1757, he lived for many years at 36 Craven Street, London, where he set up a laboratory to continue his various experiments. He was active in the Royal Society's explorations into medicine, mechanics, and agriculture and once gave an account of a useful North American crop, timothy grass.

In the 1990s, the Franklin house on Craven Street was still standing but in disrepair. Preservation efforts began with the help of the Royal Society and other organizations. While excavating the basement in 1997, workers found the bones of 10 bodies dating to the time of Ben's occupancy. It is believed that William Hewson, a member of the Royal Society and the husband of the daughter of Ben's landlady, conducted an anatomy school in the house. Since

a shortage of cadavers existed, some surgeons continued medical research by robbing graves and hiring body snatchers, facing severe penalties if caught. We can only speculate whether Ben ever observed or participated in the dissections.

HINTS FOR HOUSEPLANTS

❖ Starting this month, as the amount of daylight approaches its nadir, most houseplants become dormant or grow slowly. Cut down on watering by about half until active growth resumes in March. Hold off on fertilizing until then, too.

❖ If your windowsills are full to bursting with geraniums from your summer garden, some of them can spend the winter in the cellar. Simply lift the geraniums from their soil and hang them upside down. Replant them outside in the spring.

❖ Indoor ferns will maintain a rich green color if you add 1 teaspoon ammonia to 1 quart water when you water them.

DECEMBER, *the Twelfth Month*

Sign of the Zodiac:
Sagittarius
(November 23–
December 21)

Element: Fire

Quality: Philosophical

Birthstone: Turquoise

Flower: Holly

DETERMINED TO BRIGHTEN the darkest month of the year, people since ancient times have created festivals of light and ceremonies of renewal to celebrate the winter solstice and the return of the sun. December has long since lost its original meaning of "ten" *(decem)*, for the old Roman calendar's tenth month, and now is more synonymous with "decorate." The Yule log, evergreens (box, holly, mistletoe, and pine), colored glass ornaments, the wassail bowl—all of these have antecedents lost in time but designed to make the season bright.

It's possible that more cookies are baked this month than in all other months combined, and we're certain that more eggs are nogged, more chocolate melted, more bulbs forced into bloom, more mittens knit, more greeting cards addressed, and more snowflakes cut out of paper. Old American recipe books have some memorable recommendations for the holidays. One favorite for wassail punch comes from Amelia Simmons, whose *American Cookery* was published in 1796. "To make a fine Syllabub," she wrote, "sweeten a quart of cyder with double refined sugar, grate nutmeg into it, then milk your cow into your liquor." Wouldn't your neighbors be impressed?

1

If leaves wither and hang on the bough, it betokens a frosty winter.

● ● ○ ○ ●

1831
The Erie Canal in upstate New York froze and remained that way for the entire month of December.

1913
The nation's first drive-in gas station opened in Pittsburgh.

1955
ROSA PARKS was arrested for refusing to give up her bus seat in Montgomery, Alabama.

■ ■ ■

Announced by all the trumpets of the sky, Arrives the snow.

—*Ralph Waldo Emerson*

Odometer Readings

THE *Inspired* MIND

VITRUVIUS, a Roman architect and contemporary of Julius Caesar, described a carriage odometer for measuring mileage along Roman roads. Three spiked, interconnected gears attached to the axle interacted to count each revolution of a 4-foot-diameter wheel and record the total distance traveled. Vitruvius had learned about the device from the ancient Greeks.

Perhaps Ben Franklin had already read Vitruvius's Latin text when he invented an American odometer sometime between 1737 and 1753, while he was postmaster of Philadelphia. Ben mounted his invention—a metal box with three dials on the front and a bell that rang every 1/16 mile—on a carriage to measure the city's postal routes. Mid-19th-century inventors of other odometers include the Canadian Samuel McKeen and the Mormon pioneer William Clayton, who fashioned one for his covered wagon trek to Utah.

According to the U.S. Census Bureau, the average car travels about 12,000 miles a year, while the average truck travels about 26,000 miles. To thwart the temptation to make a vehicle more attractive by lowering its mileage, Guenter Hachtel patented a tamperproof odometer in 1970.

GET READY FOR WINTER DRIVING

❧ To restore proper windshield wiper blade action, smooth the rubber blades with fine sandpaper to remove any grit and pits.

❧ Stuck on the ice and forgot the sand or cat litter? In a pinch, take the mats out of your car, place them just in front of or behind the tires, and slowly inch the car onto the mats. With luck, you'll be back on the road in minutes.

Clean Your Rugs with Snow

The first fresh snowfall offers an opportunity to get the grit out of your area rugs, and your kids can help. Lay a rug on a patch of clean snow and ask the kids to tread on it. Turn it over and repeat. Sweep off both sides and bring the rug back into the house. (This is also the traditional way to clean Persian rugs.)

There are croakers in every country, always boding its ruin.

—Ben Franklin

WHEN BEN FRANKLIN opened his own print shop, a distinguished old gentleman named Mickle appeared at his door. Mickle asked Ben if he was the proprietor, and when Ben replied that he was, Mickle said he was sorry. Printing was an expensive undertaking, he explained, and Philadelphia was a bad place to start any new business. Half the citizens were bankrupt, and the rest were on the way to ruin. True, new buildings were being constructed and rents were rising, but those were simply signs of false hope. The area was doomed.

The old man went on in this vein for some time, and by the time he left, Ben was thoroughly depressed. Later, he said that if he'd met Mickle before going into business, he never would have done it.

Nevertheless, in the years to come, Philadelphia thrived—as did Ben's printing business—and old man Mickle continued to predict its downfall. Many years later, Mickle finally bought a house in the city, and Ben was pleased to note that he paid five times what he would have when he first began his "croaking."

> **A WORD TO THE WISE**

> Between the optimist and the pessimist, the difference is droll. The optimist sees the doughnut; the pessimist the hole!
>
> —*Oscar Wilde*

DECEMBER

2

1923
Soprano MARIA CALLAS was born.

1954
The U.S. Senate voted to condemn Senator JOSEPH McCARTHY of Wisconsin for dishonorable and disreputable conduct.

1982
BARNEY CLARK received the first permanent artificial heart.

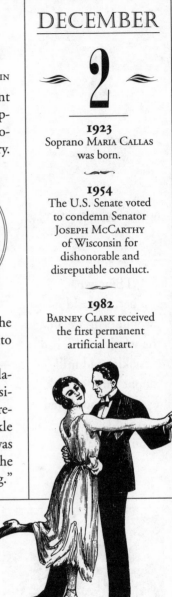

Party Time

❖ Set the table before guests arrive. Run and empty the dishwasher to make room for party dishes.

❖ If the holidays have pinched your entertaining budget, hold your next party at teatime or at least between meals. Offering snacks instead of a full meal can cut costs considerably. A potluck dessert party in the evening is another money saver.

❖ For quicker cleanup after a party, place a basin of warm soapy water next to the sink for soaking flatware as you clear the table.

❖ If you love to dance but rarely get the chance, try inviting a dance instructor (or any good dancer who's willing to step in) to your next party. Roll up the rugs and learn some new steps.

DECEMBER

3

1818
Illinois became
the 21st state.

1833
Oberlin College, the
nation's first coeducational
college, opened in
Oberlin, Ohio.

■ ■ ■

Think what
a better world it
would be if we all,
the whole world, had
cookies and milk
about three o'clock
every afternoon and
then lay down
on our blankets
for a nap.

—*Barbara Jordan*

Nutmeg Refrigerator Cookies

If you wish, you can bake one log and freeze the other. If unexpected
guests arrive, simply slice and bake the frozen one.

1 cup butter, at room
  temperature
2 cups brown sugar,
  packed
2 eggs
1 tablespoon water
1 teaspoon pure vanilla
  extract
3 cups flour
1 teaspoon baking
  powder
1 teaspoon nutmeg
½ teaspoon salt

In a large bowl, cream the butter and
brown sugar until light. Add the
eggs, water, and vanilla and beat well.
Combine the remaining ingredients in
another bowl and add to the butter
mixture. Divide the dough in half and
roll into 2 logs about 2 inches in diameter. Wrap in aluminum foil and refrigerate for several hours or freeze.

Preheat the oven to 350°F. Slice the
dough ¼ inch thick and place on ungreased cookie sheets. Bake for 10 to
12 minutes, until golden.

Makes about 4½ dozen

COOKIE ADVICE

❖ To avoid tough cookies,
don't overmix the dough.

❖ For a quick chocolate glaze
for cookies or bars, drop a few
chocolate chips on top as soon
as you take the cookies out of
the oven. Let the chocolate
melt, then spread with a
knife, if necessary.

❖ Choose metal cookie cutters instead of plastic. They
are easier to use because the
metal edges are sharper. Dip
the cutters in flour between
cuts to avoid sticking.

❖ Use antique metal
cookie cutters (the ones
with handles) to make un-
usual napkin rings.

❖ Don't store soft and crisp
cookies in the same container,
or the crisp cookies will soon
become limp.

❖ No time to bake? Melt some
dark or white chocolate and
dip store-bought sugar or almond cookies in it for a quick
and easy homemade touch.

❖ Freeze unfrosted cookies,
then add frosting and/or sprin-
kles after you take them out of
the freezer.

❖ Need a hostess gift? Prepare
refrigerator cookie dough, roll it
into logs, wrap in waxed paper,
and tie with a ribbon. Chill or
freeze, and it's all set for your
hostess to slice and bake.

If thou eatest so much as makes thee unfit for study, or other business, thou exceedest the due measure.

—BEN FRANKLIN

A WORD TO THE WISE

FOR A BRIEF PERIOD of time, Ben Franklin was a vegetarian. He came upon a book that touted the benefits of a "vegetable diet" and decided to stop eating meat, spending what he saved on books. A typical meal was often no more than "a slice of bread, a handful of raisins or a tart from the pastry-cook's, and a glass of water." He claimed that kind of meal didn't take long to eat and left him more time and a clearer head for his studies.

Shortly after making this resolution, Ben was on a ship becalmed off the coast. Other passengers began fishing, and although Ben had been a great fish lover, he stuck to his principles—until he smelled the fish frying. Then he remembered that big fish eat little fish and decided, therefore, that it was okay to eat them. "So I dined upon cod very heartily," he wrote, and was only sporadically a vegetarian afterward. "So convenient a thing it is to be a reasonable creature," he commented, "since it enables one to find or make a reason for everything one has a mind to do."

—BK

Birthday of Scottish historian THOMAS CARLYLE (1795), Spanish dictator FRANCISCO FRANCO (1892), and World War II flying ace GREGORY "PAPPY" BOYINGTON (1912).

1867
The Grange (Patrons of Husbandry) was founded as a social and political organization for farmers.

• • •

Only with winter-patience can we bring The deep-desired, long-awaited spring.
—Anne Morrow Lindbergh

YOUR GARDEN IN WINTER

❧ Lay evergreen boughs on bulb beds and perennials to help protect them from heavy snow cover.

❧ Check the "bones" of your garden or landscape for visual appeal. Hedges, topiaries, stone walls, pathways,

and dried fruits and berries all contribute to the underlying structure. Make a note of what you will change in the spring.

❧ To protect tender perennials from harsh winter weather, build a wooden box

with no top or bottom. Place it over the plants after the ground has frozen and fill with leaves.

❧ Once iris foliage is hit with a heavy frost, remove and destroy it to eliminate borer eggs.

DECEMBER

5

1782
Birthday of
MARTIN VAN BUREN,
eighth president of the
United States
(1837–1841).

1892
The Nutcracker ballet
premiered in
St. Petersburg.

1964
Captain ROGER DONLON
became the first
serviceman to receive
the Medal of Honor for
action in Vietnam.

■ ■ ■

Most people give up
just when they're
about to achieve
success. They quit on
the one yard line.
They give up at the
last minute of the
game one foot from a
winning touchdown.

—*H. Ross Perot*

Energy and persistence conquer all things.

—BEN FRANKLIN

A WORD TO THE WISE

DURING THE VIETNAM WAR, H. Ross Perot decided he wanted to do something for American prisoners of war who were being held in North Vietnam. He arranged for Christmas presents to be purchased, wrapped, and sent to Hanoi on a fleet of Boeing 707s. When the North Vietnamese refused to allow the presents to be delivered, Perot had the parcels flown to Moscow and sent to Vietnam from the central post office, one at a time, as regular mail. The packages arrived on time and were delivered to the POWs.

Robert the Bruce, first king of Scotland, learned a lesson about persistence from a spider. According to Sir Walter Scott, Robert was on the run from Edward I of England and was forced to hide out in a cave. The despairing Robert passed the time by watching a spider as it tried to spin a web. Despite being unable to attach the web, the spider never gave up, continuously going back to the task. Its persistence challenged Robert to keep fighting for his country's freedom, despite setbacks and obstacles.

Of the many ways to fail, the only one that's surefire is to quit.

Best of the Best

Make a "best of the best" annual photo album for family or friends. It's a great gift, and it will help you weed out all those photos you've never filed away.

BEST OF THE ZEST

❧ During citrus season, save grapefruit, orange, lemon, and lime rinds and store them in the freezer for a steady source of fresh citrus zest.

❧ If you don't have a lemon zester (a nifty tool with a row of little holes that remove only the colored part of the rind), strip lemon rinds with a vegetable peeler, then finely chop. Avoid scraping into the white part of the peel (the pith), because it can be bitter.

Homemade Herbal Soap Balls

*Making soap from scratch is a complicated process that requires
working with caustic lye, a project that's not for everyone.
An easier way is to start with a mild bar soap such as Ivory and
customize it to your own tastes and preferences.
Here's how to make your own homemade soap balls.*

2 cups grated Ivory Soap, about 1 bar

1 tablespoon pulverized dried herbs or flowers (such as chamomile, lavender, rosemary, mint, or rosebuds, alone or in combination)

¼ cup boiling water

5 or 6 drops of essential oil or perfume to complement the herbs or flowers you choose

Place the grated soap in a heat-proof bowl. Place the dried herbs or flowers in a small pan and pour the water over them. Let steep for 15 minutes. Reheat until bubbling, then pour over the soap. Mix together with your hands and let sit for 10 minutes. Knead and divide into 6 portions. Shape each into a ball and place on waxed paper. Let dry for 3 days at room temperature before wrapping in tissue paper. *Makes 6*

VARIATION: Add 1 tablespoon ground almonds and/or oats to make a facial scrub.

**Fatherhood
is pretending
the present
you love most is
soap-on-a-rope.**

—*Bill Cosby*

S'more Family Fun

❖ On a night when your family is at home, end the evening by toasting marshmallows for s'mores—a sandwich of graham crackers, chocolate bars, and marshmallows. If you lack a crackling fire for the toasting, place a marshmallow atop a graham cracker square and microwave for 10 seconds. Place a square of chocolate on the hot, gooey marshmallow, add another graham cracker, and enjoy. You're never too old to have s'mores.

❖ Twist garland around a column or floor-to-ceiling beam, then tuck in greeting cards you receive for display.

DECEMBER

6

St. Nicholas

● ○ ○ ●

1883
The first issue of the *Ladies' Home Journal* was published.

1947
President HARRY S. TRUMAN dedicated Everglades National Park in Florida.

■ ■ ■

LORE & LEGEND

By tradition, ST. NICHOLAS (the precursor of Santa Claus) left fruits, nuts, and candies for children in Europe. In Holland, children put their wooden shoes outside their bedrooms on the eve of the saint's day, hoping to find the shoes filled with goodies in the morning.

DECEMBER

7

National Pearl Harbor Remembrance Day

● ○ ○ ○ ●

1736
The Union Fire Company, Philadelphia's first, was founded by BEN FRANKLIN, with members agreeing to monthly meetings.

1787
Delaware became the first state.

1916
Birth of folk fiddler JEAN CARIGNAN.

The Union Fire Company

THE *Inspired* MIND

WHEN BEN FRANKLIN landed in England in 1724, it had been 58 years since the Great Fire of London. Ben was impressed with the fire brigades established throughout the city, the leading urban center in the world for fire protection. After returning to Pennsylvania, he published a letter reminding everyone that "an ounce of prevention is worth a pound of cure." Home owners, instead of using shovels to carry burning embers from room to room, should transport them in closed pans.

In 1736, Ben formed the Union Fire Company in Philadelphia with 25 volunteers, who provided their own leather buckets and salvage baskets. Soon enough, brigades had been formed to protect nearly the entire city of 10,000 people, and in 1743 Ben's company bought a fire engine like those used in London. In 1870, the

Philadelphia Fire Department became a professional organization. In 2000, it answered 84,500 alarms (including 9,200 false alarms) throughout the city of 1.5 million.

FURNACE AND FIREPLACE KNOW-HOW

❖ If your furnace makes a loud bang when it shuts off, there's probably a loose panel in the ductwork. Inspect any exposed ductwork to look for and repair the panel.

❖ Your fireplace damper should be closed (when you're not using it) in winter and open in summer. This will help keep heat in or let it out, respectively.

❖ One large log lasts two to three times longer than the same volume of smaller logs. Plan your cozy evening fire accordingly.

❖ With woodstoves and fireplaces blazing, household burns become more common.

Prevention is key, but if you do sustain a serious burn, remember to increase your water consumption. Burns can cause a loss of body fluids.

❖ You should avoid stacking fireplace wood against a wooden building. The moisture in the wood can cause the building to rot.

Love is a fire. But whether it is going to warm your hearth or burn down your house, you can never tell.

—Joan Crawford

The same man cannot be both friend and flatterer.

—BEN FRANKLIN

A GREEK PHILOSOPHER named Aristippus had flattered his way into the court of Dionysius, the tyrant king of Syracuse. One day, Aristippus happened to see Diogenes, another philosopher, preparing a simple meal of lentils for himself. "If you would only learn to compliment Dionysius," Aristippus said, "you wouldn't have to live on lentils."

"And if you would only learn to live on lentils," Diogenes responded, "you wouldn't have to flatter Dionysius."

Not all kings have been so enamored of flattery. Canute, Danish king of England from 1016 to 1035, grew sick of the fulsome praise his courtiers heaped upon him and decided to teach them a lesson. He had his throne placed on the beach as the tide was coming in and ordered the waves to stop before he got wet. As the waves lapped around his feet, Canute proclaimed, "Let all men know how empty and worthless is the power of kings. For there is none worthy of the name but God, whom heaven, earth and sea obey." The courtiers got the point.

> **It is better to know some of the questions than all of the answers.**
>
> —*James Thurber*

1894
Writer JAMES THURBER was born.

1941
The United States and Great Britain declared war on Japan.

▪ ▪ ▪

OUT WITH THE OLD

Before the holidays, enlist your children's help in weeding out old toys and clothing to donate to local thrift shops.

TIPS FOR SANE SHOPPING

❆ If you hate shopping, plan to do all of your gift buying at one store. Most people love books; try a bookstore. Or check out the garden center or a good hardware store.

❆ If gift giving seems out of control, make an agreement with friends and family to give only those gifts that will be used up: candles, homemade food, tickets to a play,

—BK

a gift certificate for free babysitting, and so on.

❆ Keep all receipts for holiday purchases in a large red or green envelope in case someone needs to return an item.

❆ If you have city friends with fireplaces, wrap a red ribbon around a giant Yule log as a season-warming gift.

9

Partridge drumming indicates a mild and open winter.

● ○ ○ ○ ●

1907
Christmas Seals were first sold to raise money to fight tuberculosis.

1941
China declared war on Japan, Germany, and Italy.

1996
Archaeologist and anthropologist MARY LEAKEY died in Kenya at age 83.

After crosses and losses, men grow humbler and wiser.

—BEN FRANKLIN

A WORD TO THE WISE

CHARLES COLSON spent 7 months in prison for his part in the Watergate affair. Colson had been a U.S. Marine officer, a successful lawyer, and the right-hand man to the president of the United States. The last thing he wanted to do after his release was return to prison. But return he did, believing he was called by God to minister to prisoners and their families.

Colson founded Prison Fellowship Ministries, which conducts in-prison seminars, helps inmates prepare for life after their release, and coordinates the purchase of Christmas presents for prisoners' children. Colson has said that of all the experiences and achievements in his life, the one God chose to use was the one he was most ashamed of. "Out of tragedy and adversity come great blessings," he notes.

In 1996, the air-conditioning at the University of Oxford Botanic Garden failed. The temperature in the greenhouse soared, and horticulturists began to fear for the collection. Then it happened. A rare cactus, the century plant *(Agave americana),* bloomed for the first time since 1896.

Will adversity destroy you or make you blossom?

> *Knowledge is proud that he has learned so much;*
> *Wisdom is humble that he knows no more.*
>
> —*William Cowper*

HOUSEPLANT HOW-TO

❦ Place several houseplants near each other to form a support group to cope with the low humidity of your house in winter.

❦ For long-lasting paperwhite narcissuses, plant bulbs in large containers of potting soil, water well, and store in a cool, dark place for 3 weeks to let the roots develop. Once the shoots begin to form, move the pots into a cool, bright spot away from direct sun. They will flower in several weeks.

❦ Grow African violets in an east window. They prefer water that is warm or tepid.

Three Easy Gifts from the Kitchen

1. **Premium vanilla extract:** Split 5 vanilla beans lengthwise and place in a pint of French brandy. Tie a bow on the bottle and add a gift tag recommending that the recipient store the bottle in a cool, dark place for 2 months before using as a flavoring.

2. **Herb mix for soups:** In a 1-cup canning jar, combine 1½ teaspoons dried lemon peel and 3 tablespoons each dried parsley, basil, summer savory, marjoram, and thyme. Decorate the jar with a circle of pretty fabric attached to the lid with lace trim, yarn, or ribbon. Give this with a copy of your favorite soup recipe.

3. **Vinegar infused with garlic:** Bring 2 cups good-quality red wine vinegar to a simmer in a small nonreactive pan. Add 1 large bay leaf and 2 large cloves garlic, peeled and quartered. Remove from the heat and let stand overnight. Strain and pour into a fancy cruet. This and a bottle of extra-virgin olive oil will satisfy each of the salad lovers on your holiday list.

PRACTICAL PRIMER

MORE USEFUL GIFTS

❖ Make your own fire starters by pouring sawdust into small paper cups and adding melted paraffin. Stir to mix and let set. Give to anyone with a fireplace or to the campers on your list.

❖ Let children gather large pinecones for winter kindling and assemble them in baskets to give as gifts. Grandparents with fireplaces especially love them. For a more colorful and fragrant fire, dip them in melted scented wax first.

❖ Make your own version of maraschino cherries by macerating fresh pitted cherries in kirsch or crème de cassis. Bottle and keep refrigerated.

❖ Consider making simple sachets or small scented pillows for holiday gifts. For stuffing, gather balsam needles if you live near the woods, or buy dried rosemary or lavender in bulk from a natural foods store. You can add a few drops of essential oil to pillow batting for a similar scented effect.

LAVENDER

DECEMBER

10

If December be changeable and mild, The whole winter will remain a child.

● ○ ○ ○ ●

1817
Mississippi became the 20th state.

1830
Birth of poet
EMILY DICKINSON.

■ ■ ■

It's not how much we give but how much love we put into giving.

—*Mother Teresa*

DECEMBER

11

1816
Indiana became
the 19th state.

1844
Nitrous oxide
(laughing gas) was first
used in dentistry.

1941
Germany and Italy
declared war on the
United States, prompting
it to reciprocate.

1946
The United Nations
International Children's
Emergency Fund
(UNICEF) was
established.

• • •

NATURE WATCH

A blizzard is the most
dramatic and perilous
winter storm, defined
by temperatures below
20°F, strong winds
in excess of 35 miles
per hour, and large
amounts of drifting
snow. Wild creatures
tend to hole up in
blizzards to conserve
energy and warmth.
Unsheltered livestock
can suffer terribly
from cold and espe-
cially dehydration.

Here Lies . . .

THE
Inspired
MIND

NOT MANY OF US, anticipating a long life, would
care to write our own epitaphs at a young age, but Ben
Franklin did when he was 22 years old. He imagined
that his aged printer's body would be like an
old, worn-out book but that after dying, the
work would appear "in a new and more perfect Edition, corrected and amended by the
Author"—a clever way to
look at life after death. Years
later, Ben wrote an epitaph for a pet squirrel
named Skugg: "Here Skugg, Lies snug, As a
bug, In a rug." Ben's epitaph for himself was not
used when he died in 1790, but here are some actual epitaphs that
share his light touch on death's icy grip.

That's All, Folks!
—Mel Blanc's Epitaph

Here lies old Rastus Sominy
Died a-eating hominy
In 1859 anno domini

-BK

Ellen Shannon,
Who was fatally burned
*   March 21, 1870*
By the explosion of a lamp
Filled with "R. E. Danforth's
*   Non-Explosive Burning Fluid"*

Let your wind blow
*   wherever ye be*
For holding mine was
*   the death of me*

Here lies the landlord Tommy Dent
In his last cosy tenement

I made an ash of myself

SNOWSTORM RULES OF THUMB

☾ When it begins to storm, notice the
size of the snowflakes. Large, fluffy
flakes often indicate a short-lived storm.
Small flakes may mean a long one.

☾ Never wait for a heavy snowstorm
before buying a sled.

Old boys have their playthings as well as young ones; the difference is only in the price.

—BEN FRANKLIN

THE HOME OF BIG TOYS for big boys is surely the Neiman Marcus catalog, which features fashions and furnishings for the fabulously foolish (and rich), along with pricey toys (such as a rebuilt 1940s slot machine for $2,550). But perhaps the ultimate item in garish consumerism was featured in the company's 2000 Christmas catalog: a personal submarine manufactured by U.S. Submarines of Fort Lauderdale, Florida. At $20 million, the 118-foot Seattle class sub is considered midsize and features accommodations for guests and crew, a galley, and living and dining areas. It has a cruising range of 3,000 nautical miles and can stay below the surface for up to 20 days.

A WORD TO THE WISE

Previous editions of the Christmas catalog have featured a private Boeing 737 jet that seats 15 to 50 people ($35 million), personal hot-air balloons, "his and her" Egyptian mummy cases, camels, robots, and a Black Angus steer (on the hoof or cut up into steaks).

1787
Pennsylvania became the second state.

1792
In Vienna, LUDWIG VAN BEETHOVEN paid 19 cents for his first music lesson from FRANZ JOSEPH HAYDN.

1899
GEORGE GRANT patented the golf tee.

1966
Yachtsman Sir FRANCIS CHICHESTER reached Sydney, Australia, 107 days after leaving England on a round-the-world solo voyage. He completed the trip the following May.

• • •

Where necessity ends, curiosity begins; and no sooner are we supplied with everything that nature can demand, than we sit down to contrive artificial appetites.

—*Samuel Johnson*

ON A MORE PRACTICAL NOTE

❖ Use a cloth dampened in white vinegar and water to remove salt stains from winter shoes or boots.

❖ If you need extra insulation in your boots, trace the outline of your feet onto Styrofoam meat trays, cut them out, and insert one in each boot.

❖ Bring canvas tote bags or recycled plastic bags when you go shopping. Some grocery stores will give you credit for each bag you bring.

❖ If you add antifreeze to your car, be sure to clean up any spills. The substance tastes sweet to pets but can cause fatal kidney damage.

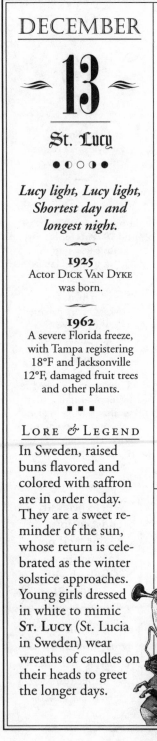

13

St. Lucy

● ○ ○ ● ●

*Lucy light, Lucy light,
Shortest day and
longest night.*

1925
Actor DICK VAN DYKE
was born.

1962
A severe Florida freeze,
with Tampa registering
18°F and Jacksonville
12°F, damaged fruit trees
and other plants.

■ ■ ■

LORE & LEGEND

In Sweden, raised
buns flavored and
colored with saffron
are in order today.
They are a sweet re-
minder of the sun,
whose return is cele-
brated as the winter
solstice approaches.
Young girls dressed
in white to mimic
ST. LUCY (St. Lucia
in Sweden) wear
wreaths of candles on
their heads to greet
the longer days.

Swedish Christmas Bread

*Add this spicy, fragrant, hearty bread to your breakfast table
on Christmas morning. Serve with sweet butter, preserves,
or thinly sliced ham.*

2 packages (2 scant
   tablespoons) active dry yeast
1 teaspoon ginger
½ cup warm water
1½ cups beer or stout
2 tablespoons butter
⅓ cup molasses
⅓ cup corn syrup

1 teaspoon salt
½ teaspoon nutmeg
2 tablespoons grated orange
   or lemon zest (or a
   combination)
2 cups rye flour
½ cup raisins
4 to 5 cups all-purpose flour

Combine the yeast, ginger, and warm water in a large bowl. In
a medium saucepan, heat the beer and butter until the butter
melts. Add the molasses, corn syrup, salt, nutmeg, and zest. When
this is lukewarm, add to the yeast mixture. Stir in the rye flour,
raisins, and enough all-purpose flour to make a firm dough.
Knead until smooth and elastic. Cover and let rise in a greased
bowl until doubled in bulk. Punch down, knead briefly, and let
rise a second time. Punch down, divide in half, and let rest for 10
minutes. Preheat the oven to 350°F. Shape the dough into oval
loaves, place on oiled baking sheets, and let rise until nearly doubled in bulk. Brush the tops with a little beer or water and bake for
about 50 minutes, until golden brown. Cool on wire racks.

Makes 2

Those who wish to sing always find a song.

—*Swedish Proverb*

A BAKER'S SECRET

Professional bakers con-
sider diastatic malt their
secret ingredient. It
helps yeast convert the
natural sugars in flour
into alcohol and carbon
dioxide (which is what
makes bread rise). Adding diastatic
malt (1 teaspoon per 6 cups flour) increases the nutritional value and im-
proves the texture of bread.

Constancy in a Box

IN THE LANGUAGE and sentiment of flowers, boxwood *(Buxus sempervirens)* denotes constancy. "Holly and ivy, box and bay, / Put in the church on Christmas Day," says one 15th-century Christmas carol. Boxwood cuttings are traditional for wreaths, tabletop topiaries, and ropes or swags—a good reason for you to cultivate plenty of it in your landscape. Here are a few guidelines for growing and using boxwood.

PRACTICAL PRIMER

❧ Box is slow growing but likes to be pruned.

❧ It can be propagated from stem cuttings taken in the fall and rooted in damp sand.

❧ Although its root system is shallow, the evergreen box is blessed with longevity, as long as it isn't planted in a climate prone to extremes, such as the Deep South or far northern zones.

❧ Box likes protection from drying winter winds.

❧ Along with holly, laurel, bay, yew, and other fragrant greens, boxwood was traditionally used as a strewing herb to bring a pleasant fragrance into the house in winter. Strewing herbs were spread on the floor, trod upon to release their fragrance, and then swept up.

BOXWOOD

DECEMBER

14

If the first snow sticks to the trees, it foretells a bountiful harvest.

● ◐ ○ ◑ ●

1503
Birthday of French astrologer and physician NOSTRADAMUS.

1819
Alabama became the 22nd state.

1911
ROALD AMUNDSEN reached the South Pole— the first person to do so— beating rival explorer ROBERT F. SCOTT.

■ ■ ■

The land looks like a fairytale.

—*Roald Amundsen*

Decorating with Greenery

❖ Place boughs of strong-scented evergreens or rosemary over the grate of an unused fireplace.

❖ Use green twine to anchor greenery on the mantel.

Remove the cuttings before they dry out and become a fire hazard.

❖ Cover a Styrofoam ball with sprigs of boxwood and attach a red ribbon to the top to make a kissing ball to hang in a doorway or arch. Add floral decorations if you wish. Boxwood works just as well as mistletoe to encourage friendly behavior.

1791
Ten of the original 12 amendments to the U.S. Constitution were ratified.

1854
A street-cleaning machine was used for the first time in Philadelphia.

1944
A plane carrying bandleader GLENN MILLER disappeared in thick fog over the English Channel. The plane was never found.

■ ■ ■

NATURE WATCH

Gardeners know that toads consume thousands of pests each summer. But unless you live in the South, you probably haven't seen a toad for a while. In winter, toads burrow deep into the ground to hibernate. Their breathing virtually stops, and their hearts barely beat.

Human felicity is produced not so much by great pieces of good fortune that seldom happen, as by little advantages that occur every day.

—BEN FRANKLIN

A WORD TO THE WISE

I T ' S   T H E   L I T T L E   T H I N G S that get to you. While living in London, Ben Franklin found the cobblestone streets filthy with dust. One day, he noticed an old woman sweeping in front of his house. She explained that she swept voluntarily, hoping for compensation from home owners. Ben gave her a shilling and was soon amazed to see the entire street swept clean and the dust deposited in the gutter to be washed away by rain.

Upon his return to Philadelphia, Ben proposed hiring "scavengers" to clean the streets in his neighborhood twice a week. He asked each occupant to contribute toward the cost, and it was a great success.

Years later, other inventors applied their minds to the problem of dusty streets. A 1907 horse-drawn street sweeper had a revolving drum with rows of bristles that swept dirt onto a wooden conveyor for transport into a holding tank. In 1923, Louis Bailly added a suction duct in front of a large brush drum. More recently, Hans Doyen's 1989 invention of a street sweeper attachment "for picking up dog excrement" might have unleashed some praise from Ben.

America did not invent human rights. In a very real sense, it is the other way around. Human rights invented America.

—*Jimmy Carter*

Happiness Is a Shiny Chrome Bumper

Whenever you check the oil in your car, use the oily rag to wipe over the chrome parts. An occasional oil coating will cut down on rust and pitting, especially through the winter months.

Navigating the Schuylkill

A 1732 ARTICLE in Ben Franklin's *Pennsylvania Gazette* promoted the idea of making freshwater rivers navigable to increase commerce. Nothing was done, but Ben felt so strongly about it that in his 1788 will he gave 2,000 pounds to make the Schuylkill River navigable. A year later, however, he withdrew the bequest after concluding that the project was "not likely to be undertaken for many years."

THE *Inspired* MIND

In 1815, the Schuylkill Navigation Company was formed to carry out the dream. Finally, in 1825, the hard work of Irish immigrants, who built 18 dams and hand-dug 23 canals around falls and gorges, opened the 128-mile-long river to barge traffic. Boats could deliver coal from the coalfields of central Pennsylvania to the city of Philadelphia.

Julius von Schmidt patented a hydraulic dredging machine in 1889. Equipped with a telescopic suction pipe attached to an underwater hood housing an 8-foot-diameter rotary excavating plow, the dredger removed 2,300 cubic yards of river bottom per day. The silt could be piped up to half a mile. The machine was used to dredge the Potomac River, but it came 100 years too late to impress Ben.

THROWING A DINNER PARTY

❧ When planning a dinner party for more than four guests, decide on the menu several days in advance to give yourself time to shop and cook. Figure out which serving dishes and serving utensils you will use.

❧ For a moist roast, cook meat fat side up so that as it cooks, the fat will flow down to baste the meat. Salt draws the juices out of meat, so wait until serving to add salt.

❧ If you order a boned roast, ask the butcher to give you the bones to use in soup stock. Be sure the boned meat weighs at least 4 pounds to ensure tenderness and prevent the meat from drying out during roasting.

❧ To recap a bottle of wine more easily, insert the cork upside down.

DECEMBER

16

Burning wood pops more before a snowstorm.

● ● ○ ◐ ●

1773
Colonials dressed as Native Americans protested British taxes in what came to be known as the Boston Tea Party.

1811
An earthquake near New Madrid, Missouri, changed the course of the Mississippi River.

1901
Anthropologist MARGARET MEAD was born.

■ ■ ■

Never doubt that a small group of thoughtful, committed citizens can change the world; indeed, it's the only thing that ever has.

—*Margaret Mead*

17

Birthday of poet and
abolitionist JOHN
GREENLEAF WHITTIER
(1807) and orchestra
conductor ARTHUR
FIEDLER (1894).

1903
ORVILLE and WILBUR
WRIGHT made the first
successful airplane flights
near Kitty Hawk,
North Carolina.

1929
An ice storm in western
New York caused extensive
damage to trees.

■ ■ ■

*Sweet bird! thy bow'r is
ever green,
Thy sky is ever clear;
Thou hast no sorrow in
thy song,
No winter in thy year.*
—*John Logan*

Fitting Feeder, Fitting Fare

ATTRACT A VARIETY of birds to your backyard by setting out different feeders containing different foods and
placed at various heights. A study by the U.S. Fish and
Wildlife Service found that most wild birds respond best to white
millet and black oil sunflower seeds. Birdseed mixtures containing
other grains may be cheaper in the short run, but much more will
be wasted.

PRACTICAL PRIMER

🐦 A ground-feeding table spread with white millet will attract large birds such as crows, jays,
cardinals, and grackles, as well as smaller
ground feeders such as juncos and doves.
(Don't use a ground feeder if predators such as
cats can lurk nearby.)

🐦 Chickadees, titmice, nuthatches, goldfinches, siskins, finches,
cardinals, grosbeaks, and other birds will enjoy black oil sunflower seeds from a hanging tube feeder or
other elevated feeder with small perches.

–BK

🐦 A suet feeder attracts small birds and
woodpeckers and provides an all-important source of fat during cold weather.
Buy a wire feeder or improvise with a
mesh bag that held onions or oranges.

🐦 A shallow dish of fresh water will attract
more species than a feeder.

🐦 Keeping a bird feeder out all winter will not throw off the migration schedule of birds. Birds determine their departure time
by the number of daylight hours, not by food availability.

Cooking IS for the Birds!

🐦 Make your own suet cakes,
melting chunks of suet from
the grocery store with bacon
fat, lard, or peanut butter and
any seeds or nuts of your
choice. Freeze the mixture in
tuna cans, then unmold and
hang outside for the birds.

🐦 Instead of making molded
cakes from suet and peanut
butter, dip pinecones in the
melted mixture, let it harden
on waxed paper, and hang
the cones from a branch with
sturdy string. This is a fun
project to do with children.

🐦 Hang stale doughnuts and
bagels outside on a tree for
the birds. Woodpeckers particularly love them.

🐦 Give the birds a treat by
putting out quartered or-
anges and apples.

Would you persuade, speak of interest, not of reason.

—BEN FRANKLIN

BEN FRANKLIN learned the power of persuasion when the famed evangelist George Whitefield made his first journey to America. After conducting successful meetings in Philadelphia, Whitefield went on to Georgia, where he learned that the colonists there (largely refugees from British poorhouses) were dying and leaving record numbers of orphans. Whitefield decided to build an orphanage in Georgia but found that the materials would have to be shipped from Philadelphia. Ben tried to convince Whitefield to build the orphanage in Philadelphia instead, but Whitefield rejected Ben's advice, and Ben withdrew his support for the project.

Nevertheless, when Whitefield returned to Philadelphia, Ben went to hear him preach, although Ben had decided not to put anything into the collection for the orphanage. Even so, in his pocket was a handful of copper coins, a few silver dollars, and five gold pieces. Whitefield spoke so eloquently of the orphans' plight that Ben decided to chip in the copper coins. As Whitefield continued to speak, Ben felt ashamed of his meager intentions and resolved to contribute the silver instead. Finally, he later wrote, Whitefield "finished so admirably that I emptied my pocket wholly into the collector's dish, gold and all."

1787
New Jersey became
the third state.

1865
The 13th Amendment
abolishing slavery went
into effect.

Birthday of
baseball player TY COBB
(1886), actress
BETTY GRABLE (1916),
and movie director
STEVEN SPIELBERG (1946).

• • •

Thaw with her gentle persuasion is more powerful than Thor with his hammer.

—*Henry David Thoreau*

GIFTS GALORE

❖ Buy a plastic underbed chest and use it to store rolls of wrapping paper and ribbon—under the bed.

❖ Buy a small notebook to record the gifts you give family and friends at holiday and birthday time. This will save

you from giving *Goodnight Moon* to the same child 2 years in a row.

❖ Avoid a last-minute frenzy by wrapping gifts as soon as you bring them home. And give yourself an ironclad shopping deadline.

❖ Use the ironing board as a work surface for wrapping small presents.

❖ Run a piece of clothesline through spools of ribbon and hang it taut across your wrapping area to keep all the spools within easy reach.

19

1843
The classic story
A Christmas Carol by
CHARLES DICKENS went
on sale in England.

1959
The last Civil War
veteran died. He was
117 years old.

1976
For the first time,
American women were
awarded Rhodes
scholarships to study at
Oxford University.

■ ■ ■

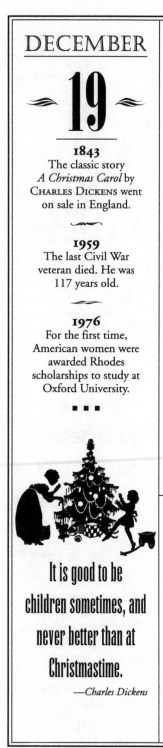

It is good to be
children sometimes, and
never better than at
Christmastime.

—*Charles Dickens*

Trim the Tree
with Homemade Ornaments

TWO DIFFERENT TYPES of "clay" let the imagination run wild and keep little hands occupied for hours making tree ornaments. Set aside the best ones for gifts.

1. **Fragrant cinnamon dough:** Buy ground cinnamon in bulk in the largest containers you can find. Slowly stir the cinnamon into smooth applesauce until the mixture forms a workable dough. Roll out to about ¼ inch thick and cut into shapes with cookie cutters. Use a straw to punch holes for hanging. Let the ornaments dry on wire racks for 2 to 3 days. Paint or decorate as desired, then thread colorful ribbon through the holes for hanging on the tree or in closets as sachets.

THE
Inspired
MIND

2. **Salt dough:** Combine 1 cup salt, 2 cups flour, and 1 cup water in a medium bowl. Knead until the dough is smooth and elastic. Divide into portions and tint each with food coloring. Roll out and cut into shapes with cookie cutters, using a straw to punch holes for hanging. You can also shape small pieces into beads or other designs. (Before baking, use a darning needle to make holes for stringing.) Place on baking sheets and bake at 250°F until the pieces are hard and dry, about 2 hours. Let cool completely, then decorate with watercolors or acrylic paint.

NATURAL DECORATIONS

❖ Collect pinecones, twigs, and acorns from the woods in the fall. Clean and dry them, then spray them with gold or silver paint. Heap them in a shallow cut-glass bowl for a striking centerpiece.

❖ Collect interesting twigs or dried weeds, spray-paint them, and stand them upright, bundled with holiday ribbon, in pots or heavy glasses on your mantel.

❖ Make distinctive cards or wrapping paper with potato prints. Cut a potato in half, cut out a simple design (such as a star, moon, or tree), blot the surface, and dip it into poster paint or brush on with a paintbrush. Print on card stock or plain wrapping paper.

Many complain of their memory, few of their judgment.

—Ben Franklin

A MAN IN DECATUR, Georgia, received an insurance settlement upon the death of his wife. There was only one problem: He was also married to another woman, who was very much alive. Upon his arrest, the two-timing husband gave this explanation: He simply didn't remember marrying the other woman.

Then there was the police officer who was fired from the Petaluma, California, police force. He filed suit, claiming he was a victim of discrimination because he was "disabled"—a result of his extensive drug use in the 1970s, when he was a drummer in a well-known rock and roll band. When asked to provide evidence of his drug use, the ex-cop said that he couldn't because heavy use of drugs had affected his memory.

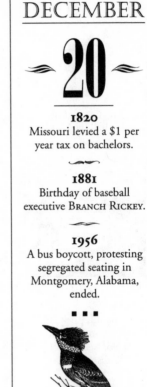

If only our memories improved with age, as computer memory has. The first computers featured a few thousand bytes of memory. These days, computer memory is measured in gigabytes (billions of bytes). Of course, a computer doesn't have to remember where it left its glasses or parked its car—or whether it married one woman or two.

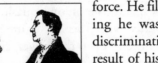

Never trust
a husband too far,
nor a bachelor
too near.

—Helen Rowland

1820
Missouri levied a $1 per year tax on bachelors.

1881
Birthday of baseball executive BRANCH RICKEY.

1956
A bus boycott, protesting segregated seating in Montgomery, Alabama, ended.

• • •

LORE & LEGEND
Coming around the time of the winter solstice, HALCYON DAYS were traditionally a period of calm weather following the blustery winds of autumn's end. At sea, sailors expected the sea to be calm enough that the halcyon, or kingfisher, could build its nest on the water.

Glowing in the Dark

☾ Attach a strip of glow-in-the-dark tape or decals to household flashlights to make them easy to find in a power outage. Consider this for any item you will need to find in an emergency—your fuse box, water supply, or cell phone, for instance.

☾ Glue a luminous strip to the switch of your bedside lamp to help you find the switch in the dark. Same for the off button on your clock radio or alarm clock.

21

Forefathers' Day

● ○ ○ ●

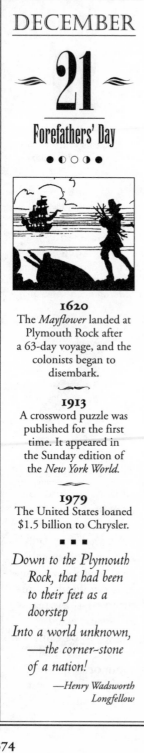

1620
The *Mayflower* landed at Plymouth Rock after a 63-day voyage, and the colonists began to disembark.

1913
A crossword puzzle was published for the first time. It appeared in the Sunday edition of the *New York World*.

1979
The United States loaned $1.5 billion to Chrysler.

■ ■ ■

Down to the Plymouth Rock, that had been to their feet as a doorstep

Into a world unknown, —the corner-stone of a nation!

—Henry Wadsworth Longfellow

Cranberry Squash Soup

This spicy golden soup is topped with a ruby swirl of cranberry sauce for a festive presentation.

¼ cup olive oil
1 large onion, sliced
4 cups peeled and cubed butternut squash (1 medium squash)
2 tart apples, peeled, cored, and chopped
1 teaspoon ginger
1 teaspoon cinnamon

2 teaspoons curry powder
1 cup cider
2 cups chicken broth
Salt and freshly ground black pepper
½ cup milk or cream
½ cup whole-berry cranberry sauce
2 tablespoons orange juice

Heat the oil in a large soup pot. Add the onion, squash, and apples and stir to coat evenly with the oil. Sauté over medium-low heat for about 15 minutes. Stir in the ginger, cinnamon, and curry powder and cook for several minutes more. Add the cider and stir until smooth. Add the chicken broth and bring to a boil. Reduce the heat and simmer, partially covered, for 30 minutes. Puree in a food processor and return to the pot. Season with salt and pepper to taste. Stir in the milk and heat just to a simmer. Combine the cranberry sauce and orange juice in a food processor and mix until smooth. Serve the soup in bowls, topped with the cranberry puree. For a special touch, swirl the puree through the soup with the tip of a knife.

Makes 6 to 8 servings

Three Tips for Gingerbread House Success

1. To raise the walls of a gingerbread house, have a few soup cans on hand to prop up the sides until the mortar dries. Then add the roof.

2. For fancy wall trimmings on gingerbread houses, decorate the walls on a flat surface first, before they go up.

3. To preserve a gingerbread house for more than one season, protect it from mice and moisture. Wrap the house in fiber batting, then triple-bag it and place it in a box to protect it from bumps.

Brighten the Night with Luminarias

ANYTIME YOU WANT the outside of your home to look festive at night, use these lovely decorations to line a driveway or sidewalk or to set out on a deck or porch railing.

PRACTICAL PRIMER

For reusable luminarias, collect large metal juice cans. Punch holes in the sides of the cans using a nail or hole puncher. If you're handy, you can punch out designs such as hearts or stars. Next, paint the cans with flat black paint. (Spray paint makes this easy, but use cautiously with small children around.) After the paint dries, pour 2 inches of sand into the bottom of each can. Settle a votive candle into the sand and light.

You can also make simple luminarias by setting votive candles in sand inside white paper bags. These require a bit more vigilance and are best used when there is snow on the ground.

THE MAGIC OF CANDLES

❖ Float tea lights in shallow bowls of water along with some flower petals.

❖ Use small terra-cotta pots as candleholders. Paint them with craft or fabric paint and add a votive candle or tea light.

❖ To make any candle a scented candle, add a drop of essential oil to the melting wax just next to the wick. Consider cinnamon, frankincense, myrrh, pine, or bay for traditional holiday fragrances.

❖ For a wintertime centerpiece,

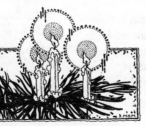

cut the top off a half-gallon milk carton, fill two-thirds full of water, and place in the freezer. Check it frequently, and when the outer layer becomes solidly frozen, remove the container from the freezer. Break through the center of the ice (a corkscrew works well), pour out the water inside, and enlarge the hole to a diameter of 2 inches. Cut or tear away the milk carton, and set the hollow chunk on a deep platter. Place a votive candle inside and decorate the platter with greenery.

Much sleet in winter is followed by a good fruit year.

● ◐ ○ ◑ ●

1894
A military court-martial convicted French army officer ALFRED DREYFUS of treason for allegedly passing military secrets to the Germans. The conviction was overturned in 1906.

1999
The first day of winter coincided with a full moon at perigee, the first such occurrence since 1866. It was the last full moon of the millennium.

⋯

Winter is on my head, but eternal spring is in my heart.

—*Victor Hugo*

23

If meadows are green at Christmas, at Easter they will be covered with frost.

● ○ ○ ● ●

1823
CLEMENT MOORE'S poem "A Visit from St. Nicholas" appeared in the *Troy (N.Y.) Sentinel.*

1913
The Federal Reserve System of banks was created.

1938
Boogie-woogie music stole the show in a jazz concert at Carnegie Hall.

■ ■ ■

The simplest toy, one which even the youngest child can operate, is called a grandparent.

—*Sam Levenson*

The art of getting riches consists very much in thrift. All men are not equally qualified for getting money, but it is in the power of every one alike to practice this virtue.

—BEN FRANKLIN

THESE DAYS, most people don't understand the power of saving. Forty percent of Americans believe that they are more likely to obtain $500,000 by playing the lottery than by patiently saving and investing small amounts over time. But the chances of winning a big lottery are 1 in 10 million to 20 million, while the "payout" from a personal savings plan is guaranteed (as long as interest rates hold). Save $25 a week for 40 years (at a 7 percent annual yield), and you'll end up with a nest egg of $286,255. Invest $50 a week, and you'll have more than half a million dollars.

A WORD TO THE WISE

Of course, some ways of saving are smarter than others. Take the man who hid $20,000 in cash in his girlfriend's oven. The loot caught fire from the oven's pilot light. Fortunately, firefighters were called and were able to rescue about half of the hot money.

TREE AND TINSEL TALK

❖ Freshly cut trees consume up to a gallon of water in the first 24 hours and quarts more thereafter. Keeping up with water demand will enhance the tree's appearance and increase safety.

❖ If you have curious cats or dogs at home, be sure to hang the tinsel out of reach. A piece can easily become stuck in their throats. You don't really want to call the vet on Christmas Eve, do you?

❖ Run a wire from the top of the Christmas tree to a hook in the ceiling or nearby window frame for added stability, especially if you have babies or kittens.

❖ To water the tree without spilling water on the packages, place ice cubes around the tree's base.

❖ Add a little lemon lime soda to the tree water to give your evergreen a lift.

Sound the Harp

MOST OF US are attuned to well-established patterns of musical sounds we recognize as pleasantly harmonious rather than dissonant. The clashing sound we call dissonance comes from musical notes that are too close to one another. Ben Franklin, fond of Scottish airs, theorized on their appeal: Old tunes "were composed by the minstrels of those days to be played on the harp. . . . The harp was strung with wire, which gives a sound of long continuance" that had no way of being stopped like a harpsichord or piano string. Composers avoided discord by blending a note with its preceding one, "as their sounds must exist at the same time."

THE *Inspired* MIND

This principle was used in Henry Gibbs's 1907 invention—hand-struck chimes consisting of metal tubes of different lengths, a precursor of today's wind chimes. In New Mexico in 2000, Bill Neely and Bob Griesing constructed a 24-foot-tall wind harp, whose 45 stainless steel strings together sound a 5-note chord when vibrated by the wind. It may not be a Scottish air, but Ben would no doubt take pleasure in it.

BAKING TIPS

€ If you run out of solid baking chocolate, substitute ¾ cup unsweetened cocoa and ¼ cup vegetable shortening for 4 ounces (4 squares) chocolate.

€ Lightly oil your knife or shears before cutting up dates and figs, and they will not stick.

€ To chop dried fruit with a meat grinder, use the coarse blade and run the fruit through.

This works better than a food processor because the fruit does not become mushy.

€ Dust chopped dried fruit with flour before stirring it into the batter so it doesn't stick together in clumps.

€ If there is a small amount of molasses, honey, maple syrup, or corn syrup in a container, place the jar or tin in a pan of warm water to make it easy to pour.

Snow tonight brings a good hop crop.

● ○ ○ ○ ●

1818
In Austria, FRANZ GRUBER sang "Silent Night" for the first time. On the same night, HANDEL's *Messiah* was performed for the first time in America, in Boston.

1922
Actress AVA GARDNER was born.

■ ■ ■

Christmas Eve was a night of song that wrapped itself about you like a shawl. But it warmed more than your body. It warmed your heart . . . filled it, too, with a melody that would last forever.

—*Bess Streeter Aldrich*

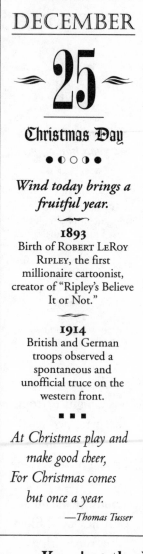

25

Christmas Day

● ○ ○ ○ ●

Wind today brings a fruitful year.

1893
Birth of ROBERT LEROY RIPLEY, the first millionaire cartoonist, creator of "Ripley's Believe It or Not."

1914
British and German troops observed a spontaneous and unofficial truce on the western front.

■ ■ ■

At Christmas play and make good cheer, For Christmas comes but once a year.

—*Thomas Tusser*

How many observe Christ's birthday! How few, his precepts! O! 'tis easier to keep holidays than commandments.

—BEN FRANKLIN

I**N COLONIAL** New England, Christmas holiday observances were forcibly banned by the Puritans and Presbyterians, who saw Christmas as nothing more than an excuse for Christians to take part in a pagan holiday. In truth, the early church often overlaid Christian themes on pre-Christian seasonal celebrations, in this case the winter solstice.

In Ben Franklin's day, Christmas was celebrated more simply than it is today, with a few token gifts for the children (usually of a practical nature), a lengthy church service, and a sumptuous family feast. Yet even in its simplicity, Ben saw how easily the Christmas holiday could obscure rather than highlight the birth of Christ. His sentiment strikes a chord with many today.

One young man who kept the spirit of Christmas in focus was Ryan Rigney of Manchester, Tennessee. One year, Ryan decided to use his Christmas money to buy socks for homeless men at the Nashville Union Mission. Ryan was later chosen as a runner-up in a national Make a Difference Day contest designed to honor those who help the less fortunate. Ryan used his $250 award to buy more socks for the homeless.

Keeping the Peace (and the Pieces) on Christmas Morning

❖ Roll up and save large pieces of wrapping paper. Pieces that aren't wrinkled can be reused next year.

❖ Keep a running list of presents received and the name of the gift giver so

proper thank-you notes can be sent to those who are not there in person.

❖ Make sure the day's plans include some outdoor activity for everyone, whether it's a walk, a snowball fight, or

the chance to try out the new sleds that Santa brought.

❖ Give every member of the family a colorful shopping bag with his or her name written on it to use for presents that have been unwrapped.

Staying Healthy during the Holidays (and Beyond)

IT'S GREAT to have the whole gang together during the holidays, but all of that socializing can spread colds and flu bugs along with good cheer. In addition to staying rested and hydrated, here are a few time-tested home remedies.

PRACTICAL PRIMER

- To ward off colds and flu during the holidays, give hugs instead of kisses. Wash your hands frequently if someone is under the weather.
- At the first signs of an earache, add a dropperful of echinacea tincture to a glass of juice or cup of tea, or steep 1 teaspoon of the dried herb in hot tea. Echinacea (coneflower) has antibiotic qualities and boosts immunity.
- To soothe sore muscles, apply arnica salve and do slow, gentle stretches. Warm compresses may help as well.
- Encourage a close relationship with your pet during the winter. Studies show that people who interact closely with their pets recover more quickly from illness or injury.
- If you know someone who's at home with a cold or the flu, fill an inexpensive wicker basket with rose hip tea (full of vitamin C), lip balm, magazines or a paperback novel, lemons or oranges, apple cider, and, of course, plenty of soft tissues.
- Laugh a lot, or surround yourself with the color turquoise—two remedies reputed to promote healing.

Too much wind today hurts the next grape harvest.

1776
GEORGE WASHINGTON crossed the ice-clogged Delaware River to attack Hessian forces in Trenton, New Jersey, at dawn.

• • •

The best of healers is good cheer.

—Pindar

LORE & LEGEND

In England and Canada, **BOXING DAY** is a public holiday celebrated on the first weekday after Christmas. People give small gifts and gratuities to tradespeople, postal workers, and others whose services make life easier. (And it doesn't hurt to have an extra holiday to recover from all the festivities.)

'Twas the Day after Christmas

- Encourage family members to take an hour or so to write thank-you notes for gifts received.
- Save this year's greeting cards to make next year's gift tags.
- Recycle plain wrapping paper. Your recycling center may not accept metallic, flocked, or heavily coated paper, but you can use such paper to cushion holiday decorations when you pack them away.
- If you are wrapping small gifts for Boxing Day, use empty oatmeal canisters or small cookie tins for anything breakable.

1822
Birth of scientist
LOUIS PASTEUR.

1900
Temperance crusader
CARRY NATION smashed
the bar at a hotel in
Wichita, Kansas.

1947
The Howdy Doody Show
debuted on NBC
television.

■ ■ ■

**Nothing so needs
reforming as other
people's habits.**

—*Mark Twain*

*Be temperate in wine, in eating,
girls, and sloth;
Or the gout will seize you and
plague you both.*

—BEN FRANKLIN

BEN FRANKLIN wasn't the first person to blame over-indulgence for causing gout (an arthritis-like condition resulting from deposits of uric acid crystals around joints). The Greek physician Galen—who developed an understanding of medicine that prevailed until the Renaissance—was the first to put the blame on overeating (wrongly, it turns out).

When Ben returned from France after the American Revolution, he brought along a gout cure called colchicine, derived from the saffron plant. But it wasn't until 1859 that a London doctor named Alfred Garrod discovered that colchicine works by increasing the excretion of uric acid (the real culprit behind gout) from the body.

Today we know that gout is exacerbated by foods high in purine, such as wine. (Ben wasn't completely wrong.) Although general alcohol consumption is on the decline, Americans are drinking more wine than in the past—an average of 2 gallons each per year. Fortunately, doctors tell us that moderate alcohol consumption (one or two drinks per day) is actually good for the heart, can prevent strokes, and has potential benefits for preventing diseases ranging from Alzheimer's to rheumatoid arthritis. But it won't prevent gout.

Make the Holidays Bright

❦ Add a handful of pine or hemlock needles, rosemary sprigs, or sage branches to your next fire to add natural incense to the room.

❦ Follow a custom of carolers in England, who often brought their hosts apple gifts for good luck. These early entertainers stuck whole cloves in apples and rolled the fruit in nutmeg or oats to symbolize fertility and good fortune in the year to come. Apples also were pierced with mistletoe at the top and perched on tripods of sticks to make table decorations.

Poor Richard Saunders

BEN FRANKLIN borrowed the pseudonym Poor Richard Saunders from a real-life Richard Saunders, who wrote almanacs in England in the 1680s. It's not all he borrowed.

John Bartlett, author of *Bartlett's Familiar Quotations* (1855), was the first to find some of Ben's original sources. "Little strokes fell great oaks" was from John Lyly: "Many strokes overthrow the tallest oaks." George Herbert  wrote, "Help thyself and God will help thee," while Ben advised, "God helps them that help themselves." And Ben copied the maxim "Keep thy shop and thy shop will keep thee" directly from the 1605 English drama *Eastward Ho!*

An avid reader with thousands of books at his disposal (while most American households had only a Bible or almanac), Ben finally confessed in his last almanac (1758). "Not a tenth part of the wisdom was my own." Although he conceded that "nothing gives an author so great pleasure as to find his works respectfully quoted," he never named his sources.

> One cool judgment is worth a thousand hasty counsels. The thing to do is to supply light and not heat.
>
> —*Woodrow Wilson*

DECEMBER

28

1732
The first issue of *Poor Richard's Almanack* (for 1733) was advertised for sale. It was so wildly successful that BEN FRANKLIN had to print more copies.

1846
Iowa became the 29th state.

1856
Birthday of WOODROW WILSON, 28th president of the United States (1913–1921).

Your End-of-Year House Checkup

❖ **Floors:** Test for wear on a hardwood floor by pouring on a tablespoon of water. The water should bead up. If it soaks in after a few minutes, the floor is beginning to wear. If it soaks in immediately, the floor is due for refinishing or replacement.

❖ **Plumbing:** To test whether your home has hidden water leaks, check your water meter just before going to bed. In

the morning, before using any water, check the reading

again. If the meter has moved, you have a leak.

❖ **Moisture:** On a cold night, go to your attic or crawl space and look for icicles on nails or ice crystals on sheathing. Black stains on sheathing may indicate mold. To improve moisture control, increase attic ventilation and reduce heat loss to the attic around plumbing stacks and chimneys.

DECEMBER

~ 29 ~

When the moon runs high, expect cold weather.

● ○ ○ ◑ ●

1808
Birthday of
ANDREW JOHNSON,
17th president of the
United States
(1865–1869).

1845
Texas became
the 28th state.

1851
In Boston, the first
YMCA (Young Men's
Christian Association) was
established.

• • •

Don't be fooled by the
calendar. There are only
as many days in the year
as you make use of.

—*Charles Richards*

Winter Car Kit

I F YOU LIVE where snow and ice can complicate driving conditions, it's a good idea to put together a canvas bag or covered storage box that holds the following emergency items. (If you live where it's balmy all winter, be thankful that you don't need all this stuff.) Having all of these things in your trunk virtually guarantees a mild and uneventful winter.

PRACTICAL PRIMER

- Flashlight with extra batteries
- First-aid kit
- Pocketknife with can opener
- Blanket or sleeping bag
- Matches or lighter
- Mittens, socks, wool hat, rain gear
- Sand or dry cat litter
- Shovel
- Tools (pliers, wrench, screwdriver)
- Duct tape
- Booster cables
- Tire chains or traction mats
- Bright cloth or flag for signaling

CALENDAR COMMENTS

☾ Get out your calendar for the new year and write down all the birthdays and anniversaries you want to remember. Use a highlighter to mark school or work vacations and important dates such as elections. Hang the calendar where you'll see it often.

☾ Purchase a family calendar with large squares for writing and keep it in a prominent place in the kitchen. Insist that each family member note appointments, sports practices and games, meetings, and other commitments.

☾ At the end of a year, don't throw out your family calendar. It's fun to look back on years past and remember all of the different things you did. Keep each year's calendar in a box along with family photos, memorabilia from trips, and other personal scrapbook items from the year.

—BK

Ben Franklin and Tobacco

No temporal concern is of more importance to us than health, and that depends so much on the air we every moment breathe. —POOR RICHARD'S ALMANACK, *1757*

IN HIS BOOK *Essays* (1798), Dr. Benjamin Rush wrote, "The appetite for tobacco is wholly artificial. No person was ever born with a relish for it." Rush, a signer of the Declaration of Independence and Ben Franklin's physician, described how his patients suffered illness and death due to their use of tobacco. As for Ben, "in the eighty-first year of his age, [he] declared he had never snuffed, chewed, or smoked," wrote Rush, in an age when tobacco was a chief agricultural product of North America.

THE *Inspired* MIND

Although smoking can cause heart, vascular, and chronic lung disease, as well as cancer of the lungs, esophagus, and larynx, the National Center for Tobacco-Free Kids estimates that about 25 percent (48 million) of Americans age 18 or older smoke, while the rate for teens is about 35 percent. The addictive nature of tobacco was known and concealed from its consumers by cigarette manufacturers, leading to historic litigation in 1998, when 46 states won a $206 billion settlement from tobacco companies.

DECEMBER

30

Record low statewide temperatures were set in Mountain City, Tennessee (–32°F, 1917); Lewisburg, West Virginia (–37°F, 1917); Winthrop, Washington (–48°F, 1968); and Bloomfield, Vermont (–50°F, 1933).

1935
Birthday of writer RUDYARD KIPLING (1865), baseball pitcher SANDY KOUFAX (1935), and golfer TIGER WOODS (1975).

1953
The first color TV sets went on sale.

Nothing is as easy to make as a promise this winter to do something next summer; this is how commencement speakers are caught.

—*Sydney J. Harris*

How to Make New Year's Resolutions

❖ Keep it simple. Settle on one or two things you really can accomplish.

❖ Define your goal: It should be measurable, doable, and specific. "I want to get in shape" is too vague. "I will walk two miles, five days a week" is concrete.

❖ If quitting smoking is one of your resolutions, take a sip of lemon juice whenever temptation strikes, or nibble on sunflower seeds. Keep a pencil in your hand to keep it occupied, or play with a yo-yo.

❖ Resolved to lose 10 pounds by spring? Indulge in a cup of herbal tea to get you through a midday slump.

❖ Any regrets about the past year? To help focus on the future, write down your regrets on a scrap of paper and toss it into a fire. Janus, the two-faced god of the new year, would approve.

DECEMBER

31

*A snowy year,
a rich year.*

● ● ○ ○ ●

1869
Artist HENRI MATISSE
was born.

1879
THOMAS EDISON
demonstrated his new
electric incandescent light
in Menlo Park,
New Jersey.

■ ■ ■

GO EASY ON
NEW YEAR'S EVE

❖ To help prevent a
hangover, drink milk
and eat fatty foods
before indulging in
alcohol. Moderation
is still necessary, but
also beware of sweet
or flavored mixers or
colored liquors.

❖ If you choose to
drink on New Year's
Eve, surrender your
car keys to a desig-
nated driver. (Ben
Franklin knew how
much trouble one
could get into
with keys.)

Work as if you were to live one hundred years, pray as if you were to die tomorrow.

—BEN FRANKLIN

ANDREW JACKSON, hero of the War of 1812 and seventh president of the United States, once said, "I try to
live my life as if death might come at any moment." That
was probably a wise course for a man with his temperament. Jackson—who never backed away from a
fight on or off the battlefield—was once
involved in an altercation that left him
with a bullet in his shoulder that doctors said was too dangerous to remove.
The bullet remained in his shoulder for
20 years, until a doctor visiting the
White House told him he thought he
could remove it. Jackson agreed, the
doctor made an incision, and the bullet
fell to the floor.

ANDREW JACKSON

Jackson sent it to his old adversary—who had become a friend
in the meantime—but the friend returned it, saying that Jackson
had acquired "clear title to it" in the intervening years. Jackson
lived to be 78, exhibiting the same feisty attitude to the end.

LORE & LEGEND

NEW YEAR'S EVE is a holiday
rich in traditions, most of
which have to do with staying
awake and making noise to welcome in the new year (and to
scare off any bad spirits) and
with eating special foods for
good luck. In the Scottish
Highlands and Western Isles,
groups parade around town
banging on skin drums and
chanting songs such as this one:
*Great good luck to the house,
Good luck to the family,
Good luck to every rafter of it,
And to every worldly thing in it.*

**Be at war with your vices, at peace with your neighbors, and
let every new year find you a better man.**

—*Ben Franklin*

Ben's Tip Finder and General Index

Bold page references indicate quotations.

Doilies, vintage lace, 266
Door(s)
    hinge, squeaky, 45, 330
    weather-proofing, 307
Doubt, **197**
Dough, for tree ornaments, 372
Down
    comforters and clothing, cleaning,
        341
    for craft projects, 114
Dragonflies, 249
Dragons, **224**
Drains, unclogging, 152
Drawers
    creaky, 45
    loose knobs on, 207
    organizing, 170
Dream pillow, 35
Dreams, **40**, **122**, **138**, 267
Dredging machine, invention of, 369
Dressed-Up Asparagus, 103
Drilling tips, 50
Drinking, 93, 156, 311. *See also*
        Alcohol
Drivers, new, 317
Driving
    drinking and, 384
    road rage and, 313, **313**
    staying awake while, 316
    time change affecting, 102, 316
    winter, 354
Drought, garden care in, 168
Dry skin, 21
Dry throat, 22
Duct tape, for wart removal, 21
Dusting, 145, 306
Dustpan, disposable, 198

E
Eagles, bald, 78
Earaches, 32, 379
Early risers, 22, **22**, **34**
Earth, **113**, **340**, **342**
Easter
    baskets, lining, 103
    eggs, displaying, 103
    grass, 78
Eating, **169**, **191**, **278**, **285**
    according to season, 240
    enjoyment of, 160, **160**
    healthy, 9, 44, 122, 285
    in hot weather, 205
Edison, Thomas, 50, 170
Education, 33, 282
    for women, 330, **330**

Eggplant, frost protection for, 287
Eggs
    cooking, with clarified butter, 54
    deviled, 247
    hard-boiled, 107
    scrambling, 247
    separating, 140
    storing, 247
    testing freshness of, 210
    whites of, 140
Egg slicer, uses for, 247
Electric cords, storing, 85
Electricity, **271**
    experiments on, 165, 238, 246,
        271, 292
    saving, 295, 343
Enemies, 276, **276**
English language, **193**, 284
Entertainment, **240**
Envy, 13
Epiphany, luck on, 13
Epitaphs, 364, **364**
Excess, **251**
Exercise, **220**
    bone strength and, 220
    injuries from, 220
    laughter as, 8
    walking as, 53, 121
Exploration, **325**
Eyestrain, preventing, 111

F
Fabrics, fancy, cleaning, 341
Fabric softener sheets, uses for, 263,
        271, 277, 351
Fairness, **31**
Faith, **269**
Falcon, peregrine, 276
Fame, **20**
Family governance, **96**
Fan belt, squeaky, 201
Fashion, 97, **97**, 247, **247**
Fast food, 285
Fatherhood, **179**, **359**
Fats, dietary, 44
Fears, 32, **32**
February, 39–68
Ferns, watering, 352
Fertility, 40
File cabinet, for college students,
        250
Fire, **49**
    adding fragrance to, 380
    building, 349, 360
    insurance, 49

prevention, 49
    starters, homemade, 363
Fireflies, 216
Fireplace
    ashes in, 59
    bricks, cleaning, 337
    damper, opening and closing, 360
    fire starters for, 363
    log gift for, 361
    log size for, 360
    safety, 337
    stoves, 337
Firewood
    splitting, 335
    stacking, 275, 360
Firs, for holiday decorating, 347
Fish
    choosing, 232
    chowder, 232
    cooking, 96, 136
    grilling, 199
    odor, on hands, 95, 136
    spawning of, 107
    storing, 136
Flag etiquette, 178
Flannel, 14, **14**
Flashlights, locating, in dark, 373
Flattery, 361, **361**
Flatulence, 213
Fleas, 238, **238**
Flies, deterring, 106, 171, 199
Floods, protecting basement from, 91
Floorboards, squeaky, 45
Floors
    cleaning, 84, 152, 257
    inspecting, for damage, 381
Flour
    repelling bugs from, 186, 210
    scoop for, 210
Flower(s), **299**
    arrangements, 144, 311, 334
    cutting, 206
    for decorating platters, 173
    drying, 193
    garden (*see* Garden, flower garden)
    as gift, 71
    increasing fragrance of, 193
Flu. *See* Colds and flu
Flying, **246**
Food(s), 56. *See also specific foods*
    bag clips for, 119
    cold, seasoning, 204
    fast, 285
    for freezer storage, 186
    for game night, 27

Franklin stove, 85, 337
glass armonica, 208
lead poisoning, 47
libraries, 125, 196
lightning bells, 271
lightning rod, 165, 238
"magic square," 177
odometer, 354
Pennsylvania Hospital, 99
phonetic alphabet, 284
proportional taxation, 109
rocking chair fan, 145
Society for Political Inquiries, 277
streetlights, 308
street sweeping, 368
swim fins, 219
think tank, 33
epitaph of, **364**
experiments, on
conductivity, 17
electricity, 165, 238, 246, 271,
292
Gulf Stream, 127
internal waves, 279
ocean calming, 233
solar heat, 231
father of, 179
homes of, 17, 76, 352
humility of, attempts at, 187
indifference of, to food, 98, 160,
285, 357
life events of
apprenticeship, 13, 72
birth, 24
death, 118
death of son, 94
education, 167
engagement of sister, 242
hero's welcome, 113
as nonsmoker, 383
perfection of, attempts at, 8, 187
roles of, 5
abolitionist, 117
ambassador, 352
ballad composer, 124
Freemason, 141
leader, 19, 65
newsboy, 263
postmaster general, 221
printer, 47, 66, 72, 89, 111,
284, 355
publisher, 302
sponsor of explorer, 329
storyteller, 159
source of quotations of, 381

as swimmer, 252, 317
vegetarianism of, 222
water drinking of, 105
wife of, 260
will of, 244
writings and publications of
Autobiography, 24, 105, 109,
124, 159, 234, 252, 263,
325
Pennsylvania Gazette, 135, 294,
302, 320, 369
Poor Richard's Almanack, 5, 22,
45, 88, 124, 138, 165, 274,
348, 383
revised Lord's Prayer, 312
on witchcraft, 321
Frankling stove, 85, 337
Franklinia alatamaha, discovery of, 33
Franklin Medal for scholarship, 167
Fraud, 12
Freedom, **265**
Freemasons, 141
Free press, 199
Freezer
choosing, 242
foods stored in, 186
increasing efficiency of, 295
power outage and, 331
Fresh Corn Chowder, 254
Friendship, 48, 81, **81**, **319**
Frogs, 91, 117
Frost, predicting, 287
Frostbite and frost nip, 20
Frugality, **50**, 203, **203**, 343
Fruit(s). *See also specific fruits*
baking with, 377
citrus
juicing, 334
for zest, 358
excess, uses for, 194
punch, 93
pureed, 242
ripeness of, 194, 241
slicing, 247
trees
autumn care of, 291
insect control for, 203
planting and growing, 123
pruning, 74
Furnace
cleaning, 307, 312
noise from, 360
Furniture
finishing, with milk paint, 86
lawn, care of, 196

used, freshening, 197
wood, cleaning, 155, 281, 351
Future, **83**, 163, **257**

G
Gambling, 67, **67**, **108**
Game night, 27
Games, for car trips, 313
Garage, cleaning, 233
Garden(ing), **64**, **108**, 174, **189**, **196**,
209, 226. *See also specific
plants, shrubs, and trees*
catalogs, 46
chores
animal control, 166
fertilizing, 268, 280
frost protection for plants, 287
insect control, 117, 174, 203,
216, 222, 342
lawn care, 135, 234, 296, 319
mulching, 335
pruning, 60, 74, 165, 226,
289, 335
raking, 308
seed starting, 78, 108, 117,
134, 147
soil improvement, 108, 115,
133
stump removal, 115
thinning and pinching, 187,
203, 226
tool and equipment care, 60,
74, 304, 335
watering, 149, 168, 209, 244,
296
weed control, 150, 165, 195,
209, 335
container gardening, 180
in drought, 168, 234
flower garden
attracting butterflies to, 100
bargains for, 189
dividing perennials in, 268
harvesting, 206
layout for, 100
planting, 268
scented foliage in, 100
in window boxes, 133, 209
winter protection for, 357
foundation plantings in, 282
fungal diseases in, 165, 234
herb garden, 126, 162, 180, 206,
303
indoor (*see* Houseplants)
rock garden, 182, **182**